Centralized and Decentralized Economic Systems:

The Soviet-Type Economy, Market Socialism, and Capitalism

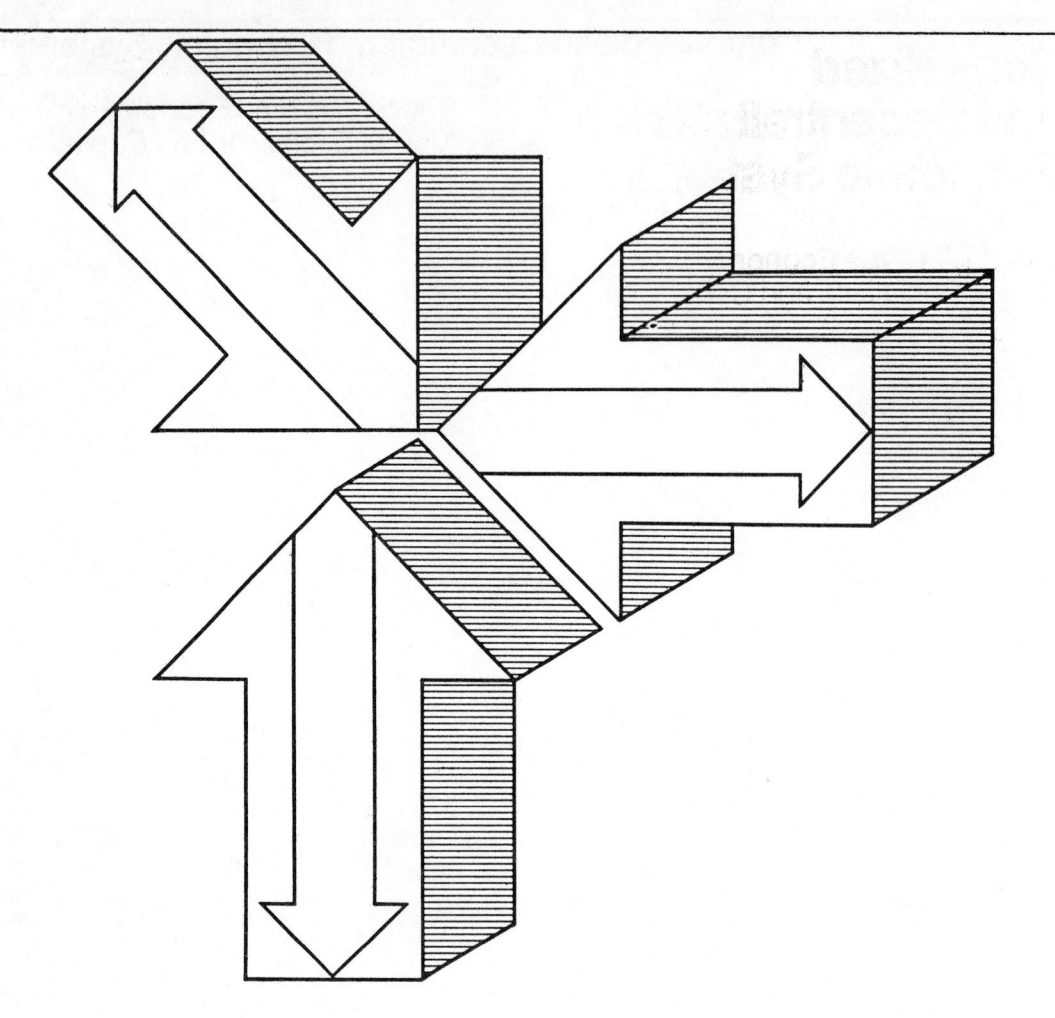

Centralized and Decentralized Economic Systems:

The Soviet-Type Economy, Market Socialism, and Capitalism

Wayne A. Leeman
University of Missouri-Columbia

KLINCK MEMORIAL LIBRARY
Concordia Teachers College
River Forest, Illinois 60305

Rand McNally
College Publishing Company
Chicago

77 78 79 10 9 8 7 6 5 4 3 2 1
Copyright © 1977 by Rand McNally College Publishing Company
All Rights Reserved
Printed in the U.S.A.
Library of Congress Catalog Card Number 76-17192

To my brother Adrian

Preface

Alternative economic systems can be studied at different levels of abstraction. At the one extreme are purely descriptive studies, a description, for example, of all the institutions of capitalism—commodity markets, labor markets, the patent system, and so on. At the other extreme are completely formal analyses with virtually no references to the empirical world, like recent mathematical models of decentralized economies. Between those extremes is the level of abstraction of this book. The objectives, the value judgments, considered herein are those in which people who choose between different economic systems would be interested. Hence, in-depth discussion of the Pareto optimum, for example, is not included and simple objectives like consistency, efficiency, and production are. Generalization is attempted, and while the results of such a middle level of abstraction are less certain than a simple description of facts and less tidy than an elegant mathematical model, work at this level appears to be fruitful in propositions that are operational.

Some readers will be surprised to see that this book begins with a consideration of the Soviet-type economy and is followed much later on, in Part V, by a discussion of capitalism. Why not go from the familiar to the unfamiliar? The familiar, however, is so familiar that it is commonplace, and Western readers too readily take important features of capitalism for granted just because they have observed and heard about them during their entire lives.

When they learn, for example, that under capitalism millions of output decisions are made consistent with one another through the responses to price signals of cumbersome autonomous decision makers, they are not likely to appreciate what is really being achieved until they have studied the attempts of a central planning body to arrive at a consistent set of output targets using a laborious method of successive approximations. Rather than begin an examination of alternative economic systems with one more review of the markets of capitalism, I have, therefore, arranged the text to enable the student to look at the way customary problems are handled in a Soviet or socialist setting by people having different views of what is proper and appropriate. When readers then turn to Part V on capitalism, they will observe aspects of it in a new and comparative light. To put it another way, in some respects one can learn more about capitalism through an investigation of socialism than by directly and immediately examining a capitalist system.

It is also probably unexpected to include in a text on alternative economic systems discussions of utopias, communal anarchy, and traditional communes. I have devoted Part III to these timely topics, however, because in recent years the new left has demonstrated an interest in anarchism; the communal life is an ever-recurring dream of men and women. Study of utopian thought, based on the literature of Bellamy, Skinner, and H. G. Wells, anarchy, and the commune brings to the fore some very intriguing questions about human behavior and alternative value systems.

As considerations of utopian systems raise interesting questions, so does investigation of centralized and decentralized socialism. Part II is devoted to a study of the static Lange model, which is followed by an operational model conceived by this author. Readers will note that I have drawn heavily on already published material by Joseph A. Schumpeter. I have tried to do what Schumpeter did not attempt, however. I have tried to develop a dynamic, or at least non-static, model of market socialism, and in so doing I have found that Schumpeter's ideas about the sources of innovation are applicable to a socialism in which there are autonomous government enterprises.

It would seem that a text on alternative economic systems would not really be complete without material on the Chinese economy. Part IV, therefore, discusses the history and evolution of that decentralized economic system.

Because this book is divided into parts, it can readily be read in a different order. One alternative sequence might be the following:

Introduction
Part V   Capitalism
Part II Market Socialism
Part III Anarchism, Utopias, and Communes
Part IV The Chinese Economy
Part I   The Soviet-Type Economy
Part VI Political Economy

To facilitate discussion of some of the material herein, three appendices follow the text, and briefly discuss such topics as the Pareto criterion, marginal-cost pricing, and indiscriminate delivery of output as a substitute for the concept of externality and social cost.

I would like to thank the many government officials, enterprise managers, and scholars in Eastern Europe who gave so freely of their time in answering my questions. I am also obliged to Professors W. Whitney Hicks and Carmen F. Menezes of the University of Missouri-Columbia. For suggestions on the manuscript or on the parts of it they read, my thanks to Professors Morris Bornstein, University of Michigan; Andrzej Brzeski, University of California-Davis; Robert W. Campbell, Indiana University; Robert F. Dernberger, University of Michigan; Max Fletcher, University of Idaho; Heinz Kohler, Amherst College; Joseph A. Martellaro, Northern Illinois University; Rod Peterson, Colorado State University; Thomas C. Rawski, University of Toronto; and Gene B. Tipton, California State University at Los Angeles. Grateful for the assistance of numerous people in kibbutzim and in kibbutz movement headquarters, I particularly want to thank Mrs. Yehudit Simhoni of Kibbutz Geva and Mr. Dani Kerman of Kibbutz Urim for their patient instruction in the operations and the problems of the kibbutz. Finally, over the two decades that I have taught undergraduate and graduate courses in comparative economic systems I have learned much from my students. If I did not always acknowledge this help in class, it is because it sometimes took me several months to recognize the significance of a question or a comment. Needless to say, I take full responsibility for any errors which remain in the book.

Wayne A. Leeman

Columbia, Missouri
August, 1976

Contents

Preface	vii
Introduction	xvii

Part I The Soviet-Type Economy

Chapter 1   Forces that Molded the System: The First Two Decades   3
- War Communism, 1918–21   4
- The New Economic Policy   5
- Industrialization and Collectivization   9
- Ideology   13

Chapter 2   Current Output Planning   17
- Required Knowledge   19
- Procedures   21
- Consistency   23
- The Determination of Technological Coefficients   25
- Efficiency   26
- Lower-Level Plans   31
- Flexibility and Simultaneity   32
- How Managers Are Rewarded   34
- The Assortment Problem   44
- Flexibility in Decision Making   45

Chapter 3   Investment Planning   49
- Multiperiod Planning   50

	Consistency and Efficiency	52
	Project Selection	55
	Minimization of Total Costs	56
	The Coefficient of Relative Effectiveness	57
	Present Value of Costs	62
	Present Value of Net Income	65

Chapter 4 Prices and Money — 67

	Retail Prices and Wages	68
	Wholesale Prices	69
	The Turnover Tax	70
	The Role of Price in Resource Allocation	70
	The Need for Money	71
	Two Monetary Circuits	71
	Control by the Ruble	73
	Monetary Policy	74

Chapter 5 Agriculture — 77

	The Collective Farm	77
	Private Agriculture and the Farm Market	79
	State Farms	83
	Recent Developments	83
	The Future of Socialist Agriculture	86

Chapter 6 The Soviet-Type Economy as a Model for Development — 89

	Increased Accumulation and Reduced Services	89
	Planned Investment	90
	The Government as Risk-Taker	92
	Socialist Growth and Freedom of Choice	92

Chapter 7 Proposals for Reform in the Soviet-Type Economy — 95

	Reduction in Output Directives	95
	Reduction of Inputs Subject to Rationing	97
	Price Reform	98
	Reward for the Sale of Goods	99
	Profit and Plan	100
	Reduction in Subsidies	106
	Sheltered Enterprises and Foreign Trade	107
	Property under Socialism and the Right of Decision	108
	Proposed Reforms in Agriculture	113
	Obstacles to Reform	115

Part II Market Socialism

Chapter 8 The Static Lange Model — 129

	Price Determination	130

	The Rules Imposed on Managers	131
	The Supervision and Reward of Managers	133
	Lange's Treatment of Indiscriminate Delivery (Spillovers)	135
	Statics and Dynamics in Market Socialism	137

Chapter 9   An Operational Model — 139

- The Competitive Sector — 139
- The Sectors of Natural Monopoly — 145
- Risk, Profit, and Innovation — 148
- Autonomy versus Accountability — 152
- Regulation of Indiscriminate Delivery (Spillovers) — 153
- Comparison of the Operational Model and the Lange Model — 154
- Objectives Achieved and Objectives Not Realized — 156

Chapter 10   Market Socialism in Yugoslavia — 159

- The Working Collective — 159
- Profit Sharing in Yugoslavia and Elsewhere — 163
- The Structure of Industry — 164
- Property and Government — 165
- Not Communal Anarchism — 170
- Solidarity or Conflict? — 170
- The Decline of Solidarity and the Rise of the Market — 172
- The Working Collective versus the Capitalist Enterprise — 174

Part III   Anarchism, Utopias, and Communes

Chapter 11   The Theory of Communal Anarchism — 179

- Institutions — 179
- Underlying Beliefs — 181
- Altruistic Motivation — 186
- Conclusions — 187

Chapter 12   An Introduction to the Utopian Literature — 189

- Bellamy's *Looking Backward* — 189
- *The Modern Utopia* of H. G. Wells — 196
- Skinner's *Walden Two* — 203
- Dreams and Reality — 207

Chapter 13   Communes: Traditional and Contemporary — 209

- Oneida — 209
- The Amanas — 212
- The Hutterians — 215
- The Israeli Kibbutz — 219
- Twin Oaks — 229
- Skinner's Behavioral Engineering at Twin Oaks — 237

	Hippie Communes	244
	Communes: Durability and Weaknesses	249

Part IV The Chinese Economy

Chapter 14	Chinese Communism	253
	A Historical Sketch	253
	Planning and Control	259
	Industrialization	261
	Agriculture	262
	Chinese Communism as Compared with the Russian Soviet-Type Economy	264
	Chinese Communism and Communal Agriculture in the West	265
	An Uneasy Balance	265

Part V Capitalism

Chapter 15	Laissez Faire Capitalism	271
	Objectives	271
	Institutions: Property and Contract	272
	Institutions: Capital Markets and the Corporations	274
	The Behavior of Consumers, Workers, Investors, and Businessmen in Laissez Faire Capitalism	274
	Structure of Industry	276
	Attainment of Objectives	277
	The Differences between Laissez Faire Capitalism and Market Socialism	278
	Criticisms of Laissez Faire Capitalism	279
Chapter 16	From Laissez Faire to Regulation in the United States	289
	Regulation of the Railroads	290
	Subsidies and Controls in Agriculture	291
	Welfare Programs	294
	Market Forces and the Environment	295
	Regulation Instead of Government Ownership	296
Chapter 17	Regulated Capitalism	297
	Directives	297
	Price Controls and Rationing	299
	Taxes and Subsidies or Grants	304
	"Equality of Opportunity"	308
	The Negative Income Tax	315
	Traditional Utility Rate Determination	317
	The Limits of Regulation	321
	A Cultural Critique of Capitalism	321

Part VI Political Economy

Chapter 18   The Relationship between Political and Economic Systems   337
- The Power of the Capitalist Class   337
- Democracy and Socialism   339
- Soviet Reform, Economic and Political   341
- The Convergence Thesis   342

Chapter 19   Conclusions—Brief and Prosaic   347

Appendices

Appendix 1   The Pareto Criterion as a Defense of Market Economies   353
- Beneficial, Non-Hurting Changes   354
- Markets Hurt People   355

Appendix 2   Marginal-Cost Pricing   359
- Marginal Cost as a Measure of Opportunity Cost   359
- Distributional Consequences   360

Appendix 3   Indiscriminate Delivery of Output as a Substitute for the Concept of Externality and Social Cost   363

Index   367

Introduction

For long there have been two strands of socialist thought, one which would have socialists capture the government and enlarge its role through central planning and government ownership of the means of production, another which would weaken or destroy government and put in its place a society of communes. In the last several decades, economists have developed yet another model of socialism, market socialism, a system in which managers of government enterprises make output, input, and investment decisions. In the real world, we can find examples of all of these models —from the centrally planned Soviet-type economy to market socialism with its working collectives to the communal farms (kibbutzim) of Israel.

In extreme opposition to the theory of socialism, we have the pure theory of laissez faire capitalism. And then, in the real world, we observe most frequently systems of regulated capitalism.

Between these opposite poles, the literature on government ownership of public utilities, which might be seen as part of an applied market socialism, meets the literature on regulated private utilities, which is aligned theoretically with a system of regulated capitalism. The pragmatically oriented economist notes that these two latter bodies of thought address the same problems and frequently arrive at similar conclusions, and he or she might decide that government versus private ownership of the means of production is a spurious issue. The theoretically oriented student of alternative economic systems, however, may recognize that property distributes the rights of decision in any economy and that property under socialism gives these rights to a different set of persons than does the private property of capitalism.

Finally, economic analysis leads the scholar into consideration of political factors: the power of the capitalist class, the relationship between political democracy and socialism, the consequences of proposed economic reforms upon the Soviet government, for example. Last, but not least, is the intriguing thesis that in the East and West different economic and political structures are converging toward a common set of institutions.

The Soviet-Type Economy

Part 1

Introduction to Part One

The Communist party in the Soviet Union has engaged in the most ambitious attempt in history to organize and rule an economy through the powers of government. The Soviet economic system reflects the goals of the Party leadership—growth through the industrialization of an underdeveloped economy. Similarly, the system reflects the ideology and methods of the Party—governmental control and central planning, dictatorship of the proletariat or of the Party in the name of the proletariat, and change through revolution. Historically, both goals and ideology have encountered opposition in the forms of scarcity (particularly of capital) and a peasantry determined to go its own way. Out of these circumstances has developed a prototype of a remarkably stable economy which, much of the time, seems almost impervious to change.

Forces that Molded the System: The First Two Decades

Chapter 1

Marx expected the revolution to come first to an industrialized country with a large proletarian working class. Instead, in 1917, it came to Russia, a relatively underdeveloped world power, a country mostly of peasants. A large part of the present-day structure of the Soviet economy can best be understood by the study of the history that followed this unanticipated revolution.

Under the determined but flexible leadership of Lenin, the Bolsheviks came to power by riding the momentarily parallel concerns of the workers and peasants. They promised bread to the workers at a time when food shortages in the cities were desperate, acceded to the demands of the peasants for land when they were already beginning to occupy their landlords' estates, and offered peace to a nation demoralized by defeats and losses in war. In November 1917, the Bolsheviks overthrew the inept Provisional Government, which had taken over upon the collapse of the Czarist regime. The following decades were to show that an urban-based Communist Party, dominated by the ideology of the dictatorship of the proletariat, was bound to conflict with the peasantry.[1]

---

[1] The best account of this period, remarkably penetrating in its analysis, is M. Lewin, *Russian Peasants and Soviet Power: A Study of Collectivization,* trans. Irene Nove (London: George Allen and Unwin, 1968). The title itself, in well chosen words, almost tells the story. A useful earlier source is Maurice Dobb, *Soviet Economic Development Since 1917* (New York: International Publishers, 1948). A third valuable work is Alec Nove, *An Economic History of the U.S.S.R.* (London: Allen Lane The Penguin Press, 1969).

An operational blueprint for socialism did not exist when the Bolsheviks came to power, but had a model been available, it is doubtful that Lenin and his followers could have made use of it. Fighting a civil war against the Whites (the opponents of the Bolsheviks) and their foreign supporters, all the Reds could hope to do was improvise on a day-to-day basis.

War Communism, 1918–21

By 1918, the workers had seized many factories, and "factory committees" dominated the management of numerous plants still nominally in private hands. Although all factories were nationalized in June 1918, workers' control continued. Private trade was largely forbidden. Chaos ensued. To the destruction of war was added the indiscipline of syndicalism in industry. Government trading agencies functioned poorly and were not an effective substitute for the private trader. Shortages were ubiquitous and the authorities rushed from bottleneck to bottleneck, creating however, new shortages with their directives. Inflation was rampant and money began to lose its effectiveness. Workers were largely paid in kind.[2] The government tried to control the economy from the center, often employing military methods. The first efforts to plan the economy were made by calculating some "material balances." These attempted balances foreshadowed what was to become the heart of the Soviet-type economy, but at this time, as a Soviet commentator on War Communism stated in the twenties, "the planned economy turned simply into the allocation of whatever was available."[3]

Conflict with the Peasants

Perhaps the most significant feature of this period was the emerging conflict with the peasants. Food was short in the cities and the authorities found it difficult to procure supplies, especially grain, from the peasants at official prices. By stages compulsory deliveries of food were systematized. In due course each peasant household was ordered to deliver its "surplus" to the government, which paid either nothing or a low price against money that was virtually worthless because little could be purchased with it. The peasants resisted and either hid their grain or sought to dispose of

---

[2] Nove, *Economic History*, pp. 49–50, 52–56, 63–66, 69–71.
[3] Ibid., p. 80.

it through a black market or through illegal barter. Riots broke out and some parts of the country fell into the hands of the "Greens," who defended the peasants against both the Reds and Whites. Enough of the peasants, fearing return of the landlords, supported the Bolsheviks so that the latter were victorious in the end. But even these peasants saw little sense in producing grain that would be taken from them by requisitioning squads. They planted less, production fell, and as grain became more difficult to locate, the requisitioning squads became more ruthless.[4] The collapse of the economy during the Civil War is evident in the statistics below.

Table 1-1

Production	1913	1921
Coal (million tons)	29.00	9.00
Oil (million tons)	9.20	3.80
Steel (million tons)	4.30	0.20
Bricks (millions)	2.10	0.01
Sugar (million tons)	1.30	0.05
Railway tonnage carried (millions)	134.40	39.40
Agricultural production (index)	100.00	60.00

Source: Alec Nove, *An Economic History of the U.S.S.R.* (London: Allen Lane The Penguin Press, 1969), p. 68.

While improvisation was the name of the game during the period of War Communism, ideology no doubt played a large role in the choice of measures adopted to meet the recurring crises. The Bolsheviks believed that government ownership and trade were superior to private ownership and trade. Many distrusted all trade and preferred the enforcing of requisition and rationing. Some viewed the demise of money as an indication of progress and were happy to see barter and payment in kind take its place.

The New Economic Policy

Peasant risings in many parts of the country and the revolt of sailors stationed on Kronstadt Island in March 1921 persuaded Lenin that a strategic retreat was necessary if the regime were to survive. He, in turn, persuaded his skeptical Party. During the spring and early summer numerous changes were decreed. A

[4]Ibid., pp. 59-61.

grain tax in kind, substantially below the requisitioning targets of the previous year, was imposed on the peasants (along with a tax in kind on potatoes, meat, etc.). The peasants were free to consume the remainder of their produce or to sell it in markets that allowed private traders. Small-scale industry was denationalized and citizens were authorized to engage in handicraft production and organize small industrial enterprises that employed not more than ten to twenty workers. Plant and equipment owned by the government could be leased by private individuals. In 1924, after the currency was stabilized, money taxes were substituted for taxes in kind.[5]

The Party, however, kept "the commanding heights"—large-scale industry, banking, and foreign trade—in the hands of the government. This resulted in an economy with a mixture of capitalism in small industry and domestic trade and what today would be called "market socialism" in large industry, finance, and foreign commerce. (At the same time the countryside experienced a resurgence of the indigenous institution of communal land ownership called the *mir*.)

The Early Years of NEP

In its early years this New Economic Policy (NEP) was a marked success, although the market economy forced severe adjustments on many people. Bottlenecks in coal, transport, textiles, and other industries were overcome. The peasants supplied grain and other agricultural products in return for the output of the cities, using private traders, known as "Nepmen," to act as intermediaries. But many Party leaders were unhappy when they observed market forces diverting resources from priority activities in the governmental sector to the private economy. Some governmental directives were issued, at first more often with respect to investment than current production. Later in the decade, the leaders introduced price controls, which led to shortages and increasingly centralized controls over the production and distribution of key commodities. Yet while much was said about planning, what was actually done was mostly forecasting.[6]

Economic gains came easily in the early days of NEP because existing plant and equipment could be reactivated. But once these resources were largely employed, a fundamental question had to be faced: What could be the source of capital for an industrializa-

[5]Ibid., pp. 83–85.
[6]Ibid., pp. 100–1, 117, 139, 143.

tion and modernization of the Soviet Union? It was the Party's answer to this question that shaped many of the institutions of the Soviet-type economy.

Almost certainly, substantial amounts of capital could not be expected from outside the country; the advanced industrial nations were hostile to the Soviet Union. Nor, in the Party's eyes could very much capital be obtained from Soviet cities. The wealth of the capitalist class had already been confiscated and the proletariat (the working class) was small and poor. Because the country was still largely agricultural, and because the estates of the landlords had already been expropriated, there appeared to be but one important source of capital—the peasantry. Once this was recognized, only two questions remained to be answered: How much capital? And by what methods? Moreover, the quantity of capital depended on the methods of obtaining it.

Accumulation and the Peasants
One possible approach was to exchange manufactured goods for peasant output on terms relatively attractive to the peasantry, much as was done during the more prosperous, tranquil years of NEP. Under these circumstances, however, the Party believed the rate of accumulation of capital would be small. Because the countryside was still poor, the peasants would choose to consume much of their income. The funds they did accumulate would most likely be reinvested in their farms or villages. The peasants would be exceedingly reluctant (with good reason) to put savings in the rural branches of urban banks controlled by the suspected Communist party. Even if the Party allowed the peasants to trade on good terms with the cities and then taxed part of their income, it would encounter concealment of capital (a problem also encountered in developed countries where farmers receive income from a diversity of sales). This benign method of obtaining capital, therefore, would result in a slow industrialization. Moreover, it would increase the wealth of the peasantry, it might correspondingly increase the peasants' political power, and might threaten the power of the Communist party. The revolution itself could be endangered.

We can now see the basis of the conflict between the peasants and the Party. Good urban-rural terms of trade for the rural population would result in a lower rate of industrialization and growth and a lower rate of achievement of Party goals. While the authorities needed the peasant's grain, they wanted it on terms that would permit capital investment in industry. Consequently, the Party displayed an inconsistent attitude toward the peasant.[7] On the one hand, the revolution had been made in an alliance with the peasantry. On the other hand, during the Civil War the peasant's loyalty frequently had wavered, and after the War his objectives differed more and more from those of the Party leadership.

The Significance of the Middle Peasant

The peasant was both a producer and a merchant. As a small property owner, he tended to identify with the bourgeoisie. The Party line with regard to the peasantry was simple: The Party should seek the support of the poor peasant, accept the middle peasant as an ally, and combat the rich peasant (the "kulak").[8] In essence the scheme was to divide and rule, but the peasants were not so easy to classify and separate. The middle peasant, like the rich peasant, sometimes rented land from the poor peasant, hired labor, or owned farm equipment, draft horses, and cattle. The middle peasant aspired to become rich. He was as reluctant to part with his grain for low prices as was the rich peasant. The middle peasant looked up to the rich peasant as hardworking, knowledgeable, and progressive. Even the poor peasant sometimes looked to the kulak for leadership, when he felt Party pressure to change his life in the countryside and when he saw how little the officials who were sent out from the cities understood agriculture. (At other times the Party successfully played on the envy that the poor peasant had for the rich.)

It became clear that the Party could not separate out and attack the kulak alone, because it was the middle peasant who produced the large quantities of grain that the government wanted. Eventually the Party, and Stalin himself, realized it was the middle peasant who was the real stumbling block. Sometimes a grain procurement campaign revealed this state of affairs when officials were instructed to attack the "better-off peasant" as well as the kulak.[9] In addition, the Party felt more and more threatened by the possibility of an alternative power, in a coalescence of Nepmen, kulaks, and a lower strata in the bureaucracy that the traders and peasants had corrupted with bribes to get around unfavorable governmental directives.[10]

[7]Lewin, *Russian Peasants*, pp. 34, 59, 66–69, 71.
[8]Ibid., pp. 44, 69, 136.
[9]Ibid., pp. 49, 71.
[10]Ibid., pp. 187–91.

Before we deal with the demise of the NEP and the turn to rapid industrialization and farm collectivization, we might consider the role of ideology in these events. Many in the Communist Party were hostile to the free trade and open markets of the NEP. These people detested the Nepman, even though the latter had opened the arteries of trade and overcome the bottlenecks that were strangling the economy during the period of War Communism. And Party activists intensely disliked the kulaks and better-off peasants despite the fact that these peasants produced vital grain supplies. Hostility to free trade was obvious in the Party attitude toward Bukharin, who had become a moderate, or "rightist," in the struggle within the Party; he had a difficult time living down the "Get Rich" slogan he coined for the NEP. Such ideological aversion to NEP, along with a deep-seated belief in the revolutionary use of force, helped bring about the increasing controls that weakened the NEP and made rapid industrialization and collectivization almost inescapable.

Industrialization and Collectivization

Difficulties mounted from 1927 on. Government procurement prices had been lowered in 1926, and in parts of the Soviet Union by 1928 they were only 25 to 33 percent of free market prices. [11]

Undoubtedly what brought matters to a head was the problem of state procurements. Every year the leaders watch anxiously as deliveries mounted in the autumn and winter, wondering if there would be enough to feed the towns and the army and, who knows, something for export too. Attention was particularly concentrated on grain, the key crop since bread was the staff of life in Russia, and because over 80 per cent of all the sown land was sown to grain.[12]

As a result of the procurement problem, the peasants hoarded their grain, sold what they could to private traders, and reduced their sowings when the government made private trade difficult. To make matters worse, the government had no grain reserves. Each year saw a battle for grain between the government and the peasantry; and the government was losing! For all grains, the government obtained in 1926–27 a total of 10.6 million tons; in 1927–28 the total was down to 10.1 million tons, and in 1928–29,

[11] Ibid., pp. 287.
[12] Nove, *Economic History*, p. 149.

down to 9.45 million tons. The totals for food grains dropped more sharply—from 8.3 to 6.2 million tons over the three crop years.[13] Stalin's statement on the subject was entitled "On the Grain Front."

The government resorted to coercion more and more often, even while the NEP was still nominally in force. Local markets were closed and the militia intimidated the peasants who appeared at any markets still open, house-to-house searches were conducted and the names of peasants found with hidden stocks were publicized, and roadblocks were set up to confiscate grain from wagons. Countrymen who sold their grain in free markets and failed to meet targets for delivery to government procurement agencies might have their belongings confiscated, or be fined or imprisoned.[14]

Forced Collectivization

So the procurement crises led to collectivization. The Party leadership, dominated by Stalin, decided that the government could get delivery of the grain it wanted on its own terms from collective farms. The peasants were forced into the collectives (although the poorest peasants were more inclined to enter voluntarily). The authorities made threats as well as promises: "Anyone who does not join the collective is an enemy of the Soviet regime." The principal tactic was a final assault on the kulaks, or "dekulakization." "Liquidation of the kulaks as a class" became the official line, and the better-off peasants or any peasant who opposed collectivization might be classed as a kulak. The kulaks' property was confiscated and they could be imprisoned. Millions were deported, with or without their families, in freight cars to the North, to the forests, and to the deserts. Large numbers died enroute of cold, hunger, and disease. Many of the families of men imprisoned or deported dispersed through the countryside and towns and became beggars and vagabond children.[15]

[13]Lewin, *Russian Peasants*, p. 178.

[14]Ibid., pp. 224–25, 235, 240.

[15]Ibid., pp. 467, 471, 487, 505–8. The reader should not assume that this grim portrayal of events is brought forward by refugees and Western critics of the Soviet economy alone. It has been largely confirmed by authors who have now been published in the Soviet Union. Anna Louise Strong, an American journalist with pro-Soviet sympathies, was in Russia at the time and described the turmoil, the uprooted households, and the deportation trains in her book, *The Soviets Conquer Wheat*, 1931.

Rather than experience the fate of a kulak, the embittered peasants flooded into the collective farms. Many of them slaughtered their livestock before they joined. The percentage of households collectivized grew very rapidly, from about 7 percent in September 1929, to 15 percent at the end of December, and then to about 59 percent in March 1930.

Stalin slowed the movement by suggesting that officials had allowed success to go to their heads; he did this in his "dizzy with success" article on 2 March 1930. The peasants left the collectives rapidly. By 1 June 1930, households in collectives had dwindled to 24 percent of all households. Then, more gradually this time, the peasants again were pressed into the collectives. The percentages of households collectivized in the month of July for years 1931, 1933, 1935, and 1936 were as follows: 53 percent in 1931, 64 percent in 1933, 83 percent in 1935, and 90 percent in 1936.[16]

Soviet leadership had made it an official policy that rapid industrialization depended on capital accumulated by the peasantry and captured by the Soviet government through collectivization. Conversely, the leadership also believed that collectivization, with the need for more equipment on collective farms, made necessary a rapid growth of industry. As historian, M. Lewin explained, "Many of the leadership at this time had begun to regard the tractor almost as if it were endowed with supernatural properties, which would solve all their difficulties for them."[17]

The Leap Forward

Along with this belief in benefits of farm equipment, a leap-forward psychology seized much of the Party leadership in general and Stalin in particular. In drawing up the First Five-Year Plan, for 1929–33, the State Planning Commission, *Gosplan*, submitted two versions, the "minimal" or initial version, and the "optimal" version. The latter was, on the average, about twenty percent larger than the former. These professional planners in *Gosplan* intended that the optimal version be implemented if fortunate circumstances were encountered, such as good weather, a favorable balance of trade, international relations permitting relatively low defense commitments, and so forth. For example, the optimal version assumed five good harvests in a row and a 110 percent increase in the productivity of industrial workers! This optimal

[16]Lewin, *Russian Peasants*, pp. 514–15; Nove, *Economic History*, pp. 172–74.
[17]Lewin, *Russian Peasants*, p. 274. See also pp. 258, 288, 357, 360.

version was adopted in April 1929, and almost immediately many of its targets were raised (for example, the investment plan for nonferrous metals was doubled). By November of the same year the watchword had become: "The Five-Year Plan must be fulfilled in four years."[18]

These efforts to leap forward created a great deal of tension in the country. The tone of discussion changed. Disagreement had existed in the twenties and differing views had been strongly expressed. But in the early thirties, real argument ceased and gave way to abuse.[19] A theory was developed to justify coercive measures; Party leaders said that with the growing power of socialism there would be an intensification of the class struggle as merchants, small-scale and medium-scale capitalists, and kulaks fought back. In Stalin's words, "As we march forward, resistance from these capitalist elements will increase, and the class struggle will grow more and more bitter...."[20] Sabotage, attributed to "wreckers," was used to explain numerous supply failures, and many engineers were tried and convicted.[21]

The Five-Year Plan had called for price reductions on consumption goods, but by the end of 1929, rationing had spread from bread to almost all foodstuffs and then to manufactured goods. Moreover, the government urgently needed revenue. Prices began to be increased and in October 1930 the turnover tax (similar to an excise or sales tax) was introduced. As prices to consumers rose while agricultural procurement prices remained low, the difference was mopped up by the turnover tax. The price of bread in cities in 1933 rose by 80 percent. The grain procurement organization during 1933 sold coarse wheat flour at 216 rubles per centner, of which turnover tax took 195.50 rubles. Because of the high prices rationing was abolished in 1934–35. Needless to say, the standard of living fell strikingly. Alec Nove asserts that "1933 was the culmination of the most precipitous decline in living standards known in recorded history."[22]

Perhaps the most significant point about these events is their legacy for the future. As Stalin's opponents, Rykov and Bukharin, foresaw, emergency measures began to seem normal.[23] Although

[18] Ibid., pp. 347–48, 374–75, 518.
[19] Nove, *Economic History*, p. 216.
[20] Lewin, *Russian Peasants*, p. 263.
[21] Ibid., p. 263; Nove, *Economic History*, p. 217.
[22] Ibid., p. 207. See also pp. 194, 201–10, 219.
[23] Lewin, *Russian Peasants*, pp. 298, 303.

plans became substantially more sober in subsequent years, even today opponents of "mobilization planning" and "strained balances" remain on the defensive, and bonuses are awarded, most of the time irrationally, for overfulfillment of the plan.

Ideology

An intriguing question is the relationship between ideology and personality in this history of the development of the Soviet-type economy. In formulating a doctrine of early socialist development, Trotsky had used the term *primitive socialist accumulation,* and Preobrazhensky had developed it into a doctrine. (This is the socialist counterpart of Marx's *primitive capitalist accumulation.*) Before the socialist sector was developed, they argued, capital could only be accumulated from the remnants of capitalism, from the petty bourgeois, and above all from the peasantry. Indeed in his early writings, Preobrazhensky even described the peasants as an "internal colony." He did not intend that they should be plundered but only that their "surpluses" should be captured through taxation and through control over the prices of the produce they sold and the goods they purchased, "within the limits of what is economically possible, technically feasible, and rational."[24]

Early in the 1970s, this important Soviet doctrine was challenged in the West. The question was raised of whether a surplus existed in the countryside, which could be tapped for the capital required in an industrialization program. Millar, a present-day scholar, contended that one attempt to measure the Russian agricultural surplus for the late twenties and early thirties indicates that the surplus may have been small or even negative. (A negative surplus would mean that capital for industrialization would have come from nonagricultural sectors.) He asserts that while Stalin may have intended to "milk the peasants" to support rapid industrialization, he actually may have succeeded only in making peasants' lives miserable. Millar argues that we may discover that the Soviet Union grew not because of the terms of trade imposed on the peasants but in spite of these conditions; he goes so far as to suggest that the agricultural procurement system may have served merely to offset the economic costs of collectivization.[25]

[24]Ibid., pp. 150–51.

[25]James R. Millar, "Soviet Rapid Development and the Agricultural Surplus Hypothesis," *Soviet Studies,* 22 (July, 1970), p. 93; James R. Millar, "The Agricultural Surplus Hypothesis: A Reply to Alec Nove," *Soviet Studies* 23 (October, 1971), pp. 304–5.

The question raised by Millar is a serious one, particularly for countries inclined to consider the Soviet experience as a model for development.

We can see how the idea of an agricultural surplus played so large a role in laying the foundations of the Soviet-type economy. Stalin and his followers believed strongly in the necessity for capturing the surplus produced by the peasants. In a speech in July 1928, Stalin justified this doctrine of accumulation. He pointed to the direct taxes on the peasants, the high prices they paid for manufactured goods, and the low prices they received for their own output, and he concluded that "this is a form of 'tribute' or 'super-tax' which we are forced to levy on them temporarily if we are to maintain and also to increase the present rate of industrial development."[26]

The Role of Stalin

Did rapid industrialization and forced collectivization require Stalin's leadership, or would these events have occurred in any case as a consequence of the ideology, the strongly held convictions, of the Communist party? Any answer to this question is bound to be speculative, but the respective roles of men and ideas in history are significant enough to be worth some thought. Would the Soviet Union have developed along similar lines without Stalin?[27] I believe the events we have reviewed probably would have happened even if Stalin had never lived. At the most, I suspect, his ruthlessness and manipulative skills speeded up what would have occurred without him. In all probability, Stalin had the support of the majority of the Party, former oppositionists included, for his

---

[26]Lewin, *Russian Peasants*, p. 258. Some students of the Soviet Union believe that the ideology of industrialization and the agricultural surplus played a less significant role in forging economic institutions than I have suggested here. They contend that what occurred was a struggle for power between persons and factions, with ideas being used as weapons. They also argue that the old leadership desired a struggle with the peasantry in order to develop a revolutionary consciousness amongst those who had joined the party after the revolution and Civil War. Such an interpretation of events deserves serious consideration. But we might note that the ideas and tactics used by the ultimate victors in the struggle for power reflected the deep-seated ideology of the Party—rapid industrialization, accumulation through capture of a surplus received by the peasantry, distrust of private agriculture and free markets, and advance through the use of the revolutionary campaign. Ideology does seem to have been exceedingly important in the formation of Soviet economic institutions.

[27]An interesting article on this question is Alec Nove, "Was Stalin Really Necessary?" in *Encounter* 18 (April, 1962), reprinted in Nove, *Economic Rationality and Soviet Politics* (New York: Frederick A. Praeger, 1964).

policy.[28] The Party believed in revolutionary change, and it was becoming increasingly frustrated at what it believed was the peasants' ability to thwart rapid industrialization. Therefore, the Party was likely sooner or later to take advantage of the weakness of the peasantry, with its inability to organize politically. The pressure of the ideology can best be seen in the remarks of the nearly defeated Bukharin as he considered the possibility of an attack on the almost victorious Stalin:

> We will say—'Here is the man who has reduced the country to ruin and famine' and he will say—'Here are the champions of the kulaks and the Nepmen.'[29]

It would be easier to defend the proposition that Lenin changed history because he led Russia into the New Economic Policy, *against* the strongly held convictions of a very large part of the Party. As a consequence Lenin probably saved the Revolution. Stalin, on the other hand, had the majority of the Party supporting him as he put the Revolution back on its original course—using a Party apparatus largely created by Lenin.

Having studied the origins of the Soviet-type economy, we are now in a position to examine the way the different parts of the system work.

---

[28] Nove, *Economic Rationality*, pp. 24, 32, 37.
[29] Lewin, *Russian Peasants*, p. 307.

Current Output Planning

Chapter 2

The problems of planning cannot be understood unless the immense complexity of a modern economy is recognized. An economy is a vast network of direct and indirect relationships. For example, the output of steel is directly related to the outputs of iron ore, coal, and limestone, is indirectly related to the outputs of gasoline and electricity used in the production of ore and coal, and is still less directly related to the outputs of crude oil and drilling mud. The output of steel also is directly related to the outputs of automobiles, refrigerators, and locomotives, which in turn are related to the outputs of glass, rubber, plastics, and copper, and these in turn are related to the outputs of sand, chemicals, and copper ore. Moreover, the relationships between products frequently are two-way relationships. Just as the output of electricity depends on the output of coal, the output of coal depends on the output of electricity. This network of related outputs spreads out in millions of connections. In the United States there are 27 grades of aluminum scrap, 44 of copper and brass, 46 of wastepaper, and 105 of iron and steel.[1] The Boeing 747 alone has 130,000 parts. The standard classification of all industrial products manufactured in the Soviet Union consists of 20 million items.[2]

[1] Marilyn Wellemeyer, "For Scrapmen These Are Tinsel Days," *Fortune* 90 (August, 1974), p. 232.
[2] *Ekonomicheskaia gazeta*, 18 May 1963, p. 17. Also cited in Leon Smolinski and Peter Wiles, "The Soviet Planning Pendulum," *Problems of Communism*, November-December, 1963, p. 24.

The unknown outputs are interdependent variables, mutally determined.

These relationships are further complicated by the fact that all production does not take place at a single point in space. Rather, inputs may be required and products may be manufactured at thousands of different points on the surface of the earth. It is not enough that the total production of steel and coal be appropriately related. The steel produced and the coal supplied must be made consistent at numerous steel mills in different locations. Space greatly increases the number of unknowns that must somehow be made known if resources are to be rationally allocated.

Millions of commodities, innumerable spatial possibilities, interdependent variables! The complexities of current output planning are formidable indeed.

Objectives

The basic objective of the authorities in the Soviet-type economy is the production of goods that maximize the rate of growth of wealth in the economy. The goods that make up wealth are evaluated by both the government and the consumers, with the preferences of the former overriding those of the latter. The government has certain output preferences for goods it wants produced in a given year: for example, 120 million tons of steel, 530 million tons of coal, 1.2 million automobiles, etc.[3] Within the constraints of these output targets, expressed in aggregates, the government wants the output of disaggregated assortments and goods not included in the plan to reflect consumer preferences. (Under some circumstances governmental preferences are expressed in prices.)

To minimize waste and hence increase growth, the authorities have two subobjectives: (1) production of a consistent set of outputs, and (2) production which is efficient or economical.

There are a number of different kinds of planning. In this chapter we will be dealing with current output planning, or the construction of a set of output targets for a single year. We will consider first the problems of drawing up the plan and then take up the problems of plan execution. In the next chapter we will

[3] It has been argued by many economists that it is irrational for the authorities to express preferences for producers' goods, but if they like to see high steel output figures, high relative to the past or relative to the output of another country, the economist as scientist cannot state that they lack rationality and should have preferences only for what are usually classed as consumption goods.

look at multiperiod planning, and see how a five-year plan is constructed.

Required Knowledge

The plan is initiated by the top authority, whose preferences are final. This authority in the Soviet economy is the Council of Ministers, which is dominated by the Politburo (political bureau of the Communist party). Below it is the State Planning Commission (sometimes called a Committee), which is the principal planning agency. This is a group of technicians who draw up the plan according to the preferences of the top authority.[4] The Planning Commission uses two kinds of knowledge: (1) the preferences of the top authority, and (2) the technical relationships between inputs and outputs. Below the Planning Commission are the industrial ministries (such as the Ministry of Heavy Machine Building), below them are the subministries (each responsible for a group of enterprises), and at the bottom of the structure are the enterprises themselves.[5]

The Bill of Goods

How does the top authority state its preferences? Probably it will state them in a "bill of goods," which is a list of commodities with the amount of each that the authorities want produced. (For a sample bill of goods, see Table 2-1.) The bill of goods may include commodities like steel and electricity if the authorities prefer these things as ends-in-themselves. (The authorities in the Soviet Union often have preferred such goods as they have sought to overtake capitalism.) The bill of goods may also include increases in inventories and in plant capacity if the authorities favor such additions. When there is both a planned and an unplanned sector of the economy, the top authority will have to indicate the resources it wants to have made available to the planned sector, in addition to its bill of goods.

[4] I speak of the preferences of the top authority and not of "planners' preferences." I think it useful to distinguish between an authority with preferences and a technical body without preferences of its own, which seeks to satisfy the preferences of the authority.

[5] During the Krushchev period, the Soviet Union had a regional rather than a functional structure for planning. Below the State Planning Committee in the hierarchy were the Regional Economic Councils ("Sovnarkhozy") and the enterprises.

Table 2-1 **Bill of Goods, Year N**

Commodity	Quantity
Steel (tons)	120,000,000
Coal (tons)	530,000,000
Housing (sq. metres)	400,400,000
. . .	. . .
Automobiles (millions)	1,200,000

The Planning Commission cannot simply receive this bill of goods, gather a list of resources available, and then proceed to draw up a plan without further consultation with the authorities. The bill of goods initially proposed probably will turn out to be either too large or too small for the available resources. After the Planning Commission has constructed one version of the plan, it will have to go back to the authorities for further information about their preferences. The authorities will then revise the bill of goods, increasing the output figures for some items and reducing the figures for others. They may also decide to increase or reduce the resources available to the planned sector. Thus, during the process of drawing up an output plan, a dialogue takes place between the top authority and the Planning Commission in which information about preferences and production possibilities is exchanged.[6]

Technological Coefficients

In addition to the preferences of the top authority, the State Planning Commission has to know the technical relationships between inputs and outputs. For example, it must know how much coal it takes to manufacture a ton of steel. This technology usually is expressed in the form of a technological coefficient, which is the amount of a particular commodity used to produce one unit of another commodity. Coefficients ordinarily are indicated by the symbol a_{ij}, where the quantity of commodity i is used to produce one unit of j. For example, $a_{47} = 0.3$ states that it takes 0.3 units of commodity 4 to turn out 1.0 unit of commodity 7.

[6]Cf. Czeslaw Bobrowski, *Basic Problems of Planning* (Warszawa: Szkola Glowna Planowania i Statystyki, 1966), p. 79. Some thought has been given to ways in which the top authority might offer its preferences in a single statement at the outset, with no further consultation required. In theory, the authorities might state the amounts they would demand as a function of all possible sets of prices, or they might rank in order of preference all possible combinations of goods. Such procedures are not feasible in practice.

One difficulty with input and output relationships is that a technological coefficient is not necessarily the same for all possible quantities of production, even at the same place and time. Frequently, when there are economies (or diseconomies) of large-scale production, technological coefficients vary with output. We therefore find that the Planning Commission cannot know outputs without knowing technological coefficients, and it cannot know technological coefficients without knowing outputs. Because the two are mutually determined, the computational costs of arriving at a good output plan are greatly increased. (Frequently physical scientists and engineers are sympathetic to central planning when they consider our vast scientific knowledge. "If only science were properly applied to the economy...." But knowledge of scientific propositions, true under carefully specified circumstances, is not the same as knowledge of the multitudinous circumstances of time and place. A Planning Commission not only must know the technological coefficient in a particular situation but also must know the technological coefficients for a great variety of circumstances.)

A number of similar commodities may be grouped together (all the different kinds of steel produced in a number of different locations, for example), in order to hold down computational costs. Then, the technological coefficient used is a weighted average of the technological coefficients of all the subcategories, with the weights reflecting the output proportions of the subcategories. (The quantity of coal per unit of steel would be the weighted average of the coal required for each of the different kinds of steel as well as the coal required in each of the different places where a given kind is manufactured.) But the quantities to be produced in each of the subgroups is not known until the central plan is disaggregated, and estimated weights must therefore be used in drawing up the plan.

We observe, then, that the Planning Commission does not first learn the preferences of the top authorities and the technology of the economy and then proceed to draw up a plan. Rather, the process of planning itself is designed to generate knowledge. As the Commission receives new statements of preferences, it continues to revise its estimates of technological coefficients.

Procedures

Although reorganization in the Soviet economy is not uncommon, the basic method of planning is fairly stable and can be simply described. For many years the annual central plan in the Soviet

Union has included output figures for about one thousand commodities. Most of these commodities have been aggregated totals for groups of similar products, such as steel, vehicles, and clothing.

The formal procedure for drawing up a current output plan is the following: The State Planning Commission starts out with a statistical analysis of the base period, which is the past year. For example, if the plan for 1978 is being drawn up in 1977, the base period is 1976. The Commission also studies developments in the first six months of the current year and forecasts what will happen in the second six months. Then, keeping the basic objectives of the Council of Ministers in mind, the Commission constructs what are known as "control figures" or "preliminary indicators." These are tentative, aggregated output targets for the most important commodity groups, as well as a list of the major investment targets.

These control figures are then sent down the hierarchy to guide the lower bodies in their planning. Using the control figures and a knowledge of past periods and recent changes, enterprises, subministries, and ministries forecast their probable output targets and submit orders for the necessary material inputs. The subministries aggregate the input orders of the enterprises, the ministries aggregate the orders of the subministries, and the State Planning Commission sums up all the ministerial orders. The Planning Commission then balances the supply and demand for each of the centrally planned commodities, using the "method of balances" described below, and submits the balanced plan to the Council of Ministers for approval. The Council may insist on some changes that require rebalancing. The approved plan is sent down the hierarchy, becoming disaggregated en route. The plan received by the enterprise includes orders for delivery of outputs and authorizations, or "fondy," for the receipt of inputs. The enterprises then contract with one another to establish delivery schedules and other delivery details.

The broad outline just described for drawing up the plan is, in practice, much less formal than my description suggests. Messages are sent up and down the hierarchy at irregular intervals and more often than when the control figures go down, the orders for material inputs go up, and the final plan goes down. There is also a certain amount of horizontal communication, as successive versions of the plan are developed by a "shuttle technique." Information and proposals shuttle back and forth as in a loom.[7]

[7]Bobrowski, *Basic Problems*, p. 94.

We now need to see in more detail how the State Planning Commission uses the method of balances to arrive at consistent output figures.

Consistency

The State Planning Commission constructs a "material balance" for each of the commodities in the central plan. This material balance is a yearly statement in physical terms (tons of steel, number of vehicles, etc.) of the total demand for and total supply of a product. A typical material balance can be seen in Table 2-2.

Table 2-2 **Material Balance, Product X**

Sources	Distribution
1. Production	1. Production-operation needs (production inputs, maintenance included)
2. Imports	2. Construction
3. Other (e.g. scrap metal)	3. Market fund (distributed for consumption)
4. Stocks at suppliers at beginning of period*	4. Exports
	5. Increase in state reserves (for national disasters)
	6. Increase in reserves of Council of Ministers (for distribution during the year to cover supply failures)
	7. Stocks at suppliers at end of period*

Source: A modified presentation of material in Herbert S. Levine, "The Centralized Planning of Supply in Soviet Industry," *Comparisons of the United States and Soviet Economies* (Joint Economic Committee, Congress of the United States, 86th Congress, First Session, 1959), pp. 162-63.
*Stocks at users (if above normal levels) are taken into account by subtracting them from requirements submitted by enterprises.

The Commission's problem is to achieve a consistency of the material balances, taking into account both direct and indirect interdependencies. For example, the planned output of vehicles should be consistent with the planned output of steel, the planned outputs of coke, iron ore, and limestone, the planned output of electricity, and so forth. The planned quantities of any set of commodities are consistent with one another when the totals agree given the technological coefficients being used. A plan of 10,000 trucks, 50,000 automobiles, and 200,000 pounds of copper is consistent if it is expected that each truck will require five pounds of copper and each automobile three pounds (10,000 × 5 + 50,000 × 3 = 200,000).

In addition to being consistent with one another, outputs must be consistent with the inputs required by current investment projects. The latter may include capital installations valued by the authorities as ends-in-themselves (and, therefore, part of the bill of goods). They will certainly include investment projects derived from multiperiod plans (five-year plans or the like), which are discussed in the next chapter.

Iteration
In trying to construct a consistent set of balances, the State Planning Commission uses an informal iterative technique. This is the repetitive adjustment of output targets to make them agree with one another. For example, a tentative output figure for vehicles may be selected, then an output figure for steel is set (steel being used in the production of vehicles), then output figures for iron ore, limestone, and coal are set, followed by an output figure for electricity (which is used to lift the coal from the mines). At this point it may be decided that the coal figure must be increased in order to compensate for the planned electricity. More coal, in turn, requires a revision of the figure for electricity. The readjustments go on, taking account of all the direct and indirect relationships between outputs. The process is one of successive approximation, of groping toward a consistent set of output targets. The iterative technique used in this method of balances is not as systematic as mathematical iterative procedures, but, as we shall see, the informality of the Soviet method gives it flexibility.

We shall also see how the process of making lower-level plans consistent with the central plan uses "administrative iteration." But before we deal with lower-level plans, we must know more about the construction of the central plan. In dealing with consistency, we assumed that technological coefficients were given. Now we need to examine Planning Commission's means of determining inputs per unit of output, and its means of determining coefficients for the utilization of materials, labor, and machinery.

The Determination of Technological Coefficients

Technological coefficients, we noted earlier, often vary with output. Except for industries with constant returns to scale, inputs per unit of output depend upon the volume of output. For example, the quantity of necessary coal per unit of steel depends upon the output of steel. But, of course, output figures are the unknowns that the Planning Commission is trying to discover. In practice, knowledge of output in the preceding year and in the first few months of the current year, combined with control figures or preliminary indicators for the year being planned, make possible some shrewd guesses as to what the technological coefficients are likely to be. As new output figures emerge from the iterative process, early estimates of technological coefficients can be revised. This is an example of the flexibility of the method of balances.

Aggregation

Summation, as we have also observed already, is a further source of difficulty in calculating technological coefficients. In determining aggregates to reduce the number of commodities in a central plan, the State Planning Commission has to use average technological coefficients. For example, as it tries to arrive at the total amounts of iron ore and steel that should be produced, it necessarily uses the average amount of iron ore which is required to turn out one ton of steel; that is, the Commission averages iron ore per ton of structural steel, per ton of steel plate, per ton of sheet steel, and so on. This average technological coefficient is a weighted average, with the weights reflecting the proportions of the subcategories which are likely to be needed. But the proportions of the subcategories are not known until the plan is disaggregated. The Planning Commission has to estimate these proportions and hence estimate the weights to be used in calculating average technological coefficients. Consequently, the technological coefficients often will be in error.

Erroneous Technological Coefficients

A technological coefficient is a forecast. It is a forecast of the uncertain future performance of labor, materials, and equipment. For a number of reasons, the forecast may be wrong. The quality of workers may be lower than expected, or the effectiveness of incentive schemes may be less than predicted. The quality of materials may be below expectations. The quality of equipment may fall short of what was anticipated. Old equipment may be in poor condition and unexpected breakdowns may occur. New equipment may come into operation later than anticipated, it may achieve planned output later than foreseen, or it may fail entirely to reach contemplated output. Finally, forecasts of technological coefficients may be wrong because individuals supply inaccurate information to their superiors.

This brings us to the subject of a possible conflict of interest between individuals at different levels in the hierarchy. Frequently the enterprise manager, in order to get an easy production task, understates the capacity of his plant and equipment and overstates his needs for material and labor inputs. (He may also produce less than his plant can turn out so as not to reveal by his actions the capacity of his enterprise; we will consider this problem when we deal with plan execution.) The authorities in the Soviet economy are not interested solely in what managers say their technological coefficients are, nor are they interested only in the actual performance of managers. The authorities are interested in improvements in performance, in increased efficiency.

Efficiency

A good is produced efficiently if it is produced at a minimum cost in foregone alternatives. Such a minimization of opportunity cost promotes a maximum rate of growth in wealth.

The Soviet authorities' interest in greater efficiency, at least in engineering efficiency, can be seen in the name they give to technological coefficients. They call inputs per unit of output "norms," norms of labor, material, and equipment utilization. Contrary to the Western idea that technological coefficient is something that exists and is discovered, the concept of norm connotes a sought-after level of performance. This effort to achieve improvement is seen in the kind of pressuring norms that are set. Typically, an enterprise is given an "average-progressive" norm, which is a technological coefficient somewhere between the industry average and the best in the industry. The top firms are given norms that represent improvement over the preceding period; for example, their norm of material utilization might be 3 percent lower than the previous year. The Soviet-type economies generally rely upon this "mobilization planning," with its sets of "strained balances."[8]

Forecasts versus Improvement
Is there a conflict between forecasting technological coefficients and efforts to improve them? In principle, there need not be a conflict, as forecasts can include predictions of the consequences of pressuring norms. The danger, of course, is that the State Planning Commission or the top authorities will persuade themselves that more can be achieved by pressure than is possible. In actuality, strained balances often are unrealistic. Moreover, pressure to improve norms may cause enterprise managers to conceal information or to supply inaccurate information about technological coefficients. If the authorities are risk-takers and the managers are risk-averters, the authorities will want to take a chance on ambitious targets while the managers will want low, safe targets. The managers will understate the capacity of their plants and overstate their labor and material input needs. The Planning Commission will try to correct for this bias in the information it receives. It will increase output targets for the plant and reduce the material inputs put at the disposal of managers. When a manager overstates his input needs, it is called "planning upward," and when the Commission corrects these managerial requests, it is called "planning from above." In the end managers who play it safe may succeed in getting targets so low that there are concealed reserves of capacity in the economy. Or, tough planners may demand so much that their plan is not feasible. Often there will be concealed reserves in some parts of the economy and unrealistically high targets in others.

Bargaining for Efficiency
The Soviet-type economy may produce a more reliable plan than is developed when planners and managers simply try to outwit one another. The State Planning Commission or the ministry actually bargains with the enterprise managers over norms of plant, material, and labor utilization. The manager says to the Planning Commission, "If you will give me x quantity of material inputs and y quantity of labor, I will produce z amounts of output in the plant you have assigned to me." At the end of the bargaining the man-

[8]Ibid., pp. 102–3.

ager commits himself to the targets that have been set. This negotiated plan probably is more reliable than one that results from the Planning Commission's arbitrary corrections for suspected misinformation from the manager. The manager's bargaining power rests on the fact that a failure of his enterprise reflects adversely on his supervisor.

Whether or not the plan is an efficient one will depend largely on the planner's knowledge of the real state of affairs in the enterprise. If the Planning Commission is ignorant of the capacity and input needs of the enterprise, the manager can get away with an easy, inefficient plan. If the people in the Commission have an intimate knowledge of the industry and the particular enterprise, they will insist on a tight, efficient plan. The supervisor of the tanker fleet of one of the major international oil companies once told me that his earlier years at sea were invaluable to him in appraising a ship captain's reasons for a low daily mileage. (But a captain I asked to comment on this point observed bitterly that officers who went ashore quickly forgot the difficulties encountered at sea!)

Efficiency through Input Substitution

Efficiency may be achieved in two ways: (1) by reduction of a particular input per unit of output while all other inputs are held constant, or (2) by substitution of a low-valued for a high-valued input. For example, the amount of coal used in the production of electricity might be reduced while all other inputs remain stable, or low-valued fuel oil might be substituted for high-valued coal. In either case opportunity cost is decreased and the rate of growth in wealth is increased. The first alternative is most likely, for while the reduction of individual inputs per unit of output is a difficult task in a planned economy, the discovery of substitution possibilities in such a system is truly formidable.

With physical planning, the Planning Commission has to consider the indirect as well as the direct physical consequences of a production decision. Consider the example of electricity produced with either coal or fuel oil. Table 2-3 shows some of the factors that might be considered in determining the cost of coal-generated electricity. If electricity is produced with coal, less coal is available for steel production. With a lower production of steel, more limestone is available for the production of cement. A larger output of cement requires more clay, which reduces the output of tile, and so forth. Moreover, if electricity is produced with coal, oil will be available for the production of refrigerators. This output of refrigerators will require labor, which will reduce the output of some other commodity. Table 2-3 states, in summary, that if electricity is produced with coal, the economy will forego steel, tile, fertilizer, harbor fill, etc., but it will have more cement, bricks, refrigerators, and the like. After the State Planning Commission has traced the direct and indirect effects of producing electricity with coal and with fuel oil, it must evaluate all the goods foregone or gained and decide which method is least costly. The top authority will insist that its preferences be considered in the evaluation of goods which appear in the bill of goods. Opportunity cost in this context means not money value foregone but net value foregone. Minimization of opportunity cost means minimization of net value foregone; this, of course, will maximize the increase in wealth.

The concept of opportunity cost presented here is a more complex concept than many textbooks have indicated. Texts often illustrate opportunity cost with only one input.[9] Or, if an author deals with multiple inputs, he or she speaks of a fixed bundle of inputs used to produce two commodities. For example, the economist Boulding writes of a given quantity of resources which could

Table 2-3 Part of the Opportunity Cost (In Physical Terms) of the Production of Electricity with Coal

```
Electricity
  ← Coal
      – Steel
              Limestone →
                  + Cement
      Labor           ← Clay
         – Fertilizer       – Tile
      Trucking                    Labor →
         – Harbor Filled In           + Bricks
      Oil →                              ← Etc.
         + Refrigerators                     – Etc.
             ← Labor
                 – Etc.
```

Note: Plus and minus signs indicate, respectively, increases and decreases in output. Arrows indicate movement of a resource (e.g., the movement of coal from the production of steel to the production of electricity).

---

[9]George Stigler, *The Theory of Price*, rev. ed. (New York: Macmillan Co., 1952), p. 97; Donald Stevenson Watson, *Price Theory and Its Uses* (Boston: Houghton Mifflin Co., 1963), p. 125.

produce either 50 bushels of wheat or one ton of steel.[10] He does not consider that if the wheat is not produced, land may be available for the production of corn, fertilizer may be used to produce hay, and labor may be employed in the steel mills. Then, with a larger output of steel, coal may be drawn away from the production of electricity. Other indirect results will follow. Thus, in the construction of a physical plan, the discovery of efficient combinations necessitates that the cost of all ramifications be explored.

The Absence of Scarcity Prices
The question arises of whether or not it is possible to achieve efficiency without scarcity prices. In a system with scarcity prices, the decision maker need not trace the direct and indirect consequences of a decision, as prices will reflect the possible input-output relationships. The decision maker need only minimize money cost. But in a Soviet-type economy, the Planning Commission must construct an efficient physical plan. Can it trace all the direct and indirect consequences of all the different ways of turning out each good in the plan and then evaluate all the different alternatives? Von Mises in 1920 contended that rational calculation is impossible without the prices that follow from the private ownership of the means of production.[11] Lange and Lerner have shown us that, at least in theory, the "socialist" accounting prices that clear the market for capital goods can be used to find efficiency in a socialist economy.[12] But it remains to be demonstrated that efficiency can be achieved in an economic system with no prices at all.

There is one more problem that supports the idea that prices may be necessary to achieve efficiency. The Planning Commission must evaluate the efficiency of trade with the unplanned parts of the economy and trade with other economies. Is it more efficient, for example, to produce automobile batteries in the planned sector of the economy or to produce lead in the planned sector and exchange it for batteries turned out within the country in a sector

[10] Kenneth E. Boulding, *Economic Analysis*, 3rd ed. (New York: Harper and Brothers, 1955), p. 28.

[11] Ludwig von Mises, "Economic Calculation in the Socialist Commonwealth," in F. A. Hayek, ed., *Collectivist Economic Planning* (London: Routledge and Kegan Paul, 1935).

[12] Oskar Lange and Fred M. Taylor, *On the Economic Theory of Socialism* (Minneapolis: University of Minnesota Press, 1938), pp. 72–83; A. P. Lerner, "Statics and Dynamics in Socialist Economies," *Economic Journal* 47 (June, 1937), pp. 253–70; Abba P. Lerner, *Economics of Control* (New York: Macmillan Co., 1944).

of market socialism or capitalism? Is it more efficient to produce machine tools within the economy or to produce oil and trade it for machine tools manufactured elsewhere in the world? It is doubtful that trade patterns can be made efficient with physical planning and without prices.

Lower-Level Plans

We stated earlier that the central plan, after it is approved by the Council of Ministers, is sent down the hierarchy from the State Planning Commission to the ministries, subministries, and enterprises. The lower-level bodies disaggregate the plan, constructing a set of subplans. For example, the Planning Commission might set an output figure for vehicles. A ministry might break this down into targets for trucks, automobiles, and motorcycles, and a subministry might draw up a plan for different kinds of trucks—one-ton, five-ton, ten-ton, dump trucks, moving vans, two-wheel drive, four-wheel drive, etc. The enterprise itself might plan the most detailed assortment—trucks with different combinations of lights, mirrors, windshield washers, etc.

Consistency

The first question we must ask is how lower-level plans are coordinated with one another. Suppose one subministry disaggregates the plan for steel and another subministry breaks down the target for vehicles. How will the outputs of different kinds of steel be made consistent with the outputs of different kinds of vehicles? The planned quantities of sheet steel of different kinds, to take a particular case, should be consistent with the planned quantities of trucks, automobiles, and motorcycles. A consistency of total steel production with total vehicle production does not ensure a consistency of heavy sheet steel for truck bodies with truck output. Clearly, some horizontal communication between lower-level bodies is necessary. The subministry which decides the steel assortment must ask the subministry that decides the vehicle breakdown how much sheet steel of different kinds is required. Similarly, it must communicate with all the other agencies that use steel products.

At first glance this might not appear to be a large problem. The necessary flow of information is like that which occurs in capitalism when businessmen seek customers and place orders for materials and components. But there is a very important difference in a Soviet-type economy. When there is a central output plan, the lower-level bodies are constrained by that plan. Managers in these bodies must not only communicate with each other about what kinds of goods are wanted, in order to find a pattern of output that meets input and consumption needs, but they must also find a set of outputs that fulfills the central plan. In practice this requires a great deal of vertical as well as horizontal communication. The manager of a steel enterprise may have to say to the subministry or ministry, "I will not be able to turn out the kinds of sheet steel which the vehicle enterprises want if I must fulfill the proposed total output plan with the inputs you propose to make available to me." With a sufficiently large number of messages sent between lower-level units and between lower- and higher-level bodies, a consistent central plan and set of consistent lower-level plans can be constructed. (This process is sometimes called "administrative iteration," since the plans are constructed through communication between separate administrative units.) But in the traditional Soviet-type economy, motivation for vertical communication is much stronger than motivation for horizontal communication. As we shall see, rewards are tied mostly to the fulfillment (and overfulfillment) of aggregate output targets, and managers heed messages from their superiors more than messages from their customers. A manager who persistently receives inputs that do not meet his needs is more likely to get satisfaction by communicating with higher authorities than by sending messages to his suppliers.

Flexibility and Simultaneity

The method of balances has the advantage of being very flexible. Planning agencies can work on efficiency at the same time that they work on consistency. The Planning Commission may be able to change a technological coefficient in order to avoid taking into account the indirect consequences of change in a particular target. Suppose, for example, that the Commission decides to increase the output of steel and that this requires an increased production of pig iron. Rather than fullfill the larger production of pig iron with an increase in the output of iron ore, the Commission might decide that more pig iron should be turned out from the same amount of iron ore. This change in the technological coefficient would avoid the need to take into account the consequences in iron ore production of an increase in the target for steel. (Not taking into account indirect interdependencies like these is sometimes referred to as avoiding the problems of second-order linkages.) Needless to say, it is not always possible to stretch technological coefficients.

Because technological coefficients are not fixed, the State Planning Commission can achieve consistency by looking for alternative processes of production that substitute nondeficit for deficit materials, excess capital capacity for deficit materials, labor for materials, or skilled labor for unskilled labor. Industrial heat might be obtained from fuel oil rather than coal if dual-firing equipment is available. The economist Montias tells of an instance where bituminous coal was short in Poland, at the same time that there was a surplus of transportation facilities and an excess capacity in distant sugar refineries. Moreover, the distant refineries were newer and used less coal per ton of sugar produced. Consequently, authorities decided to transport sugar beets to the distant rather than the nearby refineries.[13] Capital, in the form of transport facilities, was substituted for a material input, coal.

The method of balances is flexible also in the use that planning agencies can make of information coming to them from outside. With virtually all aspects of the central plan and lower-level plans open to change during the day-to-day iterative process of constructing the plans, planners are often in a position to incorporate into their plans information about input needs and technology that comes to them from other planning agencies. They can also incorporate information about preferences that comes to them from the top authority. Furthermore, specialists with years of experience in planning a given sector of the economy incorporate the valuable information learned from their own backgrounds to estimate a real "feel" for the input/output relationships that prevail in their sector and in related sectors.[14]

The Cost of Calculation

There is a reverse side to the coin of flexibility. Because Soviet methods are so lacking in formality, the planners cannot know if all the information generated at any one step in the process is

[13] John Michael Montias, *Central Planning in Poland* (New Haven and London: Yale University Press, 1962), pp. 99–100.

[14] "It is particularly difficult to put into a formal model the experience and the knowledge of hundreds and thousands of people who take part in the planning process." Jozef Pajestka, "Certain Problems of Economic Planning in Poland," *Weltwirtshaftliches Archiv*, 1964, p. 173.

utilized at the next step. Moreover, the planners cannot be sure that the process is converging on the best possible set of plans, or that it is converging at the most rapid rate possible.

It must never be forgotten that what is being sought is a simultaneous solution of most of the unknowns in the system. Because of the vast network of direct and indirect interdependencies in a modern economy, the planners do not really know the proper output figure for one commodity until they know the output figures for most of the other commodities in the system.

It is not surprising, therefore, to learn that the high cost of calculation forces the planners in the Soviet-type economy to stop short of complete consistency and efficiency. Because inconsistency is revealed by shortages and surpluses when the plan is executed, and because inefficiency is not at all evident during plan execution, consistency is pursued more vigorously than efficiency. Even so, consistency is seldom, if ever, achieved. In spite of the fact that the authorities inveigh against successive versions of the plan ("versionism"), the annual plan often is not ready until February or March of the year to which it applies, and it is widely recognized that the plan is usually completed only through an arbitrary "closing" of the balances.[15]

Hitherto we have considered only the construction of the plan. Now we must turn to plan execution, for a plan could be constructed which was only a paper plan—one which had no effect on output and input decisions.

How Managers Are Rewarded

The behavior of managers depends on their rewards and penalties, on their risk preferences, and on their concern for the needs of the community. Rewards and penalties may take the form either of a material gain or loss or of a status gain or loss in status. Promotions and demotions usually involve a change in pecuniary rewards as well as status. We will confine our analysis to the study of formulae for material reward, as pecuniary gain is the most important incentive device employed in the Soviet-type economy. We will assume that managers receive bonuses re-

---

[15]Herbert S. Levine, "The Centralized Planning of Supply in Soviet Industry," *Comparisons of the United States and Soviet Economies* (Joint Economic Committee, Congress of the United States, 86th Congress, 1st Session, 1959), pp. 167–68. Reprinted in Wayne A. Leeman, ed., *Capitalism, Market Socialism, and Central Planning* (Boston: Houghton Mifflin Co., 1963), pp. 67–69; see also Stanislaw Wellisz, *The Economies of the Soviet Bloc* (New York: McGraw-Hill, 1964), p. 154.

lated to performance, and that each manager tries to maximize his bonus.

Reward for Plan Fulfillment

Because they are interested in a successful plan for current output, the Soviet leaders might be expected to reward fulfillment of the plan well. In fact, a plant manager traditionally has received a bonus for plan fulfillment that ranges from 20 to 100 percent of his basic monthly salary.[16] Sometimes the manager gets no bonus at all if he underfulfills the plan even by as little as one percent,[17] but so stringent a penalty discourages efforts to approach fulfillment of a plan when complete fulfillment is impossible. We will try to design more sophisticated reward schemes, because such hypothetical bonus formulae will identify problems the authorities are likely to encounter as they try to induce managers to behave in particular ways.

We need to say a few words about the constants in the bonus formulae we will be considering. In reality, the economist cannot measure these constants. He can, however, conceptualize a closed system in which only the size of the reward is varied, while the impact of this variation on managerial behavior is measured. Hence our formulae meet the scientific test of being conceptually verifiable. More importantly, a formal analysis of reward systems is of value because with such an analysis we can identify the problems which the authorities will encounter as they try to induce managers to behave in particular ways. (In practice, of course, the planners would have to exercise their judgments to evaluate the size of the constants in any scheme of rewards.)

Let us first suppose that the authorities concern themselves only with fulfillment of the current output plan. They might pay bonuses according to this formula:

$$B = c - b(q - q')^k.$$

B is bonus, q' is planned output, q is actual output, k a positive, even integer, and b, c, and k are constants. The bonus is a fixed sum less a penalty for turning out less or more than the planned quantity. With $k = 2$, the bonus is a second-order function of

---

[16] Joseph S. Berliner, *Factory and Manager in the Soviet Union* (Cambridge, Mass.: Harvard University Press, 1957), p. 30.

[17] Ibid., p. 37.

divergence from plan. The penalty for diverging from the plan increases at an increasing rate as the divergence increases. With this formula, however, the manager would have no interest at all in a large volume of production from his plant. He would prefer a low, safe plan that he could be certain of fulfilling exactly. He would consequently understate the capacity of his plant during the preparation of the plan, and he would be careful not to reveal a large capacity by a large output when he executes the plan. It is clear that the manager must be given an incentive for volume of production.

Rewards for Volume

Let us look at a formula at the opposite extreme, one which rewards the manager only for volume:

$$B = aq.$$

In this formula a is a constant, and it is really a piece rate for output. Such a simple reward for volume of output is clearly inadequate, since the manager under such a reward system has no inducement to follow the plan.

A Combined Rewards Formula

The intriguing question is whether a bonus formula can be devised that will interest the manager both in volume of output and in exact fulfillment of the plan. One possibility is to combine the two preceding formulae:

$$B = aq - b(q - q')^k.$$

The second term penalizes the manager for deviations from the plan, and the first term rewards him for output. The size of the coefficient a (relative to the coefficients attached to the outputs of other commodities in the plan) is an indication of the importance the authorities or the central planning board give to the goods. In fact, a is a price, and it is interesting to observe that prices emerge as soon as material rewards are introduced into a system of physical planning. Prices are the numbers that indicate to the managers the relative importance of different goods.

One difficulty with the combined formula that rewards for volume of output and penalizes for deviations from the plan is that it produces bonuses that are asymmetrical with respect to planned output. In fact, the maximum bonus in this system is at an output greater than that called for the plan. (See Figure 2-1.) Consequently, the manager is not motivated to fulfill the plan exactly.

The best way of achieving symmetry is to pay bonuses according to the following formulae:

for $q < q'$ $B = aq - b(q - q')^k$; and
for $q > q'$ $B = a[q - 2(q - q')] - b(q - q')^k$.

In a graphing of these formulae, the curve to the right of the line q' (which represents planned output) is the mirror image of the curve to the left of q'. (See Figure 2-2.) Although the peak of the bonus "mountain" is no longer smooth, which means that the penalty for small deviations from the plan is greater than it is with

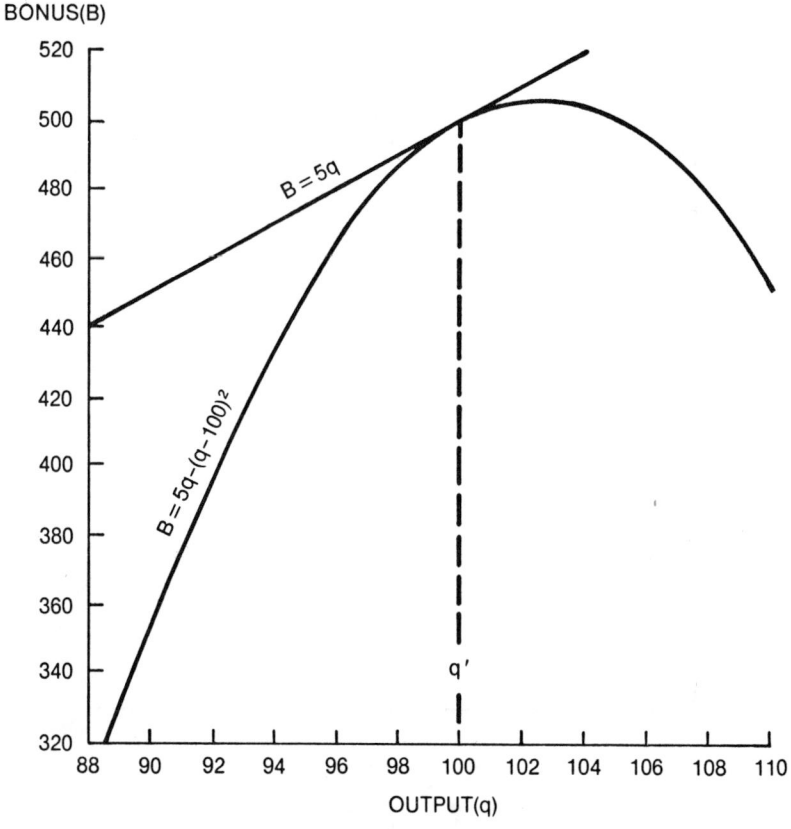

Figure 2-1 **Bonus Formulae**

a smooth peak, the penalty for small deviations does not need to be large. In Figure 2-2, for example, the penalty for a one percent under- or overfulfillment of the plan is only 1.2 percent of the bonus for exact fulfillment. And were k made equal to 4, the peak would be still less sharp.

Risk Preferences

The formula $B = aq - b(q - q')^k$, modified as indicated for symmetry, will produce results that satisfy the authorities if the authorites and the managers have similar preferences with regard to risk. The probability that a plan target will not be met increases with the size of the target, so risk for both authorities and managers increases with the target. As planned output rises, the authorities

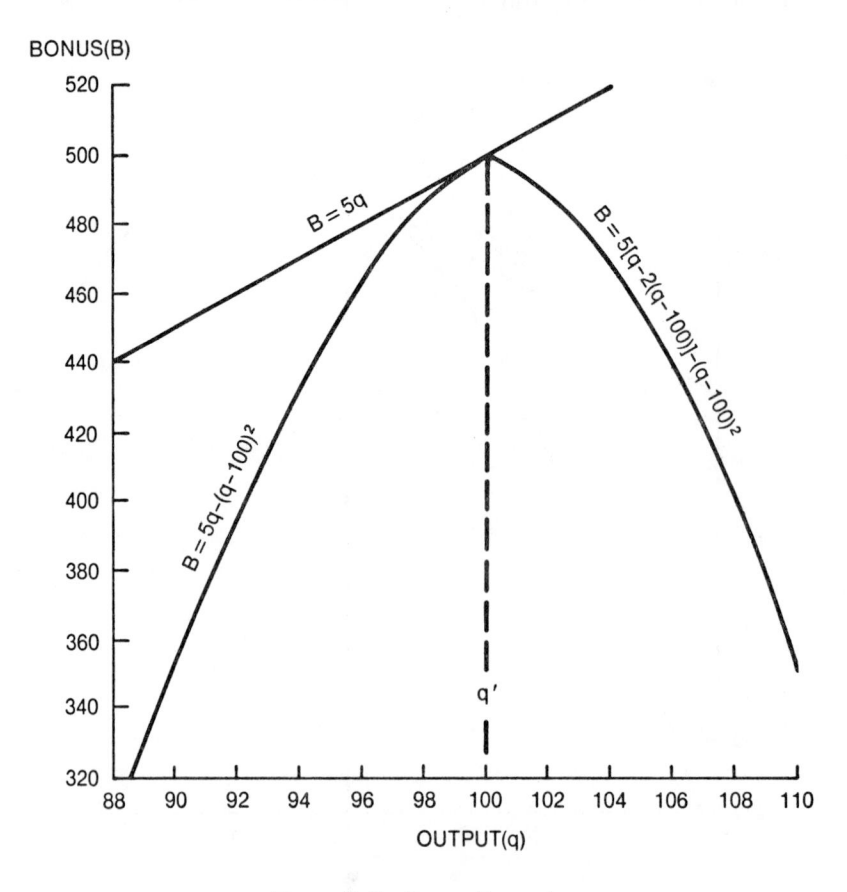

Figure 2-2 **Bonus Formulae**

are exposed to an increased probability of shortages that will adversely affect growth, and the manager is exposed to an increased probability of a penalty for underfulfillment. Suppose both the authorities and the manager are risk-takers. Both want large plan targets; the authorities want to try for a high rate of growth (and take the risk of a low one), the manager wants to try for the bonus associated with a large volume (while taking the risk of a low volume and low bonus). Neither wants a safe plan, and the manager has no reason to understate plant capacity. The central planning board and the manager will then concur in a large plan, and the manager then will do all that he can to fulfill this plan. Or, suppose the authorities and the manager are both risk-averters. Both prefer a low, safe plan;[18] the authorities prefer a more secure rate of growth, the manager prefers a more secure volume and bonus. The two agree on a low, efficient plan, and the manager tries to fulfill it.[19]

If the authorities and the manager diverge in their preferences for risk, however, then the formula $B = aq - b(q - q')^k$ modified for symmetry will not lead to the desired results. The most probable divergence in risk preference is that the authorities want high output targets and the manager wants low targets. The authorities utilize mobilization planning, and the manager puts in a safety factor, understating his plant capacity in order to get a low plan. The authorities probably correct the manager's proposals, perhaps overcorrect them, and the manager is further motivated to conceal capacity in the future. Plan targets become the result of efforts on the two sides to outwit one another.

Under these circumstances and with the formula above, the manager is not rewarded for the risk he is asked to take. His bonus for exact fulfillment increases in proportion to output, but the probability that he will be penalized for underfulfillment increases more rapidly than output. He is more likely to underfulfill a large plan than a small one. The solution may be to reward the manager for the risks associated with large targets. The bonus formula might be

$$B = aq^j - b(q - q')^k,$$

[18]It is a little surprising that economists who have said that managers try to get a safe plan have failed to see that they are talking about risk-averters; they have failed to see that the authorities, too, might prefer to avoid risk.

[19]The plan is efficient even though input of plant per unit of output is large, because risk-averting authorities prefer the margin of safety associated with a large reserve of capacity.

where k is a positive, even integer and $j > 1$. For example, j might be 1.5 or 2.0. Made symmetrical with respect to planned output, the formula would be as follows:

for $q \leq q'$ $B = aq^j - b(q - q')^k;$
for $q > q'$ $B = a[q - 2(q - q')]^j - b(q - q')^k.$

The reward for exact fulfillment per unit of output now rises with volume, and, if j is well chosen, it compensates the manager for the risk that he will be penalized for underfulfillment.[20] Consequently, the manager is less inclined to conceal his capacity and to try for a low plan. This formula for reward, of course, is not actually used. We may conclude that if managers in the Soviet-type economy try for low, safe targets, as economists say they do, it may be simply because they are not rewarded for the risks associated with large targets.

Overfulfillment of the Plan

There is, however, another reason managers conceal capacity. Most of the time in the Soviet Union and Eastern Europe managers are rewarded for overfulfillment of the output plan. These rewards might be calculated by the following bonus formula:

$$B = c - b(q' - q).$$

In this formula, the manager receives either a fixed sum plus a piece rate on output exceeding planned output, or a fixed sum minus a penalty (a negative piece rate) when actual output falls short of planned output. An alternative bonus system would be as follows:

when $q < q'$ $B = dq;$
when $q = q'$ $B = eq;$ and
when $q > q'$ $B = fq,$

where $f > e > d$. In this system the manager receives a certain piece rate when actual output is less than the targeted quantity,

[20]If the manager is averse to risk, then j is greater than one. Further specifications of the manager's utility function (e.g., that he is subject to decreasing absolute risk aversion) would enable us to specify further the characteristics of j.

a larger piece rate when output is equal to planned output, and a still larger piece rate when output exceeds the target.

The difficulty with all the formulae which reward overfulfillment is that they lead the plant manager to conceal the capacity of his plant. He gains nothing from a high output target. Indeed, the higher the target, the lower the bonus for any given output. Consequently, when the manager is asked about his capacity, he will understate what his plant can do. When he operates, he will overfulfill the plan very cautiously for fear of revealing his plant capacity by his output. When a manager does overfulfill the output plan, he probably will insist to the planning board that the circumstances that made it possible were exceptional and not likely to recur.

If enterprise managers are rewarded for production in excess of the plan, the central planning board will then have to accept the managers' prevarication about their capacity. They will need to be resigned to a considerable distortion of information from their best sources of information about the economy, the enterprise managers themselves. Consequently, the authorities in a planned economy would be wise to reward the fulfillment of current output plans and to penalize both under- and overfulfillment. They would then receive accurate information and good performance in production. Planners, I suspect, should be willing to pay a high price for information.

There is one deficiency that will be found in any bonus formula that penalizes overfulfillment. Suppose an enterprise manager quite honestly reports his capacity, receives an output target close to the one he proposed, and then in the course of carrying out the plan discovers that he can do better than he anticipated. If he produces more than the planned amount, he will be penalized. Yet, if additional input could be used, overfulfillment of a plan would be in the public interest. On the other hand, regularly to reward production in excess of the plan would induce managers to conceal capacity. The solution to this dilemma is generally to reward plan fulfillment and to penalize overfulfillment, but in rare, carefully documented instances, to reward production in excess of the plan. When an enterprise manager demonstrates that his earlier forecasts were reasonable in light of the knowledge then available, when he shows how new circumstances that previously could not have been known make a larger-than-planned output possible and when an increased output of the good is needed, then the authorities should reward excess output. But such exceptions would have to be rare in order to avoid giving managers an incentive for a low plan.

It is surprising that Western students so often are upset by the thought of penalizing overfulfillment. Under capitalism, they certainly would not consider it out of the ordinary to see General Motors penalize a plant manager for turning out more automobiles than the directors had concluded could be sold.

Cost Reduction

The Soviets and East Europeans plan for cost reduction. They do not, however, penalize managers for production at below planned cost; they do not, and obviously should not, penalize them for overfulfillment of a cost reduction plan. It would not make sense for a manager to use more inputs or more valuable inputs than necessary just because the plan called for their use. The authorities should reward managers for using only planned inputs or fewer, and penalize them for using more than that amount. The formula describing this process is the following: Let $u'_1, u'_2, \ldots, u'_n$ be planned inputs of commodities $1, 2, \ldots, n$ while $u_1, u_2, \ldots, u_n$ are actual inputs, and $g_1, g_2, \ldots, g_n$ are constants. Then

$$B = c - g_1(u_1 - u'_1) - g_2(u_2 - u'_2) - \ldots - g_n(u_n - u'_n).$$

The input plan here is really a set of norms, with managers penalized for exceeding the input norm and rewarded for using fewer than normal inputs.

The reader will immediately wonder whether $g_1, g_2, \ldots, g_n$ are not prices of inputs, and in fact they are prices. The manager maximizes his bonus when he minimizes the expression $g_1 u_1 + g_2 u_2 + \ldots + g_n u_n$. The relative sizes of $g_1, g_2, \ldots, g_n$ reflect the values the government puts on the different inputs and indicate the amount of attention the government would have managers devote to each as the managers seek to economize in the use of materials and labor. Should the coefficients $g_1, g_2, \ldots, g_n$ all be equal, the government would be valuing all inputs equally. It would reward managers equally for saving, let us say, a pound of platinum and a ton of coal.

The difficulty with an input plan or a set of input norms is that it causes managers to overstate their input needs. Because they are rewarded for overfulfilling the plan, the managers have an interest in a plan that calls for a large use of inputs. Indeed, the higher the planned inputs are, relative to the actual inputs, the larger the managers' bonuses. Consequently, managers will supply misleading information about their input needs.

Explicit Prices

The Soviets and East Europeans could better achieve their efficiency objectives by throwing out the input plan entirely and explicitly using the prices that are now only implicit in their rewards for efficiency. Bonuses might be calculated according to the formula

$$B = c - g_1 u_1 - g_2 u_2 - \ldots - g_n u_n,$$

where $g_1, g_2, \ldots, g_n$ are the scarcity prices of inputs. This formulation gives the manager everything he achieves by cost reduction. Should the authorities want to give him only part of the cost saving, they could use the formula

$$B = c - h g_1 u_1 - h g_2 u_2 - \ldots - h g_n u_n, \text{ where } 0 < h < 1.$$

We can combine the earlier bonus formula for volume of output and fulfillment of plan with the bonus formula dealing with inputs.

For $q \leq q'$ $\quad B = a q^j - b(q - q')^k - g_1 u_1 - g_2 u_2 - \ldots - g_n u_n.$

For $q > q'$ $\quad B = a[q - 2(q - q')]^j$
$- b(q - q')^k - g_1 u_1 - g_2 u_2 -, \ldots, - g_n u_n.$

In this bonus scheme, the coefficient a is a price of the output, while the coefficients $g_1, g_2, \ldots, g_n$ are prices of inputs. The coefficient b is a "price," or monetary valuation, of adherence to plan. The relative sizes of the coefficients reflect the importance the authorities attach to different outputs, the importance they give to efficiency in the use of different inputs, and the importance in their view of adherence to plan. The Soviet leaders in the past generally have given much more weight to output objectives than they have given either to efficiency or to exact plan fulfillment.

In this combined formula we approach the formula for net income or profit. If we set aside the term that penalizes deviations from the plan, the bonus is equal to total receipts minus total costs. (These are receipts and costs, however, only for those outputs and inputs included in the bonus formula.) We noted earlier that as soon as material rewards were introduced into a system of physical planning, prices emerge, numbers that indicate to the managers the relative importance of different goods. Now we see that simply rewarding managers materially for the efficient production of goods brings about something like net income. Profit, it appears, need not be only found in a capitalist system or a socialist system with extensive markets. It may emerge as soon as individuals are hired to manage the plants owned by a socialist government. Because the authorities in the traditional Soviet-type economy have weighed output so much more heavily than efficiency, however, managerial rewards have been little related to net income. But in the reforms proposed for the economies of the Soviet Union and Eastern Europe, profit will play a larger role than it has in the past.

The Assortment Problem

Defects in the current output plan very often lead to a faulty product assortment when the plan is executed. Because the effect of output volume on technological coefficients is not adequately allowed for, or because the aggregated weights used in calculating average technological coefficients are wrongly estimated, or because the managers supply inaccurate information and planners wrongly adjust for suspected inaccuracies, the technological coefficients used in drawing up the central plan frequently are erroneous. As a consequence managers often are supplied with fewer inputs than they need to produce targeted outputs. For example, the State Planning Commission might wrongly estimate the proportions of narrow and wide cloth required and the proportions of summer and winter shoes needed. They might figure on more narrow cloth and less wide cloth than users would desire and more summer and fewer winter shoes than consumers would want to buy. With narrow cloth and summer shoes too heavily weighted, the plan would call for the production of too little cotton and leather, and not enough of these raw materials would be distributed to textile mills and shoe factories. The managers would then be in a dilemma. If they were to fulfill their total output targets for cloth and shoes, they would have to turn out too much narrow cloth (which takes less cotton) and too many summer shoes (which take less leather). If, on the other hand, the managers were to turn out assortments to suit the needs of users, they would not fulfill their total output plan.

In practice, the managers in a Soviet-type economy seldom doubt which horn of the dilemma to choose. Because they are rewarded most heavily for fulfillment of the total output plan rather than for production of a suitable assortment, they turn out the collection of goods that enables them to reach their total output targets rather than the collection that satisfies users. The consequences are well known. When output plans are stated in weight, too many narrow items are produced, when in area, too many thin items, etc. Either the user must accept what is produced, not what he wants, or, when the user is given freedom of choice, unwanted stocks pile up in warehouses or must be marked down and sold at a loss.

Flexibility in Decision Making

At times the authorities in the Soviet Union have accused Soviet managers of "slavish adherence to plan." These accusations seem to indicate that the Soviets want their managers to exercise discretion in following the plan. Presumably they are to recognize the objectives of the authorities and adhere to the plan only when doing so promotes these objectives. But are managers rewarded for flexibility and exercise of judgment? We know that slavishness is sometimes penalized, but we do not know that initiative is rewarded. Decisions to diverge from the plan are without doubt more risky than decisions to adhere to the plan. It appears that only if the Soviets reward managers for taking risk will managers be flexible in their responses. Without such rewards they will cling to the relative security of the plan.

Response of Planning Bodies to Shortages and Surpluses

Given the problems of central planning, shortages and surpluses seem inescapable. When they occur, planning bodies can respond in two ways: (1) they can distribute materials held in reserve for this purpose, or (2) they can revise the plan.

In distributing scarce reserves, the planners have to decide which industries and which plants within an industry should receive the materials. Reserves ordinarily are distributed between industries according to a list of priorities, metallurgy ahead of chemicals, for example, and chemicals ahead of textiles. Montias found in Poland little awareness of the desirability of equalizing the marginal productivities of the allotments made to different users.[21] If a marginal ton of lye allotted to metallurgy has a lower value product (in terms of the authorities') preferences than a

---

[21]Montias, *Central Planning in Poland*, p. 110.

marginal ton allotted to low-priority fats and soaps, then the objectives of the authorities would be served by reallocating lye to the fats and soaps industry. Indeed, rather than a single, unchanging priority list, there should be regular revisions of the order of priorities. As the more urgent needs of particular industries are met, they should drop down on the list.

Under the Soviet-type system, there are complaints that too often within industries inefficient plants using obsolete equipment are given their "share" of scarce materials. Efficient plants, consequently, suffer from a lack of input materials. A larger output might be achieved with the same inputs if reserves are distributed only to the more efficient plants.

The interests of higher- and lower-level bodies often conflict when it comes to the distribution of scarce materials. The State Planning Commission has an economy-wide order of priorities, but ministries and regional planning bodies are likely to give first priority to plants within their jurisdictions. In an economy where shortages are ubiquitous, these regional efforts to achieve self-sufficiency become a way of life. Also, ministries frequently barter some of their goods for things they need instead of delivering those goods to high-priority users. And finally, personal influence plays a role in the distribution of reserve materials.

Revision of the Plan

Plans are often revised, as shortages and surpluses emerge, and Soviet economists claim that this is an important part of the planning process.[22] Output targets are revised, with direct and indirect inputs adjusted accordingly. Technological coefficients are changed. An interesting question is: How frequently should a plan be changed? What is the optimum number of changes in a plan?

One might say that a proposed change in a plan should be made if the gains from the change exceed the cost of changing the plan plus the cost of responding to the change in plan. But one should also consider an additional factor. If a plan is revised too often, it loses credibility and managers are inclined to ignore it. Such a revision is only filed in a drawer in the expectation that a new set of targets will arrive soon. From time to time one even encounters reports that in the Soviet-type economy some changes in the current output plan are made in order to make the planners look

---

[22]Levine, "Centralized Planning," p. 161n, reprinted in Leeman, p. 59n.

good.[23] Toward the end of the year particular targets are lowered so that it can be said that the plan was fulfilled, or overfulfilled. Little is known about the extent of this practice. For a plan to be credible, it no doubt must possess a considerable degree of stability.

---

[23]Wellisz, *The Economies of the Soviet Bloc*, p. 62.

Investment Planning

Chapter 3

Investment projects in the annual plan that are not part of the bill of goods are obtained from longer-term plans, the five-year plans (or sometimes six- or seven-year plans). These plans consist of sets of "perspective balances," or balances of capacities.[1] We need to examine the construction of an investment plan that is formulated entirely in physical terms, with neither money nor prices used in plan calculations. We will assume that the plan objective is a maximum rate of growth in wealth. Goods are valued in part by the authorities and in part by consumers, with the preferences of the former overriding those of the latter when the two conflict.

Detailed descriptions of actual multiperiod planning in the Soviet-type economy are not available, perhaps partly because it is much less formalized than current-output planning. Some documents on the subject have been published, however, and the following version of long-term planning is believed to accord with Soviet practice.

---

[1] John Michael Montias, *Central Planning in Poland* (New Haven and London: Yale University Press, 1962), pp. 148, 157; Nicholas Spulber, *The Soviet Economy*, rev. ed. (New York: W. W. Norton and Company, 1969), p. 17.

Multiperiod Planning

Ideally the authorities must indicate to the State Planning Commission what are their output preferences over time, what terminal capacity and terminal inventories they desire, and what resources will be made available to the planned sector of the economy during the period under consideration. The authorities state their output preferences in a dated bill of goods. (See sample, in Table 3-1.) This is a statement of what the authorities want produced during each year from the present to the time horizon. If the authorities value particular plant, equipment, and increases in inventories as ends-in-themselves, it will include these as well. For example, the bill of goods in 1976 might include one oil refinery, two copper smelters, one steel mill, and so forth.

Terminal Capacity and Inventories

With the dated bill of goods, the authorities will provide the Planning Commission with a statement of their preferences for terminal capacity and inventories. (See sample, in Table 3-2.) The question that immediately arises is how the authorities can rationally decide on terminal capacity and inventories without projecting the bill of goods for years beyond the time horizon. Since a time horizon at infinity which would avoid this problem is impractical, we can say only that the authorities will have to make an arbitrary choice of horizon capital; this is, apparently, what the Soviets do (perhaps taking comfort in the number of formal growth models that suggest "the distant future has a negligible impact on present decisions").[2]

Finally, the authorities will provide the Planning Commission with an indication of the resources that will be available over the years to the planned sector of the economy. For each year before

Table 3-1 A Dated Bill of Goods

Commodity	1977	1978		1979
Steel (tons)	95,000,000	100,000,000	. . .	150,000,000
Trucks	300,000	320,000	. . .	380,000
Housing (sq. metres)	350,000	370,000	. . .	440,000
. . .	. . .	. . .		. . .
Automobiles	900,000	950,000	. . .	1,800,000

[2]John Michael Montias, "Soviet Optimizing Models for Multiperiod Planning," in *Mathematics and Computers in Soviet Economic Planning*, ed. John P. Hardt et al. (New Haven and London: Yale University Press, 1967), pp. 207, 210.

the time horizon, the Planning Commission must have an idea of the probable availability of land, plant and equipment, materials, and labor.

Technology

The State Planning Commission will collect information on current and anticipated technology. It will want to know technological coefficients over the years; for example, it will project the iron ore required per unit of steel in the present and in subsequent years. It will also want to know capital-output ratios at different times; for example, it must determine the size of tire plant needed to produce a certain quantity of tires.

With a dated bill of goods and a list of resources available at different times, with a statement of desired terminal capacity and inventories, and with a knowledge of technological coefficients, the Planning Commission can draw up a set of perspective balances of capacities. (See sample, Table 3–3.)

Investment Program

At least part of the investment program (see sample, Table 3-4) attached to the one-year current-output plan is derived from this balance of capacities. In formulating the investment program, the

Table 3-2 Terminal Capacity and Inventories, End of Year, 1980

Product	Capacity (per year)	Inventories
Steel (tons)	150,000,000	750,000
Fuel oil (gals.)	1,500,000	200,000
. . .	. . .	. . .
Copper (lbs.)	700,000	300,000

Table 3–3 Five-Year Plan: Output Capacity (End-of-Year)*

Commodity	1977	1978		1981
Automobiles	900,000	950,000	. . .	1,800,000
Steel (tons)	95,000,000	100,000,000	. . .	150,000,000
Cement (tons)	210,000	240,000	. . .	370,000
. . .	. . .	. . .	. . .	. . .
Coal (tons)	490,000,000	510,000,000	. . .	590,000,000

*Actual output targets are set up when current output plans are drawn up for each year, and they may turn out to be lower than capacities.

Table 3-4 Investment Program, Annual Plan, 1976

Project	Capacity
Auto Body Plant*	170,000 bodies
Steel Mill*	10,000,000 tons
...	...
Coal Mine*	700,000 tons

*The actual program will specify the location of each project and precisely what is to be accomplished on it during the course of the year.

Planning Commission will take into account increases in the capacity of existing facilities attributable to the elimination of bugs in new equipment, better organization, etc., the predicted depreciation of existing plants, and the expected gestation period of new investment. Part of the investment program will include projects that the authorities value as ends-in-themselves. Schools, housing, and the like are often in this category.

In drawing up perspective balances and in deriving the investment program, the Planning Commission should try to obtain output capacities that are consistent and efficient.

Consistency and Efficiency

Capacity in each year should be made consistent. Examples are capacities of automobiles and copper in 1977, and the capacities of steel and coal in 1981. A problem of long-term planning not encountered in current-output planning is the change of technological coefficients through time. The State Planning Commission will have to recognize that the amount of coal used to produce a ton of steel in 1981 may differ from the amount required in 1977. Consequently, it must make forecasts of changes in technology.

Even more difficult than achieving consistency in long-term planning is achieving efficiency through time. The Planning Commission will seek to combine capital with other inputs in order to produce any given output at a minimum cost in the value of foregone alternatives. If it chooses from among the alternative processes available those which do minimize costs, then it will have chosen the ones that maximize the rate of growth in wealth. For example, the Commission will have to decide whether to use coal or fuel oil in the production of steel, or whether to use water power or nuclear energy in the production of electricity. Will the economy grow more rapidly through investments in dams, canals, and steel mills, despite their long gestation periods and the long intervals before all of their output is obtained? Or will a higher rate of growth follow from investments in steam plants, road haulage vehicles, and saw mills, where an early recovery of capital is available for early reinvestment?

With hundreds of thousands or millions of products in each of the years in the plan, with dozens of major projects like steel mills, oil refineries, and copper smelters, with hundreds of smaller projects like warehouses, different kinds of factory machinery, and locomotives, with multiple alternative processes for any particular situation, the task of the long-term planners is a large one.

Iteration

The technique employed to obtain consistency and efficiency is iteration, a repetitive adjustment of capacities in each year and from year to year. When we looked at current-output planning, we saw how the iterative process worked in construction of the plan for one year, and how adjustments in one output target had ramifications throughout the economy. In long-term planning the adjustment of a particular capacity figure for any one year will have ramifications not only throughout the economy in that year but over a number of years. For example, the Planning Commission might decide to increase aluminum capacity in 1981. This might require an increase in electricity capacity in 1980 and an increase in cement capacity in 1977. Moreover, an increased volume of aluminum production might lower its cost relative to copper so that required copper output is reduced in 1981 and the years following. This reduction in copper capacity might also have repercussions throughout the economy over a number of years.

While engaged in long-term planning, the Planning Commission will carry on a continuous dialogue with the authorities. The dated bill of goods will have to be adjusted many times as new information is generated about capacity in the economy. Occasionally the authorities may decide to increase or reduce the resources available to the planned sectors of the economy.

Because many investment decisions are made by lower-level bodies—ministries, regional and local governments, enterprises—there will have to be administrative iteration. Ideally a hierarchy of efficient long-term plans will be made consistent with one another through horizontal and vertical communication.

Rolling Planning

Economists in Eastern Europe and the U.S.S.R. long have recognized that, theoretically, a new long-term plan should be constructed each year, to incorporate the latest information about preferences and technology. If a new five-year plan is constructed only every five years, the series of plans looks like this: 1977–81, 1982–86, 1987–91, etc. Consequently, during the later years of each period, either the investment program is derived from obsolete data or the five-year plan is not used very much to derive the investment program. A better approach is called "rolling planning." A new long-term plan is constructed each year, so that the series of plans looks like the following: 1977–81, 1978–82, 1979–83, etc. Unfortunately, the scarcity of planning resources has prevented the adoption of this well-known procedure in the Soviet-type economy. Were the Planning Commission to have only a year to construct each five-year plan instead of the present five years, it would need a much larger staff.

With accurate data and enough iterations, a consistent and efficient set of long-term plans could be found, from which an optimum set of investment projects for a particular year could be derived by planning bodies at different levels. The plans would be efficient because any proposed increase in the output of a particular good at a particular time would require a reduction in the output of a more valued good at the same time or at another time. The set of plans would maximize the rate of growth in wealth.

But in practice the cost of data collection and the cost of iterative computation is prohibitively high. The Soviet mathematical economist Kantorovich describes the difficulties:

> It is not possible to obtain accurate data for all types of resources, for the many millions of conceivable technological processes possible in the production of hundreds of thousands of products, including those processes which will emerge during the planning period; it is not possible to indicate and assess accurately the demand for all types of output over a longer period.... If it were possible to obtain all these data, their compilation and computational treatment would hardly be technically feasible even if modern computational techniques were used.[3]

---

[3] L. V. Kantorovich, *The Best Use of Economic Resources*, trans. P. F. Knightsfield (Cambridge, Mass.: Harvard University Press, 1965), p. 219.

Although much has been hoped for from mathematical economics and computers, little has been achieved in the development of practical methods for long-term planning and investment choice. John Michael Montias speaks of the gap between dynamic optimizing models and their practical applications, and he asserts that "while the models constructed in the Soviet Union are by no means devoid of interest, they are so remote from planning practice that there is little to distinguish them from comparable Western work."[4] Edward Ames develops this idea with two rhetorical questions:

> Has any Soviet economist formulated a model in which the utility function is one which the Central Committee of the Communist Party (if it knew a little more calculus) would be prepared to call its own? Has any Soviet economist formulated a set of constraints which are in some recognizable sense simplifications of those confronting Gosplan?[5]

Critics of mathematical planning models sometimes refer to them as "computopia." The gibe may be accurate.

Project Selection

Long before reformers in the early sixties began to push for changes to improve input and output decisions, engineers and economists were attempting to go beyond purely physical calculations to arrive at investment choices. Engineers in the thirties and economists after World War II sought to relate money outlays on capital to the resulting decreases in money costs.[6] They viewed the problem as follows: From a dated bill of goods and a knowledge of technological coefficients, perspective balances of capacities can be constructed. But then, in drawing up an investment program which gives the desired capacities, it becomes evident that alternative processes are available, some more and some less capital intensive. Which alternatives should be chosen? For example, perspective balances might call for a certain amount of electricity generating capacity in 1981. Should a hydroelectric installation be developed or a steam-generating plant be put in?

[4]Montias, "Soviet Optimizing Models," p. 201.
[5]Edward Ames, "Comments on Montias," "Soviet Optimizing Models," p. 254.
[6]Gregory Grossman, "Scarce Capital and Soviet Doctrine," *Quarterly Journal of Economics* 67 (August, 1953), pp. 311–43.

The first requires a lot of capital but has low operating costs; the second takes less capital but is more costly to operate. Other examples of choices between more and less capital intensive alternatives are large- versus small-diameter transmission wire, shallow versus steep railroad grades, large- versus small-radius curves on railroads, etc.[7] In each case a higher initial investment results in lower operating costs in the future.

A simple scheme for choosing between alternatives of this sort is to minimize the sum of capital and current costs, as explained below.

Minimization of Total Costs

When the Soviets have chosen not to use an interest rate or its equivalent, they usually have minimized total costs without regard to date of occurrence. That is, they have minimized the total of capital costs and operating costs over the selected time horizon, or, in what amounts to the same thing, they have minimized ("straight line") depreciation plus average annual operating costs.[8]

The date on which costs are incurred is important, given the Soviet objective of maximizing the rate of growth. Different time patterns of outlays make different contributions to growth. A late outlay is preferred to an early one of the same amount because a late outlay releases resources in the interim for an alternative growth-promoting investment. Let us look at an example. (See Table 3–5.) Suppose we have two alternative ways of producing a particular output over a ten-year period. Variant one requires an initial capital outlay of 8,000,000 rubles and will have operating costs of 90,000 rubles per year. Variant two takes a smaller, 4,000,000 ruble investment but will have operating costs of

Table 3-5 Two Investment Alternatives

Variant	Capital Investment	Annual Operating Costs	Operating Costs over 10-Year Period	Total Capital Plus Operating Costs
1	8,000,000	90,000	900,000	8,900,000
2	4,000,000	500,000	5,000,000	9,000,000

[7] Ibid., pp. 318–19.

[8] Ibid., p. 324; Abram Bergson, *The Economics of Soviet Planning* (New Haven and London: Yale University Press, 1964), p. 253.

500,000 rubles each year. If the decision maker minimizes total costs without regard to date of occurrence, he will choose variant one. Most of the costs of one, however, occur much earlier than do the costs of two. Rather than tie up an extra 4,000,000 rubles through a choice of one (8,000,000 - 4,000,000 = 4,000,000), the decision maker might invest these resources in other places in the economy where they would contribute more to growth. But, the skeptic will ask, how will he knoe where the 4,000,000 rubles will contribute most to growth? Clearly, what is needed is a device that measures growth alternatives, a "norm of growth," against which the growth promised by a particular project can be measured.

The Coefficient of Relative Effectiveness

From time to time, Soviet engineers and economists have sought to make better investment choices than are made when total costs are minimized without regard to time. They have calculated what they call coefficients of relative effectiveness and have compared them with norms of relative effectiveness.[9] This is the method generally used today in the Soviet Union and Eastern Europe, as most of the earlier opposition to such calculations has disappeared. Let us examine it in a formula, best indicating the notation employed:

Let K_1 be the capital required in the capital intensive alternative, while K_2 is the capital required in the alternative requiring less capital. Let C_1 be the expected annual operating costs, depreciation included, for the alternative with relatively low operating costs, while C_2 is the expected operating costs of the alternative with high operating costs. Let e be the coefficient of relative effectiveness while E is the norm of relative effectiveness. Then

$$e = \frac{C_2 - C_1}{K_1 - K_2}.$$

Now e represents the economy in operating expenses that is realized from each ruble of additional capital investment, while E represents the norm of economy in operating expenses. When

---

[9]Alfred Zauberman, "The Soviet and Polish Quest for a Criterion of Investment Efficiency," *Economica* 29 (August, 1962), pp. 235–36; Norman Kaplan, "Investment Alternatives in Soviet Economic Theory," *Journal of Political Economy* 60 (April, 1952), p. 134; Alec Nove, *The Soviet Economy* (New York: Frederick A. Praeger, 1961), pp. 211–13; Bergson, *Soviet Planning*, pp. 253–54.

multiplied by 100, e and E are percentages. (Capitalists would call e the rate of return on investment.) The decision rules for the choice between the two alternatives are simple.[10]

If $e > E$, choose variant 1,
If $e < E$, choose variant 2, and
If $e = E$, choose either variant.

Thus if e exceeds E, then the saving in operating costs is large enough to justify the incremental investment.

In a 1946 Soviet textbook on railroad transportation, Khachaturov gives an interesting example of how this method is used.[11] A new railroad is to be built and the problem is whether to use steam or electric locomotives. Electrification would cost 90,000,000 rubles in capital, while annual operating expenses would be 2,500,000 rubles. Steam traction would cost only 70,000,000 rubles, but operating expenses would be 5,000,000 rubles. Applying the formula, we get

$$e = \frac{5{,}000{,}000 - 2{,}500{,}000}{90{,}000{,}000 - 70{,}000{,}000} = 0.125 \text{ or } 12.5\%.$$

Since the norm of relative effectiveness (E) used on Soviet railroads before World War II was 10 percent, the railroad should be electrified.

Rather than using the coefficient of relative effectiveness, the Soviets have sometimes used the recoupment (or "pay-off") period, which is its reciprocal. If R is the period of recoupment in years, then

$$R = \frac{K_1 - K_2}{C_2 - C_1}.$$

Comparison with an appropriate normative recoupment period, ten years, for example, gives the same results as the comparison of a coefficient of relative effectiveness with a norm of relative effectiveness.[12]

[10] See Bergson, *Soviet Planning*, p. 254, for discussion of the more complex decision rules applicable when there are more than two variants to be considered.

[11] T. S. Khachaturov in Holland Hunter, "The Planning of Investments in the Soviet Union," *Review of Economics and Statistics* 31 (February, 1949), pp. 54–56.

[12] Ibid., p. 255; Nove, *Soviet Economy*, pp. 211–12.

The norm of relative effectiveness is an interest rate which, when properly chosen, tells the decision maker what is the opportunity cost of employing capital in a particular project. Because E is an interest rate, use of coefficients of relative effectiveness in making investment decisions has often been opposed and has sometimes been prohibited in the Soviet Union and Eastern Europe.

Setting the Norm
How should the norm of relative effectiveness be set? It should just clear the market; it should equate the amount demanded and amount supplied to investment funds. With the interest rate set in this manner, the decision-maker knows that the rate is the marginal return on investment. It is the return that could be made with the best alternative use of the resources employed in any project under consideration. A market-clearing interest rate is the norm of growth we talked about earlier. It is an indication of alternative growth possibilities available, and it is therefore a figure against which the growth promised by a particular project can be measured. Suppose a labor-saving invention occurred which, in the form of investment in equipment, would release much labor for contributions to growth elsewhere in the economy. With increased investment possibilities, the market-clearing interest rate would rise and this higher norm of growth would tell decision-makers of new growth alternatives in other parts of the system.

That the Soviet norm of relative effectiveness should clear the market has been recognized by Khachaturov:

> The level at which the norm is set is determined by two conditions: available resources, i.e., the level of the accumulation fund ... and existing investment opportunities, which depend upon the progress of technology, differences in the levels of technology employed, and the new technology to be introduced. All other things being equal, the greater the accumulation fund, the less limited the volume of possible investments and the lower the effectiveness of the norm. On the other hand, the greater the possible investments caused by differences between existing and new technology, that is the greater the "demand" for capital investments, the higher the effectiveness of norm.[13]

---

[13]T. S. Khachaturov, "The Economic Reforms and Problems of Effectiveness of Capital Investments," *Voprosy economiki* 7, no. 7 (1967) in *Problems of Economics* 10 (March, 1968), p. 17.

Khachaturov also explicitly states that norms of relative effectiveness are equal to the return on marginal investments. He writes, "The normed effectiveness coefficients are not an average but a marginal quantity—the lower admissible limit of effectiveness. . . ."[14]

The norm of relative effectiveness need not be "arbitrary," contrary to the suggestion of Harry Schwartz.[15] The fact that supply and demand reflect the preferences of the authorities is not a reason for calling the outcome capricious or unreasonable. Ideally, through trial and error, a rate is found which just clears the market and equates the supply of and demand for investment resources.

Norms which are Varied

In the Soviet Union and Eastern Europe, the norm of relative effectiveness has varied from industry to industry; it may be 18 percent in one industry, 10 percent in another, and 7 in a third. A norm that is the same for the entire economy has been advocated by some Soviet economists[16] and by most Western students of the Soviet-type economy. Because the Soviet leadership has a maximum rate of growth as its goal, it should favor use of the same interest rate throughout the economy. As long as unequal norms are used, investments will be made in some industries, while alternatives in other industries that would have contributed more to growth are foregone. Let us suppose that the norms of relative effectiveness in electricity and textiles are 7 and 18 percent respectively, and that each norm clears the market of investment funds available in its sector. Let us also suppose that following these norms, the State Planning Commission is constructing hydroelectric plants in order to save coal, and is not constructing textile plants to save labor. An additional 100 rubles invested in hydropower reduces the consumption of coal so that costs decrease by 7 rubles. (The norm of relative effectiveness represents the saving in operating expenses per ruble of incremental capital investment; multiplied by 100 it represents the saving per hundred rubles.) But rather than invest the 100 rubles in plant for hydroelectricity, the Planning Commission might have invested it in the textile machinery that reduces labor costs by 18 rubles. The coal released through investment in the produc-

---

[14]Ibid., p. 22.
[15]Harry Schwartz, *Russia's Soviet Economy*, 2nd ed. (Englewood Cliffs, N.J.: Prentice-Hall, 1954), p. 169.
[16]Nove, *Soviet Economy*, pp. 213–14.

tion of electricity contributes less to growth than the labor that would have been released had the same resources been put into textile machinery.

If coefficients of relative effectiveness are to be used in making investment choices, then actual and anticipated prices of goods and services must reflect the preferences of the authorities. Were their preferences not embodied in the prices of commodities, then it could be argued that the authorities could rationally reject investment decisions based on financial calculations. (The prices must also reflect the preferences of the population, to the degree that these preferences are heeded.)

The Simplest Method

The comparison of coefficients of relative effectiveness with a norm of relative effectiveness in making investment decisions is an improvement over a simple minimization of total costs. Since the latter employs no interest rate, it leads to a choice of capital intensive alternatives. This can be seen in an example. Consider two variants of a project, one with a capital investment of 2000 rubles and operating costs of 70, the other with an investment of 1000 rubles and operating costs of 100. The capital has a life of 40 years. If total costs are minimized, the first variant will be chosen. (See Table 3-6.) Yet the coefficient of relative effectiveness on the incremental investment of 1000 is only 3 percent.

$$e = \frac{C_2 - C_1}{K_1 - K_2} = \frac{100 - 70}{2000 - 1000} = 0.03.$$

In capitalist terminology the rate of return on investment is only 3 percent. As long as the investment objective is to minimize total costs, investments will be made whenever the reduction in operating costs over the life of the investment exceeds the incremental capital outlay, no matter how far in the future the cost savings are realized. Such capital intensive choices will not maximize the rate

Table 3-6 **Two Investment Alternatives**

Variant	Capital Investment	Annual Operating Costs	Operating Costs over 40 Years of Life	Total Capital Plus Operating Costs
1	2000	70	2800	4800
2	1000	100	4000	5000

of growth, because long-delayed returns will not be available for early reinvestment.

Limitations on the Coefficients of Relative Effectiveness

Although the calculation of coefficients of relative effectiveness is an improvement over a minimization of total costs, it has some limitations. The coefficient of relative effectiveness does not discriminate between a variant in which all capital outlays occur in the first year and one in which some capital outlays are delayed until later. But late capital outlays are preferred for growth because they release resources for alternative use in earlier years. Also, the coefficient of relative effectiveness is not precisely defined with regard to operating costs. It is not clear whether the straight-line depreciation used to determine operating costs should be equal to total capital outlays divided by all the years from commencement of construction to the end of the life of the capital, or should be equal to total capital outlays divided by the years of life following completion of construction. Finally, when operating costs vary from year to year, it is not clear how average operating costs should be calculated. Should the average include the relatively high operating costs of the breaking-in period, or include only the operating costs after the activity has struck its gait?[17]

Rather than compare coefficients of relative effectiveness with a norm of relative effectiveness, decision makers anxious to maximize the rate of growth for planned output should try to minimize the present value of all outlays.

Present Value of Costs

Let O represent all kinds of outlays, capital expenditures and operating costs. Then, to minimize the present value of all outlays, the objective of the decision maker should be to minimize the following expression:

$$\frac{O_0}{(1+E)^0} + \frac{O_1}{(1+E)^1} + \frac{O_2}{(1+E)^2} + , \ldots, + \frac{O_n}{(1+E)^n}.$$

E, the norm of relative effectiveness, is, of course, an interest rate, which should just clear the market. The first term of expression

[17] Bergson, *Soviet Planning*, pp. 253–55.

states that outlays in the present are not discounted at all. Subsequent terms discount later outlays by geometrically increasing amounts. They are discounted in this manner because later outlays are preferred to early outlays of the same magnitude, as they permit growth-promoting investment in the interim.

The beauty of the foregoing formula is that it is completely unequivocal. Every cost is precisely dated and is discounted accordingly. Thus capital outlays that occur in other than the first year cause no difficulty. Decisions about the number of years over which capital assets should be depreciated do not arise, because capital expenditures are fully accounted for on the date of their occurrence. An average of the operating costs when these vary over time need not be arbitrarily selected. And use of a present value formula permits the decision maker, when he anticipates changes in the interest rate, to employ different norms of relative effectiveness for different years.

If the prices of goods and services used in the calculations are satisfactory, if they reflect the preferences of the authorities, then minimization of present value of the capital and operating costs incurred to achieve desired capacities will maximize the rate of growth in wealth. Prospective investments will be measured against a norm of growth representing the best alternative uses of the resources.

"Impatience" not the Consideration

It is important to recognize that the recommended use of an interest rate in investment calculations does not arise out of impatience, does not arise out of an objective of early consumption. Rather it follows from the Soviet objective of growth and from the contribution to growth made by an availability of resources for early investment. Late outlays are desirable because they leave resources free for investment until the date they are required.

The noted Soviet mathematical economist Kantorovich and his colleague Makarov have pointed to minimization of the discounted sum of capital and current costs as one possible approach to investment planning.[18] As early as 1959 the official Soviet methodology for determining the economic effectiveness of capital investments recognized the problems of annual operating costs that

---

[18]John Michael Montias, "Soviet Optimizing Models for Multiperiod Planning," in *Mathematics and Computers in Soviet Economic Planning*, ed. John P. Hardt et al. (New Haven and London: Yale University Press, 1967), p. 209.

vary over time and investments that have different time patterns. Thus methodology provided for a discount factor that would make all investment and cost streams commensurable.[19]

What about Receipts?
Long before this point in the analysis some readers will have been concerned because the formula for coefficients of relative effectiveness and the formula for present value deal with outlays but not with receipts. The costs of different projects but not their benefits are considered. In the Soviet-type economy, however, output capacities generally have been obtained from perspective plans. Project-makers require a formula that will enable them to select the best of the alternative methods of turning out a planned future output. Kantorovich puts it this way:

> The movement of capital investments and the allocation of means to sectors of industry are basically predetermined by the planning of final production, and the calculation of efficiency serves only to choose the best system of solutions for the completion of this task.[20]

Nevertheless, even in the 1959 methodology, there was a somewhat casual reference to an investment criterion related to receipts: $Q\ (P-C)$, where Q symbolizes quantity, P price, and C costs. In the "Standard Methodology for Determining the Economic Effectiveness of Capital Investment" introduced in 1969, the ratio of profit, $Q\ (P-C)$, to investment, I, appears to be the only approved measure of effectiveness.[21] We should recognize that we do not know the precise methods of project selection employed at different times and places in the Soviet-type economies.

Receipts should enter into the study of investment alternatives when authorities seek to achieve consumer and worker objectives through the response of socialist enterprises to consumer and worker market behavior. Because reformers in the Soviet-type economy propose to rely heavily on the market, and because in subsequent chapters we will delve into a complete system of socialist markets, we may usefully conclude this examination of

---

[19] Alan Abouchar, "The New Soviet Methodology for Investment Allocation," *Soviet Studies* (January, 1973), pp. 402–3.

[20] L. V. Kantorovich, *The Best Use of Economic Resources*, trans. P. F. Knightsfield (Cambridge, Mass.: Harvard University Press, 1965), pp. 206–7.

[21] Abouchar, "New Soviet Methodology," pp. 403–5.

project selection by looking at investment decisions in a system of market socialism.

Present Value of Net Income

Consider a socialist enterprise that purchases plant, equipment, materials, and labor (it purchases all but the labor from socialist firms), and sells its product to consumers or other government enterprises. What criterion should be used in decisions to invest in plants and equipment? One possibility would be to calculate annual net income as a percentage of capital invested and to compare this figure with a market-clearing interest rate, like a Soviet-type norm of relative effectiveness. If a proposed investment would yield, say 10 percent on capital at a time when the interest rate is 8 percent, then the project would be undertaken. This is the method that many if not most businessmen in capitalist economies employ, and it is close to what the Soviet reformer Liberman proposed for the Soviet Union. Liberman would have managerial bonuses relate to the rate of profit on production assets (fixed and circulating), although he would not have managers pay interest on the capital employed.[22]

Rate of Return is Equivocal

But rate of return on investment is equivocal. Receipts and operating costs usually will vary from year to year, so that averages will have to be used. Should the denominator used in calculating these averages be the total number of years from the commencement of the investment to the anticipated end of capital life? Or should the total capital outlays be divided by the number of years from completion of the project to the end of its useful life? Annual depreciation will necessarily be included in operating costs.

Better than using the rate of return on investment is using the unequivocal present value of receipts minus outlays. Let V_0 be present value, R be receipts, O be outlays, and i be the rate of interest. Then

$$V_0 = \frac{R_0 - O_0}{(1 + i)^0} + \frac{R_1 - O_1}{(1 + i)^1} + \frac{R_2 - O_2}{(1 + i)^2} + \ldots , + \frac{R_n - O_n}{(1 + i)^n}.$$

[22]E. G. Liberman, "Planning Production and Standards of Long-Term Operation," *Voprosy economiki*, no. 8, 1962, in *Planning, Profit and Incentives in the USSR*, vol. 1, ed. Myron E. Sharpe (White Plains, N.Y.: International Arts and Science Press, 1966), pp. 67–69.

In this formula each receipt and each outlay is exactly dated. Initial investment outlays, later additions, overhauls, and repairs all are inserted into the formula at the dates of their expected occurrence. Different interest rates can be used for different years if changes in the rate are anticipated.

The decision rule is to invest whenever present value exceeds zero, except when projects are mutually exclusive (like different-sized dams on the same site). In the latter case the rule is to choose the alternative with the highest present value, as long as it is positive.[23]

Provided that the interest rate is market clearing and that prices appropriately reflect the market-revealed preferences of consumers and workers, the use of present value of net income maximizes the rate of growth in wealth. The interest rate is a norm of growth that indicates growth opportunities elsewhere in the economy.

The use of the present-value formula assumes that anticipated receipts and outlays are certain; in practice, decision makers in a socialist economy are not sure of the future. We will look at risk and risk bearing in a socialist economy in Chapters 6 and 9.

---

[23] Roland N. McKean, *Efficiency in Government Through Systems Analysis* (New York: John Wiley, 1958), pp. 77–78.

Prices and Money

Chapter 4

In the foreseeable future it will not be possible for a central body to plan an entire economy in physical magnitudes. That is, it will not be possible to order the production of a detailed assortment of all the different goods, to order a specified set of inputs for each output, to direct the delivery of particular goods and services to each household, and to direct each worker to a particular set of tasks. Hence decentralized decisions in response to money prices will become part of any economy likely to exist in the decades to come. In the Soviet-type economies there are already many decisions of this sort. Largely in response to money prices and wages, consumers decide what goods to acquire and workers decide what jobs to take. Enterprise managers make some decisions on assortment and inputs by looking at prices. "Project makers," or design engineers in the central body, use prices to choose among variants of particular investment schemes.[1] Gerschenkron has pointed to a striking illustration of the influence of price in the Soviet Union:

[1]Market phenomena not dealt with in this book are: (1) sales by collective farms and individual peasants in the collective farm markets, where prices are uncontrolled and are market clearing, and (2) the informal, illegal barter of materials between enterprises where barter ratios of exchange usually reflect the official money prices of the goods but include supplementary gifts and favors. See Morris Bornstein, "The Soviet Price System," *American Economic Review* 52 (March, 1962), pp. 94–96, and Joseph S. Berliner, "The Informal Organization of the Soviet Firm," *Quarterly Journal of Economics* 66 (August, 1952), pp. 352, 352n.

Production and consumption of copper is centrally planned. Copper is included in what is called in Russia 'material balances,' that is, balance-sheet-like juxtapositions of output and consumption of individual commodities in terms of physical quantities. In Soviet literature very much emphasis is placed on this method of planning through material balances. It is said to assure absence of disproportionalities. Now, copper remained in short supply throughout most of the thirties. Domestic production grew at too slow a rate; imports remained substantial; and the Soviet government attempted for years to reduce the consumption of copper by introduction of substitutes in less essential lines of production. These attempts showed but a moderate degree of success, until, in 1937, the government decided to increase drastically the price of copper while keeping constant the planned cost of commodities in the production of which the metal was used. Apparently, the effect was all that could be desired. Copper was thenceforth confined to more essential uses, and substitutes began to be utilized on a significant scale.[2]

Retail Prices and Wages

Generally prices for retail and wages are market clearing. The Soviets attempt to set prices that equate the amount supplied and the amount demanded. In practice, there are numerous exceptions.[3] Quite often it is necessary to queue up for an item, store shelves are sometimes empty, and in the last few years warehouses have filled up with excess inventories of goods. There are long waiting lists for housing and automobiles. And usually there are more jobs open than workers to fill them.

Much of the difficulty arises out of the infrequency of price changes in the Soviet economy. When so many prices are set by a central body, the cost of price changes is high. Prices that are both stable and market-clearing could be maintained if inventories were accumulated during periods when supply is large (or demand is small) and then worked off when supply is low (or demand is high). But the carrying costs of such stocks may be prohibitively high. At times, moreover, retail prices are not set to

---

[2] Alexander Gerschenkron, *Economic Backwardness in Historical Perspective* (New York: Frederick A. Praeger, 1965), p. 308.

[3] Bornstein, "Soviet Price System," pp. 73–77.

clear the market because some prices are held down to benefit low income groups; these prices are, for example, the prices of basic foodstuffs, public transport, and housing.

Insofar as retail prices and wages are market clearing, consumers have free choice in their purchases and workers have free choice in their occupations. Consumers are then constrained only by their budgets and workers are constrained only by their capabilities. But production does not respond to consumer purchases and worker supplies of services. Rather, prices at retail are used to adjust the amounts demanded to a supply largely determined by planning bodies, and wages are employed to adjust the amount of labor supplied to the demands for labor that grow out of planned outputs.

Wholesale Prices

Soviet wholesale prices generally are set to be equal to planned average cost of production plus "normal" profit. Cost is the average cost of most of the enterprises producing the good, excluding the costs of the highest-cost firms. Cost comprises wages, salaries, social insurance payments, materials (fuel and power included), depreciation, and overhead such as postage, business travel, and workers' housing.[4] Rent and interest on capital are seldom included. A normal profit of about 5 percent is added to planned average cost to get the wholesale price received by enterprises. The Soviets believe that a modest profit promotes efficiency, that large profits encourage indolence, and that losses cause managers to become dependent on subsidies rather than strive for lower costs.[5]

When wholesale prices are equal to the sum of planned average cost and a normal profit, they are not market clearing. Materials are rationed according to the distribution plan. Exceptions to the assertion that wholesale prices are not set to clear the market occur in cases of close substitutes, such as coal and fuel oil, or copper and tin. Here the prices of "deficit" commodities are raised to discourage their use. In addition, coefficients of "deficitness," or scarcity, are sometimes added to prices for use in calculation when designing investment projects.

[4]Ibid., pp. 83–84.
[5]Ibid., p. 85.

The Turnover Tax

Apart from relatively low wholesale and retail trade margins, the difference between the wholesale price received by the enterprise and the retail price paid by the consumer is the turnover tax.[6] This tax is collected mostly on consumption goods rather than producer goods, with the exceptions being petroleum products, natural gas, and electricity. The turnover tax is price determined rather than price determining. Retail prices are set to clear the market, and then the rate of tax is set to mop up most of the difference between retail and wholesale prices. As a consequence the structure of wholesale prices is separated from the structure of retail prices, and any inclination of enterprises to produce in response to prices received is not an inclination to respond to consumer purchases.

Soviet theorists contend that the turnover tax is not really a tax but a "profit of the socialist economy," or the difference between costs and the final selling price that is appropriately collected by the government, which owns the means of production. Textbook writers avoid the word "tax" and write of "the state's centralized net income."[7] It is difficult to challenge this view, except perhaps in the case of the turnover tax collected on farm products delivered by collective farms. The Soviets, however, do not recognize that the turnover tax on the products of industry is a monopoly profit, and is consequently higher than competitive profits would be. (If this is doubted, imagine what would happen to Soviet market-clearing prices at retail if enterprises were free to enter and capture the spread between retail and wholesale prices.)

The Role of Price in Resource Allocation

Soviet managers are rewarded mainly for reaching or surpassing physical output targets. Profit is a much less important indicator of success and basis for reward. And since wholesale prices received and paid by enterprise managers are not market clearing, this system of production in response to central directives is better than a system of production that responds to prices and profit. When prices do not reflect the relative scarcities of different goods (we are talking about scarcities in terms of the preferences of the top authority), they are not a satisfactory guide to production, and profit is not a good measure of performance.[8] Advocates of reform

---

[6]Transport costs are usually included in a delivered price received by the seller. See ibid., pp. 80, 86.

[7]Alec Nove, *The Soviet Economy* (New York: Frederick A. Praeger, 1961), p. 100.

[8]Bornstein, "Soviet Price System," p. 79.

in the Soviet Union and Eastern Europe, as we shall see, recognize that a greater emphasis on profit would require major changes in the Soviet price system.

The Need for Money

The nature and significance of money in a socialist economy depends upon the location of decisions in the system. If complete centralization were possible, money would not be required. Imagine a State Planning Commission that makes all production and distribution decisions, right down to the decision that on 17 January 1972 five bars of bath soap will be delivered to the Petrovsky family at 23 Gorki Street. But in the foreseeable future central planning bodies will not be capable of such comprehensive planning. Consumers will make many of their consumption decisions and will acquire the goods they want through exchange. Similarly, socialist managers will be given considerable discretion over inputs employed and will trade for materials and labor. Even if consumers and managers with powers of decision attempted to barter for the goods and services they want, the high cost of barter transactions would lead to the use of money. The need for a measure of decentralization plus the high transaction costs of barter will cause any practical socialism to become a money economy.

Nevertheless, where there is a strong tendency toward centralized controls, as in the Soviet-type economy, there will be a constant tension in the monetary system. The men at the center will always distrust money and will constantly endeavor to keep it weak; however, they will be forced to allow money a certain precarious existence.

Two Monetary Circuits

The Soviets have two carefully segregated monetary circulations, currency and bank ("demand") deposits. Currency is used for transactions between government enterprises and households and for transactions between households alone. Bank deposits are used for transactions between government enterprises and for transactions between a government enterprise and a government agency. On payday a government enterprise gets currency from the government bank to pay its workers. Over the next few days the workers spend this currency mostly in government stores, where it is promptly deposited back into the government bank. Some currency is spent in purchases from other households—in purchases of services, goods produced by artisans (like furniture), secondhand goods, and food from farmers.[9] As soon as this currency finds its way into a government shop, it is deposited in the government bank.

When one government enterprise purchases goods from another, payment is made by a transfer of deposits at the government bank. The seller, upon dispatch of the goods, usually sends a "subsequent acceptance" draft to the bank. The bank credits the account of the seller and debits the account of the buyer before the latter has inspected the goods. Then, should the goods turn out to be unacceptable within a specified period, the buyer can ask the bank to reverse entries.[10]

Absence of Checkbook Balances

It is a little surprising that the Soviets do not allow individuals to have bank demand deposits and to use checks for personal transactions, in view of the fact that transfers of funds from one bank account to another are more easily observed and controlled than are payments by currency. One suspects that the Soviet view that bank deposits are not money has something to do with this failure to put checkbooks in the hands of individuals.

Currency can be freely spent by its holder, except for use in illegal "speculative" transactions. Moreover, the price of consumption goods are generally set to clear the market, with some notable exceptions like housing and automobiles. With Soviet currency then a bearer of options, the authorities, being concerned with control, do what they can to minimize idle balances held by individuals. Systematic efforts are made to get people to put their accumulations in savings accounts in government savings banks. Even stronger efforts are devoted to minimizing till cash held by government stores. At the end of the trading day a store is required to deposit all of its currency receipts except for a small reserve.

---

[9] George Garvy, *Money, Banking, and Credit in Eastern Europe* (New York: Reserve Bank of New York, 1966), pp. 13–14, 47; Andrzej Brzeski, "Forced Draft Industrialization with Unlimited Supply of Money: Poland, 1945–1964" in *Money and Plan*, ed. Gregory Grossman (Berkeley: University of California Press, 1968), p. 18; Franklyn D. Holzman, "Soviet Inflationary Pressures, 1928–1957: Causes and Cures," *Quarterly Journal of Economics* 74 (May, 1960), p. 176.

[10] Garvy, *Money, Banking, and Credit in Eastern Europe*, pp. 49–52; Donald R. Hodgman, "Soviet Monetary Controls Through the Banking System," in *Value and Plan*, ed. Gregory Grossman (Berkeley: University of California Press, 1960), pp. 114–15.

Thus, the government in a Soviet-type economy feels obliged to issue the currency that gives its possessor many options. In contrast, it treats the holder of bank deposits differently, and holds in close check the choices available to him.

Control by the Ruble

Loans of bank deposits are supposed to be made only in accordance with the plan and only on inventories and accounts receivable. Then, bank deposits are to be spent only if the expenditure accords with the plan; the government bank is to approve and permit only expenditures of this kind. Bank supervision of expenditure both of "own funds" and of borrowed funds is called "control by the ruble." Particularly when an enterprise proposes to withdraw currency to meet its payroll (which is its largest expenditure of currency), its performance is closely scrutinized. Furthermore, only a very limited amount of trade credit is allowed, so that an enterprise cannot escape control by acquiring goods on credit from its suppliers.

But why does there need to be control by the ruble when the State Planning Commission is empowered to issue directives and control the activities of the enterprise? The answer is "because there is money." Money is a bearer of options, and the government, having been obliged to give money to its enterprises, immediately tries to limit these options. Money, the Soviets tell us, is tied to the plan. But the very idea of "tied money" is a contradiction in terms. If money is a carrier of options (Dostoevski called it "coined freedom"), then to restrict its uses is to reduce the degree of its moneyness. One East European said to me bitterly, "Money in our system is not money." He was not entirely right, of course. In order to give their enterprise managers some flexibility in acquiring inputs, the Soviets have given them bank deposits with a degree of moneyness. The manager who successfully fulfills or overfulfills the plan is particularly likely to escape the closest supervision of his expenditure; his bank deposits will have considerable degree of moneyness.

Yet there will always be tension in the Soviet monetary system, as the authorities are torn between the desire for control and the need to give to the manager on the spot some powers of decision. At times bank officials are charged with leniency in their supervision of deposit expenditure; they are told they have not been sufficiently concerned with the plan and have given managers too much leeway in the disposal of funds. At other times bank officials are charged with formalism, they are told they have gone too much by the book and managers have not been given enough freedom to perform effectively. Soviet bank deposits in the foreseeable future will remain uneasily poised somewhere between being a bearer of options, as in the West, and scarcely being money at all.

Monetary Policy

In the traditional Soviet-type economy there is nothing that can be identified as monetary policy. The availability and cost of credit are not adjusted independently of the plan, in response to price changes or to the level of economic activity. Instead, the plan is supreme and money serves the plan.

The Soviets generally adhere to the "real bills" doctrine, or the "commercial banking" theory, in which bank credit rises automatically with a rise in inventories.[11] Credit expansion only to finance an increase in inventories, it is believed, will provide just enough money to meet the needs of trade. The real bills doctrine was discarded in the West decades ago. Let us see why it is inadequate.

Suppose that the Soviets, recognizing a growth in output, want to avoid inflation. They can maintain stable prices by seeing to it that total expenditure rises at the same rate as the growth in goods and services coming into the market. But will an increase in money that is related to an increase in inventories cause expenditure to expand at the same rate as goods and services supplied? In the first place, an increase in the quantity of money is not equivalent to a rise in total expenditure, because the velocity of money may change. Secondly, an increase in inventories is not equivalent to an increase in goods and services flowing on the market. Inventories can remain constant or decline as the flow of goods and services rise—if, for example, transportation services become more reliable, stocks that are held to deal with transport interruptions become less needed. Consequently, an increase of the money supply corresponding to an increase in inventories is not the same thing as an increase in total expenditure to match an increase in the flow of goods and services coming into the market. A policy of relating growth in bank credit to growth in inventories will not ensure that the price level remains stable.

[11] Raymond P. Powell, "Soviet Monetary Policy" (Ph.D. diss., University of California-Berkeley, 1952), pp. 242, 250–257. For a discussion of the real bills doctrine in the context of capitalism see Dennis H. Robertson, "Theories of Banking Policy," in *Economic Essays and Addresses* (London: P. S. King & Son, 1931), pp. 109–11.

Budget Surpluses

A device in the Soviet-type economy that to some extent substitutes for Western monetary policy is the use of budget surpluses to offset an inflationary increase in bank deposits. At intervals accumulated Treasury deposits are cancelled, and an offsetting amount of bank loans to enterprises is converted into grants that increase enterprise capital.[12] This mechanism can be seen best through a sequence of changes in entries on the government bank balance sheet. Table 4-1 illustrates the changes on a hypothetical, consolidated balance sheet of all enterprises in the Soviet system.

The Treasury surplus alone, achieved in the second step, is enough to offset an inflationary creation of bank deposits. The

Table 4-1 **Government Bank Balance Sheet**

Sequence	Government Bank Assets	Government Bank Liabilities	All Enterprises Assets	All Enterprises Liabilities
1. Inflationary bank loans of 100 rubles are made, in excess of additions to goods available for purchase.	Loans to enterprises + 100	Enterprise deposits + 100	Deposits in bank + 100	Loans payable + 100
2. The Treasury collects turnover taxes and does not spend the proceeds.		Enterprise deposits - 100 Treasury deposits + 100	Deposits in bank - 100	Capital - 100
3. Accumulated Treasury deposits are cancelled and bank loans to enterprises are converted into grants.	Loans to enterprises - 100	Treasury deposits - 100		Loans payable - 100 Capital + 100

[12]Garvy, *Money, Banking and Credit in Eastern Europe*, p. 72n; Brzeski, "Forced Draft Industrialization," p. 26; Brzeski, "Finance and Inflation under Central Planning," *Osteuropa Wirtshaft*, September, 1967, pp. 183n, 184n. See Holzman, "Soviet Inflationary Pressures," p. 178, for a simplified balance sheet of a Soviet government bank.

elimination of accumulated Treasury deposits in the third step simply prevents the later, possibly inflationary, expenditure of these funds. Western economists do not agree about the importance of Soviet Treasury surpluses as a weapon against inflation. Some consider surpluses important. Others argue that inflation is mostly controlled by measures such as the prevention of unauthorized payroll expenditures and the construction of realistic plans, both of which make budgetary surpluses less important.[13]

There is good reason to believe that proposed Soviet reforms that would increase the importance of the market relative to the plan would lead to the emergence of a monetary policy. In making loans, bank managers under the reforms would be expected to look more at the market performance of the enterprise than in the past. Managers of enterprises would be freer to make their own input decisions and spend their bank deposits as they choose. With this decentralization of decisions, bank deposits would acquire a higher degree of moneyness. (The mechanics of settlement also would change in reformed Soviet economies. Payment from one account into another would be effected by order of the purchaser, after he or she had an opportunity to inspect the shipment.)

If bank loans were made in response to market forces and enterprise managers were allowed to spend bank deposits at will, the authorities would have to see to it that all these autonomous decisions resulted in a sum total of expenditures appropriate to the supply of goods coming into the market. They would have to make someone responsible for a monetary policy. The policy might be to limit the availability of credit. Or, rather than set up a system of credit rationing, the policy might be to put a price on credit to limit the demand for accommodation. Utilization of an interest rate to control the supply of money would decentralize decisions all the way down to the enterprise manager who would decide whether or not to borrow at the prevailing rate. This use of the price system would be consistent with general reforms sought in recent years by many East European and Soviet economists.

---

[13]The two points of view are expressed in Hodgman, "Soviet Monetary Controls Through the Banking System," pp. 121–23, and in Holzman's skeptical "Comment," pp. 125–30, in the same volume.

Agriculture

Chapter 5

The collective farm (the "kolkhoz") is the most important institution in Soviet agriculture. However, the private household plot within the collective and private agriculture elsewhere in the economy are also of great consequence. The state farm (the "sovkhoz") is now becoming a larger part of the total agricultural picture.

The Collective Farm

The land occupied by the kolkhoz is the property of the state. It is transferred to the collective for its permanent use. The buildings, equipment, livestock, seed, and fodder are said to be held in common.[1] But all these means of production in the collective are state property both according to law and in reality. The rights of decision (making up much of the content of the "bundle of rights" which are property) have been in the past and remain today largely in the hands of the government. Through its procurement quotas the government decides what shall be produced. Even though the members elect the Chairman and the Management Board in a General Meeting, the Chairman is a Party nominee and the Board is nominated by the Chairman and the Secretary

[1] Leonard E. Hubbard, *The Economics of Soviet Agriculture* (London: Macmillan & Co., 1939), pp. 132–33.

of a Party committee.[2] Ostensibly the General Meeting approves the annual production plan, but an alternative plan or a substantial modification of the official plan would not be allowed by the Party. Certainly an organized effort to change or reject the plan would be forbidden. Until 1958 much government control was exercised through the Machine Tractor Stations. Since these Stations were abolished, control has been maintained through governmental units and a Party apparatus that penetrates more deeply into the collective farm.[3]

Delivery Targets

The collective farm is required to sell a designated quantity of its output to governmental procurement organs at fixed, relatively low, prices. The remainder of produce, after appropriate amounts have been set aside for seed and reserves, may be sold in the generally uncontrolled farm market (to be discussed later), or it may be distributed to members. Until recent years the delivery targets have been unstable, and government procurement agencies have increased their demands from kolkhozy with good harvests to make up for deficiencies from collective farms with poor harvests.[4] Needless to say, this instability has had a deleterious effect on incentives.

Distribution of Farm Income

Until 1966, members received pay (in cash or kind) from the kolkhoz according to the number of labor-days they had put in during the year. The Chairman or a senior tractor operator might get two labor-days for one day of actual work, while a watchman would get only one-half a labor-day for each day on the job. A labor-day was not, then, exclusively a time unit. Not only were labor days awarded according to the normal value of the work involved, but in many instances they were credited according to measured performance. A ploughman would be credited for the number of hectares ploughed. That is, numerous collective farm members were in effect on piece-rates.[5]

[2]Ibid., pp. 144–45, 264–65; Robert C. Stuart, *The Collective Farm in Soviet Agriculture* (Lexington, Mass.: D. C. Heath Co., 1972), pp. 11–19, 22–28; Paul R. Gregory and Robert C. Stuart, *Soviet Economic Structure and Performance* (New York: Harper & Row, 1974), pp. 235–36.

[3]Stuart, *The Collective Farm*, pp. 21–28.

[4]Hubbard, *Soviet Agriculture*, p. 184.

[5]Ibid., pp. 142, 168; Gregory and Stuart, *Soviet Economic Structure*, pp. 233, 252.

During much of the history of the collective farm, its workers were residual claimants on the income of the farms. The government got the first share of farm income through taxes and compulsory procurements at relatively low prices. Then what remained, if anything, was distributed to members according to the labor-days credited to their accounts. When little was available for distribution, a labor-day was not worth very much and members received little for their work on the collective. Sometimes on farms that were poor because of infertile soil, meager equipment, or bad management, members got nothing at all for their labor days. Cases have been reported of procurement agencies having to return grain to collectives for seeding the new crop. In the early days and on the poorer collectives in recent years, the workers obtained most of their livelihood from the private plots they were allowed to possess. When exiled to Siberia in 1965 and 1966, the dissident, Amalrik nearly starved because, as an exile, he was not entitled to a private plot and had to live on his earnings from the collective farm on which he was required to work.[6] Private farming, it turns out, is an important part of the Soviet economy.

Private Agriculture and the Farm Market

The role which the private plot plays in the life of a farmer in a collective is fairly well known in the West, but its significance for the economy of the collective itself is little understood. Moreover, the scope of private agriculture outside the collective is seldom recognized. Although smaller than in the collective, private plots are permitted for the employees of state farms and for nonfarm workers (like teachers) in the countryside, in small towns, and on the outskirts of large cities. Land is often set aside in "urban centers" for collections of privately held garden plots.

The land employed in private agriculture remains the property of the Soviet government. On the collective farm the kolkhoznik is given no documentary title to land farmed privately and "the individual has no legal appeal against directives concerning the size and allocation of private plots."[7] Members have found the area of their plots reduced by the kolkhoz chairman because they were not believed to be contributing enough labor to the collective farm. The aged and infirm have found themselves deprived

---

[6] Andrei Amalrik, *Involuntary Journey to Siberia* (New York: Harcourt Brace Jovanovich, 1970).

[7] Karl–Eugen Wädekin, *The Private Sector in Soviet Agriculture*, trans. Keith Bush (Berkeley: University of California Press, 1973), pp. 3–4, 21, 23–25.

of their private plots when they were no longer able to contribute much to the public sector; this was a very serious matter before the recent introduction of government pensions for collective farmers.[8]

The size of the private plot on the collective farm varies from one region to another in the Soviet Union and it has varied over time. In 1969 the average plot in the entire country was 0.31 hectares, which is about three-quarters of an acre.[9] Those who possess private plots devote much labor to them, so that a surprisingly large part of total farm commodities comes from these small holdings. For ideological reasons, the Soviets are reluctant to collect and release data on this subject. Karl Eugen Wädekin, who has made the most comprehensive Western study of the private sector in Soviet agriculture, estimates that in the late sixties private farms still accounted for more than a quarter of total agricultural output. Of this at most 60 percent came from collective farmers and the workers on state farms, with the remainder coming from nonfarm employees.[10] In 1969 the private sector accounted for 67 percent of the total Soviet production of potatoes, 39 percent of vegetables, 35 percent of meat, 37 percent of milk, 56 percent of eggs, and 35 percent of fruit and berries.[11] Private agriculture has proved to be very sensitive to changes in consumer demands. G. I. Shmelev, a leading Soviet authority on private agriculture, has recognized this characteristic in what he calls the "personal subsidiary farm." He observes that "because of changes in demand, farms with market orientation have shifted their production from lard to bacon, from early to late ripening apples, and in favor of berries and flowers."[12]

Needless to say, it is difficult for the Party to accept or acknowledge the large role that private agriculture plays in the Soviet-type economy. Soviet writers refer to the "personal" plot and to "personal" rather than private livestock,[13] and almost always this personal agriculture is considered temporary and is expected to wither away as socialism continues to develop. Private agriculture always remains in an uneasy coexistence with collective and governmental agriculture, and after a series of good harvests it is

---

[8]Ibid., pp. 3–4, 21, 24–25.
[9]Ibid., p. 349.
[10]Ibid., pp. 1, 59.
[11]Ibid., pp. 59, 64.
[12]Quoted in Wädekin, *The Private Sector*, pp. 159–60.
[13]Ibid., pp. 11, 19.

likely to find itself under attack. However, such campaigns are reversed when difficulties emerge and food shortages develop.

The Farm Market

One reason that private farming remains under a cloud is its close ties with a relatively free farm market. Referred to in the Soviet literature as the "kolkhoz market," these markets are legally open for the sale of products both from private plots in collectives and from subsidiary plots not in the possession of collective farm members. The commodities sold in these markets are extremely varied —potatoes, vegetables, eggs, meat, milk and milk products, fresh fruit, dried fruit, honey, preserves, wines, game, livestock (particularly young animals in rural areas), mushrooms, sauerkraut, tobacco, flowers, seeds, and rural handicraft products like brooms and painted wooden toys.[14] Government and retail trade in food has risen from 21 billion rubles in 1950 to 75 billion rubles in 1969, so that the share of the kolkhoz trade in the turnover of "comparable" products has fallen. Even so, in 1965 more than 50 percent of all potatoes, 15 percent of all vegetables, and 17 percent of all eggs sold to the Russian population were disposed of through the farm markets.[15] One reason for the survival of the kolkhoz markets is the relatively high quality of the products available there. Prices on the collective farm markets are generally free to fluctuate according to supply and demand, and in 1967 these prices were about 50 percent above those in government retail trade.[16] Kolkhoz market prices are extremely sensitive to the availability of supplies in the cooperative and government stores.

Unfortunately, the kolkhoz market is inefficient, as Soviet writers frequently point out. It constitutes high-cost distribution because each household is required to bring its own products to market. Middlemen are not allowed, as that would be private speculation. Strictly interpreted, the law does not even allow one neighbor to market produce for another. Householders lose many days of potential work to bring relatively small quantities of commodities to market. One Soviet estimate is that 250 million labordays were lost in this way in 1961. Large distances are travelled, sometimes thousands of miles, to take advantage of regional differences in prices. The Soviet government is trying to increase

[14]Ibid., pp. 129, 133, 138–39.
[15]Ibid., pp. 133–34.
[16]Ibid., pp. 134, 136, 154, 375.

Unacknowledged Interdependence

Official opposition to private agriculture and farm markets partly reflects a failure to recognize the substantial interdependence between the private and governmental sectors.[18] The authorities will not admit that the development of the collective farm itself depends upon the private plots of the member households. First of all, earnings from private plots help to keep people on the farm. With farmers only having income from labor-days on the kolkhoz, which in the early years was low in most collectives and which even today is low on the poorer collective farms, migration to the city would be a more serious problem without private plots than it has been. Also, earnings from the private plot permit the kolkhoz to pay less for work on the collective, enabling it to accumulate and invest more of its earnings. Finally, the private sector sells part of its produce to the kolkhoz; this assists the collective in meeting its delivery targets. For example, young saplings and organic fertilizers are sold to the kolkhoz by its plotholders. The Soviet authority Shmelev observes that "the public herds are stocked up with young animals raised in the personal farms, while an appreciable share of the output of the private plots is used to meet state procurements."[19]

Likewise, the household with a private plot is dependent on the kolkhoz. From the collective it receives grazing land for its livestock, hay and grain for animal feed, and grain for household bread. It also receives young animals to be raised for domestic consumption, for sale at the farm market, or even for sale to the collective.

A considerable barter trade goes on between them. For example, a member may trade milk for hay. Also, he may clear some land for the collective, in return for being allowed to keep for several years the hay and firewood he takes off this land.

The household plot and the collective farm complement one another. The household specializes in labor-intensive activities in which it has a cost advantage—livestock, vegetables, berries and fruit, and the like. The kolkhoz concentrates on the output of

[17] Ibid., pp. 140–41, 169.
[18] Ibid., Chapter 7.
[19] Ibid., p. 366. See also pp. 185–86.

commodities produced on a large scale with machinery—grains, cotton, flax, etc. Furthermore, the opportunity cost of work on the household plot is low. Much of it is performed by the elderly or by women with children to care for, who could not readily work on the collective; the rest of the work is done by the men during the off-season of the kolkhoz.

Not only are the collective farm and its private plots interdependent, but private agriculture and the nonfarm Soviet economy are dependent on one another. Private agriculture, both on and off the collective and state farms, provides a considerable part of the foodstuffs consumed by the nonfarm rural population as well as by the population dwelling in small towns and cities. Similarly, the farm household consumes services and goods produced in the nonagricultural sector.

So, in the words of the leading Western authority on the subject, Wädekin, "fifty million small-scale private producers" play a large role in the Soviet economy—and provide a continuous ideological irritant to the Party regulars.

State Farms

The state farms are factorylike units of production, and pay their workers regular wages. On these farms the government is the residual claimant, not the workers. The government is also the risk-taker. Consequently, the sovkhoz is more truly a socialist institution than the kolkhoz, and Soviet theorists recognize it as such. Unfortunately for the development of socialism in the countryside, state farm workers generally earn less than members of collective farms, and even so, state farms frequently operate at a loss and must be subsidized by the government. Nevertheless, the trend in recent years has been to expand the role of the state farm by converting some collective farms into state farms.

Recent Developments

Khrushchev was intensely interested in agriculture, and he pursued aggressively those agrarian policies he considered appropriate. Unfortunately, the policies he favored were not well chosen. Rather than choosing to supply more inputs for land already in use, Khrushchev chose "extensive" development; he insisted that more and more hectares be put under cultivation. Falling back on traditional campaign methods, he pressed for the opening of virgin lands east of the Volga and the Urals. The climate in these regions caused the venture to be a high-risk one; severe winters made the growing of high-yield winter wheat impossible. Often, delayed planting or early frost shortened the growing season for spring wheat. Drought in the summer was frequent and early rains in the autumn periodically interfered with the harvest. The techniques appropriate to dry farming, widely used in Canada and the United States, were not employed. The previous year's stubble was not left in the ground to hold the soil in place against wind erosion. Summer fallow was little practiced. Khrushchev displayed poor risk management by resting his policy on "best outcome" assumptions. Initially the weather was on his side, leading to good crops every other year (1954, 1956, and 1958), and it looked like his gamble had paid off. But after 1958 there was only one really good harvest (1964), and it was preceded by a catastrophic yield and followed by a poor one (1963 and 1965).[20]

Using the American experience as his model, Khrushchev also launched a campaign to make corn for grain and silage a major crop in the Soviet Union. But the U.S.S.R. lacks the favorable climate of the U. S. corn belt, and lacked fertilizers, high-yielding hybrid varieties, and a high level of mechanization. Corn was planted in many regions where it was too cold or too dry and often (on orders from above) it replaced more suitable crops; frequently these were oats, rye, perennial grasses, and sometimes even valuable winter wheat.[21]

Finally, Khrushchev was hostile to the private sector in agriculture. After 1958 the private ownership of livestock was discouraged. In some localities, the peasants were "persuaded" to sell their cows to the collective; in others, fodder was not made available or the use of collective farm land as pasture was restricted. Taxes were altered to penalize some categories of livestock owners.[22]

Toward Efficiency

Under Brezhnev, the Soviets substantially changed the direction of agricultural policy. From "extensive" development of new

---

[20]Lazar Volin, "Krushchev and the Soviet Agricultural Scene," in *Soviet and East European Agriculture*, ed. Jerzy F. Karcz (Berkeley and Los Angeles: University of California Press, 1967), pp. 5, 13–14.

[21]Ibid., p. 14.

[22]Alec Nove, "Soviet Agriculture Under Brezhnev," *Slavic Review* 29 (September, 1970), p. 381.

lands they turned to "intensive" development of existing resources. They began to think more about efficiency.[23]

Procurement quotas were reduced and stabilized. Quotas for grain were fixed at an unchanged level for six years in advance. Livestock quotas also were set for some years ahead, but, hoping for increased production, the plan called for larger deliveries in later years. Because managers knew the quantities they would have to deliver to government procurement agencies at set prices, and because they knew that additional quantities produced could be sold at higher prices, the managers' and workers' diligence was increased. It is generally believed that procurement targets have indeed remained stable.

More inputs were supplied to agriculture. Fertilizer production increased rapidly. Lime was applied to acidic soils at government expense. Investment in machinery, trucks and trailers, irrigation and drainage, and housing was enlarged substantially. To be sure, planned targets frequently were not attained, and numerous complaints were made about the quality of fertilizer and machinery. A lack of spare parts and inadequate maintenance were reported. On some farms, the milking apparatus broke 60 to 100 times each month. Nevertheless, productive investment did rise. From 1960 to 1965 deliveries of tractors went up from 157,000 to 239,500.[24]

Pressure against the private plot was reduced.

Changes in the method of payment of the collective farmers probably were not as significant as they were portrayed to be. The labor-day was largely abolished and a minimum wage was put in its place. This was not, however, a minimum per year but a minimum *rate per job performed.* A minimum share of the gross harvest was set aside for wage payments and poorer farms could borrow money if necessary. Thus, although piece-rates were retained, two important improvements were made. A minimum wage reduced the likelihood that the output "norm" would be changed when worker performance improved. And the pay of the collective farmer became the first charge on the farm's income.[25] The government, not the worker, became the residual claimant, so that the collective farm became more like the state farm.

[23]Ibid., pp. 386–88.
[24]Ibid., pp. 402–5.
[25]Roger A. Clarke, "Soviet Agricultural Reforms Since Kruschchev," *Soviet Studies* 20 (October, 1968), p. 161.

Considerable gains have been made in agriculture in recent years. In spite of relatively unfavorable conditions of climate and soil, crop yields have improved. Livestock production, however, has not improved as much. Meat prices in government and cooperative stores have been held in check since 1962, when price increases led to political unrest. Procurement prices are high enough so that the production of livestock is subsidized (5.3 billion rubles out of the budget in 1968). Free market prices on meat are frequently double the official prices and long queues for meat at government and cooperative stores are seen.[26]

The Future of Socialist Agriculture

Much study is necessary before we will know whether a viable socialist agriculture is possible. Some of the difficulties that the Soviets have experienced are physical, and are related to an inhospitable climate and poor soil. Some are ideological, reflecting the Soviets' drive toward industrialization and their unwillingness to deliver agricultural inputs and consumption goods to the countryside. Although socialists are often devoted to industrialization, this "unbalanced" growth probably is not a necessary characteristic of socialism. It is conceivable that the cold war between Party and peasantry might be broken.

We must recognize that up to now Soviet agriculture has achieved a fragile viability only with the existence of a private sector. How frail this viability is can be seen in the migration from farm life to city work that continues year after year. The peasantry vote with their feet against the Party's agrarian policies. The Party erects all sorts of barriers against this movement off the farm. The identity card (the "internal passport") of the peasant is kept in the office of the collective (the city dweller has possession of his own card), and the peasant can pick it up for a visit to the town or city only with the permission of the officials of the farm. No one can take up legal residence in a city without permission of the city authorities. Instances have been reported of parents threatened with a reduction in the size of their private plot should their son not return to the collective after his military service.

Despite all these obstacles migration relentlessly continues. The increased earnings possible in the city are a magnet. Although the movement from countryside to city is a worldwide phenomenon, it presents special problems in the Soviet Union. Their level of

[26]Nove, "Soviet Agriculture," pp. 406–7.

mechanization does not enable the farms to handle the harvest without the mobilization of millions of townspeople. Furthermore, the flight from the farm occurs mostly among young people. A social survey of peasants in Siberia reveals the situation: "Migration has an extremely unfavorable effect on the quality of kolkhoz and sovkhoz labor. The proportion of young people who are the most intelligent and qualified is declining." Many "mechanizers" leave.[27]

---

[27] Quoted in Nove, "Soviet Agriculture," p. 402.

The Soviet-Type Economy as a Model for Development

Chapter 6

Many people in underdeveloped countries look to the Soviet-type economy as an engine for development. Whatever its shortcomings, it is thought to provide a model for modernizing an economy in a relatively short period of time.

Increased Accumulation and Reduced Services

In the Soviet economy the output of consumption goods is restricted, while the prices of consumption goods, which are largely market clearing, are allowed to rise. At the same time government procurement prices for many agricultural products are held down. Then the price-determined turnover tax mops up what are in effect monopoly and monopsony profits, and the government uses these proceeds for capital formation. Part of this mechanism for economic progress has been described by Charles K. Wilber in the following statements:

> The farms were required to sell a major part of their output to the state at prices set well below the free market level. . . . Any short-fall in total production was absorbed by a reduction in the residual received by peasant households. . . . The resulting low incomes of the peasants, coupled with the high prices of manufactured consumer goods, repressed the effective demand for these goods. Thus the Soviets were able to restrict investment

in consumer goods industries and concentrate most of the investment in capital goods industries....[1]

With low family incomes housewives in the cities are induced to enter the labor force. Because the services of housewives are not included in the usual measures of national product, entry into the labor force shows up as an increase in output. (Lost household services are not counted as a decrease in production.) In addition to a reduction in the family services rendered by housewives, there is almost certainly reduced female leisure as well, and leisure does not enter into national accounting. (The Soviet press refers to the "second shift" which women work when they get home and do the housework). Finally, there is also a reduction in labor and materials made available for services such as laundry, dry cleaning, shoe repairs and plumbing. To be sure, a transfer of resources away from services to other activities does not increase national income if services are considered part of the national product, but it may increase the output figures for status commodities like steel, electricity, and the like. So we must recognize that the increase in output from women new to the labor force, unmeasured reductions in services in the home along with reduced female leisure, and the increased output of status commodities all tend to overstate Soviet achievements in economic growth.

Planned Investment

Believers in the Soviet-type economy anticipate great results from planned investment. They assume that in this system fewer resources would be put into commerce and more would be put into industry. Presumably, fewer commercial buildings would be constructed while more manufacturing plants would be built. Yet it is not necessarily true that manufacturing contributes to growth and commerce does not. The trader who opens up new markets or new sources of supply may stimulate development, while government manufacturing plants may be high-cost facilities and turn out low-quality goods.

Unfortunately, the Soviet ideology of planned investment calls for an emphasis on investment in heavy industry. We have seen in Chapter 4 that capital tied up in projects with long gestation and fruition periods is not available for early reinvestment else-

---

[1] Charles K. Wilber, *The Soviet Model and Underdeveloped Countries* (Chapel Hill, N.C.: University of North Carolina Press, 1969), pp. 32–34, 49, 70.

where in the economy, so that often it contributes less to growth than it would if it were put into light industry.

Balanced Growth

Perhaps those who believe that the Soviet-type economy is an engine for growth think most often of planned investment in complementary industries. Such planning, it is hoped, will break the "underdevelopment equilibrium" that occurs when demand is lacking for the products of an enterprise that attempts to start on its own. When a set of industries are established all at once, then the enterprises and the workers in the entire set provide demand for the products of any one of them. Less risk is involved in such planned investment because a market for all the products is created.

Critics of this version of the balanced growth doctrine point out that piecemeal entry has proved to be possible in many underdeveloped economies (with transistor radios, flashlights, bicycles, and the like), and that even without balanced growth demand for new products like these can come from dishoarding as well as reduced leisure and more work.[2] In the absence of planned investment, moreover, development can follow from cost reductions in existing industries which, followed by price reductions, increase real income and consumer demand.[3] Finally, critics ask whether the skills required to create and manage a whole set of industries can be made available. One critic, Albert O. Hirschman points out that application of the balanced growth theory "requires huge amounts of precisely those abilities that we have identified as likely to be in very limited supply in underdeveloped countries."[4] Moreover, the cost of administration may be high, and an underdeveloped country may not have evolved very high standards of honesty in government officials. Harold G. Johnson writes, "I should like to remind you that a large part of Adam Smith's argument for *laissez-faire* was the inefficiency and corruption he saw in the governments of his time."[5]

[2]Albert O. Hirschman, *The Strategy of Economic Development* (New Haven and London: Yale University Press, 1958), pp. 51–54.

[3]Charles P. Kindleberger, *Economic Development* (New York: McGraw-Hill, 1958), pp. 154–55.

[4]Hirschman, *Strategy*, p. 53.

[5]Harry G. Johnson, "Planning and the Market in Economic Development," in *Comparative Economic Systems: Models and Cases*, ed. Morris Bornstein (Homewood, Ill.: Irwin, 1969), pp. 406, 413.

The Government as Risk-Taker

People who argue that the Soviet economy is a model for development aver that the government should carry the risks of investment when there are taboos on lending, when potential lenders and investors are strongly averse to risk, or when there is a lack of a business and entrepreneurial tradition. Government investment might also be undertaken when a substantial segment of the population is hostile to private investment and profit (though obviously an alternative would be to try to reduce or eliminate hostility to private enterprise).

A government may not be as good a risk-taker as those who propose to give it this role anticipate. The men chosen for higher managerial posts may be people who only follow rules and are not venturesome. Government enterprises may be hierarchical, with a large emphasis on seniority. Harry Johnson points out that there is a "danger that if the Government undertakes investment itself, especially if its administrators are not too clear on their objectives, the result will be the creation of vested industrial interests inimical to further development, and resistant to technical change."[6] New men with new ideas probably will not be free to go outside the existing governmental structure to create new organizations. Monopolistic government enterprises will not encounter the positive effects of pressure from innovating competitors; when obsolete they will not be faced with destruction from up-to-date rivals.

Socialist Growth and Freedom of Choice

Even if all the claims of the supporters of the Soviet development model were conceded, critics might argue that Soviet growth has been achieved largely through coercion—through forced saving and through control over the production of capital goods, consumption goods, and services. Could a socialist system of government ownership of the means of production increase the rate of growth faster than a capitalist system if the savings-consumption decision is left to private individuals and if production is shaped in response to market-revealed preferences of consumers and workers? With these constraints on a socialist government there are relatively few methods it can use to increase the rate of growth. One possibility is the already discussed planned investment in complementary industries, where the workers in a set of new industries provide demand for the products of any one of them. Another possibility is for the government to take risks that

[6]Ibid., p. 413.

private capital is not prepared to take. These risks would have to be taken with borrowed funds and the reinvested profits of competitive government enterprises, rather than with the proceeds of tax collections or government monopoly profits, in order to ensure that the savings-consumption ratio is decided by private individuals' preferences. A final possibility is for the total costs of risk-taking to be reduced through the pooling of risks when the government invests in a number of independent projects. (This possibility will be discussed in detail in Chapter 9). It does appear that much of what is claimed for the growth of the Soviet economy rests on forced saving and on government controls over the production of goods and services.

It should be recalled that there are some characteristics of capitalism that make it a strong contender in the growth sweepstakes of capitalism versus socialism. As Harry G. Johnson points out, "the availability of goods through the market stimulates the consumer to seek to increase his income; and access to the market provides an opportunity for inventors of new goods and technical improvements to profit from their exploitation."[7] Profit incentives induce the capitalist businessman to find the lowest-cost combination of inputs; consequently, resources that are not wasted are available to increase the total national product. Johnson continues, "Moreover, the market serves particularly to provide an incentive to the accumulation of capital of all kinds: first to the accumulation of personal capital in the form of trained skill, since such skill earns a higher reward; and second to the accumulation of material capital, since such capital earns an income."[8] Under capitalism, finally, new men with new ideas can create new organizations and force existing enterprises to modernize. Obsolete organizations can be pushed into bankruptcy, releasing resources for more productive activities.

It would be unwise to be dogmatic about the likely growth of different economic systems. With a strong entrepreneurial tradition and a vigorous entrepreneurial class and in an environment receptive to economic change, capitalism might develop an economy very rapidly. In an economy without a class of entrepreneurs, a carefully designed program of government investment might be the more promising route for development.

[7] Ibid., p. 409.
[8] Ibid.

Proposals for Reform in the Soviet-Type Economy

Chapter 7

Not satisfied with the assortment and the quality of goods turned out, and seeking more efficient production, some Soviets and East Europeans have proposed the introduction of reforms. While numerous, the most important of these reforms are: (1) Reduction of the number of output directives; (2) Reduction of the number of inputs subject to rationing; (3) Price reform; (4) Reward for the sale of goods rather than simply for their production; (5) Reward in accordance with profit; (6) Reduction of the payment of subsidies. We will consider each of these proposed changes, along with some others.

Reduction of Output Directives

With unsold and often unsaleable goods piling up in warehouses, and with consumers as well as enterprises dissatisfied with the kind and quality of goods they buy, it seems entirely sensible to reduce the output directives made at the center, and increase the output decisions made by enterprise managers. The latter presumably know more of what their customers want. What is currently proposed in the Soviet Union and Eastern Europe is to reduce the number of output directives in the central plan from about 1000 to 100 or 200 items.[1] But such a reduction in central

[1] In Hungary the authorities intended to eliminate all output directives.

output decisions is desirable only if the number of planned sectors is correspondingly reduced so that the degree of aggregation is not increased. Instead, there is reason to believe that actually what is envisaged for the Soviet Union is a higher degree of aggregation. Liberman, the most publicized advocate of reform in Soviet Russia (who has, however, in recent years recanted), stated that "the list of output items approved by the state plan can be steadily diminished and ultimately limited to a consolidated, group nomenclature."[2]

A reduction in centrally planned outputs from 1000 to 200, while the number of planned sectors remains unchanged, would make the problem of aggregation more serious, because of the consequences of such a reduction. For example, instead of having structural steel, steel plate, and sheet steel as separate commodities in the central plan, it might be necessary to aggregate them into one commodity, steel. With the plan more highly aggregated, the average technological coefficients used in construction of the plan would be averages of a larger number of actual technological coefficients. Consequently, more weights would have to be estimated and there would be more possibilities of error. If structural, plate, and sheet steel were aggregated into a single commodity, then the central planning board would have to estimate in advance the proportions that these three kinds of steel would be of the total, rather than solve for the proportions while drawing up the plan. A decrease in the number of commodities centrally planned, to be sure, does decentralize decisions. Fewer output decisions are made at the center, more are made by lower-level bodies that disaggregate the central plan. But if the degree of aggregation were higher than it needed to be, the lower bodies would be constrained in their decisions by a central plan that would be further from reality than necessary. The decisions, though decentralized, would not be as good as they are when there are more commodities in the central plan.

Rather than increasing the degree of aggregation, the Soviets would be wise to reduce aggregation. As they cut down the number of output directives, they might cut down more the number of sectors for which output directives are issued. Current output planning could then be confined to commodities that create bot-

---

[2] E. G. Liberman, "The Plan, Direct Ties and Profitability," *Pravda*, 21 November 1965, in *Planning, Profit, and Incentives in the USSR*, ed. Myron E. Sharpe, vol. 2 (White Plains, N.Y.: International Arts and Science Press, 1966), p. 175.

tlenecks and to commodities where the preferences of the government clearly diverge from the preferences of the population. Output planning could be concrete.

Reduction of Inputs Subject to Rationing

In order to increase efficiency, some Soviets and East Europeans propose to give enterprise managers more freedom in the choice of inputs. These reformers would eliminate the rationing of inputs; managers would purchase what they need in the market. Liberman would gradually eliminate "the system of funding supplies" and would replace it with "a system of wholesale trade without advance orders."[3] Nemchinov, less publicized and less known in the Western press, but an important Soviet theorist of reform, would eliminate what he calls a "peculiar 'system of rationing' " and would have "items manufactured by state enterprises ... exchanged, in the main, through the system of wholesale state trade."[4] Along with having freedom to choose material and labor inputs, managers would make many of the investment decisions.

The problem with this suggested reform is that the outputs of one enterprise often are the inputs of another. Can the central planning board issue output directives and leave the choice of inputs to managers? The answer is simple. Output directives can be combined with the free choice of inputs if prices are set to clear the market. No matter what output directives are issued, managers can choose their own inputs as long as the price of each output equates the amount supplied with the amount demanded. To be sure, if successive current output plans are bad because of problems with aggregation or because of other difficulties, market-clearing prices may fluctuate widely. However, should current-output directives be relatively few in number and only concern bottleneck items, they actually might contribute to the stability of prices that clear the market.

Let us consider the probability that prices in the reformed Soviet-type economy would be market clearing and thereby would enable output directives to be combined with freedom of input choice.

[3]Ibid.
[4]V. S. Nemchinov, "Socialist Economic Management and Production Planning," *Kommunist*, 1964, in *Planning, Profit, and Incentives in the USSR*, Vol. 1, p. 180.

Price Reform

It is almost universally agreed in the Soviet Union and Eastern Europe that, as Kosygin put it, "the transition to new forms and methods of economic stimulation of industrial production demands the improvement of the system of price formation."[5] Usually, reformers begin by stating that prices must increasingly reflect "socially necessary outlays in production" or average production costs; such statements make one wonder whether market-clearing prices can emerge. But additional assertions by reformers about price determination suggest that they will push for market-clearing prices. For example, it is frequently said that the quality or effectiveness of goods should be taken into account in setting prices. Liberman illustrates this with the case of a new tractor:

> Higher prices must be paid for new machines in accordance with their increased efficiency in operation. The new T-135 tractor will soon go into production. It will be more efficient, it will plow faster, and the cost of output per hectare will be reduced. . . . We must not establish a price for this tractor on the principle of 'production cost plus normal profit,' but rather we must add part of the machine's effect in agriculture. . . . The prices for new and efficient items must be higher, and the prices for obsolete items should be reduced.[6]

Frequent assertions are made that higher prices should be put on new goods. The leading Czech advocate of reform, Ota Šik, says:

> Prices for the new and modernized goods, and also for goods in great demand, should be fixed, temporarily, higher than price of production, and, conversely, prices for obsolete goods or those for which there is little demand should be below the price of production.[7]

If the quality and efficiency of a good is taken into account in establishing its price, the demand for the good is also being considered. A price may emerge that equates the amount demanded

---

[5] A. N. Kosygin, "On Improving Industrial Management, Perfecting Planning, and Enhancing Economic Incentives in Industrial Production," *Isvestia*, 28 September 1965, in *Planning, Profit, and Incentives in the USSR*, vol. 2, p. 29.

[6] E. G. Liberman, "Increase Production Efficiency in Every Possible Way," *Economicheskaya gazeta*, 10 November 1962, reprinted in *Current Digest of the Soviet Press 14*, 5 December 1962, p. 19.

[7] Ota Šik, *Economic Planning and Management in Czechoslovakia* (Prague: Orbis, 1965), p. 24.

with the amount supplied. Indeed, in the previous quotation, Šik explicitly introduces demand into the setting of prices.

Actually, demand has implicitly been taken into account in the pricing of close substitutes for many years in the Soviet Union and East Europe. For example, if the calorific content of fuel oil relative to coal is high, the price of fuel oil is raised above its cost of production in order to hold its demand in check. Current reformers simply propose to go one step further and consider demand in setting the prices of commodities that are not close substitutes.

Reward for the Sale of Goods

Hitherto enterprise managers in a Soviet-type economy have been rewarded for the production of goods even when the assortment and the quality were such that the goods could not be sold. Under proposed reforms, managers would receive bonuses only when the goods they turn out have been actually marketed. For this change to effect an improvement in assortment and quality, a number of conditions would have to be met. First of all, the purchaser would have to be a willing buyer who has the enforceable right to refuse purchase of a good he does not want. This seems elementary, but in a Soviet-type economy enterprise managers have often been required by their superiors to take unwanted goods. It probably would not be sufficient to issue a ruling or to pass a law stating that managers may refuse to buy, such rules have been issued in the past without being effective. A method would have to be established to protect the independence of the enterprise manager. We will develop this point in a later section of this chapter.

Another condition is that bonuses confined to those managers who sell the goods they have turned out would improve assortment and quality only if buyers had alternative sources of supply and enterprises competed for sales. But the advantages of competition are given little attention by the reformers. One of the few references to competition in Liberman's work takes for granted that the enterprises would compete for orders: "the competition will be based on comparisons of quality, delivery dates, and prices."[8] Nemchinov also seems to take competition for granted.[9]

---

[8]Liberman, "The Plan, Direct Ties, and Profitability," p. 176.
[9]Nemchinov, "Socialist Economic Management and Production Planning," in *Planning, Profit, and Incentives in the USSR*, vol. 1, p. 177.

Yet it seems likely that considerable study and effort will be required to introduce effective competition into socialist economies.

Finally, rewards for the sale rather than simply for the production of goods would improve the performance of enterprise managers only if the seller's market that characterizes the Soviet-type economy were eliminated. As long as unrealistically large plans perpetuate widespread excess demand, enterprises will be under little pressure to improve assortment and quality.

When it is said that managers are to be rewarded for goods sold, the question must be asked, sold at what price? Reformers no doubt believe that, most of the time, goods should be sold at a price that covers costs and yields a profit. Even when they want market-clearing prices, reformers generally want quantities produced to be such that the prices at which the goods are sold cover cost and return a profit.

Profit and Plan

Some advocates of reform in the Soviet-type economy would have managers rewarded in accordance with profit to improve assortment and quality and increase efficiency. At the same time, they would have managers rewarded for their fulfilling of plan targets, as there would probably still be an output plan in the reformed system. How are rewards for these different facets of managerial performance to be put together in a total reward figure? One bonus formula might be

$$B = ay - b(q - q')^k,$$

with k a positive, even integer. B is bonus, y is net income or profit, q' is planned output, q is actual output, and a, b, and k constants. The manager would get a bonus related to enterprise profits less a penalty for under- or overfulfillment of plan targets. The penalty would increase at an increasing rate as the deviation from the plan increased.

This formula is more likely to achieve Soviet objectives than is the reward scheme proposed by Liberman. Liberman states that "the personnel of an enterprise always have a right to receive a bonus if the output plan, with due regard for the assigned nomenclature, has been fulfilled."[10] There may be a suggestion here that

---

[10] E. G. Liberman, "Planning Production and Standards of Long-Term Operations," *Voprosy economiki*, no. 8 (1962), in *Planning, Profit, and Incentives in the USSR*, vol. 1, p. 71.

bonuses are not to be received if output and assortment plans are not fulfilled. Such conditions for receipt of bonus would be very stringent. It would be better to have small penalties for small deviations from the output plan, with penalties increasing with the size of the deviation. (It is also better to leave assortment ["the assigned nomenclature"] up to arrangements between producer and customer, as Liberman himself in most of his later writings proposes to do.)

Liberman in his reward scheme would have bonuses related to the rate of profit on production assets (fixed and circulating),[11] rather than give the manager a share of total profit as in my formula above. It turns out that on current input and output decisions Liberman's rate of profit scheme[12] and my share of total profit formula give the same results. Both the maximization of profit in the numerator of Liberman's ratio and the maximization of total profit in my formula would lead enterprise managers to produce a marketable assortment with an efficient combination of inputs.

It is with regard to investment decisions that Liberman's reward scheme is most often challenged.[13] His rate of profit on production assets is like the rate of return on capital used by old-fashioned capitalists.[14] (Liberman would not have enterprises pay interest as capitalists do.) What bonus formula might produce better investment decisions? We must recall that the objective of the authorities in the Soviet Union and Eastern Europe is maximization of the rate of growth in wealth. Given this objective, the authorities must induce enterprise managers to consider future streams of money receipts and outlays associated with different investment decisions, to discount them at an interest rate that reflects the opportunity costs of capital, and to choose investments that maximize present value. How should managers be rewarded for the maximization of present value of investments? One possibility would be to give managers a share of increases in present value each year, but this is not feasible because there seldom would be an objective measure of these increases. The assets of the enter-

---

[11] Ibid., p. 68.

[12] Liberman's formula is implicit in his words and numerical tables. See the following paragraph.

[13] See, for example, Stephen Merrett, "Capital, Profit and Bonus in Soviet Industry," *Economica* 31 (November, 1964), pp. 401–7. Merrett's approach differs from this author's approach.

[14] Rate of return $= \dfrac{\text{net income}}{\text{total amount invested}}$

prise are not sold each year, so that there is no market test of gains in present value.

The best way of getting managers to make good investment decisions is to give them a share of current profit, to give them some assurance that they will hold their positions for a number of years, and to charge interest on funds borrowed by the enterprises while paying interest on funds that the enterprises put out at loan. Then, in making investments managers would consider future streams of receipts and outlays, discount them, and probably maximize some measure of present value.[15] Yet much work needs to be done before we can know how to get good investment decisions under socialism, and many questions remain unanswered. How, for example, is the time horizon of the manager to be made to coincide with that of the authorities? The person who cannot bequeath shares in the means of production may have little interest in what happens beyond his anticipated tenure as manager.

Use of a Profit Formula

Though we cannot be sure that a scheme that ties reward to total profit rather than to rate of profit is the most promising approach to managerial incentives, it is instructive to study the consequences of using such a scheme. We will look further at the formula $B = ay - b(q - q')^k$.

A formula that introduces profit into the calculation of bonuses has a distinct advantage over a formula that rewards a manager for economizing in the use of particular, specified inputs. The profit-seeking manager will try to economize in the use of *all* inputs on which there is a price. When only particular inputs are specified in the plan and in the bonus formula (as in Chapter 2, "How Managers Are Rewarded"), the manager may waste inputs not

---

[15]It can be demonstrated formally that when income does not change over time, maximization of net income is equivalent to maximization of present value. Let V_o be present value, y be unchanging annual income, and r the rate of interest. Then:

$$V_o = \frac{y}{(1+r)^1} + \frac{y}{(1+r)^2} + \ldots + \frac{y}{(1+r)^n}$$

$$V_o = \left(y \frac{1}{(1+r)^1} + \frac{1}{(1+r)^2} + \ldots + \frac{1}{(1+r)^n} \right).$$

The parenthetical expression is a constant and V_o reaches a maximum when ye is maximized.

specified. Moreover, the cost of plan construction and ignorance of the alternatives available to managers in different industries often will cause planning bodies to omit some inputs that can be used from the plan and bonus formula. A profit-related bonus rewards the manager for choosing the most efficient combination of inputs from among all the possibilities.

Moreover, a profit-related bonus induces the manager who is deciding on his assortment to consider cost. A manager who must sell his output before he can collect a bonus will take care not to turn out goods for which there is no demand, but he may not consider the cost of the goods he produces. A manager who is trying to maximize profit will compare the price of any commodity that might be in his assortment with the cost of his producing that commodity. His taking into account the cost of various assortments will lead to a better assortment for his enterprise. Moreover, a reward system that induces an individual to compare price with cost contributes to the maximization of the rate of growth in wealth (if prices used are scarcity prices).

Serious problems would arise in systems where managers are to be rewarded both for plan fulfillment and for profit. Because of the interdependence between technological coefficients and volume (with its consequently high computation cost) and because the weights in weighted-average technological coefficients are based on estimates of what disaggregated output figures will turn out to be, this system would lead to many inconsistencies in the plan. Shortages would occur, placing managers in a dilemma. If a manager, short of inputs, were to produce an assortment that would enable him to fulfill his plan, he would be unable to sell his output at prices that yield a profit. If, alternatively, he were to turn out an assortment that could be marketed at prices generating a profit, he would not fulfill his plan. For example, with leather in short supply a manager might produce summer sandals, using relatively little leather in each, to fulfill his output plan. But he would be unable to sell so many summer shoes at profitable prices. He might produce the winter shoes that consumers want, but each would take so much leather that he could not reach his output target. Regardless of the choice the manager might make, he would fail to get a bonus or would receive only a small one. The manager often encounters such a dilemma in the traditional Soviet-type economy. But in that system he gets around the difficulty by fulfilling the output plan without regard to assortment. He fills warehouses with unwanted goods, but he collects his bonus.

The authorities in the Soviet Union and Eastern Europe probably could overcome the difficulty presented by managers who are unable to sell the targeted quantities at prices that yield a profit by (1) a reduction in the number of commodities in the output plan, and (2) a still greater reduction in the number of planned sectors. These reductions would lessen the degree of aggregation in the plan, making it more concrete and more accurate. The output plan might be confined to a few items for which the preferences of the authorities and the preferences of the consumers are distinctly different, to products that are in short supply, and to bottlenecks.

Even if aggregation were minimized, there still might be difficulties when enterprise managers are rewarded in accordance with both profit and plan fulfillment. The output that maximizes profit might be different from the output that the central planning board wants to have produced. The manager would want the profit-maximizing output that equates marginal cost with marginal revenue, output OA in Figure 7-1, while the central plan-

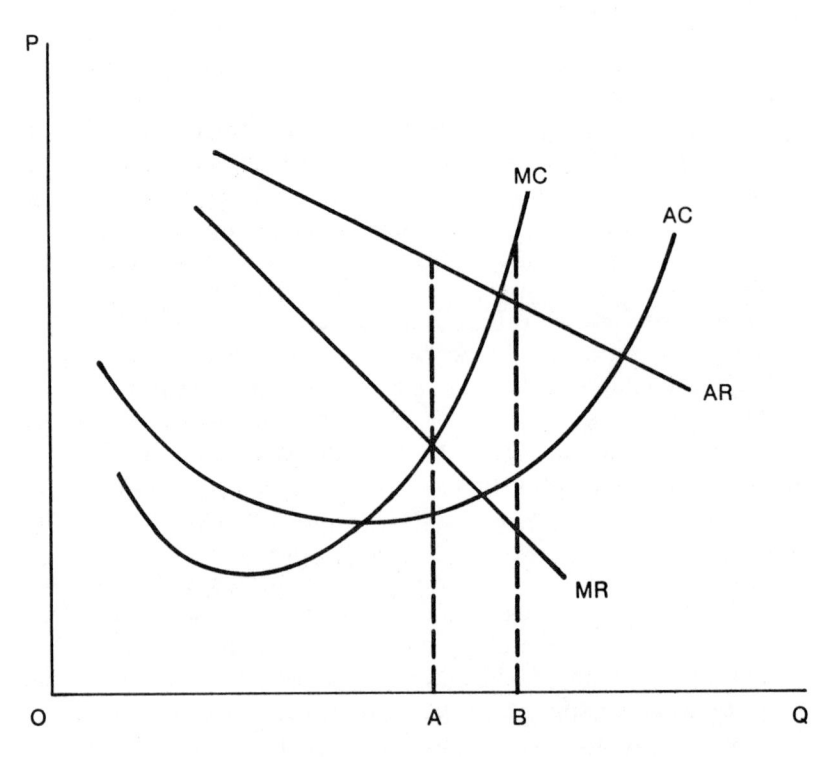

Figure 7-1 **Profit Maximizing and Planned Output**

ning board might want an output larger than this, *OB* for example. In order to get a target of *OA*, to produce at his point of maximum profit without penalty, the manager would be tempted to understate his capacity and to supply misleading information. Should the central planning board succeed in discovering the manager's actual capacity, and should the board give him a target of *OB*, the manager would not fulfill this plan exactly. He would produce an output somewhere between *OB* and *OA*, depending on the shapes of the demand and cost curves and the relative sizes of the coefficients *a* and *b*. To decide his actual output, the manager would trade off larger profits against larger penalties for deviations from the plan, as he moves from *B* to *A*. It is clear that when rewards are tied to profit the authorities and the managers can find themselves with conflicting interests.

This conflict has not always been recognized. In his treatment of Liberman's proposals for the use of profit incentives, Stephen Merrett assumes that the Soviet firm "faces a perfectly elastic demand curve," and that optimum output is at the point where marginal cost equals price.[16] If the demand curve were horizontal so that marginal revenue would equal price, and if the authorities were to want the amount produced that equates marginal cost with price, then there would be no conflict between the output choices of the profit-maximizing managers and the output preferences of the authorities. But neither of these assumptions is realistic. Only rarely under socialism will there be so many suppliers in an industry that no one supplier can detect his influence on price. Nor will the demand curve faced by the manager be horizontal, as the government sets prices without regard to the quantity produced. All the evidence suggests that the tendency of the reforms in the Soviet Union and Eastern Europe is in the direction of market-clearing prices, which means that relatively large output targets and large outputs will cause low prices. Managers will be aware of the relationship between output and prices and will recognize that they face a downward-sloping demand curve. With bonuses tied to profit, their interest will be in output that equates marginal cost and marginal revenue. There is no reason to believe that this will be the output preferred by the authorities.

Just as it is unrealistic to assume that managers in the reformed Soviet economies will face perfectly elastic demand curves, so it is unrealistic to assume that the authorities in the Soviet Union and Eastern Europe will draw up a plan ordering the production of

[16] Merrett, "Capital, Profit and Bonus," pp. 403n, 405–6.

outputs that equates marginal cost and price. Almost certainly the authorities will continue to believe that they know better than consumers what the consumers should have. In fact, it is most unrealistic to construct a model of even the reformed Soviet economies that fails to recognize that the authorities will have output preferences diverging from those of the population.

There is little reason to doubt, then, that profit-related rewards combined with current output planning will produce a conflict between profit and plan. The output that maximizes profits will not always be the output that meets the preferences of the authorities.

Reduction in Subsidies

Some of the statements of reformers of the Soviet-type economy lead one to believe that all subsidies were to be eliminated. Ota Šik asserted that "production which does not satisfy actual demand (if certain goods remain unsold or have to be sold at a considerable loss . . .) cannot be said to be socially necessary production even if all is well with the fulfillment of planned targets."[17] On the other hand, there were reformers who contemplated the continued existence of some subsidies. Liberman, for one, observed that "enterprises will not be made, as a rule, to produce unprofitable goods. . . . However, should unprofitable orders be included, by way of an exception, in a factory's production program, it will be compensated either through temporary prices or out of the ministry's reserve fund. . . ."[18] Nemchinov also recognized the possibility of subsidies. "If there is a lack of coordination between the system of wholesale and retail prices, a fund for the regulation of prices is established. It is built up from national revenue and is expended on subsidies to the wholesale (marketing and procurement) trade network."[19]

It seems possible that while the massive subsidies characteristic of the unreformed Soviet-type economy might one day be greatly reduced by reform, substantial subsidies will remain for a long time to come. Even in the West the preferences of the government often are manifested in subsidies, and the Soviets are not likely soon to give up the notion of "social priorities."

[17] Šik, *Economic Planning*, p. 12.

[18] Liberman, "The Plan, Direct Ties and Profitability," p. 177.

[19] Nemchinov, "Socialist Economic Management and Production Planning," in *Planning, Profit, and Incentives in the USSR*, vol. 1, p. 191.

Subsidies do cause a major problem. Now we need to look at further prospects and problems of reform in the Soviet-type economies.

Sheltered Enterprises and Foreign Trade

Many of the problems of the Soviet-type economy arise because enterprises and even entire industries are sheltered from competition. Purchasers frequently are required to buy from particular enterprises even when the quality of the goods does not meet their standards. They are not free to shop around among competitors. Weak firms are sheltered from the consequences of their own failings through the receipt of subsidies. Bankruptcy is virtually unknown. Ota Šik explains:

> One is bound to ask what serves the public interest best: To protect backward enterprises, to keep them in glasshouse conditions, to present as an achievement of socialism the artificially created profitability derived from artificial prices that saves firms from liquidation at the expense of lower living standards for the working people? Or to provide strict conditions under which economic pressures will impel enterprises to match the performance of leading firms elsewhere, making them get down to the job of closing the gap in productivity and production costs, and in the quality and structure of output, until they are capable of facing competitive markets?[20]

Šik understands clearly that foreign trade "is the field where our economic problems are mirrored most accurately and also where we have the most sensitive barometer of the difficulties we are facing."[21] Morris Bornstein, a Western economist, makes the same point about countries in the Soviet bloc: "Expanding trade flows were concentrated in the Eastern trading area's sheltered market, where (as in each of the domestic sellers' markets) outdated producer goods and inferior consumer goods could be sold."[22] Operating in markets sheltered from foreign competition particularly the competition of technologically-advanced, low-cost products from the West, socialist enterprises "were caught napping by the

---

[20] Ota Šik, *Czechoslovakia: The Bureaucratic Economy* (White Plains, N.Y.: International Arts and Science Press, 1972), p. 33.

[21] Ibid., p. 71.

[22] Morris Bornstein, *Introduction to Plan and Market* (New Haven: Yale University Press, 1973), pp. 14–15.

start of the scientific and technological revolution."[23] As subsidized enterprises that could not make it on their own in foreign markets, they turned out low quality goods that were poorly packaged and were not supplemented with adequate post-sale services.[24] Moreover, as in the domestic economies, horizontal communications between suppliers and purchasers were lacking. An exporter took its orders from an enterprise in its own country specializing in foreign trade rather than dealing directly with customers abroad. Šik continues, "The producer enterprises were ... completely in the dark about world prices, about profits or losses recorded in foreign trade dealings."[25]

Property Under Socialism and the Right of Decision

The fate of reforms proposed in the Soviet-type economies depends in substantial degree on the nature of property in these systems. Many economists who investigate alternative economic systems today are very interested in the location of decisions and little interested in the subject of property. Evsey D. Domar, for example, a well-known Western economist, asserts that it is the "optimum and ever-shifting division between centralized and decentralized decision-making that is ... the central economic problem of today, rather than the question of private versus public ownership of the means of production."[26] But the pattern of ownership distributes the rights of decision in any economy. It therefore has a substantial impact in determining who actually makes the decisions in the system.

In Eastern Europe and the Soviet Union, enterprise managers sometimes have been given larger decision-making powers as part of an economic reform. Yet complaints are frequent that the new autonomy of managers is being violated by illegal directives from government officials. It may be that the location of decisions cannot be altered while property rights remain unchanged. And indeed in Czechoslovakia some forthright statements to this effect have been made.

Property is a set of rights, a "bundle" of rights. It is a set of powers vested in a person by law or custom. Property rights can be classified into two major categories:

[23] Šik, *The Bureaucratic Economy*, p. 71.
[24] Ibid., pp. 71–74.
[25] Ibid., p. 77.
[26] Evsey D. Domar, "John R. Commons Lecture: Reflections on Economic Development," *American Economist*, Spring, 1966, p. 7.

1. Rights to income and wealth
2. Rights of decision
    a. Right of use
    b. Right of disposal
    c. Right of appointment

The owner of bonds in a capitalist system, for example, has rights to income and wealth; he has the right to receive interest annually and the right to receive the principal sum upon maturity. Here, however, we are concerned with the second category of property rights—the rights of decision. The right of use may be the right to use a consumption good or the right to use a means of production. The latter is the right to decide what products should be turned out and what inputs should be employed. The right to dispose of a consumption good or capital good includes the right to destroy the good and the right to sell it. Finally, the right of appointment is the right to appoint the directors or the manager of a particular plant or enterprise.

Advocates of socialism believe that property matters. They believe that private ownership of the means of production gives power to the owners, and they propose to capture this power through the elimination of private property in capital. In so doing, they propose to change the location of decisions about capital, so that those decisions will be more favorable to workers. It is clear that they intend to take the decisions away from capitalists, but it is not clear where socialists intend to locate the power of decision concerning the means of production. Vague terms are used to describe the proposed changes. Socialists say that the means of production are to be made "common" or "state" property; "social" ownership is to take the place of private ownership. The terms common property, state property, and social ownership are almost meaningless. They do not tell us who has the right to use the means of production, to dispose of them, and to select the management of socialist enterprises.

In the Soviet-type economy it is clearly the government that owns the means of production. The government is not elected from amongst rivals or independent political parties, it has the right to appoint enterprise managers, it has the right to dispose of plants and equipment, and it has the right to decide on use of the means of production. (It is sometimes said in the Soviet Union and Eastern Europe that the enterprise has the right of use of plants and equipment, but this proposition is doubtful if applied to the conventional Soviet-type economy. When the State Planning Commission and the ministries can say what shall be produced in the factory and what inputs shall be used, the rights of use left for the enterprise are not very large.) So the most accurate statement is that the government owns the means of production in the Soviet-type economy.[27]

Had the workers owned the factories in the Soviet Union, as the Soviet press claimed, the quantity of consumption goods (such as automobiles) turned out over the last several decades almost certainly would have been much larger. A wry joke told in Poland illustrates the situation well. In response to questions from workers who had seen pictures of acres of automobiles parked outside American factories, a Party official said, "The American workers may own automobiles, but the Polish workers own the factories."

Economic reforms proposed in Eastern Europe and the Soviet Union would have given enterprise managers larger powers of decision with regard to output, inputs, and investment. Furthermore, in several countries enterprises would have been given rights to dispose of unneeded capital equipment. As we have already stated, however, there are frequent complaints that the autonomy of enterprise managers is being violated by illegal directives.[28] Interesting questions arise: Can the location of decisions in a Soviet-type economy be changed without a more substantial change in their institutions than is presently contemplated? How is the autonomy of the enterprise to be secured?

One solution being tried is to issue a series of laws and decrees that state that fewer directives from the authorities are to be issued to the enterprise. An inherent problem of this solution is, of course, how to ensure that these laws and decrees are obeyed. It is hoped that enterprise managers will protest if their autonomy is violated. But a manager who goes over the head of his superior to protest an illegal directive—a directive that is perhaps couched in the guise of a "suggestion"—takes a serious risk. In the first place, the manager's superior in the subministry or ministry usually has the confidence of the person above him, or he would not be in his position. Also, the manager's boss has regular access to the

---

[27] Lenin apparently held the view in 1920 that the workers did not own the means of production in the Soviet Union. He characterized as "stupid" a statement that "the hireling-class has become the owner-class," and he asserted that the workers had vested their title of ownership in the state. See Louis Fischer, *The Life of Lenin* (New York: Harper & Row, Colophon Books, 1965), p. 437.

[28] In order to keep the problem in perspective, however, we should note that sometimes the difficulty is the opposite one. Some enterprise managers are reluctant to take responsibility and try to get the ministries to make their decision for them. This is no doubt a consequence of a long history during which managers have not been allowed to decide very much on their own.

person above him; he is likely to know how this person views the situation and he has many opportunities to state his case and to justify his actions. The manager is less likely to know what the person above his boss is thinking, and he has fewer opportunities of appearing before him to defend his position. Moreover, the manager knows that the individual above his superior will rarely overrule the superior, for fear of undermining his authority. The manager's boss is a powerful person, and the manager will be slow to challenge his power.

Liberman recognized this difficulty when he wrote:

> One can easily visualize the possibility that a ministry through some of its representatives will try to intervene administratively in matters in which it is not supposed to intervene. Such an administrator who does not want to part with his old habits would harm the cause of economic reconstruction. A clash could ensue. The enterprise may be objectively right, and the representative of industry not. But for the manager of the enterprise it will be hard to get embroiled every time in a conflict with the ministry he is subordinated to.[29]

Perhaps in reaction, an interesting method has been proposed to safeguard the autonomy of the socialist enterprise. In several countries of Eastern Europe, reformers have suggested that the ministry be held materially responsible for its directives. If, for example, a ministry ordered an enterprise to produce a particular item and the enterprise lost money in doing so, the ministry would have to pay the enterprise a sum to cover the losses. Making ministries financially responsible for their decisions would no doubt shift decisions from the center to the periphery in some marginal cases, where the enterprise manager feels strong enough to insist that the ministry assume financial responsibility for its directives but does not feel strong enough to reject the directives outright. This proposed method, however, will not generally secure the autonomy of the enterprise in an environment in which the administrative hierarchy is not in sympathy with decentralization of decisions. In such an environment the enterprise manager will seldom take the risk of any challenge to the directives issued by his superior.

[29] Quoted in Alexander Erlich, "Economic Reforms in Communist Countries," in *New Currents in Soviet-Type Economies*, ed. George R. Feiwel (Scranton: International Textbook Company, 1968), p. 606.

The reformers of socialism may decide that they must give the enterprise rights of decision that are enforceable in the courts. There are courts in some countries in Eastern Europe that claim independence from the government. Realistically, no court could claim that it is independent of the highest political authority—the Council of Ministers or the Politburo of the Party. If, however, the highest political authority were to really believe in decentralization and enterprise responsibility, it should be able to create courts independent of enterprises, ministries, and the central planning board to protect the autonomy of enterprises against unauthorized directives from government officials. And it should be able to specify the exact steps that an enterprise manager could take when he felt that the rights of his enterprise were being infringed.

An important facet of this problem warrants discussion. As we have seen, the autonomy of the enterprise should be protected by the manager; the manager should be able to appeal to the courts when in conflict with the ministry. However, there is the possibility that the manager might not be free to act due to coercion. If he were to proceed and appeal a ministerial decision to the courts, he might be threatened with or, in fact, discharged, or he might fail to secure a promotion or a pay increase, or he might find his pay cut. It follows, therefore, that reformers in a Soviet-type economy should respond to the question of job security. Should the enterprise manager, for example, be given tenure—a type of civil service commission—so that he can be dismissed only by the directives of a higher body? Similarly, the manager of a very large government enterprise might be removable only by the Council of Ministers. At the least the manager might be given the right of appeal to a higher body if he were discharged by his subministry or ministry. In addition to this job security, managers might be given a share of enterprise profits, according to a formula specified by a higher body. With this system of payment, increases in the manager's income could not be checked by a ministry in retaliation for his appeal to the courts.

If the manager of a socialist enterprise were given a measure of tenure in his position, he would be capable of defending the autonomy of the enterprise, and he would have some property rights in the means of production under his control. He would have rights of use and he would even have some rights of disposal for the period of his tenure. (As mentioned earlier, these are not rights that would stand against the highest political authority, the Council of Ministers or the Politburo, but in no economic system do property rights stand against the sovereign, whether the sovereign be king, ministers, or parliament. "No writ holds against the king.") With management given tenure, property rights in the means of production might be dispersed among individuals. The manager, not the enterprise, would own some of the means of production. This private property in the means of production would be a considerable departure from socialism as it is traditionally conceived.

The manager could not purchase these rights in the means of production. He would be assigned to his position. But purchase may come. When the authorities realize that the manager would be getting the right to a fixed share of profits for a period of years, they might decide that he should pay for this right. Already in some countries in Eastern Europe, government-owned restaurants and the like are being leased to private concessionaires, who buy the rights of use for the leasing period.

In closing, we should not contend that the only ways socialism can secure the autonomy of the enterprise is through establishing the right of appeal to independent courts and through granting tenure to management. However, it would be difficult to effectively decentralize decisions through laws and decrees that simply assert that enterprises should be given larger responsibilities, particularly when economies are emerging from a structure that concentrates decisions at the center. Private property is probably the most certain way of transferring decisions from the center to the periphery.

Proposed Reforms in Agriculture

Agriculture has been described as the Achilles' heel of the Soviet-type economy. How do advocates of reform propose to meet its problems?

The most interesting proposals for reform in agriculture concern (1) the prices of farm products, and (2) the possibility of tenure for those who work the land.

Advocates of reform in a Soviet-type economy observe that changes in agricultural prices over time could be improved. If the prices of milk, vegetables, fruit, and berries, for example, were more flexible and fluctuated to increase in the winter and decrease in the summer, collective farms and private producers would be motivated to aim for a possible harvest in the winter months. The distribution network would be motivated to invest in cold storage and freezing equipment.[30] (The assumption being made here is that decision makers would be rewarded in accordance with profit.) Prices also might be lowered after a large harvest and raised after a small one. Actually, in the Soviet-type economy, "prices" now move in the opposite direction; because bonuses are paid for above-quota deliveries, the effective prices per unit of output rise with a larger harvest and fall with a small one. Moreover, were prices raised as a result of a poor harvest, they might stimulate production for the next year. Higher prices would also distribute the consequences of adverse weather or plant disease throughout the population rather than having them fall, as they do now, on collective farmers.[31] (Western economists might disagree with these Soviet reforms. They have studied markets systematically and know more than the Soviets about "market failure." These Western economists often conclude that cyclical oscillations in farm prices and production are undesirable and that carefully designed programs to dampen price fluctuations are advantageous.)

Advocates of reform not only are concerned with temporal price changes, but also are critical of existing spatial price differences.[32] Regional price differences at present in a Soviet-type economy do not reflect transport costs, and this leads to surpluses in some regions at the same time as there are shortages in others. At present low prices are set in regions with poor soil, in order to capture the land rents of fertile regions. These low prices discourage production. Reformers propose more pricing zones with more suitable zonal boundaries, and they propose to collect economic rents through a collective farm income tax. (Again, advocates of reform might learn from Western economists. An income tax might also reduce production. Instead, the tax should be a lump sum, nonmarginal tax on land rent, which would recognize that the supply of land (as opposed to improvements) is not produced by man, is perfectly inelastic, and cannot be decreased by taxation. Other agricultural reforms have been suggested. Some reformers, possibly influenced by Henry George or by modern welfare economics, have proposed that agricultural prices be set to equal marginal cost rather than average cost.[33] If prices were equal to

---

[30]Morris Bornstein, "The Soviet Debate on Agricultural Price and Procurement Reforms," *Soviet Studies* 21 (July, 1969), p. 7.

[31]Ibid., pp. 7, 9.

[32]Ibid., pp. 8–9.

[33]Ibid., p. 12.

the costs of production on the poorest land, surpluses could be captured through taxation of the differential rent earned on superior land. Some reformers have proposed that agricultural prices should be set high enough to provide adequate planned profitability. Prices that fail to cover costs lead to subsidies, and we have seen that government distribution agencies receiving subsidies lack incentives to function efficiently. Finally, some of the most daring advocates of reform have proposed freedom of sales for the cooperative farms in place of compulsory delivery quotas.[34] Farms would then choose the most profitable output mix, and if supplies from the farms did not match the requirements of the authorities, the latter could adjust relative prices.

A more fundamental agricultural reform would be development of the semipermanent "link," or work gang.[35] The link itself is not new and has existed as long as the collective farm itself. What is proposed, and what has been cautiously experimented with, is the assignment of a link to a particular piece of land for a relatively long period of time. With the appropriate equipment, the group would be allowed to farm the land as it saw fit and to share the resulting income. Such a grant of tenure would become in some measure the rights of private property in the means of production.

Some problems which effective reforms would encounter have already been discussed. Now, we need to explore systematically the difficulties which were or might be encountered in efforts to reform.

Obstacles to Reform

The need for reform is widely recognized in the Soviet Union and especially in Eastern Europe. Yet from 1968 (when Russian troops entered Czechoslovakia) through 1974 (when leading reformers lost their positions in Hungary[36]), reforms were halted and frequently reversed in most of the Soviet bloc that had undertaken significant change. Why?

Fears

Much of the explanation lies in the fears that the reforms aroused. The Party, the ministerial apparatus, and the financial bureau-

[34]Ibid., p. 17.
[35]Alec Nove, "Soviet Agriculture Under Brezhnev," *Slavic Review* 29 (January, 1970), pp. 391–92.
[36]"Hungary: End of an Era," *Economist* 250 (March 30, 1974), p. 32.

cracy feared a loss of power—a loss of control over economic development and even a loss of political power.[37] The Party and the government were afraid that they would lose power to the managerial class. All three groups feared losing power to the workers through an increase in the strength of the unions.

The authorities also feared that suppressed inflation would burst into the open.[38] Enterprise managers frequently were afraid they could not cope with the market. They had been functioning in a world of "prefabricated markets," and under the reforms they were going to have to shift from being engineers to being "businessmen."[39] Under a centralized economy only sergeants, not captains of industry had been required.[40] Managers were not sure they would measure up to what the reforms required of them.

An exceedingly pervasive fear that bodes ill for the future of the Soviet economies is that workers fear lower pay and unemployment.[41] Worker demonstrations in the north of Poland during the winter of 1970 and 1971 illustrate this fear well. When these demonstrations occurred, many observers in the East and West thought that Gomulka's consequent fall from power in December 1970 had happened because he had become conservative, even reactionary—an obstacle to reform. However, as we shall see there is another explanation. Although Gomulka had become steadily more conservative from 1956 to the late sixties, his struggle for power with the even more reactionary Moczar, a poorly educated former partisan, had forced him in 1968 to turn to the reformers for support. Moczar pushed him into a series of reforms (many of them long overdue) that were complicated and were not well explained to the people. Managers were to receive bonuses for

[37]Morris Bornstein, *Introduction to Plan and Market* (New Haven: Yale University Press, 1973), pp. 6–8; John M. Montias, "The Czechoslovak Economic Reforms in Perspective," in *New Currents in Soviet-Type Economies*, ed. George A. Feiwell (Scranton: International Textbook Company, 1968), p. 518; Gregory Grossman, "Economic Reforms: A Balance Sheet," in *New Currents*, pp. 618, 621, 623, 625–26; Robert Campbell, "Economic Reform in the USSR," *American Economic Review: Papers and Proceedings*, May, 1968, p. 557; Leda Urbanek, "Some Difficulties in Implementing the Economic Reforms in Czechoslovakia," *Soviet Studies* 19 (April, 1968), p. 563.

[38]Montias, "The Czechoslovak Reforms," p. 511.

[39]Vaclov Holesovsky, "Planning Reforms in Czechoslovakia," *Soviet Studies* 19 (April, 1968), p. 549.

[40]R. V. Burks, "The Political Implications of Economic Reform," in *Plan and Market*, ed. Bornstein, p. 395.

[41]Urbanek, "Some Difficulties," pp. 561–62; Holesovsky, "Planning Reforms," p. 547; Ota Šik, *Czechoslovakia: The Bureaucratic Economy* (White Plains, N.Y.: International Arts and Science Press, 1972), pp. 32–35.

saving materials and labor; workers were to be moved out of uneconomic industries into service activities; workers were to be paid with worker bonuses for "real effort" and not for attendance; and price increases were announced on food, fuel, and the like. Demonstrations among workers erupted to protest these changes.[42] Even today advocates of change find it painful to think that workers present obstacles to reform.

Who Might Be Hurt by Reform
Within the Soviet bloc, economists in different countries have held different views on the extent to which reform might hurt individuals or groups. For example, the Bulgarians and East Germans have been convinced that no one need be made less well off during the transition to a reformed system. The Yugoslavs have been at the opposite extreme. They have emphasized that "some must inevitably 'lose' if the position of others is to be improved."[43] Elsewhere in Eastern Europe one can encounter a variety of ideas on whether or not individuals will be hurt by reform, and one can also find differences of opinion on who the victims of reform should be.

At the outset we must decide what we mean by the word "hurt." Are we concerned with an individual's own preferences, or the values of an outside economist or a government official? One might argue that no individual would be put in a less preferred position during the transition to reform if only his own preferences were considered. (In technical terms, in this case, all changes would be changes to Pareto superior positions, changes in the direction of a Pareto optimum.) Or, one might argue that no individual would be put in a less satisfactory position according to the values of an outside economist or authority.

Few if any economists in the Soviet Union or Eastern Europe would argue that all transitional reform changes would be changes to Pareto superior positions. It is generally agreed that during reform many workers would have to be retrained and transferred to new jobs, that uneconomic enterprises would have to be closed

[42]"Poland: Reform or Perish," *Economist* 235 (April 11, 1970), p. 34; "Poland: Ferreting Out Those Reserves," *Economist* 235 (June 20, 1970), p. 39; "Poland: When the Workers Start to Stir," *Economist* 235 (February, 1971), pp. 31–32; A. Ross Johnson, "Polish Perspectives, Past and Present," *Problems of Communism* 20 (July-August, 1971), pp. 59–72.

[43]Mijalko Todorović in a report submitted at the Second Plenum of the Central Committee of the League of Communists of Yugoslavia, published in *The Economic Reform in Yugoslavia* (Belgrade, 1965), p. 35.

down and management and workers relocated. Many of these people, particularly the older ones, would probably prefer to stay in their old positions. Thus, when reformers in East Europe have argued that no one need be hurt during a transition, it is likely that they have meant only that no one would be unemployed for any substantial period of time and that no one would experience a cut in real income. For example, when enterprises in East Germany were to be closed as part of the reforms, workers were to be retrained and to receive a guarantee that their basic wage would not be lower in a new working place. Moreover, the East Germans hoped both to forecast plant closings three to four years in advance and carefully to plan the transitions.

The number of individuals who would be hurt during the transition to reform depends in part on the skill with which the authorities forecast and plan for changes. This number also would depend on the rate of change sought and the responsiveness of managers and workers to different kinds of incentives. Two transitional problems especially will affect the number: (1) the problem of transferring managers and workers from uneconomic to economic activities, and (2) the problem of inducing people to work harder. (In a number of countries of Eastern Europe, it is generally admitted in the official press that workers no longer work very hard. Years of unsatisfactory incentive systems have resulted in workers expecting neither rewards for hard work nor penalties for poor work.)

Could the authorities in the Soviet Union and Eastern Europe succeed in transferring managers and workers out of uneconomic into economic activities without reductions in real income and without unemployment? Apart from directives (which reformers did not consider using), there are two ways of getting people to move without using directives: (1) offer a higher real income in the new activity than has been received in the old, and (2) reduce the real income associated with the old activity. The first alternative could be achieved simply by paying high incomes in the growing sectors. However, these high incomes would lead to high prices and could slow development. Instead, authorities might choose the second alternative. Reduction in real income might be achieved by paying a lower money income, paying the same money income at a time of rising prices, or laying workers off. If authorities laid off workers in the declining sectors only as rapidly as new jobs opened up in the expanding parts of the economy, and if workers were retrained in anticipation of the change the authorities could induce people to move with few or no individuals suffering losses of real income or unemployment.

Could Soviet-type economies get workers to work harder during transitions to reform? There are three ways of inducing people to work harder: (1) increase the pay of those who increase the intensity of their labor, (2) threaten those who do not work more intensely with wage reductions and unemployment, and (3) actually reduce wages of those who fail to work with greater intensity or fire those people. Some people will respond well to increased pay or threats of wage reductions, so that an increase in labor intensity can be achieved without actual pay cuts or unemployment. But it is doubtful that threats of pay reductions and unemployment will be credible without a certain number of genuine pay reductions and at least a few workers unemployed. Thus, a combination of all three alternatives will most effectively induce harder work.

If it is decided that some individuals should be made worse off during the transition to a reformed system, it is necessary to decide which ones. Many would consider the following redistribution of income desirable: (1) offer a higher income to those who transfer to the dynamic sectors of the economy and those who work harder, (2) protect those unable to move to growth sectors and those working up to capacity against a loss in income (in this category would be the aged, ill, and physically incapacitated), and (3) fire or reduce income for those able to move but slow to make the change and those working below capacity.

An example of this method of redistributing income may be seen in Czechoslovakia, when there was a great deal of discussion of what should be done in uneconomic areas of activity. Should wages in these areas be reduced or should prices be increased? Many opposed increases in retail prices. A law was enacted that wages in uneconomic plants could be reduced by as much as 8 percent.

Wage reduction is a good solution only if the plant is uneconomic because workers are working below capacity. Likewise, if the source of the difficulty is poor management, a cut in managerial income would be suitable. But if the workers are performing well, then a wage reduction would put the burden of inefficiency on the wrong people. Immobile but energetic workers would be subsidizing the enterprise in place of the general public. (On the other hand, if the wage cut immediately separated the high- from the low-performance workers, the cut might be considered desirable.)

When an enterprise is uneconomic because its plant and equipment are obsolete, then economists might feel that the burden of the transition should fall on the general public. This might be accomplished through a reduction in enterprise payments into the budget or by higher prices. For example, there were people in Czechoslovakia during the reform period who wanted to see some retail prices increased, contending that this would eliminate suppressed inflation (queues and subsidies). Nevertheless, these people wanted the higher prices to be accompanied by reforms that would make it possible for workers who improved their performance to earn higher money incomes, thereby putting the burden of the transition on the workers who did not improve.

Opposition to Soviet-type reform often occurs in underdeveloped regions for a number of reasons. People dwelling in underdeveloped regions become concerned about the impact of reform on their parts of a country. Investments made only on the basis of prospective profit often would have reduced resources for the development of places like Slovakia in Czechoslovakia.[44] Also, reform is hindered by the disequilibria that characterize the Soviet-type economies. Attempts to decentralize have encountered difficulties caused by the facts that the allocation of resources is far from an equilibrium, that prices similarly are a long way from equilibrium, and that macro quantities are not in balance.[45] Reforms that threaten a large reallocation of resources and adjustments in prices are potentially sources of major tension.

Taut Plans

Reforms directed toward decentralization generally require slack plans; in reality, during most attempts at reform, the authorities have insisted on continuing traditional taut plans. Had there been slack plans, prices could have been more flexible and less rationing would have been necessary. Gregory Grossman explains this need:

> The need for rigid physical controls would be lessened, price flexibility would more likely be allowed, and hence the decentralizing reforms would be more likely to succeed, if the overall pressure on resources—which is to say, the ambitiousness of the national plans and goals of the countries in question—were to be restrained.[46]

[44]Montias, "Czechoslovak Economic Reforms," p. 518.

[45]Abram Bergson, "Economic Reform in Eastern Europe—Discussion," *American Economic Review* 58 (May, 1968), pp. 581, 585.

[46]Grossman, "Economic Reforms," p. 622. See also Campbell, "Economic Reform," pp. 550, 556; Holesovsky, "Planning Reforms," p. 549; Gertrude E. Schroeder, "Soviet Economic Reform at an Impasse," *Problems of Communism* 20 (July–August, 1971), p. 37.

In addition, if plans were slack profit rather than plan fulfillment would influence managerial behavior more often than it has.[47] Finally, if plans were intentionally slack, central investment plans could be held down, which would release resources for decentralized investment decisions, for contingencies like changes in the conditions of foreign trade, unforeseen technological progress, and changes in consumer demand.[48]

Pressures for Recentralization

Perhaps the greatest obstacles to reform in the Soviet-type economy are the numerous and powerful forces pressing toward recentralization. When ill-conceived reforms have not gone well, disillusionment has set in and decisions have been moved back to the center. One reason for such recentralization has been that the initial decentralization sometimes was premature; decisions were decentralized before price reform had provided scarcity prices. The old prices did not transmit the proper information from one part of the economy to another, and when managers were allowed to act in response to these prices their choices did not lead to a good allocation of resources. In Eastern Europe one encounters numerous tales of hasty decentralizations that had untoward consequences because they preceded price reform. In one country in 1965 all packaging materials for machinery were exported, and this seriously hampered the export of machinery itself. Unreformed prices did not adequately signal domestic demand for the product. Some Polish economists believe that Polish efforts to decentralize in 1958–59 failed in part because price reform did not precede decentralization.

Decisions were too quickly decentralized during the reform period because many advocates of reform, reacting to cumbersome central controls, became infatuated with the market and seemed to think it would do everything right under almost any circumstances. Amongst East European economists who were advocates of reform one encounters frequently a belief in a sort of socialist laissez-faire. Some reformers have not thought about what Western economists call "market failure." For example, as part of the price reform in several countries, these reformers wanted to increase agricultural prices in order to stimulate a

---

[47]Michael Keren, "Concentration Amid Devolution in East Germany's Reforms," in *Plan and Market*, ed. Bornstein, pp. 145, 150–51.

[48]Montias, "Czechoslovak Economic Reforms," p. 509.

larger agricultural output and to keep young people on the collective farms. Other East Europeans doubted that higher prices would be followed by a larger output because the average age of collective farmers was quite high (54 years in Hungary, 49 years in Czechoslovakia). The older peasant, they argued, had simple wants and would be satisfied with food, clothing and shelter, tobacco, money, and some fruit and vegetables to take to his children in the city. Hence he would lack motivation to produce more. This possibility of an inelastic supply in the agricultural sector of the economy was not considered by the most enthusiastic advocates of the market.

Another reason for recentralization has been that the reformers failed to insist on the desirability of competition where possible. When monopolies raised prices, the government often stepped in and recentralization followed.

Also, in reform systems horizontal ties were supposed to take the place of directives from above. But inadequate sanctions were provided for contract violations,[49] and appeal to higher authority has invited centralized decision making.

Too often, reforms have been piecemeal. In a modern economy with millions of interdependencies, a market in one sector may function poorly because of controls in another sector. For example, a manufacturer of clothing may not have produced garments wanted by retail outlets because the material inputs required were rationed. The response to this failure of the reformed system may have been to reimpose output targets on clothing makers.

Confidence Gap

One important factor leading toward recentralization is what in the West we would call a "confidence gap," and what in the Soviet literature is sometimes called "reserved trust."[50] Too often in the past the authorities have promised improvements in the standard of living and then have failed to deliver. One Party member said to me, "The workers do not trust us. We have broken our promises too often." Indeed, both workers and managers have been slow to reveal capacity when in the past such revelations have so frequently been followed by higher norms and larger targets. The

---

[49]Gertrude E. Schroeder, "Soviet Economic Reforms: A Study in Contradictions," *Soviet Studies* 20 (July, 1968), p. 11.

[50]Holesovsky, "Planning Reforms," p. 547.

reformers have faced a dilemma. The authorities have said, "Work harder and we will pay you more." The workers have replied, "Pay us more and we will work harder." What the workers really were saying has been, "Pay us more over a period of time. Do not change the norm when we increase our productivity. As we gradually gain confidence we will reveal our capacity."

One proposal to alleviate the confidence gap has been to give managers discretionary funds so that they could pay "cash on the barrelhead" for improved performance. While this decentralization might be helpful (the manager has a better idea than the authorities of where the reserves in his plant are to be found), it would not induce the workers to reveal their capacity if they distrusted the manager and believed that the next time they would be expected to do the work without the extra cash.

It seems clear that it would take time, perhaps a great deal of time, to rebuild confidence. The authorities would have to convince the workers that they had been converted to a "high-wage philosophy," that they will pay a high wage for a good day's work. (They would also have to convince managers that they believed in high incomes for good management.) It would take time to overcome the effects of years of what has been in reality a low-wage philosophy. The authorities have always tried to squeeze a little more work out of people, with the increment devoted to capital formation rather than the output of consumption goods.

Implementing a high wage philosophy calls for more consumption goods. A number of economists in Czechoslovakia have proposed an interesting scheme for mobilizing concealed reserves. They have suggested that the authorities use foreign exchange to import consumption goods rather than the traditional capital goods. They believe that consumption goods, if supplied to managers and workers who have performed well, would induce them to disclose the real capacity of existing plants and equipment. This newly revealed capacity then would substitute for imports of capital. It is not certain that importation of consumption goods would effectively mobilize reserves early in the transition to the new model, because probably workers and managers initially would not trust the authorities to continue high incomes for hard work. Thus, foregone imports of capital goods might not at first be replaced by the newly revealed capacity of existing plants and equipment. But even if the reduced import of capital goods (accompanied by an increase in imports of consumption goods) appeared temporarily to slow down economic growth, it might in the long run accelerate growth by creating a valuable "capital" of manager and worker belief that hard work is appreciated and rewarded.

The Weights of Ideology and Bureaucracy

Possibly the strongest forces pressing for recentralization are the weights of Marxist-Leninist ideology, accompanied by the existing undismantled administrative machinery[51]—the heavy hand of the past in ideology and bureaucracy. One hears of obligatory targets that have been set by ministries even when such targets were not in the plan.[52]

Finally, it must be remembered that a reintroduction of decision making by the center can occur in small steps, with each of them little noticed but with the sum total defeating the reform movement. As Gregory Grossman has stated:

> In general, effective decentralization in a centrally administered economy can take place only when carried out on a very broad front all at once, which requires intervention from higher quarters and calls for big political battles. Centralization, however, can and often does proceed in little steps, virtually unnoticed but important in aggregate impact.[53]

The obstacles to reform of the Soviet-type economy are indeed formidable, perhaps so formidable that reform can be achieved only through new people with new ideas, who are capable of overcoming the legacy of the past. (The average age of the top people in Party and government in Russia and Eastern Europe is a decade or two above that of their counterparts in Western Europe and North America.) But the ideology of the dictatorship of the proletariat, the leading role of the Party, and democratic centralism—all of which mean in practice the dictatorship of an oligarchy or an individual in the name of the proletariat—stand in the way of new people who might bring in new ideas.

---

[51] Montias, "Czechoslovak Economic Reforms," pp. 514–17.
[52] Schroeder, "Soviet Economic Reforms: A Study in Contradictions," p. 10.
[53] Grossman, "Economic Reforms," p. 623.

Market Socialism

Part II

Introduction to Part Two

Karl Marx had little to say about socialism; he wrote mainly about capitalism. When Marx did write about socialism, he wrote about the likely distribution of income,[1] and he said virtually nothing about how output, input, and investment decisions would be made in a socialist economy. Indeed, socialists generally have been slow to devote themselves to the arduous task of drawing up a workable model of a socialist economy. As a consequence, the Bolsheviks had no blueprint of socialism at hand when they came to power in Russia in 1917. The Soviet-type economy, which we have been examining in the early chapters of this book, was evolved through experience.

Widespread efforts to develop a theory of socialism did not get underway until after World War I. They really began in 1920 when the Austrian economist Ludwig von Mises launched his now celebrated attack on socialism in an article in which he contended that rational calculation under socialism is impossible.[2] He argued that without private ownership of the means of production there is no market for capital goods, no prices on those goods, and consequently no way of determining rationally how they are to be employed. Should a drill press, for example, be used to produce automobiles, refrigerators, tractors, water pumps, or what? Without a price on a capital good, according to von Mises, there is no way of knowing its most economical use. "There is only groping in the dark."[3]

Actually, in 1908 an Italian economist, Enrico Barone, had developed earlier suggestions of Pareto to mathematically show how a socialist government might rationally plan production.[4] But Barone acknowledged, as did Lionel Robbins in 1934 and Friedrich A. Hayek in 1935, that while his solution was formally correct, it did not provide a practical method of deciding what outputs should be turned out with the means of production.[5] Hayek contended that in order to construct a good plan, a planning body

[1] Karl Marx, *Critique of the Gotha Program* in *Selected Works* (New York: International Publishers, 1891), pp. 561–66.

[2] Ludwig von Mises, "Die Wirtschaftsrechnung im sozialistischen Gemeinwesen," *Archiv für Sozialwissenschaften,* 1920, translated and reprinted under the title "Economic Calculation in the Socialist Commonwealth," in *Collectivist Economic Planning,* ed. F. A. Hayek (London: Routledge & Kegan Paul, 1935), pp. 87–130.

[3] Ibid., p. 110.

[4] "The Ministry of Production in the Collectivist State," in *Collectivist Economic Planning,* Appendix A, pp. 245–90.

[5] Lionel Robbins, *The Great Depression* (London, 1934), p. 151; F. A. Hayek, "The Present State of the Debate," in *Collectivist Economic Planning,* pp. 207–12.

would have to know the technical properties of all intermediate goods and capital equipment and the quantities of all commodities that would be bought at all possible combinations of prices.[6] The planning body would have to solve hundreds of thousands of simultaneous equations. Long before the data were collected and the equations were solved, the results would be outdated by changes in the economy. The difficulties that the Soviets have encountered over the years in achieving consistency and efficiency lend support to the contentions of Barone, Robbins, and Hayek.

In a direct response to the arguments of Robbins and Hayek, a number of economists developed a model that in recent years has become known as "market socialism." While the spade work had already been done by Taylor in his 1929 presidential address to the American Economic Association,[7] the model was elaborated by Dickinson,[8] Lerner,[9] and Lange[10] in the thirties. In this book I shall follow the relatively simple and well-known Lange version, and refer occasionally to the works of Dickinson and Lerner.

---

[6]Hayek assumed that the market demand of consumers rather than the directives of the authorities would control production.

[7]Fred M. Taylor, "The Guidance of Production in a Socialist State," *American Economic Review,* 19 (March, 1929), pp. 1–8; reprinted in Oskar Lange and Fred M. Taylor *On the Economic Theory of Socialism* (Minneapolis: University of Minnesota Press, 1938), pp. 41–54.

[8]H. D. Dickinson, "Price Formation in a Socialist Community," *Economic Journal,* 43 (June, 1933), pp. 237–50; H. D. Dickinson, *The Economics of Socialism* (London: Oxford University Press, 1939).

[9]A. P. Lerner, "Statics and Dynamics in Socialist Economics," *Economic Journal* 47 (June, 1937), pp. 253–70; A. P. Lerner, *The Economics of Control* (New York: Macmillan Co., 1944).

[10]Oskar Lange, "On the Economic Theory of Socialism," in Lange and Taylor, *On the Economic Theory of Socialism,* pp. 57–142.

The Static Lange Model

Chapter 8

The institutions of Lange's model for market socialism can be simply described. There is "a genuine market (in the institutional sense of the word) for consumer goods and for the services of labor. But there is no market for capital goods and productive resources outside of labor."[1] Misnamed by Lange,[2] a central planning board sets accounting prices on capital goods and supervises the managers of plants and industries. *Plant* managers decide on inputs and outputs of an existing plant, while *industry* managers decide whether or not to maintain it, expand it, or create a new plant. Managers of plant and industry make their decisions in response to actual or accounting prices and in accordance with specified rules.[3] Much of what follows will deal with the problems of price formation and rule enforcement.

[1] Oskar Lange, "On the Economic Theory of Socialism," in Oskar Lange and Fred M. Taylor, *On the Economic Theory of Socialism* (Minneapolis: University of Minnesota Press, 1938), p. 73.

[2] A more accurate term here would be "central price setting board and management supervisory agency." Lange's board does not plan output, input, or investment. We will, however, use Lange's term.

[3] Lange, "On the Economic Theory of Socialism," pp. 73, 75–78, 81.

Price Determination

The central planning board sets accounting prices by trial and error to clear the market, lowering the price when, at the existing price, quantity demanded is less than quantity supplied, and raising the price when the contrary is the case.[4] The central planning board knows that there is an inequality between supply and demand when it observes that inventories are higher or lower than the optimum.[5] This means that the board works with the idea of an optimum inventory. Although Lange did not say so, the central planning board probably would have an optimal range rather than a fixed quantity as its optimum. For example, its optimum inventory in St. Louis of a certain kind of pipe might extend from 5,000 to 6,000 feet. When inventories fell to 5,000 feet, it would raise the price; when inventories rose to 6,000 feet, it would lower the price. With this system prices would not be changing all the time, and the size of the inventory range could be varied to alter the frequency of price changes.

It is not at all clear why Lange wanted all accounting prices to be set by a central planning board. Why couldn't they be set by agreement between the parties? Why couldn't socialist managers, like capitalist businessmen, decide whether the amount supplied would be greater than, equal to, or less than the amount demanded? It is unlikely that Lange's reason for centralized price determination came as a result of his attempt to control monopoly prices; he proposed to deal with that very problem through output rules imposed on the managers. (We will discuss these rules shortly.) Moreover, if the objective of centrally established prices were to control monopoly, prices would have to be set by *non-market-clearing* formula, for with a market-clearing formula a monopolistic enterprise could get a higher price through the restriction of supply.

We may conclude, therefore, that if monopoly in Lange's model could be effectively controlled through the imposition of output rules on socialist managers, then centralized price determination would be unnecessary. However, if monopoly had to be controlled through the imposition of price ceilings, then Lange's formula for price setting is faulty.

[4] Ibid., pp. 82, 86.
[5] Ibid., p. 87. Lange credits Fred M. Taylor with this idea. Neither Taylor nor Lange uses the concept of an optimum inventory explicitly, but it is implicit in their statements.

The Rules Imposed on Managers

Lange proposed that plant and industry managers be required to follow three rules: (1) Produce a quantity of output such that marginal cost is equal to price; (2) Produce any given output with that combination of inputs that minimizes average cost; and (3) In arriving at input and output decisions, act as though prices were independent of the decisions taken.[6]

The foregoing rules can be refined. In the first place, they are best regarded as input and output rules only, addressed to plant managers. Regarded as such, the first rule, the order to produce to the point where marginal cost is equal to price, directs the manager to ignore his influence on the price of the product. He is to produce to the point where marginal cost is equal to average, not marginal, revenue. The question arises: Is Lange's third rule even necessary? It turns out that it is: changes in marginal cost include changes in factor prices that are associated with changes in output.[7] A manager with monopsony power who produces to the point where $MC=P$ and ignores the third rule takes into account his influence on factor prices when he makes output decisions.

If, however, we follow Lerner's and Hirshleifer's theory, which has been unaccountably neglected by microeconomists, we can achieve symmetry in the output rule.[8] In place of MC, we can use a curve CMF (cost of the marginal quantity of factor), defined as the cost of the marginal unit of output in terms of the quantity of factor in input required, with this input valued at factor prices.[9] We can then employ a modified rule one: Produce a quantity of output such that cost of the marginal quantity of factor is equal to price.[10] If the manager follows this rule, he ignores his influence on factor prices as well as on product prices, and we do not need Lange's original rule three. Nor, it turns out, do we need rule two as long as we assume that the incremental factors employed are the minimum necessary to produce the output and that they are obtained at the minimum possible price. (This assumption usually is made. Cost curves represent the minimum of the costs which it

[6] Ibid., pp. 75–76, 81.

[7] Jack Hirshleifer, "An Exposition of the Equilibrium of the Firm: Symmetry Between Product and Factor Analyses," *Economica* 29 (August, 1962), pp. 264–65.

[8] Ibid.; A. P. Lerner, *The Economics of Control* (New York: Macmillan Co., 1944), pp. 99, 128–31.

[9] Hirshleifer, "An Exposition," p. 265.

[10] Ibid., p. 268.

is possible to incur.) We end up, therefore, with a single rule: Produce to the point where $CMF=P$.

The rationale of the rule, or rules, is difficult to elucidate without an extensive discussion of formal welfare economics. One defense of the rule suggests that when CMF and P are equal, everywhere in the economy, a Pareto optimum is attained in which it is impossible to move any one individual to a position he prefers more without moving at least one other individual to a position he prefers less. Mathematical economists have proved that under special conditions a competitive equilibrium is a necessary and sufficient condition for a Pareto optimum. (At a competitive equilibrium, $CMF=P$.) Knowing this characteristic of a competitive economy, many economists believe that if the equality of CMF and P is imposed on managers throughout the economy, whether they are monopolists or in competitive environments and whether their costs are increasing or decreasing, a Pareto optimum will result. Actually, it has not been established that in reality a universal equality of CMF and P would result in a Pareto optimum.

A more understandable argument for the use of $CMF=P$ is the contention that the cost of the marginal quantity of factor measures the opportunity cost of producing the good, while price measures the value of the commodity. Lerner expands the argument:

> If we order the economic activity of a society so that no commodity is produced unless its importance is greater than that of the alternative that is sacrificed, we shall have completely achieved the ideal, the most economic utilization of resources.[11]

A rule that leads to the production of a good only when its value exceeds its opportunity cost would, in a static economy, maximize wealth produced. However, use of a rule equating CMF and P may not be satisfactory when innovation is desired. (This point will be developed more fully later.)

Lange's model lacks a good investment rule. Industry managers who make investment decisions are simply directed to adhere to the same three rules as plant managers, except that Lange modifies the output rule for indivisible inputs. He explains, "We have to compare the cost of each *indivisible input* with the receipts

[11] A. P. Lerner, "Statics and Dynamics in Socialist Economies" *Economic Journal* 47 (June, 1937), p. 253.

expected from the additional output thus secured."[12] Lange does not explicitly state that future receipts and costs should be discounted, although after he introduces his decision rules he does introduce an interest rate into his system.[13] (Lerner more clearly introduces a discount rate into investment decisions.)[14] We have already demonstrated, in Chapter 4, that in the absence of uncertainty, the best rule for investment is to invest whenever the present value of net income is positive.

For the remainder of this chapter, let us assume that the socialist manager employs the single rule, $CMF=P$, for those decisions in which time can be ignored. Let us also assume that the manager has a present value rule to use when the time of receipts and outlays are significant.

The Supervision and Reward of Managers

Lange does not provide details on how managers are supervised and rewarded. He says that "certain rules are imposed" on managers, and he no doubt intends that the services of managerial labor, like all labor, are to be priced in a genuine market. He also asserts that the discussion of the relative efficiency of public officials and private individuals as managers of production belongs to sociology rather than economics.[15] Lerner takes a similar view, and states that the matter of incentives is a sociological question.[16] Most economists who study alternative economic systems would not care to set aside the question of the behavior of the people in the systems. No one who purports to design a practical system of socialism can ignore the method and the cost of getting the factors of production to behave in the way required by the model.

In the Lange system, managers are to be rewarded for *adherence to rule*, and supervisors will have to decide how well or how poorly the managers are following the rule.

Supervision of the rule that the manager produce to the point where the cost of the marginal quantity of factor is equal to the price requires the authorities to examine a manager's estimate of the physical quantities of factors required to produce a marginal unit of output. With knowledge of product and factor prices at the

[12] Lange, "On the Economic Theory of Socialism," p. 77n.
[13] Ibid., p. 84.
[14] Lerner, "Statics and Dynamics," p. 264.
[15] Lange, "On the Economic Theory of Socialism," pp. 75, 109.
[16] Lerner, "Statics and Dynamics," p. 267n.

time of decision, the authorities can then judge whether or not the output rule was followed. They cannot insist that cost of the marginal quantity of factor be equal to price at every moment in time, for the manager must be allowed time to move from a position of disequilibrium to one of equilibrium. The authorities must exercise judgment in deciding whether a manager's rate of adjustment toward equilibrium is satisfactory. (A study in comparative statics assumes that all transactions take place at positions of equilibrium, hence such a study does not deal with rate of change.)

Supervisors also have to check to see that the cost of the marginal quantity of factor incurred by managers is the minimum possible. In so doing, they must compare the costs incurred by one manager with the costs incurred by managers in the same or a similar line of activity, taking into account the circumstances under which different managers are operating. Again, judgment is involved in these evaluations. It is notable, however, that under capitalism similar cost comparisons are made by various people— the staff at the headquarters of a large corporation, shareholders, lenders, security analysts, and, in some industries, governmental rate-setting agencies. While much work remains to be done on the detection and reward of efficiency under different institutional arrangements, there is no reason to believe that judicious administrators cannot enforce cost minimization.

Judgment is also involved in supervision of the investment rule. If the prices used in calculations of present value are the ones that are expected to prevail after an investment is made, so that the investment makes a profit, then the authorities generally can judge an investment decision by its subsequent record of profit and loss. But even when post-investment prices are used in decision making, the authorities cannot always take losses as evidence of failure. Losses may occur as a consequence of an unanticipated development (for example, the sudden outbreak of war), and those who evaluate the performance of socialist managers must decide whether a manager should or should not have been able to make a profit under given circumstances. Again, the same kind of judgment has to be made in evaluating the performance of capitalist managers. Joseph A. Schumpeter was wrong when he asserted that under capitalism "both business success and business failure are ideally precise. Neither can be talked away."[17] A capitalist management can talk away losses caused by unforeseen events,

---

[17]Joseph A. Schumpeter, *Capitalism, Socialism, and Democracy*, 3rd ed. (New York: Harper & Brothers, 1950), p. 74.

such as wildcat strikes, floods, changes in technology, and so on. (Schumpeter, himself, later recognized that chance does play a part in business success under capitalism.[18]) Yet when all circumstances are considered, over the long run profit is generally a good indicator of success in the competitive sector of a capitalist economy. Likewise, it would be a good success indicator under socialism when investment decisions are guided by the prices that are expected to prevail after new capacity is installed.

If, in order to take account of consumers' surplus, managers are expected to calculate with the prices that prevail before an indivisible investment is made (perhaps averaged with post-investment prices), then the activity might regularly operate at a loss. In this case, profit cannot be used as a success indicator. Supervisors reviewing a given decision must them look at the estimates that managers made of the expected physical performance of any given installation, look at the forecasts of input and output prices which were made, then compare actual performance and prices with the earlier estimates and forecasts. Here, even more than when profit is the success indicator, an element of judgment is involved.

Finally, in supervising all investment decisions, the authorities must use judgment in deciding whether a manager has taken the right amount of risk in making his decisions. Perhaps the greatest danger in the supervision of investment decisions, especially big decisions, is that they may inadvertently become partially centralized. Managers, in order to avoid subsequent criticism, may seek advance approval of projects, so that in effect the higher authorities are making the final decisions. If a decentralized socialism is desired, the authorities must be on their guard and insist that managers make their own decisions. Managers would then be subject only to a periodic review of their performance.

Lange's Treatment of Indiscriminate Delivery (Spillovers)

Lange argues that under capitalism the private businessman considers only the gains and losses that are reflected in the prices he receives and pays.[19] In contrast, he asserts that decision-makers in a socialist economy are able to take into account *all* the benefits and costs associated with any given decision. Socialist managers presumably must consider the consequences of the smoke their

---

[18]Ibid., p. 73.
[19]Lange, "On the Economic Theory of Socialism," pp. 77, 103–5.

plants emit, the noise their plants make, the wastes their plants dump into streams, and so on. The managers would not indiscriminately produce and deliver such things to those who did not want them. (Smoke, noise, odors, and the like are usually discussed under the heading of "externalities." Appendix III, explains why the concept of indiscriminate delivery, like the concept of "spillover," is more precise.) Lange believes that in his model all the consequences of decisions will be considered because industry managers, when they make decisions, will take into account the costs and benefits for an entire industry. However, as we have already recognized, it occasionally happens in a Soviet-type economy that the decision of one plant manager may benefit or hurt the activities of another manager in the same industry without these gains or losses being taken into account by the decision maker. For example, the operation of pumps in one mine may drain water from an adjacent mine that is under the control of another manager. Under these circumstances, which probably are rare, the industry manager himself may have to make current input and output decisions or put both activities under the same plant manager.

More frequently circumstances arise when the decisions of managers in one industry affect the situation in other industries. For example, the meatpacking industry may pollute the water used by the chemical industry. Consequences of this sort, which so often occur, are not taken into account by Lange's managers. Lange has plant and industry managers in his system, but he does not have "economy" managers. His control planning board does not plan. He partitions his economy into industries and hence leaves open the possibility of indiscriminate delivery between industries. At one point he does say that "by appropriate legislation, taxes, and bounties a socialist economy can induce ... small scale private entrepreneurs to take *all* alternatives into consideration."[20] Presumably, Lange would argue that a socialist economy could use similar means to deal with indiscriminate delivery between the large socialized industries. But a capitalistic economy also can use legislation, taxes, and subsidies wherever such problems exist, and Lange does not establish that socialism has an advantage in this respect.

Once it is recognized that indiscriminate delivery may have to be dealt with by the central authorities, industry managers in a model of market socialism look like a dubious idea. For industry

[20] Ibid., p. 107n.

managers are likely to reduce the degree of competition, and monopoly is probably as undesirable in a socialist as in a capitalist economy (except in both economies when reduced competition is a consequence of economies of scale).

Statics and Dynamics in Market Socialism

Lange gave us a model of market socialism defined in comparative statics. An operational model, however, must be dynamic. It must, as we have seen, allow for the fact that many if not most transactions occur at nonequilibrium positions and that those who evaluate managerial performance have to conceive of an optimal rate of adjustment toward equilibrium with which to compare actual adjustment rates. (The optimum rate of adjustment will rest on value judgments, on judgments as to the relative values of security and change.) A dynamic model of market socialism must explicitly recognize that many decisions must reflect anticipations of future prices, that speculation will and should occur, that traders who specialize in the relationship between present and future prices may be useful, and that disequilibrating speculation may be a problem. Speculation, it must be acknowledged, is not exclusively a phenomenon of capitalism.

Most importantly, a dynamic and operational model of market socialism must eventually deal with the concept of innovation. Lange does discuss why modern capitalism is not progressive,[21] but says little about the sources of progress under socialism. He tells us that industry managers decide "whether an industry ought to be expanded (by building new plants or enlarging old ones) or contracted (by not replacing plants which are wearing out)."[22] He does not tell us whether industry managers should be conservative. Lange's managers have enduring monopoly control in their respective industries, and they are chosen because it is believed that they will follow the rules. Such people are usually not innovative by nature. It is easy to imagine Lange's managers repeating themselves month after month, year after year. To be sure, we have observed government officials innovating and taking large risks in both the U.S. and the Soviet space programs. But these are sectors that attract much attention and as a consequence are closely watched by government authorities. Success is rewarded with notable recognition and prestige. It seems improbable to

[21] Ibid., pp. 112–21.
[22] Ibid., pp. 76–77.

assume that the same sort of performance can be expected in less glamorous areas by men who are supposed to function by Lange's rules. It has often been noted that the Soviets turn out good space vehicles but poor saucepans. Innovation in the less exciting pursuits of mankind may require a more dynamic model of socialism than the Lange model.[23]

This author feels that a model of market socialism that is generally practical and effective will have to be constructed on Schumpeterian rather than Marshallian and Walrasian lines. Surprisingly enough, Schumpeter himself did not construct such a dynamic model of socialism. His system of socialism is as static as Lange's.[24] When speaking of capitalism, Schumpeter shows how the profits of temporary monopoly induce men to innovate and he speaks of the process of creative destruction where new organizations come into being while old ones disappear.[25] But in dealing with market socialism, Schumpeter does not face the problems of inducing men to innovate and preventing organizations from solidfying into immobility.

Lange—with Taylor, Lerner, and Dickinson—made one major contribution to the theory of socialism. He demonstrated beyond the shadow of a doubt that through trial and error scarcity prices could be found in a socialist economy and that rational decisions in response to conditions of scarcity could be made in such a system. Beyond that, his model is essentially a formal exercise in comparative statics. It is not surprising, therefore, that it and similar models have been almost entirely ignored in the Soviet Union and Eastern Europe by reformers, even as they propose a larger role for markets in the Soviet economies.

---

[23]Lerner entitles one of his papers "Statics and Dynamics in Socialist Economics," but he supplies little analysis of economic change. Though he differentiates between short- and long-period decisions and recognizes that investment decisions should reflect anticipated prices, he does not deal with nonequilibrium states of the economy or rates of adjustment and he does not consider the introduction of new processes, new products, or new organizational units. See Lerner, "Statics and Dynamics," pp. 264, 266ff, 269.

[24]Schumpeter, "*Capitalism, Socialism, and Democracy,*" pp. 175–86.

[25]Ibid., pp. 82–84, 88.

An Operational Model

Chapter 9

Rather than focus on a set of formal decision rules for those who set prices, determine current output and input, and settle upon investment projects, I shall attempt to construct a practicable model of market socialism. The model will include such topics as the creation of new administrative units or enterprises and the destruction of obsolete ones, the appointment and removal of managers, the methods of inducing government officials and enterprise managers to behave in ways required by the model, and the finance of the different economic units in the system. Finally, a distinction will be made between the institutions of the competitive sector of the economy and the institutions of the parts of the economy in which there is natural monopoly.

The Competitive Sector

The principal features of a competitive market socialism might be the following:

1. Either government departments or government-established conglomerate holding companies create and destroy government enterprises in accordance with prospects of profit and loss and in order to promote competition. Enterprises (relatively autonomous units with their own income statements) are set up in manufacturing, the extractive industries, transportation, domestic and foreign

trade, and banking. All enterprises have distinctive company names and trademarks.

2. The government owns the enterprises established by government departments and owns the conglomerate holding companies. The latter in turn own the enterprises that they establish. The enterprises own the means of production, except for some rights that the government reserves to itself. The government invests funds in the holding companies or enterprises, and it possibly invests in them physical plant and equipment taken over from private owners. The government as owner has the right to appoint the managers of holding companies, the right to appoint the managers of enterprises established by government departments, and the right to receive profits from the government holding companies and government enterprises.

3. Private individuals save and deposit money in interest-paying government banks and buy interest-bearing government bonds. Individuals also may be allowed to buy the debt instruments of government enterprises and holding companies.

4. A capital market unifies the investment decisions made by autonomous units. In this market: (1) individuals may be allowed to trade in debt instruments of government enterprises and holding companies, (2) government departments, government-established conglomerate holding companies, government enterprises, and government banks may buy and sell debt instruments, and (3) government enterprises may trade in new and used buildings and equipment.

5. Prices are set by enterprise managers to clear the market.

6. The indicator of enterprise success is profit, and the manager, who may be given tenure, is rewarded with a share of profit. Output and investment decisions are made in accordance with anticipated profit.

Let us now examine more fully each of these characteristics of the competitive part of a market socialism.

Government Departments or Holding Companies?

Advocates of socialism have had little to say about the circumstances under which new production units are established and existing units are dissolved. One possibility is to have government departments at the national, provincial, and local levels authorized to establish enterprises in accordance with prospects for profit. Most of the government departments would specialize in a particular branch of the economy. The departments would be instructed to establish as many competing enterprises in each branch as the economies of large-scale production would permit, and they would be instructed to dissolve enterprises that could be expected to make little or no profit.

Alternatively, the government might establish government conglomerate holding companies, with each holding company free to establish enterprises in any sector of the economy that looks profitable as long as it does not seek or achieve monopoly in a sector. In fact, such a proposal has already been suggested. In Hungary Dr. Sandor Kopatsy, head of the Research Institute of the Finance Ministry, suggested that desirable capital flows would be promoted through the establishment of fifteen or twenty "socialist holding companies."[1] In Italy, there already exists a government conglomerate holding company, the Institute for Industrial Reconstruction (IRI). Owned entirely by the government, IRI is a holding company with shares, notes, and debentures in a number of subsidiary financial companies that in turn own shares in steel, shipping, engineering, electricity, and telephone enterprises.[2] Although Italy does not have government holding companies that compete with each other, IRI subsidiaries do operate side by side with private firms in the same sector. In any economy consisting entirely of market socialism, there would be good reason to foster competition between government enterprises through government holding companies that are free in a kind of socialist free enterprise, to enter any sector of the economy.

Government enterprises that are allowed to engage in foreign trade would foster competition within the economy through imports and might be motivated to strive for efficiency in order to secure sales in competitive foreign markets.

Company Names and Trademarks

Whether established by government departments or by government holding companies, the competing enterprises would be given distinct company names and trademarks; enterprises so identified could be held responsible for their products by the con-

[1] *Magyar Hirlap,* 25 May 1969, quoted in *Radio Free Europe Research,* 2 June 1969, p. 2.

[2] Vera Lutz, *Italy: A Study in Economic Development* (London: Oxford University Press, 1962), Chapter 12.

sumer. As a consequence of consumer ability to shift purchases accordingly, enterprises would be induced to strive for quality and reliability. (While the consumer outside the Soviet sphere often takes the benefits of a trademark for granted, the consumer in a traditional Soviet-type economy, where products of different factories are frequently not identified, often cannot even find out which factory is responsible for defective goods. One economic reform proposed in the Soviet Union and Eastern Europe is the extensive use of trademarks.)

In the model of market socialism being developed here, the government would appoint the managers of holding companies as well as the managers of enterprises established by government departments. Much needs to be said about these appointments. If a manager were to hold his position at the pleasure of his superior, the holding company or enterprise under the manager's control might lack independence. It might, for example, not be free to close down uneconomic operations or to lay off unneeded workers. Moreover, a manager who could be dismissed at any time and whose performance was judged by current profit would have a short time horizon. He might fail to make promising but late-maturing investments, or he might run down the plant under his control by undesirable disinvestment. As a consequence, socialists might conclude that the manager should be given some degree of security—a tenureship—in his position. Yet, while tenure would give the manager independence, it would not extend the time he looks into the future beyond the time he expects to hold his position, and his time horizon would move steadily closer as he approaches the end of his appointment. A manager with tenure, moreover, would have the right of decision with regard to buildings and equipment for a period of time; which is to say that he would have some property rights in the means of production. These attributes, of course, are contrary to the principles of socialism and are part of capitalism.

Capital Market

When there are units that are autonomous with regard to investment decisions, an economy requires a capital market. Our model of market socialism with its intent to maximize growth would have such a market. Government holding companies and perhaps underlying enterprises would make investment decisions without the approval of a higher organization, and branches of government banks might make loans without the approval of the head office. Enterprise managers would make independent decisions on the use of buildings and equipment.

It is interesting to note here that, as reforms emerged in the Soviet Union and Eastern Europe, economists there began to develop an interest in capital markets. In 1967 T. Khachaturov, a noted Soviet economist, pointed out that in the Soviet Union "enterprises are often unable to make use of the production development funds they possess. . . . As long as development fund moneys cannot be made use of, it would be proper to permit the enterprise to keep them in a special bank account and to receive interest on them."[3] In Yugoslavia, as well, it is widely recognized that capital markets are needed to unify a set of decentralized investment decisions.

In our model of market socialism there also should probably be a money market for short-term paper, a bond market for long-term investments, possibly a stock market in which government departments or government holding companies could trade shares in government enterprises, and certainly a market for used buildings and capital equipment. Specialized government financial enterprises might exist to act as brokers or dealers in different kinds of paper.

In such circumstances managers of socialist enterprises probably would be willing to set prices that clear the market. Prices higher than these would lead to an accumulation of inventories; low prices would deplete inventories and make it necessary to ration the goods produced. Market-clearing prices would indicate the relative scarcity of different commodities, and provide freedom of choice to purchasers. With goods not rationed, only the buyer's budget would constrain his capacity to purchase.

In the competitive sector of the model of market socialism here proposed the indicator of enterprise success could definitely be profit, and the manager could be rewarded with a share of profit. Were this the case, the manager would be given incentives to produce an appropriate assortment and quality of goods, to produce goods efficiently, and to innovate. (Innovation will be discussed in detail later in this chapter.) The manager who maximized profit would compare receipts with costs, and in so doing would compare the value of possible outputs with the value of goods that are foregone when a particular program of produc-

[3] T. Khachaturov, "Effectiveness of Capital Investments," *Voprosy ekonomino*, no. 7 (1967) in *Problems of Economics*, 10 March 1968, p. 16.

tion is undertaken. Such a manager would contribute to the maximization of the rate of growth in wealth in the economy.

Reward of Managers

We have introduced into our analysis two kinds of supervisory bodies—the government department that would control all enterprises in a given branch of the economy and the government-established conglomerate holding company that, in competition with other conglomerates, would control enterprises in a variety of fields. In both bodies, supervisors would select managers, evaluate managerial performance, promote, demote, or discharge managers, and decide what share of profits the manager receives (0.5 percent, 1.0 percent, 2.0 percent, and so on.) The profit share would vary from manager to manager as risk varied; the socialist manager would risk his reputation as decision maker. Given the state of the industry and economy, supervisors would evaluate a manager's performance by his enterprise profits. Should losses occur, supervisors would decide whether or not they were caused by factors beyond the control of management. (A manager whose enterprise experienced persistent losses would find it more and more difficult to explain them away.) Supervisors, with a notion of an optimum rate of change, would look at the rate of adjustment of an enterprise to changes in demand and changes in conditions of supply. Good supervision, needless to say, would require the exercise of judgment.

Reward of Supervisors

If advocates of socialism have had little to say about the reward of enterprise managers, they have had even less to say about the measurement of performance and the reward of those who supervise managers. In our proposed model the reward of supervisors in government departments would be based on factors different from those in government-established conglomerate holding companies. The indicator of success of the government department could not be profit alone. Each department would control entry into its sector, each department might also restrict entry, so that its enterprises were in positions of enduring monopoly or oligopoly. Therefore, along with profit as evidence of its capacity in the selection of good managers, the government department would have to be judged by its successes in fostering competition, while at the same time securing the available economies of scale.

To a greater extent than with government departments, the indicator of success of the government-established conglomerate holding company could be profit. These holding companies would be free to enter and compete in any industry. Thus, after checking to see that the conglomerate had not acquired long-run monopoly power, the authorities could judge its performance very largely by its profits.

The Sectors of Natural Monopoly

It is more difficult to organize and control enterprises in the sectors of an economy that are naturally monopolistic than it is to organize and control sectors of an economy where competition is possible. When the economies of large-scale production are so great that only one manufacturing unit or transportation unit of optimum size, or one optimum-sized unit for the generation of electricity can supply an entire market, then it is is exceedingly difficult to devise institutional arrangements that are completely satisfactory.

Study of natural monopoly in a system of market socialism is a study of what is usually examined under the heading of government ownership of railroads and public utilities.

In our model we propose that a governmentally owned natural monopoly, for example, a railroad or a public utility could be set up in either of two ways: (1) it might be operated by a government department, or (2) it might be operated by a government corporation.

Were a natural monopoly to be operated by a government department, every facet of the performance of its administrators would be reviewed by supervisors. The latter would review prices, output, assortment, quality, efficiency, investment decisions, amount of innovation, and the like. There would then be many indicators of success and failure. Promotions, salary increases, and bonuses would be awarded after the appraisal of all the different aspects of performance. Profit would not be sought by the operators nor expected by the supervisors. A good example of this operation of a natural monopoly by a government department would be garbage collection for a fee by the public works department of a small municipality. Until 1970, the U.S. Post Office would be another example.

Under these circumstances, profit would not be used as a success indicator, because the government would not want to induce a natural monopoly to restrict output in order to maximize long run monopoly profit. Profit also may not be used as a success indicator because the government would want a system of price equal to marginal cost, which means that decreasing cost activities would be operated at a loss.[4] (The rationale of price equaling marginal cost is discussed in Appendix II.) Here we will simply note the high cost of supervision when the authorities must review all the details of management behavior.

Rather than being placed in the hands of government departments, natural monopolies could be turned over to the more autonomous government corporations. A higher government agency, itself considerably autonomous, would set maximum sale prices for the corporations and instruct them to supply the entire amount demanded at the officially established prices. Within these constraints, and some others that will be introduced shortly, the management of the government corporations would be free to make decisions on output, methods of production, investment, and the like.

The higher government agency that would set maximum sale prices also would have to set minimum standards of quality. Otherwise the monopolistic government corporations could effectively raise prices by lowering quality. A price is an exchange ratio between money and a good or service of a particular quality. This point is not always understood and acted upon. Under socialism in Great Britain, where most monopolistic government corporations are not under agencies that control prices and quality, there are frequent complaints that the consumer is neglected. For example, consumers often receive dirty coal. One English writer has suggested that "the motto of the coal industry might be 'the producer is always right'."[5] When the government corporation is a monopoly, there is little doubt that a higher government agency must control the quality of the product it supplies in order to prevent it from increasing price through a reduction in quality.

The maximum price allowed might be just high enough to cover cost over the long run. For example, in Great Britain, government enterprises are supposed to break even, not each and every year but "taking one year with another." In our model, a government corporation that could not earn profits as a reward for efficiency,

---

[4]Another reason why profit would not be used as a success indicator might be that ideologically oriented socialists do not consider it to be appropriate for a socialist economy. But should this reason prevail, it probably would prevail in both the competitive and monopolistic sectors of the economy.

[5]R. Kelf-Cohen, *Nationalization in Britain* (New York: St. Martin's Press, 1959), pp. 158, 282–83, 292–93.

however, would have to be supervised very closely by some higher government agency. The activities of management would have to be examined in detail so that efficient management could be identified and rewarded with promotions and salary increases, while inefficient management would be penalized with constant or decreasing salaries. Prices that just cover costs might be covering the costs of inefficient operations. Only close supervision would discover this and appropriately relate reward to performance.

Fewer administrative resources might be required if enterprises were allowed to make profits, or losses, and if managerial rewards were tied to profit. If top management were given a share of profits, it would be motivated to turn out an assortment desired by consumers and other enterprise managers. This assortment would include desired high-quality items and would give managers incentives to produce efficiently. If the authorities were to decide to use an approach like this, they would instruct the price-setting agencies to keep prices relatively stable. Should an energetic management succeed in reducing unit costs, the agencies would not hasten to order a price reduction. Instead, for a time they would allow the enterprise to earn larger profits than usual. For example, in attempts to reform the East German economy during the late sixties, seller's prices were not to be reduced for twelve to eighteen months after the enterprise had succeeded in lowering costs, so that the enterprise would "make short-term gains through any technological progress."[6] Also, in our model the authorities would not hurry to increase prices if costs rose (apart from increases caused by inflation), lest they encourage carelessness and inefficiency. Moreover, the percentage of profit received by a manager would be kept relatively stable. Receiving a fixed share of profits, a manager who performs well and increases the profits of his enterprise would see his personal income rise, perhaps strikingly. Managers probably should be allowed to become rich.

When the appointment and removal of enterprise managers are considered, the question of time horizon arises in the sector of natural monopoly as it did in the competitive sector. A manager who would be judged by the level of current profits and who would hold his position at the pleasure of his superiors would be likely to have a short time horizon. Tenure would not extend the

[6]Michael Keren, "Concentration Amid Devolution in East Germany's Reforms," in *Plan and Market*, ed. Morris Bornstein (New Haven: Yale University Press, 1973), pp. 147–48.

manager's time horizon beyond the period he would expect to hold his position, and in effect it would give the manager property rights in the means of production.

In the evaluation of the management of a government corporation, the principal indicator of success or failure would be a profit or loss, although the authorities would also have to check to see that management adhered to officially established prices and standards of quality, that it supplies the entire amount demanded at official prices, and that it follows other government regulations soon to be discussed. Supervision would have to be more intensive in the sectors of natural monopoly than in the sectors of competition. Responding to the lure of profits but not to the spur of competition, management might become indolent.

Clearly, the indicator of success of the government price-setting agencies cannot be profit. Those who appraise these agencies would have to look at the skill they exercise in setting and enforcing prices as well as standards of quality. However, supervisors who select, and reward or penalize the management of government corporations could be judged to a considerable extent by the profits of these corporations. A well-selected and properly rewarded management in an intelligently administered structure of controls would make a profit over the long run, while a poor management would experience losses.

We should now discuss the relationship between profit and risk.

Risk, Profit, and Innovation

We shall consider two kinds of assets that are at risk under market socialism: (1) the capital supplied by the government or by government banks to the enterprises, and (2) the reputations of the socialist managers, which command rewards and which may be lost when decisions are made.

It is possible that the government and the managers would bear risk without receiving pecuniary rewards for doing so. Any government at times invests government funds when there is little or no prospect of a profit on the investment. The investing body may be a deliberate risk-taker with government moneys, or it may be indifferent to or unaware of the risks involved. (We will soon discuss the argument that the government need not receive a risk premium because it can pool the risks of many projects.) Moreover, some people risk their personal reputations in venturesome decisions without expecting to receive large monetary rewards if they are successful. At times, recognition and prestige appear to be sufficient to induce people to take risks, as has been the case of the managers of the United States and Soviet space programs.

It may be, however, that in less publicized and less glamorous pursuits, governments and socialist managers would be venturesome in their decisions if their prospects of monetary gain were relatively large when risks were high. We will look at a market socialism in which short-run monopoly profits are employed to stimulate innovation.

Schumpeter demonstrated that the capitalist businessman tries to develop a better product or seeks a new, lower-cost process of production in order to obtain the profits of short-run monopoly. He pointed out that, if imitators were free to rush in immediately after an innovator, were there really perfect mobility, competition would destroy the profits that follow the introduction of new products or new, lower-cost methods. This would choke off the incentive for innovation.[7] But Schumpeter applied his idea only to capitalism.[8] He accepted without question the static Lange model of market socialism. Let us see whether Schumpeter's approach can be used when the means of production are owned by the government.

Suppose we give enterprise managers as well as government a share of profits. Suppose we allow an enterprise to hold a temporary monopoly when it develops a new product or devises a new, lower-cost method of production. The enterprise might then achieve a temporary monopoly simply because of a headstart over rival enterprises in the development of a new product or process. It might also achieve the short-run monopoly through secrecy or through legal patents (exclusive rights to produce obtained from the government). The profits of temporary monopoly would perform the same role under market socialism that they play in a capitalist economy. (Patents may be useful in market socialism as well as under capitalism.) With the passage of time, a headstart would be overcome, secrecy lost, and patents expire. Where competition is possible, rivals would enter and keep the innovative enterprise on its toes. Short-run monopoly would yield to a long-run competition. Temporary monopoly profits would reward the government for its venture capital and the manager for risking his reputation.

[7]Joseph A. Schumpeter, *Capitalism, Socialism, and Democracy*, 3rd ed. (New York: Harper & Brothers, 1950), pp. 82–84, 88–89.
[8]Ibid., pp. 175–86.

The use of secrecy raises an interesting question about market socialism. Lange claimed that "the Central Planning Board has a much wider knowledge of what is going on in the whole economic system than any private entrepreneur (under capitalism) can ever have."[9] Dickinson agreed, writing that in a system of market socialism, "All enterprises work as it were within glass walls."[10] However, if managers are given a share of profits so that they will innovate, they might conceal their activities in order to preserve the gains of innovation. Moreover, secrecy that permits some managers to develop newer products or lower their costs might serve economic progress in a socialist economy as it does under capitalism. Once we depart from comparative statics, we can no longer be sure that the maximum flow of information would occur in an economy, nor can we assume that a maximum information flow would be desirable.

It is not easy to use Schumpeter's approach when thinking about socialistic institutions for naturally monopolistic sectors of the economy. If the natural monopoly were run by a government department, profit would be used neither as an indicator of success nor as a motive for performance. Economic change would seem likely to come slowly. Rather than innovate, managers probably would play it safe, because they and their supervisors would know that a department would be more likely to be criticized for errors made in attempting something new than they would for lost opportunities. For similar reasons, a government corporation that is expected to break even probably would look with caution at proposed changes. Supposing that monopolistic government corporations are allowed to earn profits, however, we can devise a Schumpeter-like scheme for promoting innovation.

In a scheme of this sort, the government agency that sets maximum prices would tend toward stable price ceilings, permitting temporary monopoly profits to the innovative government corporation. It would not hasten to lower prices received by enterprising government firms that lower costs (this point was made earlier), and it would allow a firm that comes out with a new product to sell it for a high price over a considerable period of time. In due course, when the price-setting agency believed that high profits had lasted long enough to motivate innovation, it

---

[9]Oskar Lange, "On the Economic Theory of Socialism," in Oskar Lange and Fred M. Taylor, *On the Economic Theory of Socialism* (Minneapolis: University of Minnesota Press, 1938), p. 89.

[10]H. D. Dickinson, "Price Formation in a Socialist Community," *Economic Journal* 43 (June, 1933), p. 239.

would lower the price. Here the agency would be acting as a substitute for the forces of competition, as both push down prices in the long run.

In a system that relies on profits to promote innovation, the manager's percentage share of profits would be kept relatively stable. The manager who innovates and increases the profits of the socialist firm under his control would see his income rise.

Any discussion of risk and profit under socialism must address itself to the argument that risks borne by the government could be financed more cheaply than the same risks carried by private individuals, because the government is in a position to pool the risks of many projects. The law of large numbers says that the government could expect to offset losses on some of its many ventures against gains on others. Therefore, the government would not need to collect a premium for risk, or at least it would not need to collect as large a premium as nongovernmental risk-takers. Private individuals or corporations, with smaller resources, could not spread risks over as many alternative investments; hence, they would take larger risks of loss and would receive larger premiums for risk-bearing.

Hirshleifer points out that this argument for government ownership assumes positive risk aversion on the part of investors, which leads to their requirement of a premium for carrying risk.[11] The pooling-of-risk argument for socialism, however, rests on some additional assumptions. It assumes that the risk preferences of the government owner would be the same as those of the private owner. The government might be more averse to risk, and therefore might require a larger premium for a given amount of risk than would private investors. Were this the case, the required premium for risk under socialism might be larger, even if government pooling of investments lowered total risk. Then, too, the contention that risk is significantly lowered through government pooling assumes that risk falls as the number of projects rises above the size of the package that a capitalist conglomerate holding company can put together. It may be that such large numbers of projects can be achieved in capitalist conglomerates and that little more can be obtained through government pooling of risk. Finally, advocates of government risk pooling assume that the larger the package of projects the lower the total risk, no matter by

---

[11]Jack Hirshleifer, James C. de Haven, and Jerome W. Milliman, *Water Supply: Economics, Technology, and Policy* (Chicago: University of Chicago Press, 1960), pp. 140–41.

whom they are managed. But the pool of government projects might be less well managed than the set of projects in private hands, and this possibility might increase the risk to the government owner and offset the risk lowered through pooling.

Autonomy versus Accountability

A crucial matter in the analysis of market socialism is the question of government control of socialist enterprises. On the one hand, the enterprise is to be relatively independent; on the other hand, it is to be accountable to the government. How is the balance to be struck between autonomy and accountability? Some fear inadequate control of the enterprise, while others are concerned about political interference with its operations.

Agreement is easy to reach on some controls. Probably most people would agree that long-run monopoly profits should be prevented through controls over prices and quality of output and through the insistence that the enterprise supply the entire amount that is demanded at official maximum prices. Most people would also agree that such things like the indiscriminate delivery of smoke, for example, should be prevented. Beyond the exercise of these controls, controversy develops.

Some would have organs of the central government intervene for planning; for example, government agencies would plan to electrify rural areas or to develop particular regions. Others would have the government engage in economic stabilization: they would have it insist on countercyclical investment, and they would have it hold down price maxima in order to fight inflation. Still others would like to see the government keep in operation facilities that the public has grown accustomed to having, such as little used branch lines of railroads. Finally, some would have central government organs intervene to protect the employment or the incomes of parts of the population; for example, the government might insist that low-profit mines be kept open or that streetcar fares and bus fares be held down.

Opposed to these interventions would be people who wanted to see an efficient and up-to-date operation of government enterprises. Such people would erect barriers to government intervention. They believe that autonomous enterprises would locate new plant where it would contribute most to growth in wealth, and they would close down uneconomic activities. These people think that autonomous price-setting agencies would set prices that cover costs and yield profits high enough to stimulate innovation.

We have here conflicting objectives—regional development versus efficiency, or a particular income distribution versus efficiency—and a choice has to be made between their different goals. This conflict illustrates an important differentiation that must be made between theoretical economists and practical scientists. Economists can point out conflicts, but they cannot act as scientists to make choices between them. They must be careful not to suggest that they can speak with scientific authority in favor of the objective of efficiency. Above all, they must be careful not to suggest that politically motivated interventions run counter to scientific economics. The notion that an objective realized through political activities is less desirable than an objective realized through the operations of the uncontrolled market is a value judgment, not a scientific idea. Economists as scientists should not be custodians of efficiency and the free market.

It seems likely that in practice an intermediate position between two opinions will be adopted: government corporations will not be totally autonomous nor will government departments be subject to all desires of an elected legislature and executive. Government corporations with tenured managers might be established and encouraged to maximize profits for efficiency, while independent boards with tenured members might be created to set prices and standards of quality. Parliamentary bodies, government departments, or both, might then exercise control through appointments to boards of directors, through legislation, and through regulations, with the kinds of acceptable regulations specified in legislation. It might be required that these regulations be published to prevent hidden influence Finally, in order to achieve efficiency in a system of market socialism where the people choose legislators and administrators, the electorate would have to be persuaded to be self-denying in the exercise of its powers over government economic activities.

One kind of control that is likely to be generally acceptable would be control over the emission of smoke, noise, and the like.

Regulation of Indiscriminate Delivery (Spillovers)

Enterprises in a system of market socialism, whether competitive or monopolistic, cannot always deliver their products only to those who want to receive them. Because enterprises cannot always control delivery of their outputs, the unregulated market in both socialism and capitalism, for that matter, is subject to criticism. To be sure, the involuntary recipient of smoke from a factory could simply move, or join with his or her neighbors in a voluntary club to buy pure air from factory managers. (Noncontributors would be allowed to be "free riders.") But probably most people would prefer to coerce managers who dump smoke, liquid wastes, or noise indiscriminately about the cities and the countryside. In our model of market socialism, therefore, we would have higher governmental bodies—legislatures or regulatory agencies—impose restrictions on either competitive or monopolistic government enterprises that indiscriminately deliver.

Comparison of the Operational Model and the Lange Model

We have already showed that Lange proposed to imitate competition through the enforcement of a set of rules. Socialists would be more likely to achieve quality of output and efficiency of operation, however, in a model that relies on actual competition between socialist managers where it is possible. Such a model would utilize short-run monopoly to encourage innovation. Lange's scheme included only plants, factories, or workshops administered by government officials.[12] The model proposed here would include autonomous enterprises each on its own profit and loss statement. Since competition is desired in this model, Lange's industry managers would be discarded. Finally, indiscriminate deliveries in the model proposed here would be dealt with through higher governmental bodies that impose constraints on socialist enterprises.

An important difference between the two approaches is the role assigned to profit in the operational model. Rather than using Lange's scheme of having managers perform in accordance with rules, this model would have managers work for profit within a set of constraints. Profit, as the synthetic indicator of success, would act as an incentive to induce the manager to heed the consumer, to produce efficiently, and to innovate.

In the competitive sector of the operational model, socialist managers would set prices rather than have them set by a central price-setting agency; this is a relatively minor variation from Lange's approach, although it would reduce the work load of the government. A more significant difference is the determination of price and output in sectors of natural monopoly. Instead of Lange's governmentally set market-clearing prices that are treated as parameters by managers, our model would have governmentally

---

[12]Lange, "On the Economic Theory of Socialism," pp. 76–77.

established price ceilings set for natural monopolies. This would give enterprises an appropriate level of profits, and managers would be instructed to meet all demands at the officially set prices. In effect, marginal cost would be discarded. This can be seen most clearly by looking at the way prices would actually be set. There are two possibilities. With the price-setting agency wanting to permit a level of profits it believes would give enterprise managers desired incentives, it might consider a particular price, forecast sales and the resulting total receipts at this price, and compare these receipts with total costs calculated on the basis of anticipated volume. Or, in order to permit the desired level of profits, it might use proposed prices to forecast profit per unit—average revenue minus average cost—and multiply unit profit by anticipated volume. Prices would then be related either to total cost or to average cost, but not to marginal cost. It should be noted that this process is not cost-plus pricing either, since profits would vary with risk and performance and would not be assured.

Many economists will have grave doubts about a model that discards marginal cost in the determination of price and output. Yet the model follows from the use of profit under conditions of natural monopoly when prices are controlled. The government would not want enterprises to receive the profits of a permanent natural monopoly, but it would want them to earn profits when they respond to market demand appropriately, produce efficiently, and innovate. The government therefore would set price ceilings to provide these earnings and their profit incentives. As authorities would try to decide what prices would yield the desired level of profits, they would have no alternative but to look at total or average costs. Marginal cost is out, since its use produces losses in decreasing cost activities. "Marginal-cost pricing" is the child of comparative statics. A dynamic model that relies on profit as an incentive under conditions of decreasing costs is bound to disown it.

The lack of interest that reformers in the Soviet Union and Eastern Europe have shown in the Lange model is almost certainly a consequence of their interest in profit as a success indicator and incentive.

Economic change in market socialism necessitates a mechanism for the creation of new enterprises and the destruction of obsolete units. Unless socialism can find the counterparts of capitalist free entry and capitalist destruction of unadaptable, high-cost firms, socialism over the long run may be less progressive than capitalism. Lange, with his interest in the decision rules of a static economy, did not concern himself with such organizational problems. In the operational model an attempt is made to develop a mechanism for the creation of new production units and the destruction of obsolete ones.

Objectives Achieved and Objectives Not Realized

In the operational model of market socialism outlined here, consumers and workers would have free choice of goods and jobs. With market-clearing prices, the only constraints on their choices would be budgets and work capacities. Production generally would be set in response to consumer purchases and worker job choices. This would be an efficient system, although it probably would be more efficient in the competitive sectors than in the sectors of natural monopoly. (The spur of competition added to the attraction of profit would be more likely to promote efficiency than a share of profit alone, even though the natural monopolies would be more closely supervised than the competitive enterprises.) Thus, there probably would be a high rate of innovation, although much would depend on how successful innovating firms in the competitive sector might be in securing temporary monopoly profits (through secrecy, patents, and the like). Innovation would also depend on the extent to which natural monopolies would be allowed temporarily larger profits (through sophisticated price controls). Risk would be mostly borne by government, although managers would risk their reputations. Growth would be promoted when managers made decisions by comparing receipts with outlays and when claims on resources were transferred through capital markets. Income would be distributed in accordance with the production of wealth by labor and management (management would get a share of profit) and in accordance with private saving when interest is paid.

Through legislation and administrative orders, some government objectives could be achieved in a regulated market socialism: the control of natural monopoly and indiscriminate delivery, perhaps the planned development of regions, the stabilization of production and prices, the continued operation of facilities that the public has become accustomed to having available, and the protection of the employment and incomes of particular segments of the population. Taxes and subsidies, too, could be used to achieve government allocational and distributional goals.

Some objectives will not be achieved in a system of market socialism. First, with managers receiving a share of enterprise profit, the traditional socialist goal of eliminating the private collection of profit will not be attained. Second, the intensive development of heavy industry (believed by the Soviets to promote growth) may not be realized in a market socialism, because the government cannot direct resources into mining, steel mills, railroads, and the like. However, it may be that heavy industry can be just as well developed through taxation and subsidies.

Third, efficiency may not be attained. In practice, the government may not foster competition between government enterprises. Instead, it may use its powers to protect existing government enterprises from competition, either to avoid the embarrassment of failure or to respond to pressures from workers who would lose their jobs. There is a long history of the prolonged existence of uneconomic governmental enterprises. For example, even when Hungary moved toward reform with a Communist Party that cannot be voted out of office, uneconomic mines continued to operate for many years because the government feared the reaction of unemployed miners.

Finally, in market socialism and indeed in all kinds of socialism, the objective of private risk-taking in physical assets or shares is not realized. This is because the government is given a monopoly of investment in many sectors of the economy, and individuals in other sectors may not look for some general public good and take the risk of investing in plant and equipment in order to produce it.

Market Socialism in Yugoslavia

Chapter **10**

The Yugoslavs did not set out to establish a system of market socialism. It evolved, as a consequence of Yugoslavia having broken with Russia. At that time the shortcomings of the Soviet-type economy became apparent and in reaction the Yugoslavian government set out to develop a system of workers' control in a communal economy. While intellectual acceptance of market socialism in Yugoslavia has been slow to come, it has emerged, and serves as an example of the emergence of a new model from the cocoon of communalism.

The degree to which workers actually control the collective in Yugoslavia has been carefully investigated by Ward.[1] The material that follows will, therefore, concern itself with the basic characteristics of a system of workers' control.

The Working Collective

In Yugoslavia, the enterprise is called a "working collective." Its workers elect a "council of workers," that, depending on the size of the collective, has a membership of 15 to 120. The council

---

[1] Benjamin Ward, "Workers' Management in Yugoslavia," *Journal of Political Economy* 65 (October, 1957), pp. 373–86; "The Nationalized Firm in Yugoslavia," *American Economic Review* 55 (May, 1965), pp. 68–74. See also the comment on the 1957 article by Branko Horvat and V. Rascovid and see Ward's reply, *Journal of Political Economy* 67 (April, 1959), pp. 194–200.

159

makes policy for the enterprise, approves the output and investment plans of the collective, fixes wages, and makes final decisions as to the hiring, laying off, and firing of workers. The workers' council also has a voice in the disposition of the net earnings of the enterprise, called "funds for enterprise use."[2] The council elects an executive committee—a managing board—with 3 to 11 members. A commission, appointed by the workers' council and the local unit of government (called a "commune"), selects the general manager of the collective.

A considerable discussion has taken place in Yugoslavia with regard to the level at which workers' control should be exercised. Should the worker have the right to vote in the enterprise, in his department within the enterprise, or in a still lower unit? With enterprises free to create relatively autonomous units within themselves, there arises a question as to whether the workers should control these units directly or only indirectly through their control of the enterprise which creates them. One can also ask what sort of control the workers might exercise over a nonautonomous department of an enterprise (a unit which is not on its own profit and loss statement). Another question concerns the control one collective should have over an enterprise in which it invests. (In the reformed Yugoslav model one collective can invest in another.) At what level or levels should the workers in the two enterprises exercise control, and how much control should each body of workers have? As new possibilities of industrial organization open up in Yugoslavia, the whole question of workers' control takes on new dimensions.

One wonders how efficient a system of workers' control could be in any system. How much discipline will there be among workers who elect their managers and have the power to vote them out of their positions? Those who do not anticipate a disciplinary problem may be willing to see the worker exercise his control at a low level in the collective. (The extreme, which I have heard no one in Eastern Europe advocate, would be for workers to elect their foreman.) Those more concerned about discipline might have workers elect only the top management of the collective. (Socialists still less interested in workers' control might retreat to worker election of the government that appoints enterprise management,

[2] Branko Horvat, *An Essay on Yugoslav Society* (White Plains, N.Y.: International Arts and Science Press, 1967), pp. 42–43; Svetozar Pejovich, *The Market-Planned Economy of Yugoslavia* (Minneapolis: University of Minnesota Press, 1966), pp. 89–93.

and those least interested in control by workers might prefer government in which there are no elections at all or merely elections without effective opposition.)

In a system of workers' control, decision makers may undesirably disinvest. Workers would sell off machinery and equipment and pay the proceeds to themselves. They also might pay out depreciation funds to themselves rather than reinvest them.[3] In both cases, workers might invest their monies in privately owned savings deposits or in government securities that would pay them an income after they left their job; the same funds invested in the working collective would yield a profit only to those still employed in the collective. Should the sale of machinery or the failure to reinvest depreciation funds run down the enterprise, the workers might seek employment elsewhere and take their private accumulations with them. Concern over the danger of disinvestment has led the Yugoslavs to require that the working collective maintain the book value of its assets with its capital to be revalued periodically during the course of inflation.[4]

Failure to invest a portion of net income may be a more serious problem. Workers who have a choice between investing net income in the working collective or paying it out to themselves (and perhaps then investing it in personal holdings of savings deposits or government securities) might be strongly motivated to decide on the latter. Privately owned assets still yield an income after the worker leaves the job. According to Pejovich, "The Yugoslav press has repeatedly ... criticized the firms for distributing their profits as wages while borrowing extensively from the banks."[5]

In a system of workers' control, what institutional arrangements might induce workers to invest net income in the working collective? The workers' council might give workers bonds (obligations of the collective) for net income left in the enterprise, or it might give workers stock in the collective. Enterprise bonds would have to pay a higher interest rate than government bonds, since enterprise bonds, as obligations of the collective alone, would involve higher risk than government securities. In fact, some working collectives in Yugoslavia have become interested in the issuance of bonds. Dragisa Boskovic, a Yugoslav, wrote in 1966:

---

[3]Benjamin N. Ward, *The Socialist Economy: A Study of Organizational Alternatives* (New York: Random House, 1967), pp. 213–14.

[4]Svetozar Pejovich, "The Firm, Monetary Policy and Property Rights in a Planned Economy," *Western Economic Journal* (September, 1969), p. 194.

[5]Ibid., p. 199n.

Workers of a very successful enterprise in Slovenia wish to renounce a good part of what they have earned in order to help build a new workshop. But they say they would like, in turn, a paper which would indicate what they have given and what rights they would have to the future income of the enterprises.[6]

In 1968, the Yugoslav motor firm Crvena Zastava issued debentures. Other firms followed suit. In 1969, Slavenijales, a Yugoslav furniture manufacturer in Slovenia, announced plans to sell bonds to purchasers who would be invited once a year to a conference where the work of the collective would be discussed, as well as the question of the bondholders' participation in the distribution of net profit. These plans apparently attracted some criticism.[7]

At times an enterprise (domestic or foreign) takes a position in a new or established Yugoslav enterprise and in so doing is entitled to a share of profit. What powers of control do such investors have? "With the increasing complexity of industrialization, the conflict between the principle of worker self-management and the desire of corporate investors to control the enterprises they found [or expand] will probably be exacerbated."[8]

It would appear that in a system under workers' control, the only way to overcome workers' reluctance to invest earnings in the collective would be to give workers bonds or stocks in the collective in return for the earnings that they agree to reinvest. In so doing, a worker's time horizon would be moved beyond his anticipated period of employment. Such a procedure, of course, is a departure from the traditions of socialism. People now would be rewarded for investing in the collective, for waiting, and for taking risks, rather than being rewarded for their work alone. And, the question of the relative weights of investor control and worker control would have to be settled.

[6] Dragisa Boskovic, "The Self-Managing Share-Holding Society," *Vjesnik u Srijedu*, 23 November 1966, quoted in "A Socialist 'People's Capitalism' for Yugoslavia," Research Department of Radio Free Europe, 25 November 1966, pp. 1–5.

[7] "Slovenia Flirts with Heresy," *Economist* 233 (November 1, 1969), p. 28; "New Steps Towards 'People's Capitalism' in Yugoslavia," Research Department of Radio Free Europe, 8 October 1969, pp. 1–3. See also the letter to the editor from a person in Slovenijales, *Economist* 233 (December 6, 1969), p. 4.

[8] Stephen R. Sacks, *Entry of New Competitors in Yugoslav Market Socialism* (Berkeley: Institute of International Studies, University of California, 1973), pp. 14–16.

Profit Sharing in Yugoslavia and Elsewhere

When an objective in a system of workers' control is to induce workers and management to function well, we need to know under what conditions the earnings of a worker or manager should be related to enterprise income or profit. The question, alternatively stated, is: Under what conditions is enterprise income or profit a good success indicator? This author feels that an individual's earnings should be tied to profit when it is desired that the individual, in making decisions, takes into account all facets of the operation of the enterprise—product quality, sales, techniques of production, working conditions, and so on. Profit is what the East Europeans call a synthetic indicator of success. People should be paid a share of profits to induce them to take an overall view of an enterprise. Were this the case, it is clear that the top manager of an enterprise should receive a large part of his income as a share of profits. And where an enterprise is subject to the collective leadership of a board of directors, members of the board should receive a share of profits. Lower-level managers who are primarily concerned with performance of specific tasks—for example, cutting the costs of manufacture of a particular item—might be paid, not a share of profits, but a basic salary along with bonuses for specific achievements. And workers, according to this view, should be paid mostly in the form of wages, perhaps with bonuses for performance of specified tasks. There is little reason to pay workers a share of profit, because by virtue of working within a relatively small sphere—the production line, for example—workers have little to do with the general overall operation of the enterprise.

In a system of workers' control, however, the worker exercises some power: he has the right to his vote. He votes for management at some level, and perhaps he votes on basic policy matters or major investment programs. He also may serve on the council of workers for a time, where he will participate in larger decisions. The worker votes only once or twice a year, however, and is on the council of workers for only a small part of his working life. I suspect, therefore, that the income of the worker, to provide effective incentives, should be little related to his actions as voter and council member and should be tied for the most part to his day-to-day performance on the job. Only an insider with an intimate knowledge of decision making in the Yugoslav economy could make a sound judgment as to whether the 15-to-20 percent of his earnings (which the worker now receives in the form of a profit share) is too large or too small a part of his total income.

In general those who want to tie worker income to enterprise income, or profit, have not, in my view, given sufficient thought to the role that a worker plays in an enterprise. This is as true of the advocates of profit sharing under capitalism as it is of the theorists of workers' control in Yugoslavia.

The Structure of Industry

The Yugoslavs propose to decentralize decisions concerning the industrial structure of the economy. The working collective may create relatively autonomous units within itself, or may amalgamate into larger organizations. The optimum structure of industry in Yugoslavia is expected to be found in the market place, and is expected to vary from one sector of the economy to another. Western economists, in contrast, tend to doubt that the market under capitalism will produce an optimum structure of industry. Mergers in the United States sometimes are forbidden by law and business units occasionally are broken up to preserve competition. While businessmen under capitalism and managers in a socialist economy often will be in the best position to discover the optimum organizational pattern of industry, they will not always achieve that optimum. One reason for this is that the first unit to reach large size may use its financial power to keep out potentially efficient rivals through local price-cutting and the like. This might be true of a working collective as well as of a capitalist enterprise, although the ability to preserve a dominant position by price-cutting can easily be exaggerated.[9] However, even if under conditions of free competition all of the potentially low-cost production units survive, we cannot conclude that the market alone provides an optimum structure of production. The surviving units, associations or enterprises, may have an undesired degree of monopoly (or oligopoly) power. Moreover, the cost of effective regulation may be higher than the cost-saving associated with these units. Hence the authorities in any economy might do better to keep in existence a greater number of independent units of production than would survive in a completely free market. They might decide to control the market structure rather than regulate the monopoly or oligopoly after it emerged. And their actions might come closer to producing an optimum structure of industry than

---

[9]For a discussion of price-cutting and entry under capitalism, see Wayne A. Leeman, "The Limitations of Local Price-cutting as a Barrier to Entry," *Journal of Political Economy* 64 (August, 1956), pp. 329–34.

would a market which was uncontrolled. (To be sure, there will be costs attached to control of market structure, though one suspects that they will be lower than the costs of regulating monopoly.)

An important factor in determining the structure of industry is the entry into and exit from it. In Yugoslavia four kinds of bodies have been able to establish new enterprises: governmental units, associations (like athletic clubs, universities, and research centers), already existing enterprises, and, at times, groups of citizens. In addition, a plant may secede from a collective and go it on its own.[10] Although it is rare, bankruptcy does occur in Yugoslavia. The demise of a firm might also come about as its workers move to collectives that pay higher wages. In Yugoslavia, entry into industry probably is less effective as a source (or threat) of competition than it is under capitalism, because governmental or judicial approval has been a requirement for entry and because potential founders may lack motivation when they know they can lose control of the new enterprise to workers' councils. Exit may be and often is checked by the grant of governmental subsidies.[11]

The Yugoslavs do have an antitrust law[12] and there have been prosecutions under it, but the emphasis is on the use of "social influence" rather than on formal controls. We need to look more closely at social ownership and social influence, both of which are much discussed in Yugoslavia.

Property and Government

Even though the working collective in Yugoslavia is controlled by its workers, it does not own the plant and equipment that it uses. Rather, the means of production are said to be owned by "society" and constitute "social capital."[13] At the same time, authorities in Yugoslavia assert that the working collective does have the right of use and even the right of disposal. The council of workers, moreover, is supposed to have a voice in choosing the management of the collective. We have seen that the rights of use, disposal, and appointment constitute most of the bundle of rights which are property. In short, given these rights of property, what

---

[10]Sacks, *Entry of New Competitors*, pp. 11–12, 19, 52–60; Ward, *Socialist Economy*, pp. 215, 218–20.

[11]Cf. Ward, *Socialist Economy*, pp. 215–20. His analysis is similar to but not precisely the same as this author's.

[12]Pejovich, *Market-Planned Economy*, p. 24.

[13]See Branko Horvat, *Towards a Theory of Planned Economy* (Belgrade: Yugoslav Institute of Economic Research, 1964), pp. 219–24.

is left that constitutes "social" ownership? The answer lies partly in the "commune," a unit of local government, that shares with the council of workers the power to appoint enterprise management. Property is also socially owned in Yugoslavia because bodies at various levels may intervene in the operations of the working collective. For example, government intervention may occur when a collective's earnings fall so low that wages paid are lower than are acceptable to the government.[14]

Rather than speak of social ownership of the means of production, a designation which does not indicate precisely where the right of decision is located, we can more exactly speak of government ownership.[15] Property in the means of production in Yugoslavia is split up between the working collective and various units of government. Part of the set of rights is in the hands of the collective—rights of use and disposal and some rights in the appointment of management—and the other part is in the hands of government—rights in the appointment of management and rights of intervention in operations.

This part was highlighted in 1968 when a few Czechs during and after the Russian invasion saw clearly that property distributes the right of decision. Czech reformers at that time, seeking to preserve their economic reforms (particularly after the invasion), promoted the Yugoslav idea of worker control of collectives. Unlike the Yugoslavs, however, they pressed for ownership of the means of production by the working collective. I quote Rudolf Slansky, a Czech engineer, at length:

> One of the crucial problems is the management of our national economy. The fundamental economic principle upon which the mechanism of the bureaucratic-centralistic management is

[14] Ibid., p. 222.

[15] Professor Branko Horvat wrestles with the difficulties presented by the notion of social ownership in the following words: "Difficulties arise with social property.... We encounter the idea that social property is a *contradictio in adjecto*. A society comprises all the members of the society, and property can only be defined in relation to those excluded from it.... Hence, it is probably most suitable to consider *social* property as the *abolition* of property." Horvat, *Yugoslav Society*, p. 152. Property is exclusive. It excludes some from the right of decision. It may, for example, exclude all but one man from the right to decide on the use of a privately owned automobile. But there are rights of decision in Yugoslavia—distributed among government officials, workers' councils, and individuals—and it seems more accurate to speak of government property, property of the working collective, and private property than to assert that in Yugoslavia social property has abolished property.

founded is the direct exercise of proprietary rights *vis-à-vis* the nationalized industry. The exercise of these rights has been assumed by the state, or more accurately, by the various central bodies of the state. Is it really necessary to repeat one of the fundamental maxims of Marxism—namely, that he who owns property has power? As the state is not abstract, and as it is actual people who act in the name of the state (i.e., the people who comprise the state apparat and those whom this apparat appoints to leading positions), it is only natural that this state apparat, exercising a monopoly of ownership of nationalized property, possesses a monopoly of power. The only possible method by which the bureaucratic-administrative model of our socialist society can be transformed into a democratic model is the abolition of the monopoly of exercise of the propriety rights on the part of the state and a decentralization of this monopoly by transferring it to . . . the collectives of workers of these enterprises.

. . . .

The concept of the workers' councils as controlling bodies, as distinct from the organs exercising the rights of ownership, is predestined to failure. The Polish example is notorious.[16]

If we reject the concept of social ownership, because it does not indicate precisely where the rights of decision are located, we are left with the notion of social influence. In Yugoslavia, social influence is regarded by many intellectuals as a substitute for government, as something which will make it possible to reduce or even eliminate government. When one asks, for example, about the working collective that has monopoly power, one is usually told that the problem will be handled by social influence. And one repeatedly encounters among Yugoslav intellectuals the idea that in the end social influence will entirely replace government. Professor Branko Horvat writes:

> Along with the new [economic] system . . . the process of economic and political decentralization must begin. This means

[16]Rudolf Slansky, "A Note by an Observer Lacking in Partiality," *Prace*, 18 February 1969, in *Czechoslovak Press Survey*, Research Departments of Radio Free Europe, 26 February 1969, pp. 2–6.

the 'withering away of the state', namely, the replacement of political authority by social authority, of the state machinery by social self government.[17]

The difficulty is that the phrase "social influence" is exceedingly vague (like most uses of the word "social"). In fact, one can find at least six meanings for social influence. It may mean the influence of:
1. Amalgamations (mergers) of working collectives
2. Trade unions and chambers of commerce
3. Associations of working collectives
4. The League of Communists
5. Expert opinion
6. Public opinion generally

Horavt, for example, indicates that social influence may be exercised by amalgamations of working collectives:

> Integrative associations come into being in situations where it is necessary to centralize the taking of economic decisions on a broader base than that of the individual enterprise.... The economy is no longer atomistic but acquires a definite organizational structure of its own.... To the extent that integrative processes develop, the need for administrative intervention by government agencies disappears. When these processes are in essence completed, regulatory mechanisms will have been built into the economy that reduce government intervention to a minimum.[18]

The skeptic observes that amalgamations reduce competition and increase monopoly power, thereby increasing the number of occasions when government intervention is likely to be considered necessary.

At times social influence, as it is used in Yugoslavia, appears to mean the weight of trade unions and chambers of commerce.[19] Or, it is suggested that social influence should be exercised by "associations of self-governing organizations,"[20] presumably associations of working collectives. If trade unions, chambers of commerce, and associations of working collectives are not expected to

---

[17] Horvat, *Yugoslav Society*, p. 105. See also pp. 112, 174.
[18] Ibid., p. 107.
[19] Ibid., p. 108.
[20] Ibid., p. 107.

be new forms of government with coercive powers, they probably are regarded as providing environments in which problems can be discussed, differences reconciled, and agreements reached. The skeptic doubts that provision of new forums for discussion will be sufficient to deal with such problems as monopoly and indiscriminate delivery (spillovers).

At other times, the term social influence appears to mean the influence or control wielded by the League of Communists.[21] Non-Communists, of course, seldom agree that this self-selected group of people can speak for the non-Communist part of the population.

Social influence probably is thought of, most often in Yugoslavia, as the weight of public opinion, or sometimes as the weight of expert opinion.[22] There are, of course, varying levels of social pressure. For the individual it might consist merely of expressions of approval and disapproval. Or, it might prompt an individual to learn the experts' opinion of the consequences of water pollution in terms of his health. Stronger social pressure might take the form, for example, of reduced personal associations or, at the extreme, outright ostracism. Finally, social pressure might even prompt a collective withdrawal of trade—dismissal from jobs, reduction of purchases of goods, and so on.

Were social influence to be defined as expert opinion, it is doubtful that the weight of expert opinion would be a good substitute for government. To be sure, experts might tell people something of the consequences of monopoly or indiscriminate delivery, but the working collective that has an interest in the receipt of monopoly profits or an interest in not correcting a spillover might at times choose to ignore these consequences. Perhaps then, however, the pressure of public opinion generally would be felt. While public opinion might usefully supplement government law enforcement, it does not appear that it would be a good substitute for government either. When there are laws and the laws mirror public opinion, the cost of enforcement will be relatively low. For example, public opinion and regard for good manners might induce many people to cut their garden weeds; as a consequence, the law would be used only against a recalcitrant minority. In the absence of law and government, the minority that is not responsive to public opinion, in our example, would continue to grow weeds. In competitive environments, collectives that heeded public opinion all the time might find themselves at a cost disadvan-

[21]Ibid., p. 108.
[22]Ibid., pp. 96, 110–12, 174.

tage. Conversely, competition might force collectives to imitate their competitors rather than heed public opinion.

Property, we have seen, distributes the rights of decision. The notion of "social ownership" does not indicate precisely where the right of decision in an economy is located. And, the social influence proposed in Yugoslavia as a substitute for ownership is not an effective alternative to law and government. Public opinion, like a law without a penalty, has no teeth, and monopolists along with those who indiscriminately deliver unwarranted goods occasionally have to be bitten.

Not Communal Anarchism

It has been argued that in due course the state in Yugoslavia will wither away and anarchism will emerge, because of the power of the "commune." Upon investigation, however, one realizes that the Yugoslav model does not resemble anarchism very closely. The "commune" in Yugoslavia is a local government, a hierarchical unit. In addition, provincial governments exist along with a federal government. Workers' control is exercised through election of a workers' council, which is an enterprise government, and the enterprise functioning under the council is hierarchically organized. Specialization permeates the economy, and trade is usually the way of distributing goods and services.

Nor can the Yugoslav system be accurately described as that particular form of anarchism called syndicalism. Workers do not exercise their control of enterprises through syndicates, unions, and syndicates have not taken the place of government.

The official ideology in Yugoslavia is that anarchism will come when a new kind of person has been created, one with fully communal rather than individual values. What is the likelihood that this will occur?

Solidarity or Conflict?

Yugoslav intellectuals put a great deal of emphasis on the social solidarity of the workers in their system, and they contrast this solidarity with the isolation of the worker in a capitalist economy. They maintain that workers under capitalism work only for themselves. Everyone is said to be alone. Capitalism, one economist told me when I was in Yugoslavia, created a good factor of production, but a poor man. In the Yugoslav working collective, on the other hand, workers are in partnership with one another; they work, presumably, for the group, and not only for themselves. Implicit in the notion of a working collective is the idea of an equal, or not too unequal, distribution of its income. A distribution of income completely in accordance with individual productivity or performance (and correspondingly unequal) would run counter to the desired social solidarity. And, in fact, there has been a reluctance in Yugoslavia to rely on the market and to pay high incomes to skilled workers and managers.

In Yugoslavia social solidarity is not to stop at the enterprise. The workers in any one collective are supposed to be concerned about workers in other collectives and concerned about the community at large. Collectives experiencing financial difficulties have commonly received subsidies from the government, as have housing and communal services. There also is a generous program of social insurance to take care of people in need.

In Yugoslavia, there is little recognition, however, that there may be conflicts of interest between different groups of workers. Yugoslavs have come to realize that there are conflicts of interest between a set of government officials and those persons who are not part of the government. As a result, they have concluded that bureaucracy represents a new class. Horvat writes:

> In order to have a stable and efficient system, rulers need loyal bureaucracy. This loyalty upwards is bought by economic privileges and reinforced by status differentiation. Thus there will be a wealthy and powerful minority and a poor and powerless majority. The former will have control over the means of production, the latter will sell their labour power in order to live. The former will rule, the latter will be ruled. And that is nothing else but the classical Marxism two-class structure....
> *If the fundamental principle of bureaucratic organization—the principle of hierarchy—is left to operate, in the course of time two social classes with conflicting interests will emerge again.* In order that this be prevented, the state, as an institution whose essence is coercion, must—to use the famous phrase of Engels—wither away.[23]

While the Yugoslavs see the possibility of a conflict in interest between a class of government officials and the people, they seldom recognize that the interests of the various working collectives

---

[23]Horvat, *Towards a Theory of Planned Economy*, pp. 91–92. (The italics are in the original.) See also Horvat, *Yugoslav Society*, p. 20.

also frequently might conflict. For example, the collective that manufactures tubes for television sets wants a high price for its tubes, while the collective assembling the sets prefers that the tubes be sold at a low price.

A surprising variety of social-economic movements—communal anarchy, traditional socialism, capitalist laissez faire—are based on a view of the world in which conflicts of interest between people either do not exist or can be easily dissolved. One suspects, however, that rational choices between alternative economic systems will begin to be made when governments and people recognize that there are ineradicable conflicts of interest between people.

The Decline of Solidarity and the Rise of the Market

The interesting thing about developments in Yugoslavia is that while much still is being said about social solidarity, many of the reforms that have been proposed at one time or another are in the direction of individualism and an enlarged role for the pressures of the market. To be sure, within the enterprise, a considerable social solidarity probably will survive for a number of years to come. The Yugoslav worker when he comes out of the village is said to be not yet very much of an individualist. His family and village ties are strong, and they may help to preserve the character of the enterprise as a working collective. There are several factors, however, that might undermine the social solidarity of workers. For example, the government has at times proposed to withdraw subsidies and thus force collectives to be more efficient. The government also has proposed to introduce more domestic and foreign competition into the economy. The role of the market would be enlarged. Withdrawal of subsidies and an increase in competition might, in fact, result in higher efficiency, and it also might induce those who control the collective to reward good performance with higher incomes and to penalize bad performance with lower incomes and even discharge. Once again, market forces would prevail. When an increasing urbanization of the labor force (a loss of the village outlook) is added to the aforementioned market pressures for efficiency, it seems possible that social solidarity in the collective could give way to the individualism that the Yugoslavs so deplore in capitalism.

Many critics of the Yugoslav system argue that greater emphasis should be placed on productivity; equality should have a lower priority and "need" should play a smaller role in income distribution. To this end, personal income would increase relative to communal income. (The rate of taxation on personal incomes would be reduced as would be the rate of contribution paid to social insurance funds.) Subsidies would be cut down or eliminated. In a report to the Central Committee of the League of Communists, Todoravid wrote, "We must, once and for all, put an end to the practice of adjusting policies and economic measures to the conditions of all and sundry in order to 'save' the nonviable.... I declare ... that our economy is not strong enough to grant premiums to anyone who may want them."[24]

With investment decisions decentralized in Yugoslavia, there probably would be less investment in the poor south and more in the developed north and west. Such changes would decidedly shift income distribution toward productivity. Rents on housing probably would increase as would the prices of food and the prices of communal services, such as urban transport. These changes give the market a larger role.

Some reformers also want the Yugoslavs to alter the system of social insurance. They argue that the present system is expensive, encourages people to be sick, and is too large a burden on a poor economy. One person told me that he would give each individual an equal chance for education up to the age of 14 or 15 years, at which time he would put him on his own (in the marketplace).

Some argue that what has been happening in Yugoslavia is a substitution of solidarity at a higher organizational level for solidarity at a lower level. And there may be some forces drawing the parts of Yugoslavia together. The Yugoslavs may still be in the process of nation-making. But nationalism is not communalism; the cohesion of patriotism is not the same as the solidarity of the collective. People who care little for each other's economic well-being may unite to defend the nation. In reality, moreover, Yugoslavia as a nation is still a fragile structure. Croatia and Slovenia are unhappy at seeing their wealth drained away for the development of the poorer regions of the country.[25] And there is a distinct possibility that Yugoslavia, after the death of Tito, will disintegrate.

[24]Mijalko Todoravid in a report submitted to the Second Plenum of the Central Committee of the League of Communists of Yugoslavia, reproduced in *The Economic Reform in Yugoslavia* (Belgrade, 1965), pp. 36–37.

[25]See Sime Djodan, *The Evolution of the Economic System of Yugoslavia and the Economic Position of Croatia* (New York: Publisher unstated, 1972), pp. 67–102; reprinted from *Journal of Croation Studies*, 1972. In 1971 Dr. Djodan was expelled from the League of Communists, and in 1973 he was sentenced to a six-year term in prison.

All in all it seems likely that over the next decade or two the desire for discipline and efficiency and a greater reliance on the market will steadily erode away the working collective while reducing communal solidarity. Yugoslavia, as a nation, might even fall apart.

The Working Collective versus the Capitalist Enterprise

While capitalistic enterprises can be established in Yugoslavia, the law limits them to a maximum of five employees. There is the fear that workers' loyalty would be severely tested should working collectives and capitalistic enterprises coexist uncontrolled by law. When asked, Yugoslav economists give two reasons why Yugoslavia does not allow capitalistic enterprises to compete freely with working collectives for the allegiance of the workers. They argue, first, that the powerful capitalistic corporations would not compete fairly and would use their political influence to destroy the working collectives. They cite as an example the unfair competition and treatment to which the producers' cooperatives in England were subjected. Second, they argue that the cultural milieu of capitalism is inimical to the working collective. They maintain that collectivistic values can develop only in a socialist environment. One economist in Yugoslavia told this author that capitalism, apart from the small-scale family business, would have to be kept out of Yugoslavia for one or two generations more to come. After that, he believed, the capitalistic firm, if introduced, would be crushed by the superior working collective in the same way that the producers' cooperative in England was crushed by capitalism.

These arguments for giving a legal monopoly to the working collective as an organizational form are dubious. It seems likely that an electorate or government sympathetic to the idea of a fair competition between the working collective and the capitalist enterprise could devise a set of enforceable ground rules which would ensure that the competition between these institutions was fair. The rules would be formulated along the lines of American antitrust legislation. East Europeans, however, are not impressed by this argument; they believe that a powerful capitalist class dominates the government in Western economies. Many Western scholars, on the other hand, think that Marxians exaggerate the influence of capitalists in the councils of modern Western government.

As for the individualistic (and inimical) culture of capitalism which the Yugoslavs propose to replace with a collectivistic culture, perhaps in a generation or two, the Yugoslavs do not make clear what it is in their present economy that will cause these cultural changes to take place. One doubts that a new national emphasis on the independent and self-sufficient working collective along with higher personal incomes would promote a change toward collectivistic values. Nor does it seem likely that an emphasis on efficiency in the working collective, with encouragement for a wider spread between the pay of skilled and unskilled workers, would promote the values of collectivism. Professor Horvat, a strong defender of the Yugoslav model, notes that "the problem of the negative effects of the market on the ethical domain of socialist society still remains and merits careful and serious study."[26] It appears that only if the Yugoslavs were to succeed in maintaining genuine working collectives that were efficient, prosperous, and progressive would they succeed in altering people's values. But proposed reforms, with their tendency toward rewards in accordance with productivity, would be in some measure a retreat from collectivism, and the reforms would reduce what was in any event a low probability that Yugoslavia would create a new culture.

In the end the Yugoslavs may choose cost reduction over solidarity and the market may emerge as one of the most important, if not the most important, features of the Yugoslav economy.

[26] Horvat, *Yugoslav Society*, p. 110.

Part III

Anarchism, Utopias, and Communes

Introduction to Part Three

People have dreamed through the centuries of some sort of ideal economic system, one in which people would give to one another rather than trade with each other, one where communal solidarity would take the place of individualism, perhaps even one without the hierarchy and coercion of government. Frequently these dreams have been of an extreme decentralization; on occasion they have been of a benevolent central control. Numerous attempts have been made to live such visions of a better world in communal economies, some with a measure of success, others ending, sooner or later, in failure.

A study of these economic arrangements and efforts to realize an ideal world in the real world can teach us much about the problems of designing alternative economic systems.

The Theory of Communal Anarchism

Chapter 11

There is a renewed interest in communalism, in anarchism. Because the new left has not chosen to draw up a blueprint of what it wants, one must infer their desires. The best way of doing this is to look at a list of what they dislike. Communalists do not like individualism, government, specialization and trade, inequality, material incentives (described as a system based on greed), consumption goods (materialism), factories, and cities. They contend that decisions should be made in small groups, local groups or vocational groups, through "participatory democracy."

Marx contended that the final stage of communism would see the withering away of the state and the emergence of a society with the slogan, "from each according to his ability, to each according to his needs." In studying anarchism, therefore, we are studying at the same time what is expected to be the final outcome of communism.

Institutions

In a system of communal anarchism, people instead of being isolated individuals controlled by government will be members of communes. Communes will belong to regional, national, even world federations. Each individual will be free to withdraw from the commune, and each commune may secede from the federation.[1] No hierarchy will exist; neither coercion nor obedience will exist. (We will discuss shortly how decisions are made in this type of system.)

Rather than becoming a specialist in a particular occupation, each person and each commune is to pursue a variety of activities. Kropotkin, a leading nineteenth century anarchist, speaks of a harmonious union between brain work and manual work and between agricultural and industrial pursuits, and he contends that the ideal is a society where each individual is a producer of both manual and intellectual work; where each able-bodied human being is a worker, and where each worker works both in the field and in the industrial workshop; where every aggregation of individuals large enough to dispose of a certain variety of natural resources—it may be a nation, or a region—produces and consumes most of its own agricultural and manufactured goods.[2] So there will be no specialists within the commune and few or no specialized communes.

Any commodities that are transferred between communes will not be traded. Within the commune as well as between communes, goods and services are to be distributed equally or in accordance with needs. (The anarchists expect that in a simple communal life people's needs will be approximately equal.)

Not liking consumption goods, not being materialists, the communalists will work relatively few hours a day (though they will work hard, since with their varied tasks they will find work interesting). In place of huge factories, there will be mostly small factories or workshops. And instead of concentrating factories in large cities, workshops will be scattered around the countryside. "Have the factory and the workshop at the gates of your fields and gardens," says Kropotkin who also expressed an interest in the Garden Cities movement.[3]

Federations of communes, a variety of work for each person, an absence of trade, distribution in accordance with need, relatively few hours of work per day, workshops surrounded by fields and gardens. We have just described an ever-recurrent dream of people. Really to understand how a system of communal anarchism

[1] Mikhail Bakunin in *The Political Philosophy of Bakunin: Scientific Anarchism*, ed. G. P. Maximoff (Glencoe, Ill.: The Free Press, 1953), pp. 247, 274, 341.

[2] Peter Kropotkin, *Fields, Factories and Workshops,* rev. ed. (London: Thomas Nelson and Sons, 1912), pp. xi, 23.

[3] Ibid., pp. 350, 417.

would work in practice, however, we need to know something about its decision-making process.

Advocates of anarchism have shied away from this issue, using the argument that to draw up a detailed blueprint of anarchism would limit the freedom of those who participate in the system. Making a blueprint available, of course, does not require anyone to follow it, and it might help people decide whether or not the scheme is likely to succeed.

A blueprint which defines the decision-making process must concern itself with the following:

1. The commune in which each individual is to live and work.
2. The federation to which each commune is to belong.
3. The goods and services which are to be produced and the quantities of each.
4. The methods of production which are to be employed.
5. The tasks which each person is to perform.
6. The distribution of goods and services within and between communes.

Only the first item on the above list can be a matter of individual decision. Because the individual is free to leave the commune, he has the right to decide on the commune in which he will next live and work. All the remaining decisions are non-individualistic and will have to be made by the commune. We have already mentioned that a hierarchy of leaders cannot exist to make decisions in a communal system, nor can majority rule determine what is to be done. Rule of the majority is a species of government, and under anarchism there is to be no obedience. Members of the commune, therefore, will have to reach a consensus. Decisions concerning production and distribution in a communal anarchy will have to be unanimous.

Underlying Beliefs

Conflict of Interest

The belief that conflicting interests would disappear with the establishment of anarchism underlies most anarchist thought. The elimination of government, the elimination of private ownership of the means of production, and the elimination of economic inequality are expected to remove the causes of divergent interests. People are to be agreeable. Rather than differ over the services which each communal member is to supply and the goods which each is to receive, members are to be altruistic, concerned more for the well-being of others than for their own material comfort. Advocates of a communal anarchism are of the opinion that a world can be created in which conflicting interests disappear and human behavior is completely benevolent. There will be a "universal solidarity between individual interests and those of society."[4]

An analysis of whether interests conflict or coincide requires that the concept of "social" and "societal" be made clear. What does the anarchist mean by social solidarity or a solidarity between individual interests and those of society? Let us assume in this instance that a solidarity between individual interests and those of society means there will be no conflicts of interest between any one individual and other members of his or her commune, and no conflicts of interest between any one commune and other communes.

How does the absence of conflict of interests apply to family and friends in a system of communal anarchism? There are three possible hypotheses. One hypothesis is that there would be no friendship and no particular fondness between family members. Each individual would like (or love) all people equally, including himself. In loving all people equally, the anarchist would be indifferent to individuals. Hence, he would not want more goods for himself or for members of his family than he would want for others. Nor would he want more for particular individuals outside his family. With universal love rather than love of particular individuals, theoretically there should be no conflicts of interest over the distribution of the output of the economy. Such an absence of family feeling and friendships seem improbable, however, and in fact left-wing anarchists almost certainly would not like a world devoid of friends. Much of the attractiveness in the idea of a commune lies in the thought of a collection of friends living and working together and helping one another.

A second hypothesis in a society free of conflict of interests is that friendship would exist, but that everyone would have the same friends. We are talking about a system in which everyone has the same preference ordering for all individuals in the system. Everyone is most fond of Comrade A (Comrade A included), everyone is next most fond of Comrade B (Comrade B included), and so on. Under these conditions there would be no conflict of interests over the distribution of goods and services. (Actually, if there are to be no conflicts of interests, everyone should have not only

[4]Bakunin in *The Political Philosophy of Bakunin*, p. 169.

the same preference ordering of individuals but also an identical intensity of feeling for all individuals in the system. I prefer, however, to skirt the quagmire of preference intensities, and so strong a proposition is not required for the analysis.) Most anarchists probably would concede that a system in which everyone has the same preference ordering of individuals is most unlikely to exist. Moreover, anarchists probably would like such a system in which some people were at or near the bottom of the universal hierarchy of friends—those little loved or not loved by anyone at all.

A third hypothesis for a system in which there would be no conflict of interests is one in which people would have families and friends, with each person having different friends, but with no one wanting more for himself, his family, or his friends than he would want for others. In such a system an individual would not want more for members of his or her own commune than he would want for members of other communes. This system is one of giving rather than trading; but the gifts, if they are substantial, are only to "society": to all the other members of the commune or to all the other communes. Because the individual would not *give* more to family and friends than he would to others, he would not want to acquire more for those close to himself. Should the contrary be the case, should people want more for themselves and their families than for others, then conflict of interest would exist.

It probably is fair to assume that most anarchists would not like a system in which members would not be able to do substantially more for their comrades than for strangers. Even if anarchists themselves were to accept the idea of not particularly helping family and friends, it seems doubtful that people generally would do so. Family loyalties as well as loyalties to friends and neighbors are likely to persist, and, as a consequence, so will conflict of interests. Moreover, favoritism is a persistent problem in government. Is it possible to train government officials not to favor family and friends even in their unofficial capacities—for example, not to bargain for a higher salary so that they could send their children to better schools? The probability of success appears to be low. And would it be possible to create a whole system without government in which there were favorites but no favoritism?

It appears doubtful, then, that the anarchists can expect to (or would care to) live in a world in which there were no friends, or in which everyone had the same friends, or in which people had family and friends and did not want more for them than for others. Hence it really is improbable that an economic system free of conflicting interests can be achieved. And note once again: our conclusion that conflicts of interest are inescapable rests not on the "cynical" assumption that people are selfish or self-interested, but on the "generous" assumption that people have family and friends and that they try to take care of them.

Scarcity

One reason anarchists believe that interests will not conflict within and between communes is because of the absence of scarcity of goods and services. Though seldom explicit on the matter, anarchists tend to assume that their communes will function in a world free of scarcity. Since they believe labor will be diversified and, as a consequence, interesting and pleasurable, they expect output to be large, despite the fact that members will work only a few hours a day. Then, too, in the simple life of the commune it is not expected that people will want luxuries. Many anarchists have aimed and aim at a life of dignified poverty.

> In material terms anarchists have never asked for more than the sufficiency that will allow men to be free. One has only to read the moving accounts of Gerald Brennan and Franz Borkenau to realize how deeply the peasant anarchists of southern Spain felt their freedom: they were willing to give up not merely alcohol and tobacco, but even tea and coffee, so that their newly communized villages could escape more completely from the golden chains of the money system.[5]

With enthusiastic workers turning out a large quantity of goods and not demanding luxuries, scarcity, in the view of the anarchists, will tend to disappear.

Anarchists might point out that our earlier conclusion on the dubiousness of creating an economic system free of conflict of interest rests on the assumption of scarcity. But the skeptic considers it improbable that scarcity will disappear. He or she notes that while communalists do not like consumption goods, ordinary people do, and he is inclined to think that rising expectations and insatiable wants are more likely to be found among people than is a willingness to settle for a life of dignified poverty. The non-anarchist, moreover, expects that a distribution in accordance

[5] George Woodcock, "Anarchism Revisited," *Commentary* 46 (August, 1968), p. 58.

with need will reduce rather than increase the supply of goods and services.

Specialization, Scale, and Cities

A final underlying belief of communal anarchists is that the economies of specialization, large-scale production, and agglomeration into cities are relatively small. According to Kropotkin, the division of functions

> is doomed to disappear, and to be substituted for by a variety of pursuits—intellectual, industrial, and agricultural—corresponding to the different capacities of the individual, as well as to the variety of capacities within every human aggregate.[6]

Kropotkin even thought that most regional specialization would disappear. He maintained that as technical knowledge is dispersed about the world, differences in natural factor endowments become less important, and "each nation acquires the possibility of applying the whole of her energies to the whole variety of industrial and agricultural pursuits."[7] Kropotkin also asserted that the development of electrical power often made small factories more economical than large ones, while observed concentrations of industry frequently reflected efforts to achieve market power rather than technological economies of scale.[8]

The skeptic, however, observing, for example, that industrial heat is conserved in large steel plants, that the economies of scale in the production of electricity from nuclear energy are very great, and that large oil refineries are more economical than small ones, is inclined to think that a system of workshops and small factories is not likely in the foreseeable future. Kropotkin himself recognized that some large-scale activities are inescapable.

> If we analyze the modern industries, we soon discover that for some of them the cooperation of hundreds, or even thousands, of workers gathered at the same spot is really necessary. The great iron works and mining enterprises decidedly belong to

[6] Kropotkin, *Fields, Factories, and Workshops*, p. 22.
[7] Ibid., pp. 22, 81, 355–58.
[8] Ibid., pp. 284, 352–54, 417.

that category; oceanic steamers cannot be built in village factories.[9]

It also seems improbable that under anarchism factories and workshops would really be scattered through the countryside. Cities throughout the world are likely to continue to grow. With all their powers of a totalitarian government, the Soviets have not been able to keep their cities from becoming larger and larger, even though they have tried.

Anarchist thought, therefore, would be more convincing if it assumed an economy of specialized activities, large-scale production, and an urbanized population.

Earlier we observed that many non-anarchists would expect a distribution according to need to reduce rather than increase the supply of goods and services. The anarchist, however, believes that altruism in an anarchist economy would motivate people to produce goods in large quantity.

Altruistic Motivation

The question of whether or not an economic system can be based entirely on altruism is of significance in the study of communism and socialism as well as in the study of anarchism. Marx concluded that the final stage of communism would have a distribution of activities and commodities such that each individual supplied services according to his ability and received goods according to his needs. And many socialists think vaguely of a system that relies on altruistic rather than material motives. ("We must create a system based on need rather than greed.")

When a communalist, or socialist, argues that a system that rests exclusively on altruism is possible, he is likely to point to the many acts of individual giving that occur even under capitalism, and in his own system he is almost certain to point to the mutual aid that is characteristic of many already existing subgroups, the family, neighborhood, clan, tribe, and so on. The family, sometimes the extended family, does live according to the Marxian slogan, with each member contributing in accordance with his ability and receiving in accordance with his needs. Neighborly help is often considerable. The communalist or socialist is likely to tell of some warm group life he has experienced and to suggest that appropri-

[9]Ibid., p. 352.

ate changes could extend it to the entire economy, or the entire world.

The skeptic is not so sure. He might doubt the Marxian slogan "from each according to his ability, to each according to his needs" can be extended very far beyond the family unit. The non-anarchist also might point out that throughout history the communes which have come into existence usually have been composed of particular kinds of rather devoted individuals, often religiously motivated, but that even so these communes often have failed to survive for more than a generation or two (see Chapter 13).

Conclusions

The advocates of communal anarchism argue that the cultural milieu of capitalism along with hierarchy in government explain the limited altruism and apparent need for material incentives observed in modern life. According to an anarchist, if capitalism and government are eliminated, a new man will emerge, benevolent and eager to work for the community.

As long as a complete system of communal anarchism is not established, the critic cannot prove that the anarchists are wrong, nor can the anarchists prove that they are right. The skeptic is reluctant to take a leap in the dark and plunge into a totally new system. The communalists would be more likely to win supporters if they could identify a series of smaller steps, each of which would produce specified results and the sum total of which would result in a new man and a system of communal anarchy.

An Introduction to the Utopian Literature

Chapter 12

Rather than develop a theory of anarchism, some writers have sought to design utopias, most of them incorporating features of socialism, with people in possession of a spirit of community. Some of these utopias in the literature resemble communal anarchism. A representative sample of this literature follows.

Bellamy's *Looking Backward*

In framing his utopia, Edward Bellamy, writing in 1887, sought institutions which recognized the brotherhood of man, the solidarity of humanity. Without private profit and the desire for money, without, he hoped, either poverty or the accumulation of riches, his system would have production generally in response to consumer and worker preferences along with, at least for people in later life, relaxation and the pursuit or every imaginable form of recreation.[1]

Centralized Planning

Bellamy proposed to attain these objectives with comprehensive central planning and centralized distribution. He visualized the

---

[1] Edward Bellamy, *Looking Backward: 2000–1887* (Boston: Houghton Mifflin, 1887), pp. 57, 67, 133–34, 156, 184–85, 196–98, 201.

189

properly run modern economy as organized into "one great business corporation," or, more often, he pictured it as organized into an "industrial army." Production and construction were divided into ten large departments, each a group of related industries; the lower industrial bodies were called guilds or bureaus. The chiefs of the ten departments were likened to lieutenant generals, while the heads of the bureaus could be compared to major generals in the army. Above the ten lieutenant generals was the general-in-chief, comparable to a president of the United States.

In Bellamy's utopia goods were distributed from a series of public warehouses after having been produced by the departments and guilds. Bellamy was certain that the knowledge possessed by those who make production decisions would be complete and reasonably accurate. "Now that every pin which is given out from a national warehouse is recorded, of course the figures of consumption for any week, month, or year . . . are precise. On these figures, allowing for tendencies to increase or decrease and for any special causes likely to affect demand, the estimates, say for a year ahead, are based." The subordinate bureaus would have "a complete record of the plant and force under its control, of the present product, and means of increasing it." With all this information, production decisions would be simple. "The estimates of the distributive department, after adoption by the administration, are sent as mandates to the ten great departments, which allot them to the subordinate bureaus representing the particular industries, and these set the men at work." Bellamy likened "the effectiveness of the working force of the nation . . . under a single head" to "that of a disciplined army under one general."[2]

It is difficult to understand how someone, even in 1887, could have been so ignorant of the complexities of a modern economy. Bellamy completely failed to recognize the millions of interdependent variables—the vast number of commodities, located in many different places and produced and consumed at different times. Moreover, he also failed to recognize that the quantity of output of a particular commodity depends upon the quantity of output of another, and that often the production of the second depends upon the production of the first. He also failed to consider that the relationships between input and output (technological coefficients) depend upon volume of output, but that output likewise depends upon input-output relationships. Since he did not understand the need for the solution of millions of simultaneous equa-

[2] Ibid., pp. 56, 87, 181–83, 187–88, 242–43.

tions, he did not turn to aggregation. Along with failing even to glimpse the costs of computation, Bellamy also neglected to take into account the cost of data collection and verification. (Apparently, no one in his economy would ever overstate his input needs or understate his capacity.) One resident of Bellamy's utopia, speaking, no doubt, for its founder might be described as insufferably conceited were he not so naively ignorant. After describing the marvels of centralized production and distribution, he added, "All of this merely shows, my dear fellow, how much easier it is to do things the right way than the wrong."[3]

Distribution of Goods and Work

Laundries were public, cooking was done at public kitchens, and most meals were taken in private dining rooms located in large public dining buildings. Goods were distributed from public storehouses after customers presented a credit card. Everyone received the same expenditure allowance.[4] Bellamy, however, never stated whether allowances were to be equal for all households, or equal for households of the same age distribution, or equal for all individuals, or equal for all individuals of the same age.

Wages

While Edward Bellamy proposed a utopia based on the absence of private profit and desire for money, he was never able to quite decide on the extent to which wages and prices would be market determined. Everyone, he asserted, was to receive the same total income, while (in effect) hourly wage rates were to differ in accordance with people's work preferences. The attractions of the different trades were to be equalized by differences in the hours of labor: the more arduous the work, the fewer the hours. For example, mining would have very short hours. But having in effect proposed market-clearing rates of pay, Bellamy demonstrated his distrust of this price system with numerous exceptions. For the first three years of his working life, a young person was to be subject to labor (compulsory service); moreover, normally required service, a sudden demand for labor of a particular sort that was not met through volunteers would be covered by a draft of

[3] Ibid., p. 187.
[4] Ibid., pp. 87, 93, 118, 153.

workers from any quarter. *Looking Backward* abounds with phrases like "the national organization of labor under one direction," employees "distributed according to the needs of industry," the labor of man regulated "for the common good," and so on.[5] A final inconsistency is that while workers of a higher grade in an industry had a greater freedom of choice in work, a worker of superior endowment was expected to do all that he was capable of doing, with a suggestion that he might be whipped if he did not do so. And then, Bellamy states, "A man able to do duty, and persistently refusing, is sentenced to solitary imprisonment on bread and water till he consents."

The utopia of Bellamy is indeed that of an industrial army rather than one of a cooperative commune. While incomes were supposed to be equal, men with the highest rank in that army received "special privileges and immunities in the way of discipline."[6] If this utopia has a slightly nightmarish quality about it, even though Bellamy spoke in the name of humanity, it is worth recollecting that nightmares like these became realities in the centralized Soviet-type economy, which likewise was established for the good of mankind.

Prices

In Bellamy's utopia prices generally were determined by the cost of labor. In unattractive trades, where hours of daily labor were low, wage costs and, hence, prices would be high. Were supply permanently or temporarily unequal to demand, however, scarcity prices would be set which might differ from costs. Products requiring skill and rare materials that were expected to be permanently in short supply, goods dependent on seasonal weather (fish and dairy products), and goods subject to changes in consumption are examples. Rents for houses also would "vary according to size, elegance, and location."

Credit

While Bellamy failed to recognize that the credit cards used to purchase goods from public storehouses were money, he did introduce consumer credit into his system. If extraordinary expenses

---

[5] Ibid., pp. 60–62, 67–69, 328–29.
[6] Ibid., pp. 94–95, 125–28.

exhausted an individual's line of credit, he could "obtain a limited advance on the next year's credit, though this practice is not encouraged, and a heavy discount [interest rate] is charged to check it." Bellamy did not tell us whether an individual could postpone consumption and save up claims on the warehouse for use in later years.) In the event of adverse balances of payments between countries, they would be settled in staple commodities: "a basis of agreement as to what staples should be accepted, and in what proportions, for settlement of accounts being a preliminary to trade relations."[7]

Compulsory Labor Service

In Bellamy's utopia the period of compulsory labor service for a worker was 24 years. It began at age 21 and ended at 45. After the first three years the worker generally was free to choose among different jobs. From age 45 to 55 the worker was on call for emergencies that caused a sudden increase in the demand for labor. (Such calls were rare.) Bellamy stated that the nation "guarantees the nurture, education, and comfortable maintenance of every citizen from the cradle to the grave," provided that, when able to do so, he or she had worked during the years of compulsory labor service. Early retirement was possible, at age 33, if the individual was willing to accept for the rest of his or her life one half of the normal maintenance. For the sick in mind and body, the crippled, blind, deaf, and dumb there was an invalid corps in which people were provided light tasks fitted to their capacity.[8]

Human Nature

Edward Bellamy argued, surprisingly, that in his utopia human nature did not change. He believed that human nature, in its essential qualities, was good at all times. What happened in utopia was that the conditions of life were changed so that people's nobler qualities came to the surface.[9] Conflict of interest would be eliminated, and a sense of a community of interest, international as well as national, would take its place. Lying would be rare. People would want to serve the nation. They had a passion for

[7]Ibid., pp. 85–89, 109, 143–44, 185–86.
[8]Ibid., pp. 63–64, 90, 131, 169.
[9]Ibid., pp. 260–61, 287.

humanity; ethical standards would change and man's basic nobleness would emerge.[10]

Organization

The nation is the basic unit of government in Bellamy's utopia. He proposed that a federal system of autonomous nations would exist with a goal of the eventual unification of the world under one government. With the political (and economic) system highly centralized, state governments in the United States, for example, would be abolished. The president, chief executive of the government and head of the industrial army, would be elected in Bellamy's utopia from the former heads of the ten departments of production and construction after about five years in retirement; he would be chosen by an electorate consisting of those who had retired from the industrial army along with members of the liberal professions (doctors, teachers, artists, engineers, and so on). The president would be served by a zealous inspectorate that would receive complaints of defects in goods, official insolence, or inefficiency—one that actively would oversee and inspect every branch of the army. There would be no parties or politicians, no demagoguery, and no corruption. Corruption, according to Bellamy, "is impossible in a system where there is neither poverty to be bribed nor wealth to bribe."[11]

Conclusions

Edward Bellamy dreamed of a world free of the constraints which skeptics believe are very nearly inescapable. What are his dreams? Most important, Bellamy dreamed of a world of markedly reduced scarcity. He believed that an abundance of material goods and services along with early retirement would be forthcoming for a number of reasons: Centralized planning would be almost perfect; hence the wastes of individual decision making and competition would not occur.[12] The economies of large-scale production would be more fully realized in a centralized economy.[13] With public warehouses, the wastes of going from shop to shop to make one's

[10]Ibid., pp. 91, 95, 97, 142, 203, 336.
[11]Ibid., pp. 60–61, 143, 187, 190–93, 207.
[12]Ibid., pp. 229–30, 234, 237.
[13]Ibid., p. 55.

purchases would be eliminated.[14] Public laundries and kitchens along with centralized dining installations would be more efficient than similar facilities in the household.[15] The absence of idlers ("drones") and of criminals and the resulting need for fewer law enforcement officials would promote material abundance.[16] The elimination of money, private debts, bankers, interest, merchants, and advertising would free resources for the production of goods and services.[17] In a centrally planned economy there would be no business fluctuations, and hence the periodic unemployment of people and machines would be avoided.[18] Finally, the functions and costs of government would be markedly reduced. Bellamy stated, "We have no sort of military or naval expenditures for men or materials, no army, navy, or militia. We have no revenue service, no swarm of tax assessors and collectors." And finally, little legislation would be needed.[19]

In Bellamy's utopia reduction in the scale of government (along with the other factors enumerated) would reduce scarcity. Government would exist without parties or politicians and without demagoguery. Perhaps Bellamy expected parties, politicians, and demagoguery to disappear because he dreamed of a system of attractive people without conflicting interests. A dweller in Bellamy's utopia, responding to a suggestion that a nation possessing a natural monopoly in some necessity might raise its price, thus making "a profit out of its neighbors necessities" asserted that "the community of interest, international as well as national, and the conviction of the folly of selfishness, are too deep nowadays to render possible such a piece of sharp practice as you apprehend."[20]

Looking Backward is indeed a comprehensive daydream. We have already shown how innocent Edward Bellamy was of the difficulties of central planning in an economy having innumerable interdependent variables. In addition, he seemed to have believed that the economies of large-scale production attainable by government are much greater than those that can be reached through large private enterprises. He had nothing to say about the possible

[14] Ibid., p. 100.
[15] Ibid., pp. 118, 227.
[16] Ibid., p. 227.
[17] Ibid., pp. 226–27, 235, 312, 315.
[18] Ibid., pp. 229, 234, 239.
[19] Ibid., pp. 208, 227.
[20] Ibid., p. 142.

diseconomies of centralized decision making. Public warehouses might be more efficient, as Bellamy asserted; they also might be less so, without the spur of competition. Similarly, public laundries and kitchens and centralized dining facilities might provide less attractive service than does competitive private enterprise. The notion that crime and that concomitant law enforcement facilities would decline with the disappearance of capitalism and poverty rests on an exceedingly simplistic theory of the nature and causes of criminal activity. And, few people today would care to defend the proposition that money and trade can be eliminated from an economy having an elaborate division of labor. If the unemployed labor and unemployed capital equipment associated with capitalist business fluctuations were done away with, we might find in their places the redundant workers and equipment (the Soviets call them "concealed reserves") that seem to be characteristic of a government plant faced with centrally imposed targets. Moreover, one is astonished to find the designer of one of the most centralized of utopias telling us how few resources will be required for government. Finally, Bellamy dreamed of a new unselfish person and of a world without conflicting interests.

The Modern Utopia of H. G. Wells

Unless the description of a utopia is pure escape,[21] a large-scale daydream, it is a statement of goals, rather more comprehensive than the limited goals of the reformer, but generally not as realistic. While the utopian system described by H. G. Wells in his book, *The Modern Utopia*, is more down-to-earth than other suggested utopias, it, too, suffers from a lack of realism. Aspects of Wells's system—its virtues and weaknesses—are described below.

Imperfection and Slow Change

"There is no perfection," H. G. Wells wrote in *The Modern Utopia*. Life in his system "is still imperfect," "still a thick felt of dissatisfactions and perplexing problems. . . ."[22] It is not a static but a changing state of affairs, a world of risk and uncertainty, with "uncertain seasons, sudden catastrophes, antagonistic diseases, and inimical

[21]Lewis Mumford, *The Story of Utopias* (New York: Boni and Liveright, 1922), pp. 15–21.

[22]H. G. Wells, *A Modern Utopia* (Lincoln, Neb.: University of Nebraska Press, 1905), pp. 233, 279.

beasts and vermin...."[23] The people in it have passions, uncertainties of mood and desire. They are, in other words, "people inherently the same as those in the world." Money would be required as an inducement to effort. Wells believed that there would be frictions and conflicts of interest, public drunkenness, criminality, and waste.[24] Perhaps most important, Wells did not expect sudden change, a striking discontinuity in life, after which utopia would be here. "Surely, surely, in the end, by degrees and steps, something of this sort, some such understanding as this utopia must come. First here, then there, single men then groups of men will fall into line...."[25]

The Economic Sphere

In the utopia designed by H. G. Wells, there would be "world-wide freedom of sale and purchase," private enterprise, corporations, private property, insurance, and money. He viewed private property in business enterprises as a source of innovation. "All new machinery, all new methods, all uncertain and variable and non-universal undertakings, are no business for the State; they commence always as experiments of unascertained value, and next after the invention of money there is no invention has so facilitated freedom and progress as the invention of the limited liability company to do this work of trial and adventure." Wells saw money as a device for "the reconciliation of human interdependence with liberty" and as an incentive to work. "What other device will give a man so great a freedom with so strong an inducement to effort?" A person, he said could choose idleness, privacy, locomotion, and almost all the freedoms of life if he has the money to pay for them.[26] More clearly than most critics of existing institutions, Wells recognized that money is "coined freedom." While not explicitly saying so, he seemed to recognize that market-clearing prices in a money economy avoid rationing and give freedom of choice to the consumer.

One finds in *A Modern Utopia* a certain distrust of loans at interest, as well as a distrust of trade. According to Wells, the law of his utopia did not "recognize contracts for interest upon private accommodation loans to unprosperous borrowers"; the govern-

[23]Ibid., pp. 5, 7.
[24]Ibid., pp. 8, 23, 64, 73, 141–49, 262, 308.
[25]Ibid., pp. 367–74.
[26]Ibid., pp. 70, 91–97, 290.

ment "insists pretty effectually . . . upon the participation of the lender in the borrower's risk." Moreover the samurai, Wells's voluntary noblemen, who will be discussed later, "are forbidden to buy or sell on their own account or for any employer save the State, unless some process of manufacture changes the nature of the commodity. . . ."[27]

H. G. Wells definitely was not an advocate of laissez faire capitalism. In his utopia unions would exist and would bargain with employers, although an individual with the skill to do so could strike a bargain with his or her employer for still better terms.[28] And the government would have a large role in the economy. Apart from establishing conditions for all sorts of contracts, it would act as a reserve employer during depressions, until "the tide of private enterprise" flowed again.[29] (Recall that he was writing more than thirty years before Keynes' *General Theory*.) The government would set minimum standards of housing and would tear down substandard houses at the owner's expense. It would set minimal standards of nutrition, health, and clothing, (and would feed, clothe, and shelter those unable to work and support themselves at the minimum). The government (actually it is to be a World State, so named by Wells) would be the sole landowner, the owner of all sources of energy such as coal and electric power, and the owner of highways and all the means of cheap and rapid locomotion. The government would levy high death duties. The government also would control births; only those above a certain age, who met specified physical conditions, who were free of transmissible disease, who were not criminals, and who were solvent and independent would be allowed to bear children.[30]

It is fascinating to read how Wells would have the government use a combination of "prices" and rationing to achieve particular objectives. "Privacy beyond the house might be made a privilege to be paid for in proportion to the area occupied" while "walls could be taxed by height and length." But "a maximum fraction of private enclosure for each urban and suburban square mile could be fixed," and "the enclosure of really natural beauties, of rapids, cascades, gorges, viewpoints, and so forth made impossible." Then too, in beautiful regions of the earth especially set apart

---

[27] Ibid., p. 287.
[28] Ibid., p. 221.
[29] Ibid., pp. 139–40, 191.
[30] Ibid., pp. 89–90, 93, 138–39, 183–84.

and favored for children, "the presence of children will remit taxation, while in other less wholesome places the presence of children will be taxed." Mothers would be paid more for the care of their children when the children rise "markedly above certain minimum qualifications, physical or mental." At the same time, the industrial employment of mothers with children needing care would be forbidden "unless they are in a position to employ qualified efficient substitutes to take care of their offspring."[31]

In sum, the modern utopia of H. G. Wells was a mixed economy. In proposing such a system at the beginning of the century, Wells remarkably anticipated what we now know of the imperfections and limitations as well as the possibilities of the various kinds of socialism and capitalism. He wrote in 1905:

> To the onlooker, both Individualism and Socialism are, in the absolute, absurdities; the one would make men the slaves of the violent or rich, the other the slaves of the State official, and the way of sanity runs, perhaps even sinuously, down the intervening valley.... Each man or woman, to the extent that his or her individuality is marked, breaks the law of precedent, transgresses the general formula, and makes a new experiment for the direction of the life force. It is impossible ... for the State, which represents all and is preoccupied by the average, to make effectual experiments and intelligent innovations, and so supply the essential substance of life. As against the individual the State represents the species....[32]

The Political Sphere

But what is it that is utopian in the world described by H. G. Wells? Mostly, the government. "In the case of a Utopia one assumes the best possible government, a government as merciful and deliberate as it is powerful and decisive." In his utopia, moreover, "the laws are wise."[33] Excellent government and laws would be achieved through a ruling group which Wells called the *samurai* or voluntary nobility. All of the voters, legislators, public officials, judges, lawyers, employers of labor beyond a certain limit, head teachers, and medical doctors would belong in this group. "The *samurai* are, in fact volunteers. Any intelligent adult in a reason-

---

[31]Ibid., pp. 42–43, 49, 188.
[32]Ibid., pp. 87–88, 90–91.
[33]Ibid., pp. 30, 142, 271.

ably healthy and efficient state may, at any age after five-and-twenty, become one of the *samurai*, and take a hand in the universal control."[34] He or she must have passed out of college and must know and follow the Canon or Rule that forbids the use of tobacco and narcotic drugs, forbids salesmanship and all its arts, forbids acting and singing, gambling, competitive sports, and many other activities, while it requires bathing in cold water only, reading aloud from the Book of the Samurai (the Canon) for at least ten minutes a day, reading one book a month, and so on. The Samurai would possess a clear common purpose, a power of will, and would be the organizing and controlling force in the world.[35]

In his system, H. G. Wells proposed the "maximum general freedom" and especially emphasizes freedom of movement about the earth's surface, devoting no less than 15 pages to the latter subject. He recognized the desire for privacy and, as a consequence proposed limitations on intrusions into an individual's room or home.[36]

Conclusions

People who write utopias live in a world of dreams. And while the dreams of people are valuable, so is recognition by them of the constraints under which they must live. Utopians usually achieve their idyllic worlds by ignoring one or more of three realities: economic scarcity, imperfections in human behavior, and imperfection in government. H. G. Wells is most down-to-earth in his economic system, least so in his proposed political system, and somewhere in between in the matter of human behavior.

When Wells recognized money as an incentive to work and asserted that his utopians could choose idleness, privacy, locomotion, and other freedoms if they had the money to pay for them, he seemed to recognize the importance of scarcity. Yet he blunted the impact of this recognition when he described the technological marvels of his utopia without discussing their costs—operating costs and costs in capital accumulation (nonhuman capital as well as human capital in the form of knowledge). He wrote of "faultless roads and beautifully arranged inter-urban communications," innumerable "clean little electric tram-ways," "dustless spotless

[34]Ibid., pp. 278, 310–11.
[35]Ibid., pp. 125, 128, 279–99.
[36]Ibid., pp. 32–48.

sweet" apartments, separate houses with perfected telephonic connection with the rest of the world, all heating done with electricity, London with air as clear as and less dusty than it is among high mountains; he talks also of a huge research activity, and a medical science so advanced that 99 percent of all children born would live to a ripe old age, and without wrinkles and baldness.[37] Wells shrewdly observed that most utopias "present themselves as going concerns, as happiness in being; they make it an essential condition that a happy land can have no history...."[38] He gave us only tiny fragments of the history of his own utopia, and he did not divulge the origins of the capital required for all his technological marvels.

In general H. G. Wells failed to take cognizance of the limited knowledge of his samurai—of their limited knowledge of the wants of consumers and of the relationships of inputs to outputs (technological coefficients). He wrote, "All over the world the labor exchanges will be reporting the fluctuating pressure of economic demand and transferring workers from this region of excess to that of scarcity...." "All that is tangled and confused in human affairs has been unravelled and made right," so that in utopia "waste will be enormously less than in our world."[39] Today we are far more aware than Wells was or could have been of the multiplicity of interdependent variables in a complex, modern economy, of the limited knowledge possessed by a planning agency, and of the costs of computation.

The people in the utopia of H. G. Wells are a little too good to be true. Although his men and women have passions and frictions and conflicts of interest, they would be "saturated with consideration," and their utopian selves would be their better selves, perhaps because "a fairly comprehensive science of human association" had been developed.[40] Nowadays we are not so optimistic about what can be achieved in psychology and social science. When Wells dreamed of people saturated with consideration, he saw what even today only a few people have recognized; namely, that we cannot entirely protect our environment from spillover effects through regulatory devices. To a great extent humanity must depend upon the consideration of one person for

[37]Ibid., pp. 42, 44, 60, 104–106, 185–86, 218, 313–14.
[38]Ibid., p. 135.
[39]Ibid., pp. 30, 153, 262.
[40]Ibid., pp. 40, 247, 264.

another. "Laws and manners are to some extent substitutes. A community that has developed habits against littering does not need anti-littering laws."[41]

H. G. Wells is most utopian in the description of his political system. He postulated the best possible government, one which would combine progress with political stability, but, like most utopians and many socialists, he did not tell us how to achieve the best possible government. He wrote, "There is to be no inquiry here of policy and method. There is to be a holiday from politics and movements and methods."[42] The idea of a government run by the elite, Wells's Samurai, has much appeal until we address ourselves to the question of how the elite is to be identified, how it (and only it) is to be placed in power, and how, once in control, it is to be kept from being corrupted by power. Wells did tell us that the psychology of minor officials is "a matter altogether too much neglected by the social reformer,"[43] but he failed to recognize that frequently it is the vote of everyman that protects him from people who achieve happiness in the routine security of government employment.

In his utopia H. G. Wells, proposed to develop a dossier on each of the residents of the World State. He proposed a complete central index of all people, "the record of their movement hither and thither, the entry of various material facts, such as marriage, parentage, criminal convictions ... arrivals at inns, applications at post offices for letters ... applications for public doles and the like." The index cards "might conceivably be transparent and so contrived as to give a photographic copy promptly whenever it was needed...." To be sure, "only the State would share" the individual's secrets.[44] Such dossiers are not worrisome if government is perfect. But what if government is not? What if these records were only as secret as our present day "confidential" records?

Finally, H. G. Wells proposed to have incorrigible criminals, drunkards, and the like exiled by the government to islands that would be patrolled by guard boats and simply policed against the organization of serious cruelty and tyranny.[45] In this instance,

---

[41] Robert A. Mundell, *Man and Economics* (New York: McGraw-Hill, 1968), pp. 187–88.

[42] Wells, *Modern Utopia*, p. 7.

[43] Ibid., pp. 64, 238.

[44] Ibid., pp. 162–65.

[45] Ibid., pp. 144–45.

Wells can be accused of simple naivete as to the horrors of maximum security prisons and the costs of protecting the weak against the strong in a society of hardened criminals.

The creator of utopias may readily succumb to illusion, and disillusion. Hungering for perfection, or near perfection, he or she is likely to find it where it is not, and be easily disillusioned with moderate efforts at reform. H. G. Wells visited Russia in 1920 and returned to England convinced that the Bolsheviks represented the one constructive party there. In 1922 he joined the Labour Party and ran for Parliament, but he was inactive in the Party after 1924. By 1927 he concluded that government by Samurai was tentatively and effectively working, although it was narrow in outlook, in China, Russia, and Italy![46]

When he wrote *A Modern Utopia,* H. G. Wells gave us a great and remarkable analysis, one which was far ahead of its time. It is sad that in later years he lost his patience and his judgment concerning world events.

Skinner's Walden Two

In 1945, B. F. Skinner wrote *Walden Two*, a fictional account of a commune in the United States. Unlike many advocates or participants in communalism, the membership of his commune, Walden Two, did not reject modern technology and in fact embraced a scientific, experimental approach to life. Moreover, Skinner, a prominent behavioral psychologist, depicted his communalists devoted to "behavioral engineering." Some two decades later, a wave of interest in communalism swept the United States, and a few of the new communes used the fictional Walden Two as their guide. One of these was Twin Oaks, founded in 1967. In this chapter we will look at Skinner's original tract, while in Chapter 13 we will observe efforts to apply his ideas in everyday life at Twin Oaks.

Institutions

Skinner's fictional commune was to be run by a Board of Planners and a set of Managers.[47] Of the six members of the Board, three

---

[46]Geoffrey West, *H. G. Wells: A Sketch for a Portrait* (London: Gerald Howe, 1930), pp. 232–33, 238, 245.

[47]B. F. Skinner, *Walden Two* (New York: Macmillan Paperbacks Edition, 1962), pp. 54–55.

usually were men and three usually women. Board members would serve ten years but no longer. Not elected by the membership of the commune, replacements for the Board were chosen by the Board itself from a pair of names supplied by the Managers. The Planners made policies, chose and reviewed the work of the Managers, and had certain judicial functions. There were Managers of Food, Health, Play, Supply, Labor, Advanced Education, the Arts, the various industries, and so on. There was a Constitution that could be changed by a unanimous vote of the Planners and a two-thirds vote of the Managers.[48] There were rules of conduct, the Walden Code, which acted as a memory aid until, through behavioral engineering, desired conduct became habitual. A member of the commune might discuss a rule with the Managers and Planners, but he was not allowed to argue about the Code with the members at large.[49] Parties or pressure groups were not to exist. This type of government by oligarchy was defended in the classic fashion: "The majority of the people don't want to plan. They want to be free of the responsibility of planning. What they ask is merely some assurance that they will be decently provided for. The rest is day-to-day enjoyment of life." Moreover, "our elite do not command a disproportionate share of the wealth of the community; on the contrary, they work rather hard for what they get. A Manager's lot is not a happy one."[50]

All goods and services, like meals in the dining room, would be free in Walden Two. Each member would pay for what he received from the community with "labor-credits"—twelve hundred labor-credits per year which worked out at about four credits per workday. On the average, one hour of work would earn one credit, so that the average member worked four hours a day. But different credit values would be assigned to different kinds of work, and these values would be changed periodically in accordance with demand. (The "supply" of different jobs would be determined by the Planners and Managers.) An unpleasant job like cleaning sewers would earn about one and one-half labor credits per hour, so the sewer cleaner would work only a little over two hours a day.[51] More pleasant jobs might earn only 0.8 credits per hour. Although Skinner did not label them as such, his labor-credits are, in fact, prices or wage rates. They are mostly market-

[48]Ibid., p. 270.
[49]Ibid., pp. 162–64.
[50]Ibid., pp. 167, 233.
[51]Ibid., pp. 51–54.

clearing; hence there is free choice of jobs, the only exception being that of medical doctor. (This exception came about as a result of so many young in the novel wanting to be doctors. The Planners, rather than lower labor-credits for medical practice, which would force doctors to work long hours, decided to limit entry into medical practice. Skinner does not explain why the Planners choose not to use the price-system at this point.) Although he did not seem to realize it, Skinner depicted in Walden Two a wage system in which the demand for labor would be determined by the oligarchy; it was a labor market of oligopsony, or, if the oligarchy were unified, monopsony (as long as the worker is immobile and unwilling to leave Walden Two).

In his novel, Skinner depicted a fairly opulent community, yet its members only worked about four hours a day. He explained this apparent anomaly: the greater productivity per hour with a shorter work day, the extra motivation "when a man is working for himself instead of a profit-seeking boss," the absence of a leisure class and of prematurely aged or occupationally disabled persons, the absence of alcoholics and criminals, a higher degree of mechanization, better educated and hence more productive workers, the unnecessary need of personnel in transportation, distribution, advertising, finance, and insurance, and in bars and taverns, and a more efficient use of women when they are taken out of the traditional household setting. There is also "little or no spoilage or waste in distribution or storage, and none due to miscalculated needs."[52]

Analysis of the Proposed Institutions

Skinner purports to have designed an economic system, yet he is not an economist and does not appear to have thought deeply about the problems of scarcity. It is significant that he began his novel with a fully established commune. As a consequence, he does not have to depict for the reader an earlier period when capital would have been scarce and when the four-hour day would have been very nearly inconceivable. Skinner does not tell us where the capital comes from which makes a high degree of mechanization possible.

Professor Skinner in his novel did not consider relations with the outside world, an important feature of a web-designed economic system. New members agreed to work according to communal

[52] Ibid., pp. 59–64.

schedules, did not claim any share in the fruits of their labor, and were free to leave at any time. Applicants, apparently, were not screened, nor were members expelled. (We shall see that both screening and expulsion proved to be necessary at Twin Oaks.) Walden Two required what Skinner called "foreign exchange" for the purchase of certain materials, for the purchase of power, and for the payment of taxes. The commune exported the products of several small industries and sent members to work on the outside, but all outside earnings of members were turned over to the commune. Were funds needed, the commune usually found a farmer with a crop ready to be harvested at which time "a fairly stiff bargain could be driven."[53] The members of Twin Oaks might have envied the fictional outside workers at Walden Two, for at Twin Oaks outside work has been a continuing unpleasant necessity and a source of much friction.

When one thinks beyond the confines of a single commune and considers the comparative advantage each commune might have, one addresses oneself to the possibilities of specialization, trade, credit, and capital transfers. It then becomes apparent that the communal movement cannot entirely escape the costs of transportation, distribution, and finance, as Skinner thought it could.

Uncertainty and risk are also given little attention by Skinner. A spokesman at Walden Two has stated: "We have a hard time explaining insurance to our children. Insurance against what?"[54] How about insurance against crop failure, fire, and epidemic disease? Does the commune want to carry all these risks itself or self-insure? If the latter, are the possible losses independent events, or might a fire in one building spread to others, a disease in one individual spread to other members of the commune? Perhaps a commune in the real world might insure itself against some losses, then elect to reinsure part of its risks with a larger carrier.

But there is the uninsurable risk—a reality that Skinner maintains can be dealt with by planning. In Walden Two there would be "no unemployment due to bad planning," nor as we said, would there be spoilage or waste in distribution or storage. However, as soon as one goes beyond the affairs of a single relatively small commune and considers the millions of interdependencies in a large, complex modern economy, one surely has to recognize the inevitable presence of uncertainty and limited knowledge.

[53]Ibid., pp. 77, 79, 227.
[54]Ibid., p. 61.

Skinner was proud of the differences between Walden Two and earlier utopian communes. He pointed out that its members would embrace rather than reject modern technology. And he had its leaders use modern behavioral engineering to instill the conduct desired in members. According to Skinner, the crucial failure of former utopias lay in the psychological management of them. He stated that members of Walden Two would have "the power to change human behavior. We can make men adequate for group living—to the satisfaction of everybody. That was our faith, but it's now a fact."[55]

Skinner's Walden Two was, indeed, utopian, naively utopian, in several respects. To begin with, he came close to ignoring the central economic problem of scarcity, failing even to tell the story of the origins of Walden Two and how it got the capital for its initial construction and the capital for its high degree of mechanization. Secondly, he did not appear to have studied the problems of planning a complex modern economy, even though a rich literature on the subject existed at the time he wrote. Moreover, although the members of Walden Two were not screened for entry, they worked well, were seldom if ever prematurely aged or occupationally disabled, and did not drink to excess or commit criminal acts. To be sure, these admirable traits of the people at Walden Two were explained by the purported use of behavioral engineering. (We will examine the claims made for behavioral engineering in the design of communities, following a discussion of Twin Oaks in Chapter 13.)

Dreams and Reality

People need to dream, but the world can probably do without utopias. More useful to humankind would be *realistic* visions of a better future to deal with the constraints of economic scarcity, conflicting human interests, and far from perfect government.

---

[55] Ibid., pp. 157, 196.

Communes: Traditional and Contemporary

Chapter **13**

A number of critics of established religions have sought to develop a new kind of religious life in communal living. Among the most interesting of these groups have been the Oneida Community in the state of New York, the Amanas in Iowa, and the Hutterian communities in South Dakota and Manitoba.

John Humphrey Noyes, a clergyman in the early nineteenth century, challenged along with other religious reformers at that time the Calvinist doctrine of man's depravity. As a result, they established a religious group known as "Perfectionists." Noyes, after deciding that he himself was perfect, was discharged from the ministry, and some 15 years later, in 1848, at the age of 37, founded and became leader of the "Oneida Community."[1] Its objectives were individual perfection and the communal good. Economic success was supposed to be a less important goal, but on at least one occasion studies were foregone so that members could devote more time to the needs of the community business.[2]

Oneida

[1] Maren Lockwood Carden, *Oneida: Utopian Community to Modern Corporation* (Baltimore: Johns Hopkins Press, 1969), pp. 3–4, 18–23.
[2] Ibid., pp. xvi, 23, 48.

The community selected its membership carefully. Prospective members had to study Perfectionist belief for months or even years before they were accepted. About two members a year "seceded" from Oneida, some were encouraged to depart, and one man (only one in its entire history) was forcibly expelled. The turnover rate of members was greatest among those who had lived at Oneida for only a short time. In 1849, one year after its establishment, membership was 87, while in 1875 membership was 253. "Of the 109 adults who joined in the first two years, at least 84 either died in the Community or lived there until the breakup."[3]

The Political Structure
Voting unanimously, the early membership chose a "theocratic" government—control by John Humphrey Noyes—and no one subsequently joined the Community without accepting his power. At that time Noyes set out "the general principles whereby Perfectionism should be practiced at Oneida," but left most of the detailed application to a few "central members" who ran the Community during the long periods when Noyes lived elsewhere. Such central members were relatively immune to criticism, at least from below, and enjoyed some privileges such as travel. (Two of them toured England and visited Paris.[4])

The Economic System
Noyes carefully selected talented craftsmen and farmers to join the Community, and these people brought their savings with them. Nine years after they began, members had invested almost $108,000 in Oneida.[5] Having concluded that farming would not give them a large enough income, the Community ventured into business. Preserved fruits and vegetables did not realize a profit nor did the sale of silks, pins, needles, and notions, but a light machinery factory was consistently profitable, as was the manufacture of silk thread. The largest source of income became the manufacture of animal traps.[6] As a perfectionist, Noyes believed in progressive improvement, so that members adopted modern pro-

[3] Ibid., pp. 26, 37, 41, 77–79.
[4] Ibid., pp. 19, 85–88.
[5] Ibid., pp. 37–39.
[6] Ibid., pp. 39–42.

duction methods in business and constantly devised new techniques to increase efficiency. In order to increase work satisfaction, a rotation of jobs was encouraged, although some members, like shoemakers, did the same job for years. Outside workers were employed, especially to help with menial tasks and to fill rush orders for traps. After the early years during which sacrifices to the future were made, Oneida enjoyed "a fairly comfortable living" and some touches of luxury.[7]

Meals in the Oneida Community were taken in a common dining room. Children under 12 lived during the day in separate quarters, the children's house, and usually slept at night with adults (but with periodic changes in order to discourage the formation of special attachments between particular children and adults). There was room rotation for adults in order to avoid excessive contact with any particular group of members. Visits outside Oneida were rare, and members who talked too freely with the local outsiders (working in the community businesses) were frowned upon.

"Complex marriage" was practiced at Oneida Community. Members changed sexual partners quite often and "exclusive love" was severely reproved. Noyes insisted that sexual relations should be ordered by the principle of "ascending fellowship." The spiritually inferior should be responsive to the sexual desires of those more nearly perfect. In general, older persons were believed to be higher in the ascending fellowship, so that young men and women were expected to associate with "persons of 'mature character' and 'sound sense' who were well advanced in Perfectionism." To avoid undesired births, the men were expected to practice "male continence," withdrawal before orgasm. Men lacking such control were subject to public disapproval and private rejection.[8] Still, of the 36 children conceived at Oneida from 1848 to 1869, 31 were conceived accidentally.[9]

Oneida broke up as a commune in 1880 and became a joint-stock company. One of the reasons for change was the decline of religion. Noyes himself had lost interest in Perfectionism as a religion and had begun to devote himself to the study of science and socialism, publishing a book entitled *History of American Socialisms* in 1870. The young members, while tending to remain at the

[7] Ibid., pp. 42, 65–66.
[8] Ibid., pp. 20–22, 52–61, 76.
[9] Ibid., p. 51. From the same data, Carden unaccountably arrives at the conclusion that "the birth control system was effective, if not quite perfect."

community, also drifted away from interest in religion. Theodore Noyes, son of the founder, became an agnostic.[10] Another difficulty, and a source of tension, was the conflict between individual self improvement (a tenet of Perfectionism) and concern for the Community. The latter required youth to submit to the will of the central members.[11] Moreover, no leader or leaders developed who could take the place of Noyes. Believing him to be a representative of God, finding him both a source of inspiration and a developer of necessary compromises, the members were deprived of his support as he gradually withdrew from the Community. Because of this lack of communal unity and effective leadership, a conflict arose between members of opposing parties in Oneida over the question of who should introduce virgins into sexual experience. By common consent of the membership Noyes had initially assumed this role of "first husband," but he had begun to delegate it, because of age, to one of the central members. As a consequence of the fact that members of the community were divided on how to settle the dispute, a group of outside clergymen threatened attack, stating that such a form of sexual initiation was immoral. Fearing criminal charges for statutory rape, Noyes fled to Canada. From there he sent a message to Oneida proposing that complex marriage be abandoned. The Community voted in August 1879. With only one member abstaining, Noyes's suggestion was adopted; members not already married arranged to marry. Thirteen months later an Agreement to Divide and Reorganize was made, and on 1 January 1881 the Oneida Community became the Oneida Community, Ltd.[12] Now a prominent manufacturer of silverware, Oneida is listed on the New York Stock Exchange.

The Amanas

A German religious group called the True Inspirationists settled in a series of villages west of Iowa City in 1885, and lived there as a commune, called the Amanas, until 1932. Following a tenet that men and women should work and pray, they developed a relatively prosperous and devout community. There was sufficient food and clothing, housing of good quality, medical and dental care, and care for widows, orphans, and the aged. One of the rules of the Amanas was "Count every word, thought, and work as done

[10] Ibid., pp. 89–96.
[11] Ibid., pp. 92–96.
[12] Ibid., pp. 98–104.

in the immediate presence of God, in sleeping and waking, eating, drinking, etc., and give him at once an account of it, to see if all is done in His fear and love."[13]

Organization and Control

A Council of the Brethren, thirteen representatives (elders) from all the communities, served as trustees and was the main governing body of the Inspirationists in matters temporal and religious. New elders were appointed by the Great Council of the Brethren and usually were the children of former elders.[14] Each village was governed by its own committee of elders in local matters such as assignment to dwellings, work direction, and marriage sanctions. Members had to receive permission from the elders to visit other villages or to go outside the Amanas. Discipline was maintained through reprimands, demotions in church seating, banishment from church services, required public confessions of wrongdoing. Such confessions were so embarrassing to members that some preferred to leave the Amanas rather than confess. A few were expelled.[15]

The Economic System

Work was specialized. Individuals were assigned to whatever activities they were best qualified to do by training and experience. Some jobs were kept in particular families, being handed down from father to son. The evening hours were devoted to chores, handiwork, clockmaking, furniture making, toy making, and other crafts. Idleness in all forms was considered sinful, so that attendance at church services and craftsmanship were expected to fill all leisure hours. Reading was considered a waste of time. Children had their chores, and Sundays, apart from church attendance, were supposed to be spent in quiet contemplation.[16]

Relationships with the outside world were minimal. Geography, religious preoccupations, use of the German language, and a considerable economic self-sufficiency tended to isolate the community. Some items, like woolen blankets, were manufactured and

---

[13] Barbara Yambura, *A Change and a Parting: My Story of Amana* (Ames: Iowa State University Press, 1960), pp. 22, 30, 36.

[14] Ibid., pp. 33–34, 143–45.

[15] Ibid., pp. 136–38, 146–47.

[16] Ibid., pp. 32–33, 101–5.

sold outside the community, and a general store, of little variety, supplied the people with goods from outside. Each family had a credit book good in the store for a fixed value.[17]

Erosion of Community Life

Over time, communal unity in the Amanas began to dissolve. Meals, once taken in a common dining room, were in later years cooked in common kitchens, and then carried to the separate households. As the community prospered, outsiders were hired to help around the kitchen buildings as handymen and to clean the chicken houses, barns, stables, and outdoor toilets. Recreation, frowned upon by the elders, began to be enjoyed covertly.[18] Instead of turning outside earnings, acquired from the sale of garden produce and handicrafts back into the community, members began to use such monies for their own personal consumption—for radios, bathtubs, bicycles, and the like.[19] Inspirationist religion declined. Public confessions were patently incomplete and untruthful; some traditional religious observances were suspended; younger members went to other churches and joined other faiths; worldliness became more pronounced.[20] The powers of the elders declined: Couples married without their permission and in outside churches. Young men avoided appointment to positions as elders: the duties were onerous and elders were expected to be examples of excellent character and conduct.[21] Much of the erosion of the old ways reflected influence from the outside. Such influences were especially pervasive at Homestead, an Amana village originally purchased simply because it was on the railroad.[22]

The Amanas disbanded as a commune in 1932. Several factors contributed to the actual breakup. A national depression had reduced the community's money income from the outside sale of its products. Communal production was down because many members were devoting little time to work for the community and some were even using Amana property for private production. The community was operating at a deficit and its debts were growing. "I can think of several brethren and sisters who never do

[17]Ibid., pp. 36, 230, 234.
[18]Ibid., pp. 43–44, 101, 106–7, 194, 264–65.
[19]Ibid., pp. 146, 224–27, 236–39.
[20]Ibid., pp. 192–93, 202, 210.
[21]Ibid., pp. 179, 145–47.
[22]Ibid., pp. 30, 279.

any honest day's work," said one member, "yet they always come to the kitchen house with their baskets."[23]

When committees were elected to develop a plan for reorganization, conspicuously few elders were chosen. A statement of the alternatives was prepared, with an attached ballot, and distributed to the members. Seventy-five percent of the Amanas voted for reorganization. Then, when an actual plan for incorporation was drawn up, 90 percent of the voting members approved it. The last meal was served from the communal kitchens on 28 May 1932.[24] Old enterprises like the woolen mills then were rejuvenated, and new enterprises were started—gas stations along the highway, bakeries, a refrigeration enterprise, and restaurants. (Venturesome members purchased the old kitchen houses for the latter.[25])

The Hutterians

With their origins in the European Anabaptist movement of the sixteenth century, Hutterian Brethren (sometimes known also as the Hutterites) settled in large numbers in the Dakota Territory from 1874 to 1877. About 350 of these (adults and children) chose to live in communal colonies. By 1915, there were 1,700 Hutterians in 17 communities. German in origin, they suffered from irrational fears of World War I, and as a consequence, all but one of the colonies left in 1918 for Manitoba and Alberta, Canada. By 1964, Alberta had 56 colonies, Saskatchewan 13, and Manitoba 39. By that time in the United States, mostly in South Dakota and Montana, there were 46 colonies. The total population of the North American Hutterian colonies in 1964 was 14,707, with some 80 to 200 living in each community.[26]

The goals of the Hutterians were and are very simple: a religious and industrious life, the two being considered inseparable.[27]

Organization and Control

At the top of the administrative structure of the community is the colony council. Ex officio members of the council are the minister,

[23]Ibid., pp. 268–71, 277–78.
[24]Ibid., pp. 279–91.
[25]Ibid., pp. 292–93.
[26]Victor Peters, *All Things Common: The Hutterian Way of Life* (Minneapolis: University of Minnesota Press, 1965), pp. 3, 9–37, 41–51, 80, 117, 207–10.
[27]Ibid., p. 167.

the colony steward, and the farm manager. Two or three other members are elected to the council for life by the male congregation. However, the council is not static: such occurrences as the election of an assistant minister, or periodic colony division all lead to the influx of new men and women. When a new minister is needed, the members of the colony concerned, the "Brethren," nominate two or three candidates, vote on the nominees (one or two members from each of the surrounding colonies, visiting for the occasion, also vote), and then choose the minister by lot from among those who receive more than five votes. The colony steward is elected by the male congregation of the community. He keeps the financial records, helps and supervises in the workshops and in the kitchen, and consults with the farm foreman about work assignments. The farm foreman, too, is elected by the male congregation. He decides, after consultation with the steward and the enterprise heads, what crops are to be sown and where, when plowing, seeding, and harvesting should be done, and in general he controls the allocation of manpower.[28]

There are numerous rules in a Hutterian commune. For example, members are not to absent themselves from work for trivial reasons; wives are to limit time spent visiting their husbands in the workshops; the buying of radios and musical instruments is forbidden; beggars should be directed to one source of distribution in the colony.[29] Discipline for violations of these rules ranges from disapproval to the requiring of statements of contrition before the congregation at church, to social ostracism, to physical isolation (at meals, at church, or at night), and to expulsion. (Only one case of which is on record.[30])

The Economic System

Agriculture is the foundation of the Hutterian communal economy. Each colony has a farm. While striving for self-sufficiency, some colonies, due to a shortage of land, often find it necessary to purchase grain and fodder. The most modern machinery and implements are employed, and experiments with new crops, insecticides, and the like are undertaken. Peripheral enterprises and crafts supplement agricultural income: a blacksmith's or carpenter's shop may do repairs or custom construction for the neigh-

[28] Ibid., pp. 80–86.
[29] Ibid., pp. 25, 158.
[30] Ibid., pp. 158–60.

bors. In the winter older men may bind brooms, some of which are sold in nearby towns. A dentist in the commune also may provide services to outsiders. All outside earnings are turned over to the colony steward.[31]

Almost everyone engages in some manual work, ministers and colony stewards included, but specialization of labor is the general rule. Outside workers are not employed.[32] If a member shirks work, a steward, a farm foreman, or even the minister might have a word with the individual. Should this fail, the member is regarded as a bit abnormal and such frailty is borne with patience by the community. But unwillingness to work is said to be rare.[33]

Each colony is an independent economic unit, but colonies do assist one another from time to time, with interest-free loans, or with grants of produce and cash in the event of disastrous crop failures, floods, or fires.[34]

Like production, consumption is communal. The elected steward controls the colony purse. Meals are eaten in the colony dining hall, with men and women eating at separate tables; communal laundry facilities are available, with each family doing its own laundry. Some colonies are heated from a central heating plant. Housing is assigned by size of the family unit. Members retire informally around the age of forty-five, but most voluntarily continue to work at jobs they prefer. Each colony member receives an annual clothing allotment, but may ask for substitutes or even an equivalent in cash. The latter to be spent, however, only on clothing of cut and color that meets community regulations. All members receive a small weekly cash allowance.[35]

Child Rearing

Permissiveness in child-rearing in a Hutterian colony is regarded as a vice. If children are caught smoking, for example, they will not be baptized and their parents might be asked to administer corporal punishment. A conflict of the generations is said to be almost completely absent from Hutterian society.

Hutterian children are educated at accredited public schools located in the colony. Schooling is not required past the comple-

[31] Ibid., pp. 108–13.
[32] Ibid., pp. 81, 87, 90, 112.
[33] Ibid., pp. 88–89.
[34] Ibid., pp. 109, 166.
[35] Ibid., pp. 77–79, 95, 103, 113–14, 166.

tion of eighth grade. Many, if not most, of the teachers are outsiders. The children often are said to lack initiative, a competitive spirit, and the desire to excel. Education beyond the eighth grade is being considered, but it is feared that it would expose the youngsters to temptations and worldly influences that would eventually create conflicts with their intended simple existences and careers of manual toil.[36]

Recreation consists mostly of visiting within the colony, and often on weekends includes visiting between colonies. Reading is another recreation and is popular. Cameras, radios, television sets, musical instruments, and cards are forbidden, as is dancing. Boys and girls sometimes meet at one of the homes and sing, perhaps (before baptism) Western songs to the accompaniment of a mouth organ.[37]

Viability of Hutterian Communities

What factors account for the continued viability and stability of the Hutterian colonies? Almost certainly, their geographical isolation, which is deliberately sought, is a factor. Their community stability can also be attributed to their forbidding radio and television. The fact that their schools are located in the colonies also contributes to maintaining the status quo. One wonders how the Hutterians would fare if the young people acquired saleable knowledge and skills in high schools outside the colonies. A certain amount of persecution during World Wars I and II and the effects of the depression undoubtedly have increased their sense of isolation, as well as their communal solidarity. The fact that everyone performs manual labor and that no outside workers are employed also promotes unity. A non-dependence on charismatic leaders probably is another factor in their survival. Moreover, a Hutterian *movement* exists, with a tradition of mutual aid, so that a single colony need not feel isolated, in dealing with the government, for example in such matters as education and military service. Finally, and possibly the most important contributing factor is their distinctive religion.

The Hutterians have a high birth rate (41.5 per thousand), and it is possible that this also contributes to the continuance of their communal colonies. When a colony reaches a size of approximately 150 members, the men begin to consider branching out

[36]Ibid., pp. 98, 135–38, 145, 148–49, 158.
[37]Ibid., pp. 104–5.

and establishing a new community. Care is taken to assure that the size and age distribution of families is about the same in both the new and the old colony.[38] With rapid growth in population, the Hutterians could lose a large number of their young people to the outside world and still survive as a movement. Some Hutterians do leave, but the fact is that many come back (even though leaving is an offense and must be expiated upon return through penitence and acceptance of punishment). The Hutterians are not active missionaries, but membership in their communities is open to anyone. Converts, however, are few in number, and this also contributes to the homogeneity and unity of their colonies.[39]

The Israeli Kibbutz

The goals of the leaders of the kibbutzim are of two kinds: collective living (a "new way of life") and nation-making. Kibbutz leaders want a system of collective production, consumption, and child rearing, with democracy, equality, and mutual aid.[40] And they have wanted to colonize Palestine, develop an agrarian people, and create and secure the nation of Israel. Consistent with most of these goals is a more mundane set of objectives: increased production, a "decent" standard of living, and economic security.[41] (A relatively small proportion of the kibbutzim have, in addition, a strong religious orientation.)

Organization and Work

In the Israeli kibbutz an elected Work Committee and a Work-Coordinator assign members to jobs, with senior members having more or less permanent jobs and newer members moving about from one branch or task to another as required. In kibbutz terminology, branch Organizers in the various branches like poultry, cattle, citrus fruits, fish, and so on usually hold their positions permanently, and try to lead rather than direct the workers in their sector. Positions in the Secretariat (the positions of Farm Manager, Secretary, Treasurer, Work Coordinator, and others) are

---

[38] Ibid., pp. 116–18, 127, 152–53, 167.
[39] Ibid., pp. 162–64, 180.
[40] Dan Leon, *The Kibbutz: A New Way of Life* (Oxford: Pergamon Press, 1969), pp. 14, 97, 115, 196.
[41] Eliyahu Kanovsky, *The Economy of the Israeli Kibbutz* (Cambridge, Mass.: Harvard University Press, 1966), pp. 32, 37.

rotated among the members; in practice, they rotate among a relatively small number of the more capable people.

An Economic Committee draws up plans for production, consumption, and investment—plans that must be approved by the General Assembly of all the members. Numerous other committees exist which (through rotation) involve many members in the work of the kibbutz. In the past, the emphasis was on technical achievements, such as maximization of sugar beet production per unit of land area. At present, more attention is paid to opportunity costs (sugar beets may be deprived of irrigation water during months when the water is more valuable on other crops), and market research is extensively employed.

Consumption

Most consumption is collective. Meals are taken in communal dining halls (except for tea at home), work clothing is replaced when it wears out, while dress clothing is rationed at a clothes depot where efforts have been made in recent years to provide a considerable choice of color and style. Housing usually is allocated in accordance with seniority. Older members dwell in the newer, more spacious units, but, at least, in one kibbutz some of its new housing is now being set aside for younger members. Automobiles used for work during the day are allocated by a transportation committee, and (as equally as possible) are allocated for recreational use on evenings, weekends, and holidays. In earlier years, the kibbutzim were reluctant to send young people away to college, fearing perhaps that they would not return, but pressure from youth has now induced them to finance the university education of able young people. (The student repays the kibbutz if he fails to return after his schooling is completed.)

Each member receives a "personal budget," pocket money for small purchases. In some kibbutzim, the personal budget has been extended into clothing, and this is a cause of controversy in the kibbutz movement. Instead of there being a system of clothing norms, members in such kibbutzim receive (equal) sums of money for the purchase of clothing. Defenders of the personal budget in clothing point out that the budget, while preserving equality, gives the member freedom of choice. Critics view it as a signal—a first step—which could transform the kibbutz from a collective into a cooperative.[42] They argue that if there is to be a personal

---

[42]Leon, *The Kibbutz*, pp. 86–87.

budget in clothing, it might as well be extended to other consumption items. This controversy nicely illustrates the difference between the free choice characteristic of a money economy and the collective consumption choices of the commune.

Children live in the children's part of the kibbutz, attend school, work part-time on the children's farm, and are with their parents in the late afternoon and evening and on weekends. For the most part, children do not sleep at home.

Kanovsky suggests that the moshavim, the cooperative farm, may be more dynamic than the kibbutzim because the moshavim "shifted their resources very rapidly into the more lucrative livestock branches" between 1955 and 1959, whereas the kibbutz farms moved more slowly.[43] It does appear that the moshav is best at shifting its existing capital in buildings and equipment from one output to another as market demand changes, for example, from one pattern of vegetable production to another. The kibbutz, on the other hand, is best at making major changes that involve totally new activities, like changes from agriculture to industry. With high levels of education and workers who are accustomed to a variety of tasks, with substantial leadership and organizational skills, and with a large capacity to service loans, the kibbutzim moved rapidly into industry after agricultural surpluses emerged in the mid-fifties. Indeed it is interesting to note that the kibbutzim have partially achieved Kropotkin's anarchist dream of small factories and workshops at the gates of fields and gardens.

One way an economy remains dynamic is through the elimination of obsolete organizational units. The kibbutz is rarely liquidated. It is liquidated, in fact, only if its "social structure" is weak, meaning presumably that leadership is lacking and that the people in it do not get along with each other. One wonders whether all kibbutzim having a good social structure also are capable of adapting to changes in preferences and technology.

Incentives

Most economists would expect the kibbutz to have a problem with incentives. What motivates people to work when goods and services are distributed equally? Motivation, however, does not appear to be a problem. All participants seem to agree that the force of public opinion in a small, closely-knit society, where work is highly valued, is exceedingly effective. Leon has written, "Noth-

---

[43] Kanovsky, *The Economy of the Israeli Kibbutz*, pp. 104–5.

ing is more highly valued by public opinion than 'a good worker' and an outstanding worker is proportionally respected—indeed it is doubtful whether any other single factor is more important in determining the respect in which people are held."[44] One does hear of exceptions to the general proposition that people work hard. Members tell of the occasional person who is expelled for not working and of a few people who have trouble getting up in the morning but who continue to dwell on the kibbutz (even though not respected). It should be kept in mind, moreover, that the kibbutz may have avoided a problem with incentives by virtue of the fact that people are free to leave the kibbutz. It may be that in Israel those who work poorly when rewards are distributed equally are uncomfortable in the kibbutz and move out into the capitalist sector. Should an economy be entirely communal, with no capitalist sector to absorb those not content with collective living, the commune might have problems with incentives.

In an Israeli kibbutz the more unpleasant jobs like garbage disposal, dishwashing, waiting on tables, and the cleaning of the public toilets are shared by the members of the kibbutz. Because of this system, members have been motivated to make such tasks as least unpleasant as possible: modern garbage disposal equipment is acquired; cafeteria style self-service is substituted for table service. This motive of the community to reduce the amount of unpleasant work is a small but not insignificant difference between the kibbutz economy and the economy of capitalism. (In the latter, people with low skills have little alternative but to take unpleasant jobs, and the employer often lacks the motive to make them less disagreeable.)

Hired Labor

A tormenting problem in the kibbutz has been the hiring of outside labor, for when outsiders are employed, the distribution of income is no longer equal. Despite this problem, there are numerous considerations that lead the kibbutz to hire outsiders. (1) A large harvest may be more than the members can handle, although some kibbutzim mobilize their entire membership during the harvest and work from dawn to dusk rather than hire labor. (2) When immigrants poured into Israel from 1949 to 1951, the government put pressure on the kibbutzim to relax their principles and give employment to newcomers, and many did so. (3) As

[44] Leon, *The Kibbutz*, pp. 76–77.

kibbutzim move from agriculture into industry, they may find themselves hiring workers when their membership cannot produce on an economically large scale or when factory work is boring and unattractive to members. One kibbutz went into the manufacture of knives and found that its members rebelled against the monotonous grinding operation. In order to avoid this pressure for hired labor, the kibbutz movement now is seeking out capital-intensive, high-technology, small-scale industries. (4) Some kibbutzim employ outside workers because it is profitable. After the Six-Day War in 1967, Arab labor from the Gaza Strip became available, and quite a few kibbutzim in the Negev switched from the capital-intensive raising of cotton to the labor-intensive raising of melons. Other kibbutzim resisted this source of additional profits.

An outside economist might be inclined to question the concern generated by the hiring of outside labor. If additional labor is profitable, why not hire outsiders? A long-time member of a kibbutz says, "You have no idea of how hired labor can demoralize the kibbutz. When a truckload of goods arrives at midday and must be unloaded under the hot sun, not a member will be found. All choose to let the hired workers perform this unpleasant job."

Another labor-related problem recently emerging in the kibbutz is that of assistance given by the members of one kibbutz to other kibbutzim. In earlier years, members of the established, strong kibbutzim were most willing to advise and assist the newer and weaker groups. Even today a weak kibbutz is "adopted" by a strong one and given assistance in its planning and training, and the movement requires each of its young members to give one year of service to some new kibbutz. Nevertheless a certain decline in solidarity has become evident in the movement. Young people do not like to be away from their families as they travel about the country to perform this service. As a result some traveling advisors have been given longer than normal weekends of leisure in order to induce them to perform these duties.

The critic suspects that members of a kibbutz sacrifice their individuality. In response to this question, let us first consider the member as a worker, and then as a consumer. The ordinary worker, unskilled or skilled, probably is more involved in decision making than his counterpart under capitalism. Even if the kibbutz ideal of work-branch democracy were seldom realized in practice, the branch organizers of the kibbutz probably would consult their workers more than do the superintendents and foremen of the traditionally hierarchical capitalist enterprise. Moreover, because the kibbutz member is free to leave the kibbutz if his or her work assignment is not pleasing (in this respect like the worker under capitalism), the Work Committee and Work-Coordinator probably would listen sympathetically to his or her statements of work preference. Finally, the worker in a kibbutz votes in elections for the Secretariat, and he votes on proposed economic plans.

It is more difficult to decide on the individuality or lack of individuality of Branch Organizers, and members of the Secretariat—the kibbutz counterpart of capitalist management. Because they must heed the wishes of their work people, the Branch Organizers and Work Coordinators are less free, individually, to make some decisions than capitalist managers in the same situation would be. On the other hand, rather than being constrained by directives from superiors in a hierarchy, they are participants in a set of collective decisions.

Consumption is the part of the system in which collective decisions largely take the place of individual decisions. As we have already seen, members eat in a communal dining hall (in which, however, there is some individual choice of foods), obtain their clothes from a collective clothes depot (again with some choice), have the use of an automobile when the transportation committee approves a request, and occupy a house in accordance with the decisions of the membership. University attendance also requires approval of the collective (but members assert that proposals to go to college now usually are granted, although they may be modified and entry may be delayed a year or two).

Perhaps one can generalize to the effect that when production decisions are moved from the hierarchical capitalist enterprise to the commune, an individual increases his or her own decision-making powers (especially the individual who would have been an ordinary worker near the bottom of the capitalist hierarchy). However, when consumption decisions are moved from the household to the commune, a person loses some individuality.

A few words might be said about the kind of man or woman who makes a good kibbutz member. Most students of the kibbutz agree that it takes a person who is flexible and mature, capable of making all the adjustments necessary in what in some respects is like a large family. The outside observer might also believe that it requires a person who is an idealist. But there are people in the kibbutz movement who deny this. They say that they have seen many people outside the movement who are just as idealistic as those within it. They contend that the kibbutz member is simply a person who values togetherness so much that he is willing to give up a little of his freedom in making individual decisions. They maintain that people under capitalism are always alone; the kibbutz member is not.

It appears, however, that a measure of idealism is required in a member of the kibbutz if he is to remain concerned about the movement as a whole. It is true that each kibbutz gains some strength by being a part of the movement of kibbutzim. All, for example, borrow at lower interest rates because their loans are guaranteed by the movement. Concern for other kibbutzim, therefore, might be generated by self-interest rather than idealism. But the established, well-off kibbutz knows that in all likelihood it will give to the new and weak kibbutzim much more than it receives. So concern for the movement does require the member of a prosperous kibbutz to be something of an idealist.

Kibbutz members often worry about their isolation from the lives of the rest of the people. They wonder whether the kibbutz can survive in a culture which is indifferent to the kind of life they value.

The Future of the Kibbutz

The kibbutz movement could decline or disappear in either of two ways. The movement might decline in membership, or it might gradually modify itself so that it became a system of cooperatives or even in some respects a capitalistic system.

In absolute numbers the kibbutzim are making slow gains. In 1957, there were 83,942 members, and in 1967, there were 93,210, living in 225 kibbutzim. As a percentage of the total population kibbutz membership is slowly declining, from 7.15 percent in 1948 to 3.93 percent in 1967.[45] (But this decline occurred during a period of heavy immigration from Muslim countries, countries without youth movements and with close-knit family groups to which the life of the kibbutz seems particularly strange.) At present about 80 percent of the children return to live on the kibbutz after military service, and new members are recruited from youth movements in Israel and abroad. Established kibbutzim usually maintain their membership without difficulty. On the other hand, new kibbutzim, frequently established in harsh desert environments, are experiencing recruitment difficulties.

Modifications of the system have occurred in some kibbutzim. For example, some children now sleep at home with their parents

[45]Ibid., pp. 200–1.

on some kibbutz farms, the personal budget for expenditure on clothing has been introduced in a few places, hired labor has been employed (although there are kibbutzim that have given up hired labor after having once used it).

The economist is inclined to think that the kibbutzim may lose people in increasing numbers to the cities. It is generally agreed that the present-day standard of living for kibbutz members is as high as that of skilled city workers. This means that the unskilled kibbutz members, of whom there probably are relatively few, enjoy a higher standard of living than they would enjoy in the city. As a consequence, such members probably are not motivated to leave the kibbutz because of economic considerations. But the Work Coordinator, the Treasurer, the Branch Managers, however, might increase their incomes by taking managerial posts in city enterprises. In particular, those members who now receive technical education at universities and establish industries on the kibbutzim might find the transition from kibbutz to city rather easy. Those concerned about the future of the movement, however, do not seem to worry about these economic considerations.

The student of the kibbutz can draw up two lists, one that gives reasons suggesting why the kibbutz movement may thrive, the other suggesting why it may disappear.[46] Let us consider some of the factors.

The kibbutz may flourish because it has roots, because it has prestige, and because it is dynamic. It has put down roots in two generations of existence, and in many kibbutzim a third generation is beginning to play a role. For members born and reared on the kibbutz, communal ways—the dining hall, the children's quarter, the general assembly of members—are normal. Secondly, the kibbutz has immense prestige, as a consequence of its achievements in agriculture and because of the leadership it has provided. Finally, the kibbutz is dynamic, constantly improving its agriculture, developing industry, and changing its consumption patterns as the preferences of its members undergo change.

The kibbutz may decline because the new generation is too pragmatic, because it is insufficiently concerned for the movement as a whole, because it may lack respect for manual labor, and because women generally have remained oriented toward the household. Some members of the younger generation are impatient with their elders' discussions of ideology. How, for example,

[46]The lists presented here are largely taken from the ideas of Mrs. Yehudit Simhoni of Kibbutz Geva, although my words undoubtedly differ from hers.

should large gifts of money to members be treated, or gifts of automobiles or TV sets? Should they become common property? The younger generation tends to opt for more practical solutions to those questions. If principles are ignored, however, if each question is dealt with in a completely practical way, a time may come when the kibbutz will no longer be a collective body, when it will have modified itself into a cooperative or into some other form of organization.

A second reason why the kibbutz may decline is that the younger generation seems to be kibbutz-oriented as opposed to movement-oriented. A younger member is likely to be more concerned with the well-being of his own kibbutz rather than with the movement as a whole. But through the movement the kibbutzim provide aid and support for one another, and this is particularly important when the kibbutz finds itself in a capitalistic environment, indifferent to the fate of kibbutzim. Perhaps more serious than a lack of identification with the movement is "the tendency in the large kibbutz for the centrifugal forces within the kibbutz to grow and for the individual to be so occupied with his own work, his own family, his own social circle and his own interests that he loses sight of the organic totality of kibbutz life."[47] The kibbutz may have to struggle constantly against a tendency for its membership to draw away from the movement toward the kibbutz itself.

A third reason that might affect the future of the Israeli kibbutz concerns a loss of respect for manual labor. As a consequence of industrial innovation in the kibbutz, and because many of the brightest young people are studying engineering and science, older members fear that the younger generation will not be willing to share in the manual work of the kibbutz during the fruit harvest, for example, when all must work long hours if labor is not to be hired. If efforts at equality of work were to be abandoned, in order to keep the qualified technical people on the kibbutz, then the justification for equality of consumption would be undermined. If an engineer is too good to wait on table, then perhaps he is entitled to a higher pay, reflecting his larger contribution. At present, few see a lack of respect for manual labor, but some fear that it may emerge as the kibbutz moves from agriculture (where almost everyone works with his hands) to industry (which requires a large complement of scientists, designers, and engineers).

[47]Leon, *The Kibbutz*, p. 73.

Finally, many women on the kibbutzim have not reconciled themselves to a situation in which their children sleep away from home at night, so that a number of kibbutzim, as previously indicated, are now building apartments with bedrooms for children. (It is difficult to understand this concession as a violation of a principle vital to the kibbutz, however, when the children spend their waking hours just as before.) More serious is the fact that "women's work" on the kibbutz has continued to be uninteresting. While males have had the excitement of pioneering new methods in agriculture and developing new industries, women mostly have had the tasks of (collectively) cooking the meals, doing the laundry, mending the clothing, and caring for the children. In 1966, a survey showed that 28 percent of the women in one kibbutz movement wanted to change their work and that 34 percent did not originally want the jobs they were doing.[48] In recent years, efforts have been made to modernize and professionalize the work of women, but without much success.

An original theory of the kibbutz was that with communal dining halls, laundries, and child-rearing facilities, women would be freed for careers and participation in the leadership of the movement. But women, with some notable exceptions, have not taken advantage of the opportunities opened up by the kibbutz.[49] They have largely confined themselves to the traditional pursuits of women, and the primary interests of many have been the household rather than the kibbutz or the kibbutz movement. It is possible that women kibbutz members might prefer traditional "homes" and as a consequence they might persuade their husbands to leave the kibbutz, or try to modify the kibbutz to meet their desires.

Zionism and the Kibbutz

To what extent do past successes and future prospects of the kibbutz depend on Jewish nation-making? The kibbutz has been an integral part of efforts to colonize Palestine and establish the nation of Israel. Secular communes elsewhere in the world have not endured. Could the reason for this be that human nature is such that collective living and economic equality are not sufficient as ends-in-themselves? Perhaps a larger goal, like nation-making,

[48] Ibid., p. 133.
[49] Ibid., Chapter X.

may be required to draw people's interests away from the household toward the commune and the communal movement.

The Problem with Incentives

The economist starts out with the hypothesis that the matter of work incentives probably will be the major problem in a communal way of life. We have seen that the Israelis do not seem to have encountered this problem in the kibbutz, perhaps because of the surrounding capitalist economy which absorbs those not content with collective life. It would seem, therefore, that the major threat to the kibbutz movement appears to be the attraction of the household. The members of an enduring commune must be persuaded or induced to devote themselves to the commune and the communal movement and to resist the centrifugal forces tending to disintegrate the commune into disparate households.

Twin Oaks

As mentioned in Chapter 12, Twin Oaks, a commune founded by eight people in 1967, consciously modeled itself on Walden Two. Five years later Kathleen Kinkade, one of the original founders, wrote a history of the community.[50]

Organization and Control

The general direction of the community is in the hands of a three-person Board of Planners. "Their job is to appoint and replace managers, settle conflicts between managers, decide touchy questions having to do with ideology, and replace themselves when their eighteen-month terms expire." The system of planners, said Ms. Kinkade, is deliberately self-perpetuating in order to protect the original goals of Twin Oaks.[51]

Most of the decisions affecting the daily lives of the members of Twin Oaks are made not by the Planners but by the Managers—members who are in charge of various areas of work. There are Managers of Labor, Food, Clothing, Health, Construction, Maintenance, and so on. "Managerial positions are continually being

---

[50]Kathleen Kinkade, *A Walden Two Experiment: The First Five Years of Twin Oaks Community* (New York: William Morrow & Company, 1973).

[51]Ibid., pp. 50, 242.

created, and are awarded on the basis of interest and work." "We pair authority with responsibility, and we are usually short of manager.... What the term means here is 'person responsible.' Anybody willing to take responsibility can get it."[52]

Rules at Twin Oaks are known as the "Behavioral Code." Examples include such regulations as: "The person who does the work gets the credit"; "Do not speak negatively about other members behind their backs."[53] Kathleen Kinkade is a little defensive about their undemocratic government. She writes, "We divide the labor—some people have the labor of making governmental decisions—but we do not seriously have hierarchies."[54] Managers can be overruled by the Board of Planners, and the Board in its turn can be overruled by the membership as a whole, but such occasions are exceptional. (Here we see that Twin Oaks is less an oligarchy than Walden Two: Skinner gave no indication that members in Walden Two could overrule the Planners. Even in Twin Oaks the members do not elect and cannot recall the Board of Planners.) Kinkade writes:

> What keeps our system from turning into a tiresome bureaucracy is its simplicity—that decisions can be made swiftly by at most three people, and usually by a single manager, using his or her own judgment. What keeps it from being a dictatorship is that there is nothing to gain from being dictatorial. All decisions that are of interest to the group as a whole are discussed with the group as a whole. No legislation can be put across unless members are willing to go along with it.... In spite of our hierarchical-sounding governmental setup, we are anti-authoritarian in both principle and practice. Bossiness quickly dies out as a personal trait, because the group does not reward it with obedience. Bossy people are simply avoided; bossy managers can't get people to work with them.[55]

(Of course bossiness does not go over well on the shop floor of an American capitalist enterprise either; it is not part of the American culture. But no one would argue that the "suggestions" of the

---

[52] Ibid., pp. 45, 50–55, 191.

[53] Ibid., pp. 47, 57, 150.

[54] Ibid., p. 149.

[55] Kathleen Kinkade, *A Walden Two Experiment: The First Five Years of Twin Oaks Community* (New York: William Morrow & Co., 1973), p. 55. Reprinted by permission of the publisher.

capitalist foreman lack authority.) Needless to say, the above argument, that the interests of leaders and followers are identical, that there is nothing to gain from being dictatorial, is a standard defense of nondemocratic government. Moreover, just as the hierarchy of the capitalist enterprise is generally acceptable because the dissatisfied worker can quit and work elsewhere, so the oligarchy at Twin Oaks is less oppressive because members are free to leave. A self-appointed Board of Planners for an entire economy would be quite another matter.

At Twin Oaks, several devices for the distribution of jobs and the assignment of labor credits were tried. The most recent method is to have each member list all the available jobs, ordered according to his or her personal preferences. Labor-clerical people then make out a work schedule for each person, and attempt to come as close to the individual's preferences as possible. A person receives high labor credits for work he or she finds disagreeable to do. Kinkade writes, "Two people might be shoveling manure side by side and the person who enjoys the work is getting less credit for it than the person who doesn't." An average labor credit in Twin Oaks is worth one hour, and community members work about forty hours a week.[56]

It is regrettable that Ms. Kinkade did not describe more fully in her book how the system at Twin Oaks works in practice. Even though labor credits for a given job vary from individual to individual (in effect, the community attempts to capture the producer's surplus of each of its members), the average labor credit for a particular kind of work must reflect, in some way, demand and supply for the work—with demand determined by the planners and managers, and information about supply revealed by the job preference orderings of the individual workers. One wonders whether a member would lie in order to increase his labor credits for a job. For example, what if most members dislike hoeing in the garden in midsummer, while one member likes it? If such a member puts this job high on his preference ordering, he probably would get a lot of it to do, with few labor credits for his efforts. If he liked lying in the sun (leisure) even more than hoeing in the sun, he might list hoeing lower on his preference ordering and earn closer to the average labor credits for the job. It is difficult to believe that when members list their work preferences, they fail to forecast the average labor credits per job, as well as the personal labor credit that depends on where they put the job on their

[56]Ibid., pp. 41–45.

preference ordering. One also wonders whether a group of members ever engage in concerted action to increase labor credits for a job. Members who enjoy putting in a garden in the spring, for example, but who enjoy leisure even more, might agree to develop a public aversion to gardening when they submit their job preferences orderings, in order to get more labor credits for gardening. Do the labor-clerical people ever adjust the labor credits given for intensity of effort, giving the industrious worker more labor credits per hour in a job than the person who tends to work slowly. It might be done fairly easily when different people get different labor credits for the same hours spent in a work activity.

The Economy

Twin Oaks has not been particularly successful in its agricultural pursuits. Kinkade states, "Everytime we talk about raising chickens, we are up against the fact that we can buy fryers at the supermarket for twenty-seven cents a pound and eggs by the case at thirty cents a dozen." "We noted that our neighboring farmers no longer feel it worth their while to process a great deal of food, but simply buy it from the grocery store as they need it. They garden mostly for summer use." "Every year our population changes a little, and almost all new members come from the city. They are as excited by a newborn calf and a packet of garden seed as I was in 1967, and it is their turn to live out their romance."[57]

Twin Oaks is not particularly successful in its industrial pursuits, either. It makes rope hammocks. Kinkade writes, "The hammocks are a good product, and it is not bad work to make them. Our problem has always been sales."[58] An observer from the outside also stated that the profit margin is quite low.[59] At the time she wrote the above, Kinkade reported that the hammock business accounted for about a third of the income of Twin Oaks.

The members at Twin Oaks go outside their commune to work and dislike this system enormously. As a consequence, work on the outside is done on a rotation system. "Work two months, then quit, and somebody else goes out.... Outside work is required of all members without exception."[60] The men usually get jobs in con-

[57]Ibid., pp. 59–70.
[58]Ibid., p. 72.
[59]Ron E. Roberts, *The New Communes* (Englewood Cliffs, N.J.: Prentice-Hall, 1971), p. 93.
[60]Kinkade, *Walden Two Experiment*, pp. 74–81, 114.

struction work where a high turnover is expected; women work in offices or as waitresses, either getting their jobs through temporary employment agencies or by lying to employers about the length of time they expect to work. The necessity of outside work has been an unpleasant reality at Twin Oaks, and in at least one case, the cause of a bitterly hostile dispute in two membership meetings.

In the early days of Twin Oaks some of its founders and supporters contributed capital and income. One man, for example, provided a free six-year lease on a farm; he also put up $3,000 for the first building they constructed, as well as bought them a cub tractor and paid for the drilling of their first well. A friend of the community sent Twin Oaks $200 a month to get started on.[61] Kathleen Kinkade states in her book that they were not ashamed to receive such donations. Privations at Twin Oaks, severe even with these grants, would have been greater without them. As mentioned in the previous chapter, Skinner in *Walden Two* did not deal with this problem of scarcity.

Indeed, Twin Oaks remains a relatively poor community. In her account Ms. Kinkade speaks of a $1,200 annual per capita income and writes of people who fail to join "because we are not far enough from the bare subsistence level."[62] Why this is so is not entirely clear. One suspects that the farm from the very beginning was poor and run down. It is significant that no information is provided by Ms. Kinkade about the amount of arable land on the farm or its fertility. Farming skills, farm management included, over the years have generally been in short supply. New members often arrive with more enthusiasm than ability, and the rate of turnover is high. (With a membership of 40 when the book was written, the community has lost, "until recently," 1.6 members per month, or 19 a year.[63]) In addition, members have resisted specialization, although there is some evidence of a movement toward the pattern of the Israeli kibbutz, where long-term members tend to specialize, while new members engage in a variety of tasks.[64] The most important aspect, perhaps, is the fact that the members of Twin Oaks have valued leisure and consumption quite highly while valuing work and accumulation less. To be sure, Twin Oaks is not like a hippie commune, whose members tend to

[61]Ibid., pp. 4, 71, 96, 226, 235.
[62]Ibid., pp. 3, 20.
[63]Ibid., p. 108.
[64]Ibid., pp. 45, 64–65, 217.

live for the pleasures of the moment. The people at Twin Oaks, however, have been influenced by the values of the counter-culture. (The average age of a member is 23.5 years; the average education level is two years of college.[65]) Members at Twin Oaks have been determined to enjoy some of the good things in life here and now.[66] Quite a few of their best people left because they felt that the community was not getting ahead as rapidly as it might; these people wanted everyone to work harder, more efficiently, and more conscientiously, and to invest a higher proportion of their resources. Forty hours, after all, is not a very long workweek for people who are trying to build something for the future, whether it is a farm or a business or a professional practice or a scholarly career. To their credit, the members of Twin Oaks have faced up to this issue and have discussed it frequently. This is in contrast to Skinner, who depicted an affluent commune with a short workweek with no period of belt-tightening.

Certainly, if Twin Oaks were going to grow in membership at a higher rate so that groups could splinter off and start new communes, so that their dream of a *movement* of scientific communalism were to be realized, a shift in values from leisure and consumption to work and capital formation would have to occur. If communalism is to compete successfully with other forms of organization and attract the masses, it will have to offer a competitive material standard of living. This means hard work, and capital formation. Young people may embrace asceticism as a protest against their elders' materialism. When they get older, they begin to value material comforts more as their years are accompanied by a certain quota of physiological discomforts and they recognize that material goods can check the loss of choices which would otherwise occur as their physical strength declines.

In contrast to the relatively harmonious, utopian community depicted by Skinner in *Walden Two*, Ms. Kinkade depicts the conflicts and disputes that occurred and probably do still occur at Twin Oaks.[67] Food is often a matter of dispute—health foods versus conventional foods. As in the Israeli kibbutzim, members at Twin Oaks debated the question of communal clothing versus a personal cash clothing allowance. There were disagreements over dormitory living quarters, with their traffic noise, versus private rooms. Members differed over standards of workmanship, cleanli-

---

[65]Ibid., p. 13.
[66]Ibid., pp. 30, 212, 226, 252.
[67]Ibid., pp. 28, 85–89, 91, 100, 107–8, 127, 148.

ness, and courtesy. (Cleaner than the hippie communes, Twin Oaks apparently falls considerably short of middle class norms. Ms. Kinkade writes, "Cleanliness is a problem, but we do enough cleaning so that chaos doesn't quite overtake us."[68]) Work versus leisure was a matter of contention, and there were quarrels over who should have to work outside the commune. Then, too, should a commune *select* good members or *create* them? Many of the disputes are essentially arguments about current consumption (leisure included) versus capital formation: meat on the table now, or construction of a new building, private rooms now or later, quality of life or expansion?[69] And the matter of government is a source of disgruntlement: members disagree over appointments to office at Twin Oaks.[70]

A Single Generation Commune

Twin Oaks has conspicuously failed in two respects. Sporadic efforts to rear children have failed, and they cannot yet support and do not have old people. When new members brought children with them, disagreements often arose concerning the location of authority over the children, and, less often, over questions of children-rearing policy itself.[71] Kinkade writes about a child, Timothy, who "with no regulation and no behavioral engineering ... became a little spoiled and a lot of the adults ceased to enjoy him." She sums up the experiences with the nine children they had at one time or another: "Parental worries, parental jealousy, community theory, community inexperience." Commune members do hope to rear children fairly soon in the future when Twin Oaks has proper facilities, as well as adults who fully believe in communal child rearing. And they hope to be well enough off some years from now to care for their parents when the latter are too old to care for themselves.[72] Needless to say, for the communal life to become a wildly accepted way of life, it must adequately provide for the care of old people as well as children.

We mentioned earlier the high turnover at Twin Oaks. Why do people come and why do they leave? People come, writes Ms.

---

[68]Ibid., p. 247. Cf. Richard Fairfiled, *Communes USA: A Personal Tour* (Baltimore: Penguin Books, 1972), p. 81.

[69]Kinkade, *Walden Two Experiment,* pp. 89–91, 212–13, 226.

[70]Ibid., p. 148.

[71]Ibid., pp. 130–46.

[72]Ibid., p. 224.

Kinkade, because of their dreams, their dreams of a noble, brighter future for mankind, of changes in the inner reaches of the soul, of cultural changes, particularly in traditional sex and family roles. "But commonest of all is the personal dream, the dream of no longer being lonely. Whatever else brings people to community, the hope of a compatible mate or a close, warm group of friends is usually just underneath the surface...."[73] Twin Oaks in the past tended to attract many emotionally disturbed people, and in due course had to set up a fairly elaborate and stringent selection procedure. The commune now seeks to screen out the unstable, the mystics, the weak, the capable but intolerant, and families with children (at least for the present). At one time there was a $200 entrance fee, "to discourage the use of Twin Oaks as a crash pad and to indicate a degree of commitment among the people who joined."[74]

A few people leave Twin Oaks because they are expelled: One man was expelled for not working; another for attempted theft. Others are forced out by community disapproval.[75] Of those who leave voluntarily, some go out to look for new adventures, some go because of ideological differences, and some because, as Ms. Kinkade puts it, "We are not Utopia yet. We don't have a perfect life. There are things missing. There are problems we haven't solved. We have not achieved Walden Two." Finally, "a large percentage of the people who leave the community do so to escape loneliness. Many find love and happiness here, but some do not, and watching happy couples all around them only increases their desperate alienation."[76]

What of the future of Twin Oaks? One suspects that the future of this commune depends very much on Ms. Kathleen Kinkade. Apart from her daughter, who has been an intermittent member of Twin Oaks, Ms. Kinkade is the only remaining original founder. From all evidence, she is a remarkable individual—a person with a dream, yet flexible and pragmatic, capable of compromise, with a sense of humor—and she is determined to keep the community together. She bridges the differences between those who want to build for the future and those who want to enjoy the present. She writes:

[73] Ibid., p. 2.
[74] Ibid., pp. 34, 103–8, 145.
[75] Ibid., pp. 29, 33, 80–81.
[76] Ibid., pp. 108–10.

It is the people who want to escape who are unable to deal with the realities of commune living. For there is no escape in a commune! Responsibility is a fact of human society. Communes face it in a grimmer form than ordinary citizens do, in that they accept even the responsibility for holding their very society together against odds.
Escapist fantasies are bad for communities, but dreams are fundamental to their existence. To be successful at community living, you have to keep adjusting your dreams to reality without ever quite giving them up.[77]

The test of the viability of Twin Oaks may come when Kathleen Kinkade is no longer there.

Skinner's Behavioral Engineering at Twin Oaks

In 1938 B. F. Skinner published *The Behavior of Organisms: An Experimental Analysis.* In it he studies "the process of conditioning and its reciprocal process of extinction," in the attempt to find a system of behavior that "can be arrived at only through the kind of experimental analysis to which this book is devoted, in which the parts or aspects of behavior which undergo orderly changes are identified and their mutual relations established." In that book he maintains that "the dynamic properties which are fundamental to a science of behavior can be properly investigated only in the laboratory. Casual or even clinical observation is ill-adapted to the study of processes, as distinct from momentary features." And he points out that "the reader will have noticed that almost no extension to human behavior is made or suggested."[78] More than 30 years later, Skinner then commented on the literature of utopias in his book entitled *Beyond Freedom and Dignity*: "The designs to be found in the utopian literature appeal to certain simplifying principles. They have the merit of emphasizing survival value: Will the utopia work?" He also wrote in that work there is an "advantage in stating objectives in behavioral terms."[79] In be-

[77]Kathleen Kinkade, *A Walden Two Experiment: The First Five Years of Twin Oaks Community* (New York: William Morrow & Co., 1973), p. 2. Reprinted by permission of the publisher.

[78]B. F. Skinner, *The Behavior of Organisms: An Experimental Analysis* (New York: D. Appleton Century, 1938), pp. 61, 433–35, 441.

[79]B. F. Skinner, *Beyond Freedom and Dignity* (Toronto and New York: Bantam/Vintage, 1972), p. 174.

tween these two works, Skinner published his own utopia, *Walden Two*, and contributed the foreword to Kathleen Kinkade's book, *A Walden Two Experiment*.

Communal Science

Given that Walden Two was the model on which Twin Oaks was based, what claims does Skinner actually make for his model of a utopian community? He has a spokesman for Walden Two say: "We do have faith in our power to change human behavior. We can *make* men adequate for group living—to the satisfaction of everybody. That was our faith, but now it is a fact." And he has the same character in the novel assert that "communal science is already a reality."[80] And in his foreword to *A Walden Two Experiment* he writes, "When I wrote *Walden Two* (in 1945), only seven years—and war years at that—had passed since I had published the *Behavior of Organisms*, in which I reported research on the principles used in the design of the community."[81] In this last citation Skinner appears to claim that his utopian model is an application of the principles developed in his *Behavior of Organisms*. Since he explicitly asserts in *Behavior of Organisms* that "almost no extension to human behavior is made or suggested," we have to look in *Walden Two* itself for the experimental analysis and evidence which constitute a communal science. Unfortunately, we will look in vain, for the utopia of Walden Two is not a laboratory and does not contain laboratories for the study of human behavior. Moreover, the objectives sought at Walden Two were not stated in behavioral terms, as Skinner suggests they should be, and, in fact, the objectives sought by the leadership of Walden Two were exceedingly vague and amorphous. In the novel, for example, a visitor at Walden Two observes that the spokesman for the commune is nervous:

> He was vulnerable. He was treading on sanctified ground, and I was pretty sure he had not established the value of most of these practices in an experimental fashion. He could scarcely have done so in the short space of ten years. He was working on faith and it bothered him.[82]

[80]Skinner, *Walden Two*, pp. 196, 293.

[81]Kinkade, *Walden Two Experiment*, p. viii.

[82]B. F. Skinner, *Walden Two* (New York: Macmillan Publishing, 1973), p. 110. Reprinted by permission of the publisher.

The visitor pursued this point later:

> "You use the word 'experiment' a great deal," I said, "but do you really experiment at all? Isn't one feature of good scientific method missing from all the cases you have described?"
>
> "You mean the 'control'," said the spokesman.

In the novel, the spokesman then goes on to discuss the problem of experimentation with the children.

> We're too small to keep two groups of children separate. Some day it may be possible—we shall have controls to satisfy the most academic statistician. And by that time they may be necessary, too, for we shall have reached the point of dealing with very subtle differences. At present they aren't necessary. To go to all the trouble of running controls would be to make a fetish of scientific method.

The visitor, unfortunately, accepts the argument:

> In the early days of any science, it may be possible to make extraordinary speed without elaborate statistical control. A new technique may permit a straightforward observation which is sometimes as direct as our sensory contact with nature.[83]

The "casual observation" that Skinner rejected in his *Behavior of Organisms* here becomes an approved "straightforward observation."

One reason that Skinner failed to produce an experimental communal science is because the objectives sought at Walden Two were imprecisely stated. Nor were they stated in terms of observable behavior. In talking about "experimentation with life," the spokesman for Walden Two asserts that what counts is "whether the relation between cause and effect is obvious. The happiness and equanimity of our people are *obviously* related to the self-control they have acquired." At another point, he speaks of "heaven *on earth,* better known as peace of mind."[84] One might ask if feelings such as happiness, equanimity, heaven on earth, and peace of mind can be experimentally observed?

[83] Skinner, *Walden Two*, pp. 175–77. Reprinted by permission of the publisher.
[84] Ibid., pp. 107, 177, 291–92.

The only detailed experiment depicted in Walden Two is a technique employed to eliminate jealousy in children. (The precise behavior indicative of jealousy is not specified.) At the toss of a coin, a lucky group of tired and hungry children sit down to eat their soup while another equally tired and hungry group stand and look on for five minutes before they are allowed to eat; the latter presumably learn to wait without envy. The whole thing reads rather like a parody of scientific method, and it is difficult to take it seriously.[85]

Nor does Skinner answer in *Walden Two* the question of incentives in a communal environment. What is to be done when a member does poor work, or no work at all, in every job he is given. (Recall that in Walden Two the planners rule only through positive reinforcement, never using or threatening to use force.) We are told that such a member would be sent to one of the commune's psychologists. In the event that that did not help, we read in the novel: "We should deal with it somehow. I don't know. You might as well ask what we should do if leprosy broke out. We'd think of something. We aren't helpless."[86] Is this an answer to the standard question about incentives asked of communal anarchists?

Skinner, like Marx, is ambivalent toward government. Recognizing that government relies on force or the threat of force to achieve its objectives, he has his spokesman for Walden Two assert:

> You can't make progress toward the Good Life by political action! Not under *any* current form of government! You must operate upon another level entirely. What you need is a sort of Nonpolitical Action Committee: keep out of politics and away from government except for practical and temporary purposes. It's not a place for men of good will or vision.[87]

Presumably the government at Walden Two, the self-selected Board of Managers with their Walden Code, is temporary, but while it exists it is nondemocratic. We have already mentioned Skinner's classic defense of oligarchy—people wanting to be free of the responsibility of planning, the elite works hard, and so on. Moreover, government at Walden Two was concealed, for where power is not destroyed it is "so diffused that usurpation is practically impossible." Diffused power is little seen. And personal favo-

[85] Ibid., pp. 103–10.
[86] Ibid., pp. 173–74, 272.
[87] Skinner, *Walden Two*, pp. 193–94. Reprinted by permission of the publisher.

ritism "has been destroyed by our cultural engineers."[88] But, finally, "as governmental technology advances, less and less is left to the decisions of governors, anyway. Eventually we shall have no use for Planners at all. The Managers will suffice."[89] The state is to wither away; oligarchy is to be followed by anarchy.

Behavioral Engineering

In Skinner's foreword to Kinkade's *A Walden Two Experiment*, we learn that, while he admired the persistence of members of Twin Oaks, he did not credit them with the application of a scientific behaviorism. He writes:

> Is it a Walden Two experiment? Certainly it is not much like the experiment described in the book. The life portrayed in Walden Two was the goal of Twin Oaks, but it was not approached through the application of scientific principles. Kate and her friends simply muddled through.[90]

But Ms. Kinkade does tell us something about the use of positive reinforcement—the approval of peers, peaceful and pleasant human relations, persuasion, and the talking over of a work problem with the Labor Manager.[91]

Kinkade also informs us that negative reinforcement became a necessity in the communal life at Twin Oaks. Indeed, they institutionalized criticism. At one time they appointed a Generalized Bastard to relay criticism to a member whose activities were disapproved of by the other members. At another time they had a Bitch Box within which written criticisms could be placed, with a Bitch Manager to relay the contents of the note (but not the note itself) to the member concerned. Twin Oaks tried systematic sessions of Group Criticism, an idea borrowed from Oneida Community.[92] Of course, they, like Walden Two, had rules, and, finally, in some instances, they resorted to expulsion. It is amusing to observe that Kathleen Kinkade alludes directly to the incident in Walden Two where the spokesman for the community responds to a question

---

[88] Ibid., pp. 235, 272.
[89] Ibid.
[90] Foreword to Kinkade, *Walden Two Experiment*, p. x.
[91] Kinkade, *Walden Two Experiment*, pp. 45–46, 57, 150.
[92] Ibid., pp. 57, 150–58.

about a member who works poorly, or not at all. Unlike the Walden Two representative, she says: "We are often asked the same question, but our answer is a little more definite, probably because our techniques of behavioral engineering aren't worked out quite so well as they were in the book. 'We would ask him to leave,' is what we reply." She also tells of forcing a member out of the Community through the "pressure of disapproval." She concedes that it is "not my idea of creating a new society through positive reinforcement," and observes that "it is too easy to envision our precarious financial situation crumbling under too great a load of parasites."[93]

Very interesting is Kinkade's idea on the use (as positive reinforcement) of tokens convertible into sweets or privileges, as is now practiced in mental hospitals and schools. Twin Oaks could not vary material rewards according to behavior. "Do we not distribute equally every reinforcement we can get our hands on?"[94]

Also interesting is Ms. Kinkade's response to questions about their experimentation. "Was not the whole community a grand experiment?"[95] The critic's answer must be in the affirmative, but this is not the tightly controlled experimentation dealt with in Skinner's *Behavior of Organisms*. Kinkade goes on to say, "Well, Twin Oaks has its share of cultural trivia," and cites the commune use of daylight saving time in the winter, a germ-free, temperature-controlled baby crib, the non-use of surnames (to help develop a sense of community), and behavior graphs (for example, to help reduce the incidence of sarcastic comments). Her concluding observations on these small "experiments" lead one to believe, however, that Kathleen Kinkade has thought more deeply about "communal science" than has Skinner:

> Do we take all this seriously? We do and we don't. We know very well that the games we make up are dealing very simplistically with complicated behavior and that we do not control the genuine reinforcers at all. I suspect that what really goes on behind these projects is the desire to be liked and approved of. If we succeed in changing an undesirable behavior, splendid. If we don't, at least the group knows that we are not defending

[93] Ibid., p. 45. See also pp. 28, 29, 80–81.
[94] Ibid., p. 149.
[95] Ibid., pp. 257–65.

the behavior but are making an attempt to change it. It makes a difference in how we feel about each other.[96]

The continued existence of rules and government at Twin Oaks bothers Ms. Kinkade. Along with others in the communal movement, she thinks that people ought to be able to get along with each other in the absence of formal constraints and hierarchies. Part of the reason for government at Twin Oaks, she believes, is "sheer poverty."

> Just as we couldn't get good work behavior for making stretchers until we improved the working conditions, just so we can't really run our entire community on positive reinforcement until a higher degree of affluence makes it possible for us to get rid of some of the rules.[97]

In addition to overcoming poverty, they must reduce desires.

> In order to make even an adequate supply of anything go around, it is necessary for everyone to have simple and modest tastes and desires. That means the creation of an entirely new culture—noncompetitive, nonconsumerist.[98]

Until Twin Oaks succeeds in making "a decent supply of desirable things available," at the same time "keeping people's desires within bounds," they will have to "continue to legislate rough equality."

There is irony in the history of Walden Two and Twin Oaks. A noted behavioral scientist writes a novel, *Walden Two,* which purports to supply the design of a scientific commune, one founded on the principles of behavioral engineering. More than two decades later, when a wave of communalism sweeps the country, a number of groups choose the novel as the source book for their basic ideas, the best known of these groups being the community of Twin Oaks. A remarkably thoughtful and detached ac-

---

[96]Kathleen Kinkade, *A Walden Two Experiment: The First Five Years of Twin Oaks Community* (New York: William Morrow & Co., 1973), pp. 264–65. Reprinted by permission of the publisher.

[97]Kinkade, *A Walden Two Experiment,* p. 57. Reprinted by permission of the publisher.

[98]Kinkade, *A Walden Two Experiment,* p. 58. Reprinted by permission of the publisher.

count of the experiences of the latter is written by its leading figure, Ms. Kathleen Kinkade. She is said to think that Skinner is a genius,[99] yet finds little real help in *Walden Two* and glimpses that their own experiments in behavioral engineering should not be taken seriously as science. Twin Oaks encounters most of the traditional problems of utopian communities—the problems of scarcity and the intractability of human nature.

Hippie Communes

As one rejects the consumerist (materialist) society that one observes around one, the hippie communalist, with consistency, rejects a society devoted to work and capital formation. He proposes to live for the moment, to cultivate leisure, and his or her emphasis is on freedom—freedom from responsibility.

Work in a hippie commune is done unsystematically and frequently not done at all. An observer at Cold Mountain Farm, a hippie commune, in New York writes, "the farm was all but deserted. The work fell entirely on the shoulders of a few people"; in the summer "the garden wasn't being weeded. The grass was growing higher and higher." When some people left Cold Mountain Farm to live in another commune in southern Vermont, there were "the same kinds of problems as at Cold Mountain, like the same small group doing all the work and taking care of the lazy transient people who only suck energy from the community *and contribute* almost nothing."[100]

Part of the difficulty experienced by people in the hippie communes is a lack of knowledge of agriculture. Such communalists do not know, for example, the season for planting, the high cost of hand labor, the type of equipment or kinds of insecticides to use. And little systematic effort is made to acquire such knowledge, or recruit people who have it. In winter hippie communes are often caught unprepared with inadequate food supplies to get them through until spring.

In a hippie commune lack of organization and structure is a matter of principle. Members are generally free to join as they choose, and to work when and if they want at whatever activities attract them at that moment. There is little or no leadership and no hierarchy; group decisions, when made at all, tend to be by consensus. Most of the time, rules are conspicuous by their ab-

---

[99] Fairfield, *Communes USA*, p. 98.
[100] Joyce Gardiner, in Richard Fairfield, *Communes USA*, pp. 41–42, 50–51, 54.

sence with the exception being that occasionally a pressing problem leads to the creation of a rule. For example, at Sheep Ridge Ranch in California members had a rule that "no tools can leave the shop." Enforcement to that rule is lax, however, as indicated by a member of the commune who said:"Let's put it this way: there's a couple of people who know the combination of the lock."[101]

With little work and little organization, life at hippie communes tends to be austere and disorderly. Amenities are few, litter and trash common, arrangements for sanitation primitive and frequently inadequate, and the consumption of drugs (and liquor) high.[102] Members live on the resources they bring with them, which often are scanty, on aid from benefactors and families, and on welfare checks and food stamps.[103] Life could be described as summers of fun, along with a varying amount of work, and winters of boredom and dissatisfaction.[104] The population of the communities fluctuates accordingly, being frequently crowded in the summer and dwindling to a handful during the worst of the winter.[105]

Open Land Communes

An interesting variant of the hippie commune is the open-land community. Morning Star Ranch and Sheep Ridge Ranch in California and Tolstay Farm in Washington were developed on the principle that the land belongs to the people and that people should be free to occupy it and erect such housing as they want.[106] Sometimes meals are eaten communally; at other times, families or groups function as separate households in their own quarters. But land is open, "access is denied to no one."

> The land itself selects the people. Those who do not work hard to build shelter and provide for their basic needs do not survive on the land. If the land gets over-crowded, people leave or spread out.[107]

[101] Fairfield, *Communes USA*, pp. 283–84.

[102] Ibid., pp. 170, 187, 191, 245–48, 267, 273.

[103] Ibid., pp. 165, 205, 207, 235–36, 280, 287.

[104] Ibid., pp. 179, 196, 221, 279. "After a brief summer of orgies and fun in the sun, the long winter sets in and darkness brings dissatisfaction and disillusionment."

[105] Ibid., pp. 243–44.

[106] Ibid., pp. 242–90.

[107] Richard Fairfield, *Communes USA: A Personal Tour*. (New York: Penguin Books, 1972), p. 242. Copyright © Alternatives Foundation 1971. Reprinted by permission of Penguin Books.

In an open-land commune, land is not allocated through the price system nor is it allocated through an administrative device. There is no land manager, no land committee, nor even a general meeting. Occupancy is free. It is anarchy, pure and simple, with the results being pretty much what the skeptic would expect: disorder and problems of sanitation.

The "anarchic crash-pad mentality,"[108] even without the ideology of open land, has contributed more than anything else to the weakness of the hippie commune as an institution. An open-door policy exists; most residents feel it would be unacceptable to refuse admission to potential members. For example, Drop City in Colorado had an open-door policy and was inundated "by hordes of teenage runaways, thrill seekers, sightseers and miscellaneous dropouts—mostly of the irresponsible variety." By the fall of 1969 "conditions got so bad that even the crashers couldn't stand it (no food, no maintenance, plenty of hostility). So everyone pulled out."[109] The more stable residents frequently debated the visitor question, and sometimes agreed to limit visitation to a maximum of three days or to weekends (in the daytime) only. But even when they settled on limitations of this sort, they found themselves with an "inability to turn people away."[110]

Because members in general tend to be irresponsible, short-sighted, and transient and because of the problems associated with visitors, the typical hippie commune endures only a few months. Olompali Ranch in California, for example, existed just 20 months. (In actuality it was the death of two small children in an unfenced pool that precipitated the closure, but even before this tragedy "the relationships between adults were often strained and abrasive. The pressures and diverse aims had taken their toll; disparaging remarks punctuated nearly every conversation."[111])

A factor contributing to the weakness of the structure of the hippie commune is undoubtedly the anti-intellectualism of the counter-culture. Sensitivity is everything; science, technology, and thought are anathemas. Hence an aversion to form and structure. But formal institutions which have been developed over the decades and centuries often represent the accumulated wisdom of

---

[108] Elia Katz, *Armed Love* (New York: Holt, Rinehart and Winston, 1971), p. 21.

[109] Fairfield, *Communes USA*, p. 204. At New Buffalo in New Mexico "the open-armed philosophy of love that welcomed one and all had been beaten and flogged by every insensitive and spoiled kid in the country," Ibid., p. 188.

[110] Ibid., pp. 201, 208–9, 213.

[111] Ibid., pp. 238–40.

mankind. Negative responses, constraints on people's behavior, frequently reflect bitter experiences in the past which taught men some of the necessities of good interpersonal relationships. And educational bodies attempt to transmit some of people's earlier experiences to young people so that they will not waste their youth repeating the errors of their parents and ancestors. (This is not to say that existing institutions are never faulty or outdated. The remedy, however, is not to discard them heedlessly, but to analyze them carefully in order to decide whether they should be remodelled or replaced, and, if the latter, what alternative has the highest probability of success.)

The need for structure and for a solidly realistic approach to communal living has been recognized by Richard Fairfield, a sympathetic observer of the movement and editor of a periodical entitled *The Modern Utopia*. He writes, "People have to learn to say 'no'.... There are times when we have to say 'no' not only for our own good but for everyone else's as well.... 'Community' means working out problems with others, not just doing what you want to do. It means having to compromise and having to do some things that may be disagreeable."[112] And it means not pretending that utopia is already a reality.[113] Fairfield states:

> People who are new to each other and refuse to develop any sort of structure, group consensus, or methods of dealing with problems inevitably become enemies rather than friends. The larger the size of the group, the worse the problem, and the greater the need for structure.... Three basic rules of thumb for new communes organizing are: (1) the more people, the more structure; (2) the less thoroughly members know and understand each other, the more structure; and (3) the less time people spend together, the more structure.[114]

Other Contemporary Communes

Like the hippie communes in some respects but different in others are the religious-occult communities, service communities (services to the poor, drug addicts, and so on), and the group marriage communities. The religious communes seem to be more effective

---

[112]Ibid., pp. 213–14, 270.

[113]Ibid., p. 303.

[114]Fairfield, *Communes USA*, p. 286. Copyright © Alternatives Foundation 1971. Reprinted by permission of Penguin Books.

in controlling visitors and screening applicants. For example, in California the Ananda Cooperative Community, devoted to meditation and yoga, charges visitors nominal rates which are based on the length of stay and the amount of time facilities at Ananda are used. The Lama Foundation in New Mexico, similarly devoted to meditation and yoga, charges $660 for six months of support and tuition ($360 for room and board, $300 for tuition), and does not allow those who want to take up residence at Lama to build winter housing until they have been there an entire working season.[115] On the other hand, the Catholic Worker Farm at Tivoli in New York has found it difficult to select its residents. Established "to provide a home away from the city for the poor and needy regardless of religion, race or creed," the Farm depends primarily on donations for support, although able-bodied members share in the work and the need for space and privacy has been recognized. At the same time, one of the leaders observes that "we are a community of need here ... which means we avoid some problems but we also get problems that could be avoided by weeding people out."[116] At Cro Research Organization in Oregon, a group marriage commune usually known as Crow, visitors are asked to make a donation of $3.00 for each day they stay. At the Family, as they call themselves, in New Mexico, a rule against long hair and drugs "eliminates most of the hip types right there."[117]

Two particular problems in the group marriage communes concern the development of exclusive attachments between members and an excess demand for sexual partners. Strictly interpreted, group marriage calls for a communism of personal relations and sexual activities. It seeks to eliminate what one spokesman calls "possessiveness and unhealthy attachments." But what if exclusive ties between pairs do form while some individuals fail to obtain partners? Such a situation occurred at Crow when one married couple was allowed to be strictly monogamous, leaving four men and three women to sleep around, and five other men to occupy what was known as the "men's dormitory." None of the members with whom a visitor spoke "felt this to be a very happy arrangement—neither for the five men who were without sleeping partners, nor for the three 'liberated' females who were

[115]Ibid., pp. 115, 152–53.
[116]Ibid., pp. 334–44.
[117]Ibid., pp. 313, 318–19.

being continuously propositioned." One girl observed: "We need more women now. I could spend all my time in bed."[118]

In another group marriage commune, Harrod West in Berkeley, California, couples and singles were not to demand exclusive rights with each other, but it was sometimes difficult.

> Bill was pretty tight.... He was always pushing for everything to be on schedule. They had this elaborate rotating partners schedule. You had to sleep with whomever you were assigned on the list, whether you felt like it or not that particular night. Bill liked this system. He was afraid if it were done more freely, he might get left out.[119]

Communes: Durability and Weaknesses

Communes seem to endure when they have religious ties that set them apart from others or when they play a unique role in nation-making, when they are structured (with formal patterns of membership selection and decision making), and when their people are hard-working, realistic, and know how to live together through compromise. The durability of communal life frequently is threatened by the attraction of the household as a living unit and by a dependence on unusually dedicated if not charismatic leaders; the commune is weakened by dreams of perfection along with difficulty in accepting both scarcity and the intractability of human nature.

---

[118] Ibid., pp. 307–8, 312, 320.

[119] Fairfield, *Communes USA*, pp. 298–300. Copyright © Alternatives Foundation 1971. Reprinted by permission of Penguin Books.

The Chinese Economy

Part IV

Introduction to Part Four

The economy of Mainland China under the Communists is unique. It cannot be considered a Soviet-type economy, even though in its early years the Chinese leaders did follow in Soviet footsteps. Nor does it belong with the communal archipelagoes like the Hutterian colonies, or the Israeli kibbutzim, even though Chinese Party leaders have been much attracted by the ideals of the commune and at one stage sought to establish communal life on a large scale in China. Nonhomogeneous in its vast expanse, volatile and unpredictable through time, the Chinese experiment, or series of experiments, in communism defies classification and makes generalization precarious. Yet the student of alternative economic systems can learn much from the events of its turbulent history.

Chinese Communism

Chapter 14

The goal of equality, of a society without classes, has been so important a factor in China during the last quarter century that "Communism" seems to be more appropriate as a label for this economy than for most others so named. What one observes is something close to cycles—campaigns for equality and mass participation that alternate with efforts to achieve efficiency through the training of specialists, specialists motivated by material rewards and the status accorded to those with technical skills.

A Historical Sketch

From 1949 through 1952, the Chinese regime concerned itself with reconstruction of a war-damaged economy, and devoted itself to the restoration of agricultural and industrial production and the reconstruction of the transport network. At the same time, it proceeded to gain control of the economy. It did this through a number of measures: (1) takeover of enterprises previously owned by the Nationalist Government, thereby capturing much heavy industry (90 percent of iron and steel output, 67 percent of electric power, 45 percent of cement output, and so on), (2) state trading in the major commodities, (3) price and wage controls and taxation, and (4) control over banking.

Perhaps the most interesting change in institutions at that time was land reform. The land, draft animals, implements, and houses of the landlords were confiscated as was some of the land owned but not worked by the rich peasants. These assets then were distributed among the poor peasants and landless laborers. "The result, however, was not egalitarianism; the rich and middle class peasants still had greater than average holdings, as well as more and better equipment and animals. They, too, were more likely to be literate than their poorer fellows...."[1]

Attempt at a Soviet-Type Economy

The greatest centralization in Communist China and the most comprehensive planning occurred from 1953 to 1956. With the assistance of Russian advisors, an attempt was made during this period to establish something close to a Soviet-type economy. Heavy industry received the largest part of available investment funds. Output targets were emphasized at the expense of cost reduction and profit objectives.[2] Agriculture was collectivized; toward the end of the period, the peasants were induced by the party to enter "agricultural producer cooperatives"[3] quite rapidly. The Party wanted to collect a "surplus" from the peasantry, and it feared revival of a "rich peasant economy" in the countryside. There is reason to doubt that entry into the producer cooperatives was voluntary. After supplying a specified amount of labor time on the cooperative, the member was supposed to be free to work on his small private plot; plots, however, were restricted and, in some cases, abolished while privately owned pigs, poultry, and equipment frequently were confiscated. Fear of further confiscation and lack of fodder previously obtained from their plots, along with restrictions on sales in rural markets led peasants to slaugh-

---

[1] Audrey Donnithorne, *China's Economic System* (New York: Praeger, 1967), pp. 36–37.

[2] Ibid., p. 17; Dwight H. Perkins, *Market Control and Planning in Communist China* (Cambridge, Mass.: Harvard University Press, 1966), pp. 15–16, 119.

[3] We will follow standard usage in referring to these early collective bodies as producer cooperatives, distinguishing them from the later "communes." The reader, however, should keep in mind that they were much like what is termed collective farms in the Soviet Union.

ter large numbers of their livestock. It does appear, however, that rapid movement into producer cooperatives did not disorganize agriculture as much as had collectivization in the Soviet Union.[4]

In the years 1957 and 1958, pragmatists and moderates came to the fore in China for a time. There were several reasons for this change. To begin with, forced-draft industrialization had led to imbalances and shortages (for example, overinvestments in steel capacity had been accompanied by shortages of pig iron, cement, and timber). Secondly, bureaucracy (at the top) and "commandism" (at lower levels) had made for inflexibility in Mainland China. Finally, agriculture had been neglected. There was discontent in the countryside as a result of floods and drought in 1956, and some peasants left the newly created producer cooperatives.[5] "By 1955 the Chinese began to realize that the Stalinist model was not applicable to Chinese conditions, i.e., that a development strategy built on industrialization at the expense of agriculture was not viable amidst the resource endowments prevailing on the mainland."[6]

Decentralization

Considerable decentralization occurred in 1957 and 1958. Many decisions were moved from the central government to the provinces, and from governmental units to enterprises. The number of mandatory targets for enterprises was reduced, particularly for firms turning out consumption goods. Profits became more important to governmental industrial and commercial enterprises. Producer cooperatives were reduced in size, while the size of private plots was increased. Markets for subsidiary production of the peasants were reopened. For a short period, free speech was even encouraged with the "hundred flowers" campaign. ("Let a hundred flowers bloom," said Mao in encouragement of free speech.) To be sure, it appears that at the same time as decisions were dispersed to lower government organs and enterprises, an increase in Party control within those bodies took place; but surpris-

[4]Donnithorne, *China's Economic System*, pp. 17, 39–41, 83–84; Perkins, *Market Control and Planning*, pp. 13, 56–59, 61.

[5]Jan S. Prybyla, *The Political Economy of Communist China* (Scranton, Pa.: International Textbook Company, 1970), pp. 228–32.

[6]Alexander Eckstein, "Economic Growth and Change in China: A Twenty-Year Perspective," *The China Quarterly* 54 (April-June, 1973), p. 240.

ingly, decisions within the Party itself soon were to be decentralized.

Great Leap Forward

The Soviet-type bureaucratic model had been a disappointment in China. Morever, the reemergence of ideologically distrusted "capitalist forces" worried many in the Party. As a result, from 1958 to 1960 a move in quite a different direction was attempted: the campaign was called the Great Leap Forward, and included the establishment of People's Communes.

Those who gained power in the Party at this time believed that the lessons of guerrilla warfare could be applied to the development of the economy. Drawing on their experiences in the hills, they turned back to the "Yenan Way," and reacted against bureaucratic inadequacies they believed were detrimental to the initiative of the people. Chairman Mao Tse-tung believed in the malleability of man, in the possibilities of collective incentives and entrepreneurship.[8] Ideologically committed local leaders at the scene of action could and should exercise independent judgment, seize the initiative, and thrust forward with little regard for the overall balance of the economy. Party cadres in industry and agriculture were freed from the constraints of central planning (targets did not need to balance, but simply needed to be large, so that local Party people could leap toward them); cadres were freed from the constraints of cost control and profit objectives (attempts at cost reduction were abandoned). It was during this period that the back-yard iron and steel furnaces were encouraged. Industrial output rose rapidly, although much of what was produced was of low quality and worthless, or very nearly so.[9]

People's Communes

The campaign to amalgamate agricultural producer cooperatives (and rural district governmental units) into large people's communes was launched in the summer of 1958. The communes were to be multipurpose units—governmental (they were to be the

[7] Perkins, *Market Control and Planning*, pp. 14, 16–17, 75–77, 129; Donnithorne, *China's Economic System*, pp. 151–52, 158.

[8] Peter Schran, "On the Yenan Origins of Current Economic Policies," in *China's Modern Economy in Historical Perspective*, ed. Dwight H. Perkins (Stanford, Calif.: Stanford University Press, 1975), pp. 280, 299.

[9] Perkins, *Market Control and Planning*, pp. 18, 83, 129–30, 133–34.

basic units of taxation), industrial (they were to develop small rural industry and handicrafts), commercial and financial (they were to absorb supply and marketing cooperatives and local branches of the People's Bank), and, of course, agricultural. Declared to be "sprouts of communism," the communes substituted "all-people ownership" for collective ownership, and they were to distribute part of their income in accordance with need, in particular free meals in communal dining halls. At first, the emphasis was on large-scale communes (in the extreme the commune was to be coterminous with the county), probably conceived in such size because of the limited numbers of qualified staff. Later the emphasis shifted to smaller units and units diversified in size appropriate to local conditions. Private plots was abolished, as was the free market.[10] The system approximated communal anarchy.

A series of bad harvests occurred in 1959, 1960, and 1961, partly as a result of bad weather, and partly as a consequence of the institutional weaknesses of the commune. The Party leaders in charge of the large communes had been out of touch with farm operations, and transferred, even during the crucial harvest season a large part of their labor force from farm work to flood control and irrigation projects, mining, steel smelting in small furnaces, and the like. With the elimination of private plots and free markets an important source of agricultural produce was lost.[11] The Great Leap represented an all-out mobilization effort which stretched the resources and the organizational and administrative capacities of the system beyond its capabilities. This evinced itself in numerous ways, such as planning errors, mistaken directives, mismanagement of projects, technical errors in project construction, and so forth.[12]

Retreat

As a consequence of these reverses and errors, the central authorities had to retreat. Cautiously they moved to reintroduce the free market in the form of rural trade fairs. Then, they encouraged the reintroduction of the private plot and put limits on the labor time which the commune could require of its members. Incentives for

[10]Perkins, *Market Control and Planning,* pp. 74, 86; Donnithorne, *China's Economic System,* pp. 44–50.

[11]Perkins, *Market Control and Planning,* pp. 19, 86, 95–97; Donnithorne, *China's Economic System,* pp. 59–60.

[12]Eckstein, "Economic Growth and Change in China," p. 240.

collective productive activity were restored by the reintroduction of piece rates and by the transfer of ownership, along with calculation of profit and loss, down from the commune to the production brigade (a unit frequently about the size of the former producer cooperative) and then later down to the production team. The communal dining hall was abandoned, and the peasant household was reestablished as the basic unit of consumption. The economy recovered rapidly. (The commune itself because an administrative unit, with, for example, responsibility for the collection of taxes from the brigade or team. But the commune was still considered part of the collective sector and its funds were not incorporated into the government budget.) The authorities also decided to cut back investment in industry and increase it in agriculture.[13]

Needless to say, all these "sprouts of capitalism" were ideologically suspect to many in the Party. From 1962 on, a debate on the use of profit as a success indicator occurred, parallel to the similar discussions inaugurated by Liberman in the Soviet Union.

Once again the opponents of capitalistic tendencies attacked, during the Cultural Revolution of 1966–67. The vanguard of the Cultural Revolution were the students, organized by Mao Tse-tung and his followers into units of the Red Guards. The principal theme of this campaign was that "politics must take command"; revolutionary principles must not be sacrificed for the "ill wind of economism." Bureaucracy and elitism in both government and Party were to be checked, and the masses were to mobilize for a frontal assault on development problems. The class struggle was to be pursued to prevent the reemergence of bourgeois values. Socialist objectives were to replace material incentives in order that the private plot, the profit motive, and the free market be eliminated.[14]

The Cultural Revolution did not have so deleterious an effect on production in industry and agriculture as did on the Great Leap Forward. In 1967 serious disruptions in transportation and production occurred. Probably aware of the adverse consequences of the Great Leap, the authorities then rather quickly began to issue orders stressing the need for order, and the army was given the task of restoring the political structure and the economy. Again,

[13]Perkins, *Market Control and Planning*, pp. 91–92, 94, 97; Donnithorne, *China's Economic System*, pp. 51–53, 62–64.

[14]Robert F. Dernberger, "Radical Ideology and Economic Development in China: The Cultural Revolution and Its Impact on the Economy," *Asian Survey* 12 (December, 1972). Reprinted in Morris Bornstein, *Comparative Economic Systems: Models and Cases* (Homewood, Ill.: Irwin, 1974), pp. 358–59.

the emphasis shifted, to "gradual development, material incentives, functional specialization. . . ." A "retreat from Mao's ideal of a revolutionary, mass-oriented, and egalitarian society" occurred.[15] One Western estimate is that industrial production in 1967 declined by 18 percent and regained the 1966 level only in 1969.[16] And the Cultural Revolution "did not penetrate too deeply into the countryside."[17] Eckstein, who considered the Great Leap a disaster, suggested only that the Cultural Revolution had "inflicted serious damage" on the economy.[18] Another writer concludes that the Cultural Revolution "was in part Mao's last great attempt to (a) reimpose his authority on an increasing technocratic and independent bureaucracy, and (b) reinvigorate the revolutionary movement with its original spirit of unquestioning loyalty, self-sacrifice, plain living, and egalitarianism."[19]

In mid-1973 during the "anti-Confucius, anti-Lin Piao" campaign, material incentives, foreign technology, and rehabilitated bureaucrats were attacked. Slowdowns and stoppages occurred in the factories and rail traffic was interrupted, but by the second half of 1974 the official press began to push for production, and disruptions died down.[20]

Amidst this volatility, can we detect a pattern? Perhaps only the faintest trace of what might become one day a Chinese model. But what we can do is delineate the persistent conflicts between the goals and ideology of the Party and the intractable reality of scarcity in the Chinese environment.

Planning and Control

The emphasis was on heavy industry during China's first five-year plan (1953–57). Following that, large investments were shifted to light industry and rural enterprise. A possible reason for this shift could be that China's leaders sensed early on that she was too near the subsistence level to afford projects with long gestation periods and late returns, sensed that a populous country with little capital

---

[15] Ellis Joffe, "The Chinese Army After the Cultural Revolution," *The China Quarterly* 55 (July-September, 1973), p. 475.

[16] Dernberger, "Radical Ideology," p. 361.

[17] Eckstein, "Economic Growth and Change in China," p. 218.

[18] Ibid., p. 241.

[19] Arther G. Ashbrook, Jr., "China: Economic Overview, 1975," in *China: A Reassessment of the Economy*, Joint Economic Committee, 94th Congress of the United States, 10 July 1975, p. 37.

[20] Ibid., p. 27.

should discount future gains at a high rate in making investment decisions.

Subsequent five-year plans in China became little more than formalities, their focus being on annual plans (or on plans of even shorter duration). Planning also was much decentralized, toward the provinces and localities. An interesting pattern of dual control began to emerge, with the center dividing authority with the provinces. In general, the central authorities, using the method of balances, worked out the targets of the most important commodities and decided upon what have become known as "balance transfers," transfers of commodities from one province to another. As early as 1956, the statistical bureau in Anhuei, a coastal province, wrote: "The commodities which our province cannot produce, or produces in insufficient quantities, are supplied by the state through balance transfers from outside the province, and surplus commodities are transferred by the state from the province to outside areas."[21]

The distribution of goods between provinces probably is not as extensive or as serious a problem in China as it is in the Soviet Union. China is a vast and diverse country; a relatively high degree of regional self-sufficiency is efficient. An underdeveloped transport network, and high costs in capital of extending transport facilities, further supports regional, even local autarky.[22] When a province (or an enterprise) cannot rely on supplies from outside, it is strongly motivated to become self-sufficient. It should be added that some of the emphasis on self-sufficiency in China (in enterprises as well as regions) reflects weaknesses in planning and

---

[21] Donnithorne, *China's Economic System*, p. 463. See also pp. 175, 287, 349, 461–63, 482. The decentralization hypothesis has been challenged, most persistently by Lardy. He contends that the central government redistributes revenues between regions through tax collections from the governments of the more developed provinces and subsidies to the governments of less developed provinces. He also argues that decentralization in late 1957 and after was "administrative decentralization" rather than decentralization of planning. Lardy concedes, however, that evidence for revenue sharing in the 1960s and 1970s is incomplete, and he admits that provincial administrative powers included powers to plan. "Provincial planners were now responsible for allocating raw materials to . . . the enterprises" which remained under central government control. Reflection may convince the reader that powers to allocate materials give the provincial authorities a substantial role in planning. See Nicholas R. Lardy, "Centralization and Decentralization in China's Fiscal Management," *The China Quarterly* 61 (March, 1975), p. 56; Nicholas R. Lardy, "Economic Planning in the Peoples' Republic of China: Central-Provincial Fiscal Relations," in *China: A Reassessment of the Economy*, pp. 100–5, 107, 111, 113–15.

[22] Jon Sigurdson, "Rural Industrialization in China" in *China: A Reassessment of the Economy*, p. 427.

an unwillingness to rely on markets, prices, and profits to induce transfers of commodities. But then perhaps a reluctance to specialize and engage in exchange (even socialist exchange) is in part a matter of ideology. The Chinese Communists have been closer to the anarchist strand of socialist thought than have Soviet leaders. Recall that Kropotkin, the anarchist, leaned toward regional self-sufficiency, wrote of factories and workshops side by side with fields and gardens, and sought a union of hand and brain. Chairman Mao from his guerrilla days to the present has emphasized the principle of self-reliance (which, of course, means less control from the center).

But, then, there are the pragmatists in the Party who see the advantages of specialization and exchange so that periodically campaigns against "departmentalism" come to the fore.

Industrialization

During the fifties, under the influence of Russian advisors, Chinese industry exhibited features characteristic of a Soviet-type economy. With emphasis on volume of output, quality was low and costs were high. Managers overstated their input needs, the "safety factor," and innovation was discouraged in the drive for a large output of a conventional product using conventional methods of production. Campaigns toward varying objectives with accompanying strains on the economy were common.[23]

However, "by 1957, Chinese industrial personnel had outgrown earlier naive expectations that Soviet institutions, advanced technology, and massive investments could rapidly eliminate all obstacles to industrialization."[24] Without doubt, the most interesting change at that time was an increase in the role of small plants and rural industry. The strategy which was employed amounted to a scaling down of modern large-scale technology (for example, in the manufacture of nitrogen chemical fertilizers and cement), and a scaling up of traditional cottage industries (repair shops, small mines, food processing, woodworking, and so on). The small-scale industrial sector included both urban industries, like the Shanghai Machine Tool Plant (an expanded version of an old agricultural machine shop), and rural industries, as diverse as the regions and

[23]Thomas G. Rawski, "China's Industrial System" in *China: A Reassessment of the Economy,* pp. 177, 179, 181–83.
[24]Ibid., p. 184.

localities in which they were located. Not only did small plants hold down expenditure on buildings and equipment and mobilize idle capital and labor, but they also developed manufacturing and organizational skills amongst the peasantry. The small plants program received new emphasis in the several years up to 1975.[25]

Departing from Soviet precedents the Chinese in the early sixties diverted large amounts of resources to investment in the agricultural sector.[26]

Agriculture

Intensive farming is the most important characteristic of agriculture in China. Because only ten percent of her land is arable and her population is relatively large, the ground is intensively cultivated in relatively small parcels. Even rice is grown in small fields. (Wheat fields are, however, larger.[27]) The technology of Chinese agriculture may have much to do with Chinese agricultural institutions. The needs of intensive agriculture may explain why the Party has been forced to decentralize decision making to the provinces, localities, brigades, teams, even to the household. In lieu of the planned direction of agriculture, we find the government forced to limit itself to taxation and procurement (planned purchases), with the private plot again and again reemerging from efforts to restrict or suppress it. And local Party leaders are given more power than otherwise might be the case.

The rural household is responsible for disciplining and motivating its labor force, and for distributing income to its individual members. Most of China's vegetables, poultry, and hogs come from the private plot of the household.[28] Subsidiary production includes the tending of fruit trees, the collection of firewood, the making of rope, and the weaving of mats, bags, and baskets. Much

---

[25] Ashbrook, "China: Economic Overview," in *China: A Reassessment of the Economy*, p. 31; Sigurdson, "Rural Industrialization in China," in *China: A Reassessment of the Economy*, pp. 411–14; Thomas G. Rawski, "The Growth of Producer Industries, 1900–1971," in *China's Modern Economy in Historical Perspective*, p. 231.

[26] Dwight H. Perkins, "Growth and Changing Structure of China's Twentieth Century Economy," in *China's Modern Economy in Historical Perspective*, ed. Dwight H. Perkins (Stanford, Calif.: Stanford University Press, 1975), p. 147.

[27] Donnithorne, *China's Economic System*, p. 56; Perkins, *Market Control and Planning*, p. 97.

[28] Frederick W. Crook, "The Commune System in the People's Republic of China, 1963–74," in *China: A Reassessment of the Economy*, p. 367.

of the output of the household is taken to market and sold for cash. Peasants have the right to own small tools and their house.[29]

Most of the agricultural means of production, however, are the property of the "team," consisting of 20 to 30 households. It is the labor-intensive agriculture of China that makes a unit of this size most suitable for managing and motivating the farmers. Hence, it is the most important formally organized unit in the agricultural system. Team members are motivated to work through a combination of material and nonmaterial incentives. Nonmaterial rewards are expected to become preponderant in the long run, but it is material incentives that, today, induces farmers to produce from team fields. Within the team, to be sure, the distribution of basic labor points is not too unequal, young strong members receiving, for example, ten per day while elderly weak workers get six. While members seem willing to share income almost equally with their relatives and close neighbors in this manner, they are not as willing to share it with their compatriots in nearby teams.[30]

Teams are relatively autonomous decision-making units. The team is the unit of account, but team members are not paid by the state and are less tractable than if they were state employees. Moreover, the government apparently recognizes that team leaders, who are local people, must have the support of relatives and neighbors if they are to be effective. And then the commune or brigade can no longer arbitrarily draft labor from the team for its own projects (as occurred during the period of the Great Leap Forward).[31]

Even with increased investment in agriculture, output has increased slowly, about two percent per year between 1957 and the early 1970s. Despite this slow progress China's intensive agriculture is quite efficient. One scholar believes that "China in the 1960s and 1970s was not in a position to achieve easy and rapid breakthroughs in farm technology," breakthroughs which would have made possible an accelerated rate of agricultural growth.[32]

---

[29]Ibid., p. 402; William L. Parrish, Jr., "Socialism and the Chinese Peasant Family," *Journal of Asian Studies* 34 (May, 1975), pp. 619–21.

[30]Crook, "The Commune System in the People's Republic of China," in *China: A Reassessment of the Economy*, pp. 366–67, 372, 397–98, 401–2.

[31]Ibid., pp. 405–6.

[32]Charles Robert Roll, Jr., and Kung-Chia Yeh, "Balance in Coastal and Inland Industrial Development," in *China: A Reassessment of the Economy*, p. 90; Perkins, "Growth and Changing Structure of China's Economy," in *China's Modern Economy in Historical Perspective*, p. 145.

Chinese Communism as Compared with the Russian Soviet-Type Economy

Intensive, small parcel agriculture has produced a less centralized and controlled agriculture in China than in the Soviet Union. With the peasantry closer to subsistence in China, less effort has been made to accumulate resources for industrialization through capture of a peasant surplus. The Chinese authorities have relied less on the turnover tax on grain, which in the Soviet Union substantially separates the prices paid to farm suppliers (by government procurement agencies) and the prices received from consumers.[33]

The Chinese Communist Party came to power in the countryside, and as a consequence probably understood the peasants better than their urban-based counterparts in the Soviet Union. The Soviets seem to have inherited from the Russian intelligentsia a contempt for the ignorant peasant. While there is little reason to believe that the Chinese peasants liked the change from private to collectivized agriculture, they may have found it somewhat less painful coming from a Party with a certain sensitivity to their feelings.

There are fewer independencies in the Chinese economy than in the Russian. In part, this reflects the fact that there are fewer complexities in a less developed economy. It also reflects the vastness of the country and the underdeveloped railway and road network. Lastly, it perhaps reflects the anarchist tendency in Chinese thought—a skepticism concerning regional as well as personal specialization. As development occurs in China, interdependencies probably will increase, so that either planning will have to be elaborated and, to a greater degree centralized, or the role of markets, prices, and profits will have to be enlarged.

That the Chinese are more revolutionary than the Russians is almost certainly true. The Cultural Revolution was a very serious, "revolutionary" effort to destroy a solidifying bureaucratic system, whereas Stalin's bloodiest purges substituted one set of bureaucrats for another. Perhaps the Chinese are more revolutionary just because the Russians are not; they may be reacting against the Soviet-type economy as part of their conflict with Russia. They also may have been able to see the stultifying consequences of a system in which officials secure their careers by following the Party line and rejecting innovative proposals.

[33]Donnithorne, *China's Economic System*, pp. 358, 361.

Chinese Communism and Communal Agriculture in the West

After looking at the differences between the Chinese and the Soviet-type economies, we might usefully glance at the difference between Chinese Communism in agriculture and the relatively small and scattered communes which exist in otherwise capitalist economies. Probably the most important difference between East and West is that almost the whole of agriculture was collectivized in China. The producer cooperatives did not function side by side and in competition with a capitalist agriculture, apart from a limited and occasional competition between collective production and production on private plots. Those Chinese who preferred individual farming could not choose to enter private agriculture. The peasant who disliked the producer cooperative could sometimes escape to the cities (where, however, he mostly found socialized industry), or he might "escape" to his private plot and perform the bare minimum of required collective duties. (The latter has been a recurring problem usually dealt with by severe pressure from the cadres.)

In general, the collective farm (the producer cooperative) in China does not have a self-selected, idealistic and devoted population comparable to that found in the Hutterian colony or Israeli kibbutz. Functioning with the ordinary rural population, the collective farm would not be expected to be as efficient as the relatively small collective islands of devoted communal dwellers in capitalist economies. That is, it would not be expected to be particularly efficient, unless the Party had succeeded in creating a new socialist man among the masses. And in China there is no evidence that the Party has been able to do so.

An Uneasy Balance

The institutions and the leadership of Chinese communism at the moment appear to be in an unstable equilibrium. There is an uneasy balance between the desire for central control and a recognized need for local initiative, between the top leadership (Party and Government) and the almost inescapable bureaucracy, and between the respective roles of the experts ("elitism") and the masses. There is a fitful balance between the initiatives of government (and Party) and private initiative—on private plots and in subsidiary household production. There is, moreover, a wavering balance between preferences for growth in material welfare (but not "materialism" or consumerism) and preferences for egalitarianism. Finally, there is an uneasy balance between a desire for efficiency (at times labeled "economism") and a belief that "politics must be in command."

The radical group, formerly thought of as the Maoists, want equality, mass participation, and material well-being (but not "consumerism" or materialism). They do not want a new class of bureaucrats and technocrats—"elitism"—and they are opposed to capitalism. They seem to be eager to reach conditions which could allow the government to wither away. Again and again, however, they run into intractable realities—scarcity, interdependencies (which must be dealt with either by directives or market transactions), the need for production and efficiency (with the skilled personnel required by modern technologies), and a peasantry and urban labor force that continue to respond most effectively to material incentives.

It would be folly to predict the outcome of all the conflicting cross-currents in the volatile Chinese economy and political structure. It may be useful to speculate a little, however, on likely future developments in China.

It seems probable that over time Chinese communism will move closer to the Soviet model than it will to the anarchist dream. First of all, as the country becomes more developed and industrialized, the number of interdependencies will grow.[34] Not willing to turn to the market to unify interrelated decisions, the Party is more and more likely to centralize control. (Already in agriculture, planning and coordination at the commune and brigade level are beginning to reduce the autonomy of the team.[35]) It seems improbable that the Chinese will succeed in developing a new socialist man who will respond to the increasingly diverse input requirements of the economy by concern for the needs of his fellow man. What socialists call "social consciousness" will most likely not evolve as a substitute for the market, or for central directives in tying together the parts of a highly interrelated economy.

An enduring decentralization requires a dream different from that of the communal anarchists. It requires a dream of individual differences and their cultivation, of pluralism, rather than concern for an abstraction called the "masses." It needs a different view of

[34] Cf. Ashbrook, "China: Economic Overview," in *China: A Reassessment of the Economy*, p. 41.

[35] Crook, "The Commune System in the People's Republic of China," in *China: A Reassessment of the Economy*, pp. 406–7.

the world—a view of men with conflicting interests that have to be reconciled. It demands modesty—the tentative ideas of science in place of a dogmatic ideology. And decentralization probably requires a relatively large role for markets, perhaps socialist markets, possibly even the markets of capitalism.

Capitalism

Part V

Introduction to Part Five

Private ownership of the means of production is the essence of capitalism, with freedom of contract amongst the most important of the bundle of rights that make up private property. Freedom allows individuals to enter the market and buy factors of production as required; it allows them to sell products desired by consumers (or other producers). It puts the businessman at the heart of what is accurately described as the free enterprise system. Decisions are decentralized and the "captains of industry" are private persons rather than government officials. Profit attracts the entrepreneur and induces him to take risks, thereby stimulating innovation and growth.

Unfettered individual initiative, however, distributes income unequally, according to productivity rather than need, allows the profits of natural monopoly, permits spillovers of smoke, water pollution, noise, and the like, and promotes economic insecurity.

Rather than government ownership in place of private ownership, the American alternative has been government regulation, governmental constraints within which the individual is free to go his own way.

Laissez Faire Capitalism

Chapter 15

Before we examine the elaborately regulated capitalism of modern times, we will find it useful to look at a model of a simpler system, laissez faire capitalism.

Objectives

An unregulated capitalism can be used to attain the following objectives:

1. Consumers have freedom of choice in consumption, and workers have free choice in jobs. In expenditure on goods and in selection of jobs, men and women are constrained only by their budgets, their capacities to work, and the prices of goods and services.

2. People are free to organize new production units and to take the risks associated with ownership of capital goods. (Free enterprise and private ownership of the means of production will be considered by some to be means rather than ends or objectives, but there is evidence that many people like the independence of the private businessman and want to take the risks of private property in capital. Hence we treat free enterprise and private ownership of the means of production as ends-in-themselves.)

3. Production is undertaken in response to actual or anticipated purchases of goods by consumers and actual or anticipated sales of services by workers.

4. Production is efficient. Any given output is produced at a minimum cost in foregone alternatives.

5. Those who make investment decisions have a long time horizon, one which extends beyond the affairs of a single decade or generation.

6. Innovation occurs. Production is not only undertaken in response to expenditure or expected expenditure on existing goods but *new* goods are introduced when it is expected that they will be purchased. And not only the most efficient of existing processes are used, but *new* processes which are expected to be efficient are employed.

7. Income is distributed in accordance with productivity. Wages, interest, and profit reflect the values produced by those who work, save, and innovate.

Institutions: Property and Contract

The essential feature of capitalism is private ownership of the means of production. Not only do people have property rights in their persons, in human capital (rights which people have in most socialist economies, too), but they may privately own factory buildings and machinery, heavy construction equipment, shipyards, and so on.

Property, as we have seen, is a set of rights, a set of powers vested in a person by custom or law. (Lawyers and sometimes economists speak of a "bundle" of rights.) Property under capitalism includes the rights to possess, use, give away, or destroy a good, the right to exchange a good for money and vice versa, the right to vote concerning the management of goods and money, and the right to receive income and wealth (income in the form of interest, and, when declared by a board of directors, in the form of dividends, and wealth in the return of the principal of a loan or as a share of assets when a corporation is liquidated). Property is a legal concept. It is the set of rights with respect to a good, and it is not, as commonly believed, the good itself. Property is not absolute and it is not unchanging. The rights that an individual has in a good are circumscribed. (An individual may not, for example, keep a dangerous animal in his home.) And the rights of property may be changed. For example, a new law may make it illegal to carry a concealed weapon. But if property really means anything, the collection of rights in a good can be altered only through a carefully prescribed legal procedure known as "due process."

Moreover, property is without content if there is no way for an individual to enforce his or her rights; that is, property lacks content if the precise steps are not known by which an individual can secure his rights. It also lacks content if independent courts to which an individual can appeal do not exist.

Property Rights and Human Rights

Many people fail to understand the nature of property. This is demonstrated by the frequent assertion that under capitalism property rights take precedence over human rights. This dichotomy is a false one, for property rights *are* human rights—the rights of human beings with respect to goods and money. One can argue, on the basis of particular value judgments, that property rights are unsatisfactorily distributed, but one cannot argue that these rights are the rights of some nonhuman entities.

Property distributes the right of decision in any economic system, and private property in the means of production locates in private hands the right to decide on the use of capital. Hence, private ownership, of the means of production as compared with government ownership decentralizes decision making.

Included in the set of rights which are private property under capitalism are the rights to lifetime ownership and the right to bequeathe wealth to heirs.

Freedom of contract, the right of exchange referred to earlier, is a species of property which is an important part of capitalism. The businessman may freely negotiate prices with his suppliers and customers. There are no governmentally established price ceilings or price floors. A businessman may cut prices in order to enlarge his share of the market or to gain entry into a new line of activity. Or, he may organize a new enterprise and enter into contracts with suppliers and customers. Freedom of contract makes possible free enterprise.

Freedom of Contract

In laissez faire capitalism, freedom of contract includes the freedom to negotiate agreements in restraint of trade. Businessmen may collude in setting prices and in dividing up markets, and workers may agree to withdraw their services in concert, may, that is, agree to strike.

Property rights in technical ideas probably are not an essential feature of laissez faire capitalism. But, since patent rights promote innovation, and in view of the fact that a patent system is commonly a part of capitalism, we will include patents in our model.

Institutions: Capital Markets and the Corporations

One of the most important institutions of capitalism is the capital market, a market in which people supply funds in return for ownership shares or instruments of debt. Information about the return expected on different stocks and bonds is in effect information about expected expenditure on goods and expected factor supply in different parts of the economy. With a capital market in existence, owners of funds not only consider investment opportunities in their immediate, familiar environments, but they also consider economy-wide alternatives for investment. The capital market knits together into a unified whole the decentralized investment decisions of the many individuals who decide on investment in a capitalist system.

One could imagine a capitalistic economy without corporations, a capitalism with only sole proprietorships and partnerships. But enterprises with limited liability play so large a role in modern capitalism that they must be part of any realistic model of such a system. We will assume, at the outset, that the managers of corporations own stock in the enterprises they control, though this is not, of course, always true.

The Behavior of Consumers, Workers, Investors, and Businessmen in Laissez Faire Capitalism

Consumers, constrained by their budgets and the prices they must pay, purchase goods and services, and save.

Workers, constrained by their capacities, supply labor in response to wages and working conditions.

Investors acquire and hold a portfolio of paper assets that include money, short-term notes, bonds, and stocks. Investors, we shall assume, maximize present value, or (when purchasing risk assets) maximize expected value. Investors may be consumers and workers, or they may be businessmen.

The Businessman
The businessman makes current input and output decisions, he decides on prices of purchase and sale, he sells stock and notes and bonds, and he makes investment decisions. That is, he selects

material and labor inputs and settles on what the enterprise is to turn out at any given time; he sets list prices and negotiates actual prices; he enters into capital markets for capital; and he determines what plant and equipment should be acquired. He also will have the business acquire some paper assets (money at least), perhaps some short-term notes, and perhaps bonds or stock in other enterprises. The corporate businessman manages two portfolios, his personal portfolio which includes stock in the company, and the "portfolio" of the business itself—plant, equipment, inventory, money and other paper assets. Part of the time, the businessman is simply a manager, performing routine acts of supervision and making routine input, output, and pricing decisions. At other times, the businessman is an entrepreneur, organizing a new firm or entering a new market, introducing a new product, or installing a new process which requires investment in new, untried equipment. The businessman, therefore, is a composite personality: a manager, an investor, and an entrepreneur.

List Prices and Actual Prices
When the businessman publishes a price, it is a standing offer to sell (or buy) at this figure. List prices are usually relatively stable and reflect the businessman's estimate of underlying, long-term trends in supply and demand. The businessman then negotiates an actual price which reflects the current, perhaps temporary, state of the market. When his inventories begin to pile up or his order book shortens, he concedes discounts off list prices or he provides extra services which effectively reduce the price of sale. When inventories fall or unfilled orders accumulate, he cuts down on the extras that accompany delivery. The flexibility of actual, as opposed to list prices, means that prices much of the time are market-clearing, equating the amount supplied with the amount demanded.

We will assume that in current input and output decisions, where the elapse of time between input, output, and sale is not significant, the businessman maximizes profit. In making investment decisions where risk is negligible, the businessman, we will assume, like other investors, maximizes present value. And in making investment decisions involving risk, he maximizes expected value.

As he invests, the businessman looks beyond the affairs of a single decade or generation.

Information

The businessman keeps some information secret. In order to gain an advantage over competitors, he conceals as long as possible his plans to introduce new products. He conceals, where possible, new low-cost processes of production, and (so as not to attract rivals) he conceals high profits.

The businessman supplies information to potential buyers and engages in acts of persuasion. He supplies information about the availability and characteristics of his product and about proposed prices, credit terms, and the like. And by means of advertisements along with direct selling he attempts to persuade customers that his product is a superior one.

Structure of Industry

In many if not most sectors of a capitalist economy, there will be short-run monopoly and long-run competition, as Schumpeter has so impressively demonstrated.[1] (We are discussing laissez faire capitalism in this chapter but much of what we say applies as well to a regulated capitalism.) A firm that develops a new product or new process will have a temporary monopoly. One source of this monopoly is simply the time it takes potential competitors to acquire finance, construct plant, purchase equipment, and build up a labor force. During that interim the businessman with a new product or process will do what he can to maintain a monopoly by keeping the product or process secret, and he may, finally, take out patents which give him a legal monopoly. As time passes, the temporary monopoly will be eroded away, or suddenly destroyed. The inertia of rivals will give way to movement. Secrecy will break down. Patents may be infringed. (A patent has been described as little more than a license to sue the many people who will try to infringe it, and a patent which is not constantly defended in the courts is said to be valueless.) Products and processes which are close substitutes, but not covered by the patent will be developed. In time patents will expire. Having freedom of contract, rivals are free to engage in price competition as well as various kinds of non-price competition. New firms may emerge and they may even destroy existing enterprises. Indeed the organizational flexibility of capitalism has not been given sufficient weight in traditional economic theory. As Schumpeter put it, "the problem that is usu-

---

[1] Joseph A. Schumpeter, *Capitalism, Socialism, and Democracy*, 3rd ed. (New York: Harper, 1950), Chapters VI–VIII.

ally being visualized is how capitalism administers existing structures, whereas the relevant problem is how it creates and destroys them."[2]

Long-run competition, to be sure, will not prevail everywhere in the economy. The economies of large-scale production and the existence of unique sites will give some enterprises a natural, permanent monopoly. Steel production and the local brickyard often are natural monopolies as are railroads and electric utilities.

Attainment of Objectives

We are now in a position to demonstrate how the objectives stated at the beginning of this chapter are achieved in a system of laissez faire capitalism.

Free choice in consumption and work—choice constrained only by budgets, work capacities, and prices of goods and services—is realized in a system when there are market-clearing prices. With the amount supplied equal to the amount demanded, the buyer can purchase all he or she wants at existing prices and the worker can sell at existing wages all the labor he is willing to supply. Goods and jobs are rationed neither by government officials nor by businessmen.

The objectives of free enterprise and private risk-taking in capital goods are realized through the legal institutions of private property and freedom of contract.

Then, with businessmen seeking to maximize profit, production responds to purchases of goods by consumers and to sales of services by workers.

Efficiency is attained under capitalism through profit maximization by businessmen, who combine factors of production in such a way as to turn out any given output at a minimum cost in money. Competition for factors in alternative activities causes the businessman to pay factor prices that reflect the value of factors in his best foregone alternatives. Hence minimization of money cost minimizes opportunity cost.

Capitalist managers have a long time horizon in making investment decisions insofar as they own shares and can bequeath them to heirs. They will look beyond the affairs of a single decade or generation because they want the income and value of their shares in the distant future to be high.

[2] Ibid., p. 84.

Innovation (the introduction of new products and new processes), when that is an objective, is achieved under capitalism because the structure of industry permits the profits of temporary monopoly. The inertia of potential competitors, secrecy employed by the innovator, and the use of patents all protect the profits of innovation, inducing businessmen to do things differently and turn out new products.

Competition under capitalism brings about a distribution of income that accords with productivity. Competition for workers leads to wages which reflect the values of their respective marginal products. Competition for capital funds leads to interest rates which reflect the productivity of capital. Temporary monopoly rewards the manager who innovates with monopoly profits, and long-run competition reduces to a reward for routine management the profits of the businessman who does not continue to innovate.

The Differences between Laissez Faire Capitalism and Market Socialism

Although capitalism and market socialism are alike in that decentralized decisions are unified through markets and prices, there are important differences between these two systems.

To begin with, in a system of market socialism the government carries the risk of loss of investments in plant and equipment, whereas under capitalism these risks are borne by private individuals. The socialist manager does take some risks when he or she decides between alternative investments. Like the manager of a capitalist enterprise he risks his reputation, and the present or expected value of his anticipated future earnings. Notwithstanding, under market socialism an individual is not allowed to take the risks of investment in major plant and equipment, and if he wants to risk his reputation in major investment decisions, he must work for the government. Private ownership of the means of production, then, and the private assumption of the risks attached to private ownership, are the two features which most strikingly distinguish capitalism from market socialism.

A second difference between these two systems is that a board of directors, elected by the shareholders, appoints the manager of the enterprise in a capitalist economy, whereas the government appoints the managers in a system of market socialism.

A final distinguishing feature, one we have already noted, is that capitalist managers probably will look further into the future than will socialist enterprise managers, since the latter expect to hold their positions for only a few years.

Criticisms of Laissez Faire Capitalism

While an unregulated capitalist system achieves a number of popular objectives, it often reaches them only partially or part of the time, and it fails entirely to attain some goals.

Prices under capitalism do not always clear the market, and consequently choice in consumption and work is not always free. To be sure, much of the time excess demand will induce businessmen temporarily to run down their inventories, thus ensuring that the consumer is constrained in his choices only by his budget and by the prices he must pay. Excess demand might also induce businessmen to raise prices, and these higher prices will reduce the amount demanded or stimulate a short-run increase in the amount supplied. On the other hand, excess supply often leads to price cuts, perhaps in the form of discounts off list price. Even workers who successfully rebel at a money wage-cut may work harder when unemployment increases and thus effectively lower wage rates. Nevertheless, prices and wages often are inflexible. Purchasers may have to agree to accept a later delivery date when demand is high relative to supply, or they may have to do without the good. Every consumer in a capitalist economy has had a businessman say to him: "Sorry, I'm completely out of that item." But the frequency with which the consumer finds the good he wants shows how close to freedom of choice in consumption a capitalist economy comes. From time to time, newspapers in the United States run articles in their financial sections detailing commodities which are in short supply. They might be such items as copper, rubber, bearings, and so on. Shortages of this sort usually occur during a period of boom, and most commonly take place in oligopolistic industries where prices tend to be inflexible. The fact that shortages are newsworthy, however, suggests that they are uncommon.

In a capitalist economy wages are sufficiently rigid so that during a recession workers lack freedom of choice in jobs.

In sum, markets under capitalism are cleared much of the time, so that people have free choice in consumption and work, but occasionally prices and wages are inflexible and freedom of choice is not realized.

At the outset we assumed that managers of corporations own stock in the enterprises they control, but of course, this is not always true. A manager may own no shares or only an insignificantly small number of shares in the company. Under these circumstances his or her interests are not the same as those of the owners. He may not strive for efficiency, he may not innovate, he may seek to maximize something like total sales rather than profit, and he may not have the long time horizon which an owner of a significant number of shares would have. Those who control corporations usually are aware of the problem and try to induce managers to acquire and hold stock in the enterprise.

Spillovers

Indiscriminate delivery of output (the spillover) is a matter of concern to many people in a system of laissez faire capitalism. The enterprise which produces steel, for example, also turns out smoke, and delivery of the latter is unwanted by those who receive it. The outdoor advertising company indiscriminately delivers messages to those who want to receive them, and to those who do not. We can identify the value judgments of people who consider indiscriminate delivery to be a problem by looking at alternatives open to recipients of unwanted smoke, noise, or the like.

Actual or potential recipients of indiscriminately delivered goods have the following options:

1. They can move to a new location.
2. They can buy for protection a large area of land, thus seeking to keep the undesired activities of others at a distance.
3. Lacking the resources to buy a large amount of land, they can purchase only the land they need but purchase it in the form of real estate that is covered by restrictive covenants. They can buy land, for example, for a real estate developer who arranges that the uses of all land in a specified area be controlled: all subsequent purchasers are bound not to use the land, say, for livestock or as a repair shop, mobile home court, junkyard, and so on.
4. Recipients of indiscriminately delivered goods can organize for the purpose of buying off the supplier, with payments which (1) induce the supplier to move to a different location or (2) induce him or her to prevent the indiscriminate delivery. The recipients of smoke might collect a fund through voluntary contributions and pay a factory owner to move elsewhere or pay him to install smoke-abatement equipment.[3]

Needless to say, there is a cost in moving, a cost in purchasing a larger amount of land than required, and a cost in organizing a group and buying off the supplier of unwanted goods. Moreover those who do not voluntarily contribute to a fund employed to change the actions of a supplier, nevertheless benefit from the

---

[3] It is curious that students of welfare economics have virtually ignored the first three of these options, although they are frequently elected in practice by actual or potential recipients of indiscriminate delivery, and have concentrated almost entirely on the fourth option, which is rarely chosen.

purchased absence of the undesired good. These are "free riders." Finally, in addition to the cost of negotiating and enforcing restrictive covenants, there is the probability that some kinds of undesired activities will fail to be anticipated and incorporated into a restrictive agreement. (Noisy nursery schools, for example, may not have been covered.)

Having looked at the options available to actual and potential recipients of indiscriminate delivery, we are now in a position to identify the value judgments of those who find it an objectionable feature of laissez faire capitalism. Critics are making one or more of the following judgments of value:

1. People who have lived in an area before an unwanted good is delivered have a vested right to the predelivery situation and should not have to incur the costs of moving, the costs of purchasing extra land for protection, or the costs of organizing and buying off the supplier. Nor should they have to anticipate in restrictive covenants all possible incursions into the area.

2. Newcomers as well as old residents are entitled to an environment free of indiscriminate delivery and should not have to incur the aforementioned costs or anticipate in restrictive covenants all possible incursions.

3. People who do not voluntarily contribute to an effort to buy off a supplier and who nevertheless benefit from the purchased absence of the undesired good should not as "free riders" receive benefits for which they do not pay.

Assortment of Goods

It has been suggested that capitalism fails in the variety of goods turned out. Sometimes it is argued that too little variety is produced; at other times it is suggested that too much product differentiation occurs. Critics also have been heard to say that the trouble with capitalism is that the consumer can choose only from goods placed before him by businessmen. The suggestion is that there are kinds of goods which consumers would like but which they do not have an opportunity to buy. A little reflection, however, suggests that, apart from made-to-order goods, the consumer in all conceivable systems will select from goods placed before him. (And made-to-order goods are available under capitalism, though usually at higher prices than standard items.) Perhaps the critics in this instance are saying that minority preferences are not taken care of, that the emphasis in capitalism is on mass-produced items. Yet, it appears that the free private enterprise is particularly well suited to minority tastes. Should large businessmen limit their activities, they leave openings for small businessmen who are on the alert for minority preferences that can be profitably served. On the other hand, under socialism when government enterprise with a legal monopoly chooses to concentrate on goods consumed by the masses, the minority will be neglected. Indeed, when people from Russia and Eastern Europe encounter for the first time capitalism in the United States, they are amazed at the profusion of goods available.

Rather than argue that under capitalism variety is deficient, some critics contend that capitalist businessmen engage in *excessive* product differentiation as a competitive device to increase their sales and profits. If, however, the consumer purchases the differentiated product, it is difficult to argue that the variety produced is excessive. Should businessmen add too many frills and create too much variety, an opening is left for someone to move in and compete with a simple, standardized, low-cost product.

Very much like the contention that there is too much product differentiation in a capitalist economy is the charge that businessmen "plan obsolescence." By producing one product after another at short intervals, it is said, they make the consumer dissatisfied with the old product and induce him or her to buy a new one. These design changes are costly. But once again, if the consumer regularly purchases the new models, the critic is hard put to defend the argument that the rate of design change is nonoptimal. Should businessmen change models more often than consumers prefer, they leave an opening for a competitor to enter with an unchanging, low-cost, product. Volkswagen with its "Beetle" seems to have done just that.

The Rationality of Consumers

Some critics of laissez faire capitalism are concerned about the consumer's capacity to make rational purchasing decisions. They argue that the consumer does not know his or her own needs, that lacking knowledge of nutrition and physiology, for example, they fail to buy the right foods, while consuming tobacco and liquor. Such critics contend the consumer at times spends on impulse and allows emotion to determine his choices. Or, they maintain that while consumers may know their own requirements, they are not able to identify the goods best-suited to these needs, are not able to detect, for example, adulterated food or recognize mechanically superior appliances. Particularly in large, non-repeat purchases, like the purchase of a house, the consumer may suffer from serious mistakes.

Of course, the defender and the critic of free consumer choice under capitalism start from different value judgments. The defender of capitalism usually admits that consumers may be ignorant and emotional and may make mistakes, but he argues that free people will learn from their mistakes and become stronger and abler than people without freedom. He or she values a world of strong, free people. Moreover, the defender of capitalism points out that each individual is an expert in the circumstances of his or her own life, and the defender of capitalism values a system in which the expert in things like nutrition and health serves in an advisory rather than a directing role. The critic of free choice under capitalism, on the other hand, values a system in which the government protects and takes care of the ignorant or emotional individual. He prefers to see the government control the production or sale of goods, so that consumers receive products that the government believes are most beneficial.

The Salesman versus the Consumer
It is suggested by some that the consumer also lacks the capacity to withstand the wiles of the salesman, that, indeed, the consumer is virtually brainwashed by advertisers so that his alleged free choice is nonexistent. It is true that in a system of laissez faire capitalism the information supplied about goods to potential purchasers often is supplied by interested parties. The profit-seeking businessman may supply incomplete or inaccurate information about his product, or he may play on the emotions of the buyer. This criticism suggests that even were the consumer a qualified buyer in the absence of advertising and sales effort, he or she would not be capable of withstanding the pressures of the salesman.

A defender of capitalism observes that though the businessman is indeed an interested party, he often is interested in repeat purchases, in the "custom" of the customer. Seeking a reputation as a reliable tradesman, the businessman may be careful not to mislead the buyer. Company names, brandnames, and trademarks show the businessman trying to identify himself and his products, presumably in the expectation that the purchaser will think well of the company or product line after an experience with it. The consumer, as an expert in his own affairs, will have some qualifications with which to decide whether or not a product is meeting his or her desires, and he or she can adjust his repeat purchases accordingly. Moreover, the consumer under capitalism can buy disinterested advice. For example, he can hire an independent appraiser to look at a house that he proposes to buy; he can employ a mechanic to examine a second-hand car; he can subscribe to consumer advisory magazines. Knowledge itself is a product that can be bought. To be sure, not many avail themselves of expert advice before making purchases. Most people seem to prefer to rely on themselves (or on friends) in evaluating goods.

We really do not know to what extent the choices of the consumer are influenced by advertising. It seems unlikely that the positions at the two extremes are valid. The consumer is neither totally manipulated by the salesman, nor is he totally free of the salesman's influence. But just how much influence the salesman has is not known. It is frequently observed in business schools that the businessman's choice of an advertising budget is nonrational, because the impact of any given pattern of sales expenditure cannot be measured. The same measurement problem may make it difficult (if not impossible) to choose rationally between alternative economic systems with different supplies of information.

Criticism of advertising in a system of capitalism sometimes is criticism of the cost of advertising that merely counteracts other advertising. There are costs in the transfer of information, and when advertising simply offsets advertising, so that no redistribution of customers takes place, the total costs of the good are increased with no benefit to the consumer. Much soap advertising may be of this sort. No seller can reduce his advertising budget without losing out to rivals, but it may be that none can gain through sales effort. Defenders of advertising contend that advertising *lowers* costs, and lowers prices to consumers, when it attracts customers to low-cost products. The lower production costs presumably more than offset the costs of sales activity. But advertising that fails to redistribute customers from high to low-cost firms—advertising that merely counteracts other advertising—adds to costs.

Monopoly
That laissez faire capitalism experiences serious difficulties with monopoly is recognized by most investigators. Agreements in restraint of trade by businessmen, agreements that check price competition or divide up markets, are widespread. (It is also

recognized, however, that these agreements are frequently broken by businessmen who are trying to get ahead of their rivals.)

While temporary monopoly serves a function in promoting innovation, permanent, natural monopoly does not serve such a function. Such monopoly exists where there are unique sites or where the economies of large-scale production are so great that one or a small number of firms of optimum size can supply the entire market. Where there are no close substitutes for the product turned out by a natural monopoly (e.g., electricity or steel produced in a geographically isolated market), a businessman in a system of laissez faire capitalism may collect monopoly profits over a long period and the enterprise may not be efficiently run.

Income Distribution

Perhaps the most common criticisms of capitalism concern distribution of income. Socialists argue that property rights in the means of production enable the owner to "exploit" his workers. Marxians argue that private property in capital enables the owner to take the "surplus value" that workers produce, since the workers have only their labor to sell. In response to these arguments, it should be noted that the owner of capital is not as strong as the socialists contend, nor is the worker as weak. Marxians have not established that the capitalist is in a position to capture any surpluses that emerge. While it is true that the modern worker must have access to capital goods if his activity is to be at all productive, it is also true that the means of production of the capitalist have to be activated by workers if these facilities are to be of any use. The notion that the worker is abjectly dependent on the owner of capital for his sustenance, while the capitalist is proudly independent of the worker, does not stand up to close examination (apart from the special case of competing workmen facing a noncompeting employer). What we observe, rather, is that the owner of capital and the owner of labor are dependent on one another. And it is important to recognize that the worker *is an owner.* He or she has property in his or her person—property in *human capital.* The worker has the power of decision over the supply of his services, and these services may be extremely valuable to an employer. (A striking example is the modern corporate manager who owes his high income mostly to the services he supplies rather than to the capital goods he owns. The manual worker also has valuable services for sale.) Marx does recognize that the worker has property rights in his own person. The worker, he says, is the "untrammelled owner of his capacity for labor, i.e., of his person. He and the owner of money meet in the market, and deal with each other as on the basis of equal rights, with this difference alone, that one is buyer, the other seller."[4] Marx, however, goes on to say that the worker has nothing but his labor to sell, but does not provide an explanation for his suggestion that what the worker has for sale is of little value.

Productivity or Need

Another interesting criticism of the distribution of income under capitalism challenges the productivity ethic. Distribution under capitalism, we noted earlier, accords with productivity. The determinist, however, or the near determinist who believes that an individual's capacity very largely depends on his or her heredity and early environment, does not find a distribution in accordance with productivity fair. Why should an individual born with a high I.Q. and reared by loving parents in a prosperous suburb earn more than an individual less gifted at birth, reared in a slum, and neglected by his parents? The former cannot claim credit for his higher productivity, says the determinist or near determinist, nor can the latter be blamed for his lower output. A distribution in accordance with productivity rewards good fortune instead of merit.

Rather than make the value judgment that productivity should be rewarded, the critics of capitalism are likely to judge that rewards should be distributed in accordance with need, or equally, or at least that wealth should be distributed so as to make opportunity equal. Other critics of capitalism point out that economic rents are unearned income: they note that the solid surface of the earth usually is not produced by people, and that, therefore, the supply of scarce sites cannot be increased. (Earlier we treated the return from scarce sites as a gain of natural monopoly.)

Some are concerned about the insecurity experienced by the individual in a capitalist economy. Illness or injury may make it impossible for him or her to work. Jobs may be wiped out, the value of skills destroyed, and incomes seriously reduced by sudden technological changes or by changes in demand.

[4]Karl Marx, *Capital: A Critique of Political Economy,* vol. 1 (New York: Modern Library, 1906), p. 186.

Finally, the radical critic of capitalism objects to the tensions experienced by people in a competitive capitalism. He objects to the use of material rewards as incentives, and to acts of trading rather than giving. He would like to establish a cooperative, communal economy.

Less radical critics seek to reform capitalism, seek to modify it through various regulations, tax measures, and subsidies. To a study of these modifications we now turn.

From Laissez Faire to Regulation in the United States

Chapter **16**

When Americans have doubted the private market economy as a system with which to achieve desired objectives, they have seldom turned to government ownership as an alternative. More frequently they have chosen the independent governmental regulatory body. One could almost speak of an ideology of regulation, were it not for the pragmatic, experimental way in which these agencies have been developed and modified as circumstances required. We will examine several major movements toward regulation in the United States.

After the Civil War, from 1864 to 1896, the trend of prices received by farmers was down and the lot of the farmer was a hard one. An indigenous American radicalism developed, culminating in the formation of the People's Party in 1891. Populism became an ideology, described by one writer as a "faith and a creed."[1] It found the economic troubles of America in monopoly, principally

---

[1] Chester M. Destler, "Western Radicalism, 1895–1901: Concepts and Origins," *Mississippi Valley Historical Review* 31 (December, 1944), p. 351.

the monopoly power of the railroads (but also in the power of the meatpackers and other large enterprises), and it found American troubles in "middlemen" (the commission houses and wholesalers) and in the bankers (the Eastern money power). This distrust of monopoly, of middlemen, and of finance even today is deeply ingrained in American thought and explains much of present-day American economic policy. While the program of the Populists called for government ownership of the railroads and telegraphs[2] the nation opted for privately owned railroads under the jurisdiction of an independent regulatory commission. Still and all an important legacy of Populism in the United States was its antitrust activity—the Sherman Act of 1890, the Clayton Act of 1914 with its accompanying Federal Trade Commission, and the persistent efforts, almost unique in the history of nations, to maintain a competitive market structure in large parts of the economy.

Regulation of the Railroads

During the early days of railroads, governmental units—local, state, and federal—mostly provided subsidies. They purchased or guaranteed railroad bonds, granted tax exemptions, provided terminal facilities, gave government land for rights-of-way, and gave alternate sections of land on either side of the track for each mile of railroad constructed.[3] As new railroads developed, competition appeared, but not uniformly across the country. It appeared only where more than one railroad served the same territory. Discriminatory transport rates emerged, lower rates for particular towns and cities, and for favored shippers. This behavior of the discriminating monopolist was deeply resented by those not favored, and attacks on the monopoly power of railroads came to the fore.[4] At first, efforts were made to regulate rates through the official charters permitting incorporation, sometimes with provisions for subsequently altering these regulations by legislative action. But regulation by charter and legislation failed for lack of flexibility; rates could not be changed with changing conditions. So a number of states established commissions that were empowered to set maximum transport rates. A time came when the requirements of interstate commerce were recognized, and in 1887 Congress

[2] Ibid., pp. 353–55.

[3] Ross M. Robertson, *History of the American Economy,* 2nd ed. (New York: Harcourt, Brace & World, 1964), pp. 283–86.

[4] Ibid., p. 287.

created the Interstate Commerce Commission. By 1906, the Commission was given the powers it needed to set maximum rates.[5]

Many, if not most, of the railroads found themselves in serious financial difficulties at one time or another, sometimes because lines were built ahead of available traffic, and other times because regulatory authorities set rates which were too low.[6] In 1898 the Supreme Court ruled that the railroads were entitled to a "fair return on a fair value," which in effect set minima below which rates might not be reduced. With this decision, the United States moved toward a pattern of cost-plus pricing in railway services which, as shown in the next chapter, has had a deleterious effect on efficiency.

Subsidies and Controls in Agriculture

From 1860 on it was the policy of the federal government to develop agriculture through the distribution of the public domain to farmers, and through the establishment of land-grant colleges engaged in agricultural research, the creation of experiment stations, and the funding of agricultural education in the high schools. In effect, agricultural research was socialized and the results disseminated free of charge to farmers.[7] The government also built dams and irrigation work and made loans at low interest rates.

But problems emerged and persisted. During the twenties farmers were heavily in debt and were encountering difficulties, and in the thirties most of the farm population suffered extreme hardships.[8] Much of the time agricultural production increased more rapidly than the production of manufactured goods. And the demand for farm products was inelastic relative to prices and incomes. That is, lower prices did not stimulate higher consumption, and as incomes rose people spent a smaller proportion of their incomes on food. The surge in agricultural production, induced in substantial degree by governmental actions, tended to depress farm prices and incomes.[9]

A curious contradiction developed in United States agricultural policy. While measures to stimulate production continued, a pro-

[5]Ibid., pp. 287–94.
[6]Ibid., p. 295.
[7]Ibid., p. 272; Earl O. Hardy, *A Primer on Food, Agriculture, and Public Policy* (New York: Random House, 1967), pp. 48–53.
[8]Ibid., pp. 264–67, 428–32.
[9]Ibid., pp. 7–11, 57.

gram of compensation to farmers for low prices and incomes was instituted.

In 1929, Congress established a Federal Farm Board which was to create cooperative marketing associations and support farm prices, but the funds appropriated for the Board were totally inadequate to arrest the collapse of prices received by farmers. Only with the passage of the second Agricultural Adjustment Act in 1938 (the first had been ruled unconstitutional) was an effective formula found. Under this act a Commodity Credit Corporation (CCC) made "nonrecourse" loans to farmers on the security of their crops. If the price of the commodity rose, the farmer repaid the loan (with interest) and sold the commodity. If, on the other hand, the price fell, the farmer did not have to repay the loan (or pay interest on it); all he did was allow the CCC to take title to the commodity while he kept the proceeds of the loan as his reward.[10] In practice, floor prices like these presented numerous problems. Because the minimum prices often were above equilibrium prices, amounts supplied exceeded amounts demanded. The consequences were that the government accumulated huge surpluses. Efforts to check production seldom were successful. Governmentally assigned acreage allotments still allowed farmers to apply larger and better inputs to their land not under control, still allowed them to apply more labor and fertilizer, superior seed, and so on. Frequently, too, farmers were allowed to divert acreage to different crops, increasing supplies in other commodities and putting these prices under pressure.[11] Moreover, farm price-support programs mostly assisted the better-off farms; really poor farmers had little to sell, perhaps only one or two bales of cotton, and, as a consequence, failed to benefit substantially from price supports. Finally, because production quotas were assigned to particular acreage, the value of price supports was capitalized into the price of the land. Those who owned the land when a program was inaugurated gained; subsequent purchasers of this land had to pay in higher land prices for the privilege of a production quota.

Agricultural Policy in the United States and the Soviet Union

There is a considerable irony in the contrast between the agricultural policy of the United States and that of the Soviet Union. For

[10] Robertson, *History of the American Economy*, pp. 433–36.
[11] Hardy, *Primer*, pp. 73–77.

a substantial part of the last several decades, the United States, under the influence of the farm lobby, had held farm prices too high, with frequent large surpluses being the consequence. For much of the same period, the Soviet Union has held farm prices down, and has regularly experienced food shortages. (Other factors are involved, of course: Russia has a less hospitable climate and its soil is not as fertile.)

The reader might conclude herein a strong argument for free market prices in agricultural produce, but that was not the intent. With productivity in agriculture in the United States growing rapidly, at the same time as price and income elasticities for farm products are low, increases in productivity mostly will hurt the farmer and help the consumer. Many people off the farm would agree with farmers that this is unfair. What we have here is a case wherein the market fails to produce a distribution of income generally considered to be equitable.

However, the widely employed notion of "parity" prices is unsatisfactory. The idea that the ratio of prices received by farmers to those paid by farmers should be fixed and equal to the ratio which prevailed during a period when farmers prospered (the period usually chosen by the United States government has been 1910 to 1914), means that the income of farmers should remain fixed relative to the incomes of nonfarm producers, without regard to changes in the demand for different factors of production. It also means that the allocation of resources in different activities tends to be frozen. In a dynamic market economy, neither incomes nor prices can remain fixed relative to one another. No simple answer to market failure in agriculture can be found, but many economists tend to think that the most promising approach would be to assist marginal farmers in the transition to urban employment (entirely closing down the operation of many marginal farms), while assisting those who remain in agriculture to be more effective and efficient. (The program might include early retirement for older farmers and vocational programs in rural and small-town schools geared to the urban job market.)

But the notion of parity between farm and nonfarm prices[12] persists, and the idea of protecting the incomes of particular segments of the population is now widespread.

[12] At the time of this writing, most agricultural prices were well above support levels, but even with a decline in the power of the farm lobby, as population shifts to the cities, the notion of parity is not dead.

Welfare Programs

A dynamic economy produces insecurity for many people as new products, new processes, or new sources of supply threaten enterprises and individuals in an established activity. Apart from the threat of innovation, people may also suffer hardships because of inadequate education or training, membership in large families, injury, ill-health, or discrimination related to race, sex, religion or national origin, or because the single parent in a one-parent household must stay home to care for small children.[13]

During the nineteenth century and early years of the twentieth century, poverty was dealt with by private charity and by the limited actions of local governmental units. A private source might deliver a few bushels of coal to a poor household, or a county board might send an impoverished elderly person to the county poor farm. After 1929 and during the worst days of the Great Depression of the thirties, local agencies, unofficial and official, found themselves with totally inadequate resources to meet the misery generated by mass unemployment. In 1933, the Federal Emergency Relief Administration began to make grants both to state and local governments for direct relief payments and for programs of public works. From 1935 to 1942, the Works Progress Administration (WPA) employed a variety of people, at its peak about six percent of the labor force.[14] In the late fifties, writers like Michael Harrington[15] attracted national attention with his studies of the "invisible poor," some 20 percent of the population not sharing in the general affluence of America.

The federal War on Poverty was launched in 1964. It included basic education for functional illiterates, training programs for the unskilled, payroll subsidies to underwrite training programs by private enterprise, day-care centers for the children of working mothers, Head Start programs to prepare disadvantaged children for school entry, youth programs designed to get dropouts back to school, and so on.[16] When the program was being wound down a decade later, most people familiar with it recognized that it had failed. The poor were still with us. But little agreement could be found as to why the War on Poverty had not succeeded. Some pointed to its relatively small budget, others to the opposition of

---

[13] Ralph Gray and John M. Peterson, *Economic Development of the United States*, rev. ed. (Homewood, Ill.: Irwin, 1974), pp. 503, 515, 519–21.

[14] Ibid., p. 438.

[15] M. Harrington, *The Other America* (Baltimore: Penguin Books, 1962).

[16] Gray and Peterson, *Economic Development of the United States*, pp. 522–23.

old-line state and local bureaucrats who frequently had been bypassed by the federal Office of Economic Opportunity. I suspect it failed because we still do not know enough about the causes of poverty. It has become clear that problem families exist and perpetuate themselves through successive generations. Poverty begets poverty. The problems of the parents are bequeathed to the children and, in turn, to the children's children. But why? Why do some children break out of this vicious cycle and others remain trapped?

More recently, public concern has shifted from the seemingly intractable problem of poverty to the apparently more manageable problem of cleaning up the environment.

Market Forces and the Environment

For more than a half century economists have recognized that decisions made in decentralized market economies often fail to take into account nonmarket interdependencies, spillover effects, or "externalities." Businessmen indiscriminately deliver smoke across the countryside, waste products into lakes or down rivers, and the noise of machinery into a surrounding area. Moreover they usually do not take these spillovers into account when they make investment or output decisions.

In the last decade or two, a large part of the general public has become aware of this kind of market failure. Unfortunately, the nature of the problem was not clearly seen at first, and goals were formulated in terms of pure air, pure water, and the like, without regard to the alternatives which would have to be foregone in order to achieve such goals. More recently people have begun to recognize the costs involved in cleaning up the environment. They have begun to think of air quality of differing degrees, each with a different cost, and to consider the trade-offs between a particular (marginal) improvement in air quality and the (marginal) opportunity cost of achieving it. But, environmentalists largely middle-class in status do not yet appear to recognize that governmental regulations with regard to indiscriminate delivery have a significant impact on income distribution. The clean air desired by an upper-middle-class family might, through required emission controls, price the automobile out of reach of low income groups, or reduce the real income of workers who turn out automobiles. It is interesting to observe that few underdeveloped countries feel that they can afford substantial restrictions on industry designed to protect the environment.

Regulation Instead of Government Ownership

Relatively few Americans have been attracted to socialism, Marxian or otherwise. Perhaps it is the heritage of the individual self-reliance of the frontiersman that has led the American to prefer individual initiative constrained only when necessary by the actions of government. Or, perhaps it is the pragmatism of the practical man who rejects the ideology of socialism and chooses rather to tinker with the system just enough to remedy a particular difficulty.

If pragmatism is a virtue in the Soviet-type economy where an excess of ideology appears to stand in the way of institutional change, pragmatism in a country like the United States where ideas tend to be suspect has its dangers. Solving each problem on its merits may seem to be eminently sensible, but the sum total of all these independent solutions may result in a set of institutions with consequences different from those desired by the electorate. A particular set of regulations may fail to take account of important interdependencies in the economy. Or, all the regulations together may so constrain private decision making, so reduce the set of rights that constitute private property, that socialism will be established by default. Rather than contribute to a de facto socialism established by default, the student of alternative economic systems might want to analyze most carefully the economic agenda of government in a regulated capitalism.

Regulated Capitalism

Chapter **17**

In response to criticisms of particular features of capitalism, governments have introduced regulatory measures along with taxes and subsidies. We will consider efforts to reach the following objectives:

1. Control of indiscriminate delivery (spillovers)
2. Control of natural monopoly
3. Production of goods preferred by the government
4. A distribution of income or wealth preferred by the government.

And we will investigate three control devices:

1. Directives
2. Price controls and rationing
3. Taxes and subsidies (or grants).

A particular device, of course, may be used to acheive one objective in one situation and a different objective in another.

Directives

A government may issue directives to control indiscriminate delivery or to control the production or consumption of goods for which it has positive or negative preferences. A government may order the production of certain goods, such as oil storage capacity for defense, or it may order that certain goods, such as marijuana, not be produced or consumed. For example, production or con-

297

sumption may be prohibited during certain hours, noisy construction activity may be prohibited at night, or the consumption of liquor in taverns may be forbidden after midnight. Consumption of certain goods may be entirely forbidden to those under certain ages, as in the cases of liquor and tobacco. Or, consumption without the approval of experts, as with prescription drugs, may be prevented. The production of particular goods, like specific kinds of advertising copy, may also be forbidden.

Government directives in a system of controlled capitalism often take the form of inequalities: Let y be the actual height of weeds, and y' be the height specified in the law. Then y must be $\leq y'$. Smoke control ordinances and water quality laws, for example, take the form of inequalities, as do many parts of municipal building codes. Such directives in the form of inequalities represent modest endeavors at control in comparison with the many output directives in the form of equalities which are issued in the Soviet-type economy. With the use of inequalities, few if any problems of consistency arise because the enterprise is free to make its own decisions within the constraints of the inequalities, and profits remain the motive for efficient operation. (Some directives in a regulated capitalism are in the form of zero equalities. The amount which may be produced is equal to zero. Zoning ordinances forbidding production of goods in particular sectors of a city are of this kind, as are laws prohibiting the manufacture of alcoholic beverages.)

In considering whether particular objectives can be achieved with government directives in a system of regulated capitalism, the economist must consider the likelihood of evasion and the cost of enforcement. The economist will also want to identify the value judgments underlying particular programs of government regulation—a value judgment, for example, that the government should take care of individuals through control of medicinal drugs rather than allow them to take care of themselves.) In recent years, there has been a greater tendency to recognize the limitations of government, to recognize that government is not omniscient and not omnipotent and that there are some results which a government cannot achieve at an acceptable enforcement cost. Particularly when the preferences of large numbers of people differ from the preferences of the government, as in the case of liquor prohibition, evasion will be a serious problem and the cost of law enforcement will be high.

Government control over the production of advertising copy encounters the specific problem of identifying the truth. Government officials may allow preconceptions about what is true to influence their conclusions. Perhaps more serious, a government that forbids the production of what it believes to be error in the description of goods and services might decide that it should also forbid the dissemination of what it believes to be error in matters of public policy.

Price Controls and Rationing

Price controls usually are introduced to serve distributional objectives. The government wants to preserve the incomes of particular groups at a time of large changes in supply and demand. During war or revolution the supply of consumption goods often declines while the money demand for them rises. Price ceilings are introduced to keep high-income groups from bidding up the price of necessities and causing low-income people to suffer hardships.

When legal maximum prices are below the level that equates the amount demanded with the amount supplied, queues emerge. It follows that the people who acquire the available goods probably are the ones who have the most time to stand in line. Rather than continue this distribution on a first-come, first-served basis, the authorities are likely to introduce rationing. They will try for "fair shares," usually equal shares of at least the necessities. Hence, price controls kept in force for any extended period are almost certain to be accompanied by rationing.

Two kinds of rationing are to be found: separate-commodity rationing and point rationing. The former is more likely to occur when rationing first is introduced, and oftentimes is replaced by point rationing. Under separate-commodity rationing, the government would separately assign rations for each commodity—for example, it might allot to each individual one pound of coffee per week, five pounds of potatoes each week, four gallons of gasoline, and so on. The consumer would then receive a set of coupons each of which, when accompanied by money, would entitle him to acquire a specified amount of a particular good.

In time, a government may replace separate-commodity rationing with the more sophisticated system of point rationing. Under that system the consumer would be given coupons worth so many points which could be used for a specified period of time to acquire any rationed good, or any good of a particular class, such as food or clothing. In order to obtain a good, the consumer would have to lay out enough point coupons to cover the point price and enough money to cover the money price. The consumer might receive a total of 100 points per week in coupons, or he might receive 60 food points and 60 clothing points. He would use his point coupons to acquire goods at governmentally set point "prices." Beef, for example, might be five points per pound (or five food points per pound), a shirt might be 35 points.

Separate-Commodity Rationing

We are now in a position to analyze the two different kinds of rationing. Separate-commodity rationing takes the form of inequalities: Let x be the actual amount of butter consumed by an individual and x' be the individual ration quantity. Then $x \leq x'$. If the rationing is to change human behavior, the equality at times must represent the amount purchased, with this being an amount that is less than individuals would have purchased in the absence of rationing.[1] The total rationed demand for each commodity should be equal to the total amount supplied. The authorities can arrive by trial and error at a ration which would result in this equality by comparing actual inventories of a good with their notion of the optimum inventories of it. If, for example, actual inventories of butter in St. Louis were 80,000 pounds, while the authorities considered 100,000 pounds to be the optimum, they would reduce the butter ration for the next period.

Separate-commodity rationing presents many problems. It works best with homogeneous commodities, like sugar. Were the commodity not homogeneous, like potatoes for example, the rations received by different individuals might not be equal, and the authorities might have to undertake the costly task of specifying different grades with different rations of each. The ration might be one pound of new potatoes or one and one-half pounds of last year's potatoes, or several different classes of potatoes might have to be defined.

Because numerous evasions of separate-commodity rationing would occur, the authorities would want to consider the cost of enforcement in any decision to introduce rationing. Some people might sell ration coupons for money, and others might exchange them. (Sales or exchanges of ration coupons are declared illegal when the government believes that it knows best what people should consume.) Black-market sales of goods against money with-

---

[1] Paul Anthony Samuelson, *Foundations of Economic Analysis* (Cambridge Mass.: Harvard University Press, 1961), p. 163.

out coupons and at above-legal prices also might occur. Some people who could buy all they wanted at the ceiling prices might be tempted to get in touch with people who were prepared to sell their products at prices that were above the legal maximum. In a large economy millions of transactions occur every week in innumerable locations, so the costs of enforcement would be high.

Moreover a system of price controls and rationing would lead to a diversion of expenditure and a diversion of factors of production away from the controlled parts of the economy toward uncontrolled or less effectively controlled sectors. With the high cost of enforcement, it would be virtually impossible to control all transactions in the economy or to control all transactions with equal effectiveness. When price controls (and especially rent controls) were kept in force in France after World War II, large amounts of resources went into the development of vacation resorts. Needless to say, a diversion of resources into uncontrolled sectors makes necessary a tighter ration in the controlled parts of the economy.

Price controls and rationing may reduce people's inclinations to work, and increase preferences for leisure: money earned through work is worth less when the government limits the amounts of particular goods that can be purchased. There is present in this instance the posssility of an interesting conflict between different government objectives. Desiring a large production, the government would allow money incomes to be distributed as usual under capitalism, unequally and in accordance with productivity. Then, seeking to preserve the incomes of those who were not so productive, the government would distribute ration coupons equally. The latter concern for need might conflict with the former interest in production.

Difficulties with price controls and rationing are most serious in the long run. Over a short period of time these controls may achieve their objectives. For example, during a short war, patriotism will keep many people out of the black market and keep them working despite an egalitarian distribution of commodities. Then too, factors of production are relatively immobile in the short run and not so likely to be diverted into uncontrolled sectors of the economy. As time passes, however, patriotism wears thin, the black market grows, work efforts might slacken, and resources might move from controlled to uncontrolled (or less effectively controlled) parts of the economy. Indeed, prolonged yet effective price controls and rationing would require extensive and costly restrictions, their magnitude depending on the degree of inflation being suppressed. A sufficiently large inflation would be uncontrollable.

Point Rationing

A system of point rationing escapes some but not all of the difficulties of separate-commodity rationing. As indicated earlier, the consumer would receive a certain number of point coupons for each period and he would distribute these points among different goods, laying out for each good the points required by a governmentally set point price. The consumer, in effect, "is limited to a weighted sum of a number of commodities, the point-prices providing the relative weights."[2]

Let x_1 be the amount purchased of commodity i per unit of time; let p_1 be a point price—the number of points that must be surrendered for each unit of i purchased, and 1 be the point budget-constraint—the total points given to the consumer per unit of time for a particular class of commodities. Then

$$p_i x_i + p_2 x_2 +, \ldots, p_n x_n \leq 1.$$

The point prices would be set by trial and error to clear the market, and the authorities would compare actual with optimal inventories to decide whether a given market were cleared. The coupon points would become "a kind of supplementary money, and the price in terms of ration coupons rather than the money price" would adjust consumption to available supplies.[3]

Point rationing leaves more options to the consumer than does separate-commodity rationing. Within the category for which any given point coupons could be used, the individual would have free choice in consumption. He could, for example, use his clothing points for any articles of clothing he wants. (Or the system might be set up with general point coupons, so that points could be used to acquire any rationed good.) Point rationing as compared with separate-commodity rationing would decentralize consumption decisions. With its relatively free choice for consumers, it would be the preferred form of rationing for those who believed that the individual knew best what pattern of consumption was good for him.

[2]Ibid., p. 165.
[3]Kenneth E. Boulding, *Economic Analysis*, 3rd ed. (New York: Harper, 1955), p. 140.

Like separate-commodity rationing, point rationing would work best when the commodities rationed were homogeneous. The cost of setting different point prices on each of the different grades of a nonhomogeneous product, like potatoes, would be very high.

Enforcement
Some of the costs of enforcement would be lower under point rationing. Consumers would be less inclined to sell ration coupons for money because the point coupons would be more valuable than the coupons of separate-commodity rationing. Point coupons could be used for the purchase of more things. It should be kept in mind, however, that the enforcement costs would be lower because the authorities would have more modest objectives with respect to the control of consumer behavior.

Perhaps fewer illegal sales at above-ceiling prices without coupons would occur under point rationing, since a consumer with greater freedom of choice would probably be less prone to violate the law. But a black market would no doubt exist, and the cost of preventing illegal sales would be high in an economy. Like separate-commodity rationing, point rationing would shift the effort-leisure margin toward leisure, since as mentioned earlier, money acquired through effort is less valuable under rationing. Probably point rationing would not reduce work activity as much as separate-commodity rationing would, because it would leave the consumer with more options in the disposal of money income.

In a system with price controls and point rationing, factors of production no doubt would tend to move away from controlled to uncontrolled or less effectively controlled sectors of the economy. It is clear, then, that legal price ceilings with rationing, whether by separate commodity or through points, is a tool for the short run. For a time, patriotism would check illegal transactions and encourage work despite an egalitarian distribution of rationed goods, and, for a time, factors of production would be relatively immobile. With the passage of time, however, patriotism would exert less influence and factors would tend to depart from the controlled sectors of the economy. Prolonged use of price controls and rationing would require an exceedingly elaborate and costly mechanism for enforcement and would require comprehensive controls over production as well as consumption. It is doubtful that even in a totalitarian state such controls would be feasible over the long run. It is noteworthy that, except during war, the Soviets have tried to maintain market-clearing prices on most consumption goods other than housing and automobiles.

Taxes and Subsidies or Grants

The government may tax and subsidize in order to attain its objectives in production and consumption. It may tax goods like tobacco and liquor which it does not want produced and consumed, and it may subsidize the production of things like housing and school lunches. It may tax and invest the proceeds in agriculture or industry so as to reduce consumption and increase the rate of accumulation. And it may tax some individuals and give grants to others with the objective of changing the distribution of income. I shall distinguish between a subsidy and a grant: a subsidy is intended to alter particular behavior; a grant is not intended to alter the actions of recipients. A payment of government funds to a farmer to induce him to produce more wheat would be a subsidy; a government payment to a disabled worker (not a return on insurance premiums) would be a grant.

Sales Tax and Unit Subsidy
When the government wants to reduce the production and consumption of some goods and increase the production and consumption of others, it can use a sales (excise) tax and a unit subsidy. It might tax jewelry and perfumes which it considers to be luxuries at ten percent of the sale price, for example, and it might offer a subsidy of 25 cents for every book published. The effectiveness of a given tax or subsidy in the control of consumption and production depends on the elasticities of demand and supply. If demand were inelastic, a tax would raise a large revenue for the government, but not greatly reduce consumption and production of the item taxed; if supply were inelastic, a subsidy would give a recipient a nice increase in income, but do little to increase production. Indeed, with inelastic demand and supply, taxes and subsidies might decrease and increase the consumption and production of the wrong goods. Excise taxes on cigarettes might have little effect on smoking, but the families of smokers with incomes reduced as a consequence of the tax might consume less food. Unit subsidies on coal might not increase the production of coal but they might, through increased incomes to owners of coal mines, increase the consumption and production of yachts.

To be sure, a high enough sales tax probably will substantially affect the consumption and production of a good, even when demand is relatively inelastic. But so high a tax opens up a wide gap between cost of production and sale price, a gap that invites illegal production. Whiskey, in the late sixties, cost about one dollar a gallon to produce in the United States, but sold after sales tax was added for around twelve dollars a gallon. The result was a large output of moonshine. In general, the government can achieve its output objectives through use of excise taxes and unit subsidies if demand or supply were elastic, which is to say that the government can reach its objectives using these instruments were its goals not too different from those of the population. If, for example, the government disliked the consumption of perfume and if women did not care for perfume enough to buy it even when its price has risen, then an excise tax would effectively reduce production and consumption of this good. Likewise, if the government wanted to encourage the output of books and if factors of production were ready to increase supplies for a relatively small increase in rewards, then a unit subsidy would achieve the government's objective.

Subsidies, however, might cause inefficiency. If a supplier knows that he will receive whatever funds are necessary to induce him to produce the quantity desired by the government, he might lack the incentive to produce efficiently. He would realize that any increase in his unit costs would be covered by an increase in the unit subsidy.

Taxation for Accumulation

A capitalist government that taxes and then invests in industry and agriculture in order to increase the rate of accumulation may dispose of the funds in one of several ways: It may lend to private enterprises in industry and agriculture at interest rates which just dispose of the funds; it may lend the funds to government enterprises at market-clearing interest rates; or, it may lend to both kinds of enterprises. The interest rate that would emerge in a system with government accumulation would be lower than were all saving voluntary and private. It would not, however, be an "arbitrary" rate. Set to clear the market, the rate would reflect the forces of supply and demand, even though the supply of funds, according to the value judgments of some, should not include compulsory government accumulations. To call an interest rate arbitrary because it reflects government insertions of funds into the capital market implicitly sets up the nongovernmentally influenced market as a norm or ideal; it would be better to find a scientifically neutral terminology and make all value judgments explicit.

Income Tax

Let us now consider taxation and subsidies or grants when the government has as its objective the redistribution of income and wealth. The tax used for income redistribution is usually the progressive income tax. It would take a larger percentage of high incomes than it would of low ones. Those who lack knowledge about taxation commonly overestimate what can be achieved with the income tax. Income, particularly income from business, is an elusive concept, difficult to define. Skillful accountants and lawyers find many legal ways of avoiding tax. And with millions of taxpayers receiving monies from many different sources, the possibilities of illegal tax evasion are great. The cost of effective enforcement is high and increases with the rate of the tax, so that to a considerable extent, the tax is self-assessed, with the government being dependent for collection on the honesty of the taxpayer.

The progressive income tax probably would shift the effort-leisure margin in the direction of more leisure and less effort, though the magnitude of the shift is difficult to determine. Leisure does not produce taxable income and individuals might elect more leisure were taxes to reduce income from work.[4] The progressive income tax also might reduce risk-taking, when the income from a risky investment were substantially reduced by tax.

Death Duties

Death duties also might be used in a capitalist economy to redistribute wealth. However, there are difficult problems of valuation when the assets transferred at death are not market quotable. Moreover, death duties can be avoided by persons deaccessing wealth prior to death. Effective death duties, therefore, would require that gifts given in contemplation of death be taxed. In recent years, the return to government from estate taxes in

---

[4]The possibility that income tax would shift the effort-leisure margin toward effort cannot be excluded. People might work harder to maintain their after-tax incomes.

the United States has been eroded away by the practice of some persons who upon their deaths put property into trust, with life estates in the property being given to a sequence of heirs. Transfers of property from life tenant to life tenant are not subject to tax.

Death duties probably would have a smaller impact on the effort-leisure margin than would income taxes. A tax collected only at death probably would discourage effort less than would an income tax, collected for example, every week or month. It should be recognized, however, that death duties might encourage early retirement. (On the other hand, the heir who obtains a smaller bequest might work harder.)

Grants

Let us now turn our attention to the subject of governmental assistance as part of a program of redistribution of income and wealth.

One question that immediately arises is whether or not the government should give subsidies in kind or grants in money. The government might build housing, supply medical care and education, distribute food stamps to the poor, and so on, or it might simply hand over grants of money. Government assistance is given in kind when the preferences of the government differ from those of the recipients, and when the government believes that it knows best what is good for people who receive aid. Of course, there are problems of evasion and costs of enforcement. When housing is subsidized, people sometimes invite relatives in to live with them, thus reducing the standard of housing below what is preferred by the government. Other examples of this sort include food stamps being sold for money; businessmen in competition with rivals accepting food stamps for nonfood items.

If, however, a government is (1) indifferent about what an individual acquires, or (2) believes that its preferences and those of the recipient are the same, or (3) believes that the recipient knows best what is good for him or her, then it will supply aid in the form of money.

Just as income taxes may cause the taxpayer to elect more leisure and less work, so grants may cause the recipient to choose leisure in place of work. The decision to cut off welfare payments to a family where there are able-bodied adults capable of finding employment is sometimes a painful one, because children in the family may be the ones who suffer. (To take the children away from feckless parents and rear them in an institutional environment or in a foster home may not be a happy alternative either.)

Perhaps the most important question is whether assistance should be designed to sustain the individual in his (or her) existing situation, or whether it should be set up to develop the individual's productivity to promote self-sufficiency. Grants to the aged and the severely disabled, for example, might do little but sustain those individuals. On the other hand, assistance to children, young people, the partially disabled, and the middle-aged might more often be designed to increase future productivity. To be sure, at present we know little about the returns on investments in human capital, and the task of increasing the productivity of people who have been reared in problem families and environments would be a formidable one. Subsidies designed to increase productive capacity might have to be in kind—in medical aid and educational programs—and government support during a training endeavor might have to be made conditional on regular class attendance—a requirement that would restrict the recipients' freedom.

The objective sought through taxation and grants is frequently described as "equality of opportunity," but an objective so stated is most imprecise. The reasons for such a statement are discussed below.

"Equality of Opportunity"

A desire for equality among men and women, at times amounting to a "passion for equality,"[5] is one of the strongest drives encountered in public affairs. It is often observed, however, that there are differences between people, differences in capacities and preferences, in anatomy, in character and personality, and differences in motivation. Observation of human diversity frequently leads men and women to value individual differences, to believe in individualism. When both equality and individualism are valued, a conflict between objectives may be seen. Ought men and women to strive for equality, or ought they seek to develop their differences? What appears to resolve the conflict is the pursuit of "equality of opportunity." It turns out, however, that the meaning of this goal is not at all clear, and that in particular the costs of alternative distributions of opportunity have not been taken into account by those considering the matter.

[5]Alexis de Tocqueville, *Democracy in America*, vol. 1 (New York: Alfred A. Knopf, 1945), p. 53.

Equal at the Starting Line

At first thought, equality of opportunity does appear to resolve the conflict between equality and individualism. Frequently the metaphor of a footrace is invoked: Everyone is equal on the starting line, while each tries to excel and expects to occupy a different position at the end. Equality of opportunity is defined, most commonly, as a state of affairs in which each person has a right to the greatest development of his or her own capacities. "Each child shall become the most and the best that he (she) can become."[6] Each child, and each adult, shall develop his capabilities to the fullest. But what meaning can be given to the idea of equality in diversity? First, let us look at a relatively simple application of the principle. Later we will try it out in more complex circumstances.

Suppose two students with equal capacities, the only difference between them being that one is white and the other black. Both, many will say, should have the same chance for admission to desirable schools. The footrace metaphor applies nicely. The two begin at the same starting line and are headed toward the same finish.

Now, however, imagine three students with marked differences in capabilities. One has the talent to become an excellent violinist, the second to become a good one, while the third has it in him to be a very good carpenter. Under precisely what conditions can it be said that the three have equality of opportunity? One supposes that the first should have an excellent violin teacher, the second should have a good teacher, and that the third should be in a vocational class or apprenticeship commensurate with his abilities. But how are these different opportunities to be measured and compared? What test can be conceived that would tell us whether or not the two potential violinists had been "equally" treated? Or that the violinist and the carpenter had received equal consideration? Here a footrace is harder to detect: The competitors are going off in different directions.

The imprecision in the idea of equal opportunity can be seen in its applications to education. At one time the emphasis was on equalizing resource *inputs* in different schools—equally good plant and teachers of equal quality (with morale, enthusiasm, and belief in student aptitudes included in the measure of teacher quality). Such an equalization of inputs does produce equal opportunity for a relatively homogeneous student body (homogeneous

---

[6]Melvin Tumin, quoted in Edmund W. Gordon, "Toward Defining Equality of Educational Opportunity," in *On Equality of Educational Opportunity*, eds. Frederick Mosteller and Daniel P. Moynihan. (New York: Vintage Books, 1972), p. 427.

in native abilities, in family and cultural environment, and in objectives). But in the last decade or two a lack of homogeneity amongst children and young people has become more and more obvious. Children from culturally deprived backgrounds have been recognized by the community, as have been children of exceptionally high ability. In time, but still in the name of equality of opportunity, the call then went out for equalization of *outputs* rather than equalization of inputs, for equality, that is, in educational achievement.[7] Compensatory education was widely adopted—headstart, remedial reading, and so on—and even some hints of a ceiling on educational achievement were heard. It seemed eminently desirable to many people at that time that those who were at a disadvantage, perhaps because of a less fortunate past, should receive special consideration. But to label all the different programs in special education *equality* of opportunity was seriously to distort the language. We would be more likely to understand the problem and possible alternative solutions if we described them as *unequal* programs for differing students. (It does not help at all to say that, in order to make opportunity equal, "it may be necessary to make education something more than equal."[8])

Investment in Human Capital

There are still more serious difficulties. When someone says that each person has a right to the fullest development of his or her own capacities, he is saying that investment in human capital should be pursued until its marginal productivity is zero, with no regard to the possible gains from investment in nonhuman capital. As an extreme example, a huge number of man-hours might be devoted to teaching a dull boy to read blueprints, even though a product of much greater value might result if the same man-hours were put into the construction of a solid-waste disposal plant. When it is said that everyone is entitled to the fullest development of his or her capabilities, the opportunity cost of investment in human capital is considered to be zero.

In decisions concerning investment in training and education, moreover, the decision maker must consider not only factor en-

---

[7] James L. Jarrett, "The Meanings of Equality," in *The Conditions for Educational Equality*, ed. Sterling M. McMurrin. (New York: Committee for Economic Development, 1971), p. 27.

[8] Gordon, "Defining Equality of Educational Opportunity," p. 426.

dowments, but also demand for the output of different factors. Demand for the products of some skills might be low, while demand for others might be high. Consumers (or government officials in a centrally planned economy) might want, for example, relatively few concerts and many houses. Decisions concerning investment in human capital, then, either might reflect the differing production capacities of potential factors of production ("equality of opportunity"), or the demand for different products ("consumer sovereignty" or the "sovereignty of the authorities"). It is more than likely that in any economy a desired solution will take into account both factor capacity and demand for the products of different skills. (Reconciliation of these conflicting goals is a problem faced by the modern Israeli kibbutz, for example, when it sends its youth away to college. One is told that almost any youngster who wants to go away to school can do so, but that he or she may have to study a subject needed by the kibbutz rather than one close to his or her heart.)

Trade-Offs

A decision maker must trade off gains against losses when he decides to increase the opportunity of some at the expense of others. The losses, of course, are the costs of the decision.

One trade-off is between equality and individualism (or between universality and uniqueness). An egalitarian program of remedial reading, for example, might take resources away from a program of reading enrichment designed for gifted children.

Another trade-off might be between equality and economic progress. Suppose that, with limited teaching resources, there are two children, one with some manual dexterity and a modest capacity to work with printed materials, the other with imagination and intellectual faculties which could make him a gifted engineer. An egalitarian objective might have the first child taught to follow instructions and read blueprints, while an economic growth objective might employ the same resources to teach the second child higher mathematics (as long as the expected value of his marginal product is greater than the likely value of the less able child).

A third trade-off will be between consumer preferences and the preferences of factors of production. For example, consumers might want a lot of electric appliances, whereas young people might want to develop their capacities in art and music.

In sum, the notion of equality makes sense when one is talking about people with approximately the same package of skills. That such people should be treated equally is a judgment of value which would be accepted by many persons. It is not meaningful, however, to speak of equalizing opportunity when human endowments are exceedingly diverse. Rather than consider the objective of equality of opportunity, the economist as scientist, or the sociologist, might rather consider an interdependent system that would reconcile diverse capacities with differing consumer preferences.

Before we discard totally the concept of equal opportunity, we should look at alternative objectives.

Total Equality

At the extreme is one socialist dream of complete and total equality. People with identical genetic inheritances, environments, and preferences would live identical lives. For most observers, merely to see the objective stated is to discredit it. Yet, some form of this goal is found incompletely and imprecisely, in a considerable part of the literature of socialism and communalism. And some efforts to attain an almost complete equality have been made in practice. Socialists and others (i.e., some liberals) on the left have tended to deny the existence of genetic differences; they believe people are born equal. The human differences that are observed are said to arise out of the inequalities of capitalism. Kropotkin, a leading advocate of anarchism, thought that all men should combine hand work and brain work and perform both agricultural and industrial tasks.[9] And indeed, equality as identity does require elimination of the division of labor. In a complete egalitarianism, moreover, everyone would consume the same goods obtained from the "socialist warehouse" of tradition. And of course money, Dostoevsky's "coined freedom," would not exist, for with money people could diversify their consumption. Capital formation would be communal rather than individual.

The foregoing seems to describe a world of fantasy. Yet, at times application of these ideas can be found. The almost identical dress of the Chinese in recent decades along with the banishment of educated youth to the countryside, to say nothing of backyard steel mills, suggest that the socialist ideal of a near-complete equality has had an impact on Chinese life. And the identical clothing frequently observed in the religious communes around the world similarly demonstrates the hold which the ideal of an almost literal

---

[9]P. Kropotkin, *Fields, Factories and Workshops* (London: Thomas Nelson and Sons, 1898).

equality has had on some people. Needless to say, critics view the socialism of identity as a regimented, ant-hill existence, while its supporters see it as the only true community.

Discard the Credential Society?
An alternative, distinctly different from "equality of opportunity," is equality in the awarding of class and school credentials, and equality in the distribution of jobs and job advancement, all without regard to capacity or performance. For example, after sitting in the same classrooms and receiving identical diplomas or degrees, men and women would have the same access to jobs, and would get the same pay regardless of their performance in school or on the job. (Perhaps new jobs and promotions would be given out by lot.) Again, it almost appears that statement of the objective alone discredits it, except that lately we have heard advocates of ideas that are not too different from these. Some of these advocates suggest that all students be passed no matter how poorly they do in class, that high school diplomas or even college degrees be given for orderly attendance alone. The credential-supplying function of schools or the "credential society" is to be discredited, while jobs and promotions are offered on the basis of minority quotas. The ultimate objective may be equal money income for everyone. But even equality of money income may cause awkward difficulties. Money, that bearer of options, allows men and women to differentiate themselves in expenditure and in savings and investment. Some may invest in private education, and, with the acquired human capital, get an edge on their fellow man.

Neither equality as identity nor equality in the award of degrees, jobs, promotions, and income is likely to appeal to many people. What seems to be needed is a substitute for equality of opportunity, a substitute for this goal that can serve to reconcile egalitarian with individualistic values. Suppose we look at quite a different set of objectives. One goal might be equality in mastery of the basic skills—reading, writing, and arithmetic.[10] For several reasons, however, equality in basic skills might turn out to be hard to achieve. At the lower end of the scale would be the seriously retarded, the imbeciles and the morons. Although investment in research on techniques of special education might provide a good return here, it does not seem likely such persons would ever

---

[10] Equality in the basic level of achievement is a suggestion put forward by Gordon in "Defining Equality of Educational Opportunity," p. 433.

achieve equality in mastering these skills. At the upper end of the scale the gifted child might virtually teach himself or herself to read (to say nothing of parental assistance or of attendance in private classes or private schools). Few would care for a world, proposed as a possibility by some, wherein the overachievers would be sent home from school and deprived of access to books. A goal of *equality* of achievement in basic skills, therefore, is not likely to be reached.

Minimum Skills Plus Individual Development
More realistic might be the goal of a *minimum* level of achievement in reading, writing, and arithmetic (excluding only those who suffer from serious mental retardation). Insofar as these minimum levels were realized by withdrawing resources from the development of the ablest children, the goal would move people toward equality, even as complete equality were recognized to be beyond realization. Educational achievement along these lines could be measured with some accuracy, so that we could know the extent to which equality were being achieved. And a goal of this sort might appeal to many as a way of preserving the options of young people until they were older and better able to assess their talents and interests.

Beyond a minimum attainment level in the three R's, the objective might be as full a development as possible of individual potentialities, given the constraints on available resources (given, that is, the opportunity costs of investment in human capital) and given the demands of consumers for the outputs of different skills (outputs turned out by private enterprises under capitalism or governmental enterprises under market socialism). The market could put a value on the various capabilities of people and could reconcile the skills of factors of production with the preferences of consumers. As different abilities were developed, discrimination on grounds of race, sex, religion, or national origin would, of course, be ruled out, so that all with equal talents would have equal chances for education, employment, and advancement.

Far more clearly than the notion of equality of opportunity, the set of objectives here proposed—equal minimum skills and beyond this the development of individual differences—reconciles the frequently conflicting goals of (1) egalitarianism and individualism, (2) egalitarianism and progress, and (3) the development of individual work capacities along with satisfaction of the wants of consumers.

The Negative Income Tax

A program with great appeal is one which would take the place of the present-day multiplicity of redistribution programs, of aid for the families of dependent children, aid for the permanently and totally disabled, aid for the impecunious elderly, and so on. Sometimes, it is called a guaranteed minimum income; more often, it is known as the negative income tax. Such a tax would entitle everyone to a minimum income without regard to the cause of deficiencies in private income. Reductions in the minimum income (up to a point) would amount to less than increments in private earnings, so that incentives to earn income would not be eliminated. Corresponding to a positive tax on high incomes, there would be a "negative tax" (government payments) associated with low incomes.

Proposed as early as 1962 by Milton Friedman, the negative income tax has attracted support across almost the entire political spectrum, from the right to the left.[11] Yet it remains a chimera, always in sight, but far away on the political horizon. Search for a reason for failure to enact what so many endorse is instructive.

Any scheme for a negative income tax possesses two key elements—a minimum guaranteed annual income and a rate of reduction (or rate of negative tax). A family with no private income, for example, might receive a minimum guaranteed income of $3,000 per year. Then for every dollar of its own earnings, its government supplement might be reduced by 50 cents (a negative tax rate of 50 percent). Should the family earn $1,000, its government supplement would decline by $500, so that its income after supplement (after "tax") would be $1,000 + [$3,000–(0.50)($1,000)] = $3,500. The objective of the minimum income and the negative tax is to assure to all households a minimum standard of life, while at the same time preserving incentives to work.

The problem, posing an almost inescapable dilemma, lies in choosing the minimum guaranteed income and the rate of reduction. The minimum should be large enough to meet what the community (for example, 51 percent of the electorate) considers to be the minimum below which no household should be allowed to fall. At the same time, the rate of reduction should be low enough to induce members of the household to seek employment, but it also should be high enough to keep a household from receiving government assistance when its total income is large by com-

---

[11]Milton Friedman, *Capitalism and Freedom* (Chicago: University of Chicago Press, 1962), pp. 191–94; James Tobin, Joseph A. Pechman, and Peter M. Mieszkowski, "Is a Negative Income Tax Practical?" *Yale Law Journal* 77 (November, 1967), pp. 1–27.

munity standards. The dilemma can best be seen in figures used in a 1972 discussion of the subject.[12] Consider a guaranteed income of $3,000 for a family of four and rates of reduction respectively of 70, 50, and 30 percent. (See Table 17-1.) At a 70 percent rate of reduction, a family that earned $4,000 would receive a government supplement of $200 and a total income of $4,200. But a 70 percent rate of tax on incremental earnings is rather high and might discourage effort. At a 50 percent rate of reduction the family that earned $4,000 would receive a supplement of $1,000 and a total income of $5,000, while at a 30 percent rate of reduction the same family would receive a supplement of $1,800 and a total income of $5,800. In the last case, the motive for work would be quite high, but probably the electorate would be reluctant to see the payment of government funds to a family with so high a standard of living. Such funds otherwise might go to people in exceedingly bad circumstances. And that is the dilemma: A rate of reduction high enough to be politically acceptable would be likely to have an adverse effect on work incentives; a rate low enough to encourage work would give government funds to families with relatively high incomes. A negative income tax which was effectively designed to have the desired effect on incentives probably would prove to be politically unacceptable.[13]

Table 17-1 **Income after Supplement at Different Rates of Reduction (With a Guaranteed Minimum of $3,000)**

Rate of Reduction	Family Earnings	Supplement	Income after Supplement
70%	$4,000	$3,000 − 2,800 = $ 200	$4,200
50%	$4,000	$3,000 − 2,000 = $1,000	$5,000
30%	$4,000	$3,000 − 1,200 = $1,800	$5,800

[12]David N. Kershaw, "A Negative-Income-Tax Experiment," *Scientific American* 227 (October, 1972) pp. 22–23.

[13]Many, if not most, writers on the subject have recognized the trade-off between the rate of negative tax and size of governmental supplementary payments, but few seem to have seen that this conflict puts serious political obstacles in the way of achieving a negative income tax. See John F. Due and Ann F. Friedlaender, *Government Finance: Economics of the Public Sector* (Homewood, Ill.: Irwin, 1973), pp. 148–51: "Low transfer rates [negative tax rates] are important from the viewpoint of incentives. But low transfer rates impose considerable cost to the Treasury unless the minimum guaranteed income is very low." Cf. also Kershaw, "Negative-Income-Tax Experiment," p. 23, and Richard E. Wagner, *The Public Economy* (Chicago: Markham Publishing Company, 1973), pp. 166–67.

One experimental study did produce tentative results, suggesting that a negative income tax would not discourage work. The small differences observed between the experimental group and the control group appeared to show that the former used their negative tax receipts to stay out of the labor force a little longer while looking for better jobs.[14] Still, many plans to enact negative income tax schemes propose to start out with relatively low income guarantees, adding them to existing welfare programs. But payments under the old programs would be reduced dollar-for-dollar with increases in earnings, which is effectively a 100 percent tax on these earnings; as a consequence, administration of the old programs, almost certainly, would blunt the incentive benefits expected from the negative income tax.[15]

The Traditional Method

Traditional Utility Rate Determination

When the economies of large-scale production are so great that one enterprise of optimum size can supply the entire market, or when only one enterprise (e.g., a hydroelectric plant) can occupy a unique and valuable site, a natural monopoly will emerge. Profits are collected, not the temporary monopoly profits of the innovator, but enduring monopoly gains. With the objective of changing this distribution of income, governments frequently attempt to control the prices charged by natural monopolies, most commonly the prices (rates) charged by utilities and transportation companies.

Rate-making bodies (commissions or agencies) ordinarily set maximum rates expected to give the utility a "fair" return, usually six or seven percent on the total capital invested. For a ceiling on rates that would give a fixed return on capital and not reduce efficiency, a more elaborate set of controls is required than has been recognized by most regulatory bodies and courts.

First of all, effective control of rates requires control over the quality of output. A price is an exchange of money for a good or a service. With only a ceiling on the money price, an enterprise could escape control and raise the effective charge by reducing

---

[14] Kershaw, "Negative-Income-Tax Experiment," pp. 22–23.

[15] "If the states continue to administer public assistance with a 100% tax on other income, the value of NIT (negative income tax) as a device to maintain work incentives will be diluted." Tobin, Pechman, and Mieszkowski, "Is a Negative Income Tax Practical?", p. 14.

the quality of its product. A railroad, for example, might allow its trains to become dirty, unsafe, and late. An agency regulating rates, therefore, should specify a minimum quality of service as well as a maximum price.

If the rate of return allowed by a regulatory agency were fixed, the agency would control operating costs, for such a method of rate determination is really "cost-plus" pricing.[16] If the regulatory agency were to allow a rate increase whenever costs rose and insist on a rate reduction whenever costs declined, in order to preserve a fixed rate of return on capital, management would have no interest in costs and no incentive for efficiency. If management in this situation were careless about operating costs, it could obtain a rate increase; if it energetically lowered costs, rates would be dropped, wiping out the profits that would result from cost reduction. Under these circumstances the authorities would have to control operating costs. They would have to see to it, for example, that a utility did not consume coal wastefully. They might even take the initiative when it became economical to substitute fuel oil for coal, insisting that a management not interested in costs (given the method of control) make the substitution.

Simply to state these requirements is to reveal that regulatory bodies in the United States are far from achieving effective control. While a commission will disallow certain outlays in calculating the costs which rates are to cover—for example, very high salaries to company officials—it will not interest itself in current expenses in general. Indeed the courts usually have held that a commission, apart from obvious abuses of discretion, may not substitute its judgment for that of management.[17] But clearly the courts have not understood the nature of the cost-plus rate-setting when they have prohibited regulatory agencies from controlling current outlays. As long as rates are set to allow the utility a fixed rate of return, managers will have little motive for efficiency in operations. If efficiency is to be obtained under these conditions, the commission will have to check all inputs of labor and materials to see that they are necessary. It will also have to take the initiative

---

[16]William G. Shepherd and Thomas G. Gies, eds., *Utility Regulation: New Directions in Theory and Practice* (New York: Random House, 1966), pp. 30, 96–98; P. Philip Locklin, *Economics of Transportation*, 4th ed. (Homewood, Ill.: Irwin, 1954), p. 341.

[17]Charles F. Phillips, Jr., *The Economics of Regulation* (Homewood, Ill.: Irwin, 1965), pp. 180–83; Paul J. Garfield and Wallace J. Lovejoy, *Public Utility Economics* (Englewood Cliffs, N.J.: Prentice-Hall, 1964), p. 48; Eli Winston Clemens, *Economics and Public Utilities* (New York: Appleton-Century-Crofts, 1950), pp. 128–31.

in insisting that low-cost factors of production be substituted for high-cost factors.

A regulatory body also will have to control capital outlays if the lowest-cost combination of capital with other factors is to be obtained. Commissions have been permitted to disallow imprudent investments, but they have seldom been able to insist that a cost-reducing innovation be undertaken. Yet with cost-plus rate determination, management lacks the incentive to innovate.

Although it is not widely known there is an alternative approach to the control of natural monopoly.

Incentive Rate Determination
Rather than allowing a fixed rate of return on capital, the authorities could permit the rate of return to vary. They could permit high prices and high profits for efficient, innovative, and risk-bearing enterprises, while holding prices and profits down for inefficient and conservative firms. Shepherd and Gies use the phrase "incentive regulation"[18] to label this proposal, but in reality such a determination of rates would reduce the need for regulation. Suppose we look at the achievement of efficiency in the use of coal, along with the substitution of fuel oil for coal when it becomes economical. Under a system of strictly cost-plus rate determination, the regulatory body would have to issue orders if it wanted improvement in procedures for handling coal, and it would have to insist on investment which would reduce costs through the substitution of fuel oil for coal. Management would have no interest in lowering costs. Were a system of incentive rate determination employed, a rate-setting agency would observe the behavior of management and adjust rates accordingly. Rates might be lowered and profits squeezed when an enterprise was believed to be wasting coal. (Orders to lower rates would substitute for price reductions forced by rivals in a competitive environment.) Rates might be left unchanged when management reduced costs through a substitution of fuel oil for coal, thereby permitting the enterprise to collect the profits of innovation. In place of the comprehensive and detailed supervision required by cost-plus rate determination, we would have only that amount of observation of management as would enable the authorities to appraise its performance in general. (Comparisons between different enterprises would be made—for example, a comparison of

[18]Shepherd and Gies, *Utility Regulation*, pp. 46–50, 98.

ratios of expense to revenue—and, of course, differences in the conditions under which diverse enterprises operated would have to be taken into account.)

A system of incentive rate determination presents some difficulties. Management, for one thing, might be paid by salary, so that rate changes which altered profits would not influence managerial behavior. It seems likely, however, that were efficiency and innovation rewarded with enterprise profit, managers would be given stock or stock options (or bonuses tied to profits) in order to interest them in profit maximization.

Incentive rate determination requires the exercise of judgment on the part of utility commissions. They must judge the performance of different managements, estimate what profits will induce desired behavior, and adjust rates accordingly. The temptation is to reward all enterprises equally so as to avoid the necessity of explaining differences in treatment. But administering any system of rewards and penalties requires the exercise of judgment and requires the administrator to overcome any inclination toward egalitarianism.

To some extent, incentive rates result from what Shepherd[19] calls "regulatory lag." Though commissions may intend to maintain fixed rates of return on capital, the time required by investigations, hearings, and the like causes a lag in upward and downward adjustments in permitted charges. This lag results in departures from cost-plus pricing and may encourage desired behavior. A lag in rate increases when costs rise might put pressure on management to function efficiently and hold costs in check. A lag in rate reductions when costs are lower must encourage efficiency and innovation by allowing larger profits during the period of the lag. The profits that result from regulatory lag, however, probably are only a rough approximation to those which would maximize desired incentives. Inflation, which is beyond the control of managers, might increase costs and reduce profits, and when there is a lag in permitted price increases, the result might be to discourage investment and innovation in regulated industries. Or price cuts which follow cost reductions with a regulatory lag, for example, of only six months, might come too soon and discourage the kind of risky innovation that is sought. Better than regulatory lag as a way of getting desired behavior would be a systematic adjustment of rates as a means of maximizing incentives for efficiency and innovation.

[19]Ibid., pp. 31, 46.

Indeed, the best treatment for a regulated natural monopoly would simulate the competitive sectors of the economy, where there is short-run monopoly and long-run competition. The authorities would allow regulated enterprises to earn monopoly profits in the short run, then squeeze these profits out after they had served their role of stimulating innovation. When the authorities ordered a price reduction, it would be equivalent to the entry of rivals in the competitive sectors of the economy.

The Limits of Regulation

A government will not always succeed in doing what it wants to do. For one thing, the objectives of a government may conflict, as when the rationing of goods introduced to achieve particular distributional goals stands in the way of the desired large production which an unfettered expenditure of money incomes would achieve, or when taxes and grants designed to change the distribution of income have the undesired result of reducing work and increasing leisure. Then too, evasion of regulatory measures will occur—black markets to evade price controls, for example—and the costs of effective enforcement may be higher than the government is prepared to pay. One regulatory measure often leads to another as the government seeks to prevent untoward side effects of its regulations. Control over production, for example, may be introduced to secure supplies when factors of production are tending to move away from sectors subject to price control. Corruption might emerge. A businessman might bribe an official in order to get a larger allocation of a rationed material input. As time passes and changes in preferences and technology occur, regulations tied to conditions in an earlier base period become increasingly out-of-date, and what started out as a simple, apparently sensible set of regulatory measures ends up a ramshackle web of only partially effective controls.

While much can be achieved through regulations, much that men and women would like to accomplish remains beyond the power of government.

A Cultural Critique of Capitalism

Traditionally, socialists criticized the distribution of income and wealth in a capitalist economy, arguing that the capitalist class exploited the working class and kept them impoverished. Less emphasized, but considered important, were inefficiencies—the waste of duplication in competitive enterprises,[20] the restrictions on output by monopolies, the lack of planning ("capitalism is anarchy"), and the loss of production during periodic depressions.

Many reforms of capitalism introduced over the years, along with recognition of some of the problems of socialism, have substantially reduced the impact of the traditional criticisms of a capitalist economy. Income has been redistributed through the progressive income tax and a variety of welfare programs; strong unions have increased the incomes of large blocs of workers; giant enterprises have rationalized operations, achieved the economies of large-scale production, and, in conglomerates, widened the scope of able management; anti-trust agencies and regulatory bodies have done much to reduce, eliminate, or control monopoly; local, regional, and national planning have dealt with interdependencies ("spillovers") which the market had not taken into account; the market; fiscal policy along with greater sophistication in monetary policy reduced the incidence of depressions and unemployment. Most important, capitalist economies have grown, so that, apart from serious pockets of poverty, large parts of the working population have found themselves experiencing a steadily rising standard of living.

The consequence has been that the working class has not rallied behind a program of socialism. In the United States and Canada, socialist leaders have attracted but a small following, and, in Europe where they have attracted more support, they have done so only by soft-pedaling their socialism and focusing on reform. As a consequence, younger socialists (the "new left") have changed their approach. They have tended to criticize the *culture* of capitalism rather than its material failings. Indeed, they have pointed to material achievements as one of the unsatisfactory features of modern life. They have turned from the ideas of Marx when as an older man he was concerned with material welfare, to his ideas as a younger man, when he described people as "alienated" from their work and its products.

The present-day critics of capitalism frequently describe it as a "consumerist" society. Rather than admire union leaders and loyalty to unions, they look down upon organized workers who they maintain are concerned with wages, hours, and working conditions, who aspire to middle class standards, and who accept bour-

---

[20]The writer received his first lesson in comparative economic systems as a child when his father pointed out to him that it was ridiculous for the milk wagons of several different companies to come down our street every day.

geois values. The work ethic and saving (the discipline of work and accumulation), individual self-reliance and the nuclear family, and law and order all are decried. Life in the suburbs often is thought of as the epitome of capitalism, embodying many of its worst features. Compromise, which is characteristic of market solutions where there are conflicting interests and is characteristic of governmental decisions in a regulated capitalism, is unfavorably juxtaposed to an inflexible idealism and a purity of motive and decision.

Capitalism, however, may not be so lacking in ideals as is frequently believed. Honesty in business dealing is admired. Many businessmen live by the creed that a man's word is his bond. It is difficult, to be sure, to measure the degree of honesty in different economic systems. We know that under capitalism, people frequently lie about the qualities of goods they want to sell or about the services they offer, but we also know that a large number of the most solid and enduring business houses and business careers have developed out of a reputation for reliability and probity. Much depends on the time horizon of the individual, on whether he is operating, for example, a one-night stand at a fair or developing a multi-generation business establishment. (To keep the matter in perspective, we should recall that inaccurate information may be supplied in noncapitalist economies, as well. Because the time horizon of the Soviet manager is short, because he is under pressure for quick results, he sometimes misleads his superiors. A member of the Soviet hierarchy has said: "The trouble with our system is that we lie so much—about our capacity, about our input needs, about our production, to say nothing of what we tell others about our beliefs.")

Perhaps most striking in the cultural critique of capitalism is the concern about a lack of common purpose, a lack of community, national, or all-humanity embracing humanitarian objectives. To critics of capitalism it is not considered sufficient for households to have their own goals, or for subgroups to be interested in particular activities (crafts, sports, reforms, and so on). They maintain that humanity in general must find a higher nobility of purpose, a selfless devotion, and a sense of larger objectives to which all mankind will rally. The critics of the culture of capitalism believe that there is a "religious" vacuum in a capitalism of households and enterprises all going their own way.[21]

[21] Cf. Irving Kristal, "About Equality," *Commentary* 54 (November, 1972), pp. 43, 47.

Suburban Life

Much of the cultural critique of capitalism can be recognized in a widespread condemnation of suburban life, and an examination of the literature that censures suburbia is of considerable value in a study of capitalism.

Socialists have almost always been contemptuous of the middle class. Intellectuals, liberal intellectuals especially, have criticized life in the suburbs, and the new left has displayed a fierce animosity toward both. Critics of suburbia have tended to compare it either with an idealized small-town past or with a utopian vision of the future. Even scientific writers frequently offer a sardonic social satire in place of detached analysis.

> The medicine cabinet contains few of the trusted patent medicines of an earlier generation, but it is nevertheless well stocked with astringents, deodorants, and antiseptic materials as well as with numerous half-finished bottles and tubes of costly physician-prescribed drugs, originally secured to combat an ailment of some family member. Much zealous trust is placed in the contents of the medicine cabinet.[22]

Berger observed that, in 1970, "plastic" seemed to be the "most common term of general rebuke."[23]

In order to gain perspective, we might observe that around the turn of the century Western intellectuals had high hopes for the suburbs as an ideal "middle landscape," between city and country. H. G. Wells wrote of a passion for nature, the charm of gardening, and a "craving . . . for a little private *imperium* such as a house or cottage 'in its own grounds'."[24]

One should not react to present-day critics of modern suburban life by idealizing the suburb. But one should maintain some detachment in study of the middle-class suburb, looking at both its positive and negative features. (Because the middle class in the suburb is the subject of this discussion, we shall not deal with the

---

[22]John R. Seeley, R. Alexander Sim, and Elizabeth W. Loosely, *Crestwood Heights: A Study of the Culture of Suburban Life* (New York: John Wiley & Sons, 1967), p. 45.

[23]Bennett M. Berger, *Looking for America: Essays on Youth, Suburbia and Other American Obsessions* (Englewood Cliffs, N.J.: Prentice-Hall, 1971), p. 159n.

[24]Scott Donaldson, *The Suburban Myth* (New York: Columbia University Press, 1969), pp. 57, 92.

working-class suburb, which has been so carefully studied by Berger.[25])

The Middle Class

It is the values of middle-income people working in middle management and in the professions which have made them so much the object of new-left and liberal-left hostility—their competitive striving for material success, their love of material comforts (automobiles, houses, appliances), their conformity, and their conventional sexual morality (frequently not practiced and, therefore, regarded as being hypocritical). Such critics also point out that white people dwell in suburban locations generally inaccessible to black and low-income families, and that the very mentality of suburbia contributes to maintaining this status quo. Given such a critique, the suburbs represent a geographical focus for many of the disappointments that arise when idealism confronts an imperfect reality.

The aversion to a life of competitive striving for material gain is frequently felt even by those caught up in it themselves. They speak of the "rat race," "dog-eat-dog," and "keeping up with the Joneses." Others, perhaps more secure in their status, sometimes tend to be smug about their positions in the world, and this smugness, in particular, is detested by those who dislike the suburban middle class.

Critics of the middle class in the suburbs also sometimes speak of a lack of privacy, of excessive participation (or feelings of guilt over nonparticipation), and of inadequate planning.

The middle class is materialistic. It likes new cars and modern houses filled with appliances. Mumford asserts that "we have only replaced the old slavery of production with the new servitudes and compulsions of consumption."[26] It must be recognized, however, that the automobile confers a remarkable freedom on the members of a household, a mobility which enables people to do many things valued by the left, such as participation in amateur sports, drama, classes in adult education, attendance at concerts, reform movements, and political meetings. The list could be extended indefinitely. It is possible that a redesign and reconstruc-

[25]Bennett M. Berger, *Working-Class Suburb* (Berkeley and Los Angeles: University of California Press, 1960).

[26]Lewis Mumford, *The Urban Prospect* (New York: Harcourt, Brace & World, 1956), p. 4.

tion of our cities and suburbs through a regroupment of people and activities, might reduce the need for individual, private transportation. Moreover, a well-planned system of reliable public transport, such as an elaborate network of trains or buses, with high frequency of movements per hour, might be a more efficient way of moving large numbers of people about. In the absence, however, of excellent public transport, middle-class attachment to reliable automobiles does not by itself demonstrate a set of values strikingly at variance from those of the left.

Some critics of the culture of capitalism will concede that the houses in suburbia are better planned than in the past, better laid out in view of the diverse interests of the members of the family, and are perhaps larger to enable individuals more privacy. That the appliances in a suburban home have eliminated a great deal of household drudgery for housewives or household help would not be debated. Their criticism of the materialism of the middle-class homeowner in suburbia, is perhaps little more than a feeling that a past simplicity of life has been lost, or that more leisure in life would be desirable, or that the "wrong" kind of consumption goods have been produced and consumed (too many electric can-openers, for example, and not enough high-fidelity phonographs). (One often is forced to speculate as to what is meant by middle-class materialism because so often the indictment is drawn up in unclear terms and the charges are not specific.)

Throughout history people have mourned a lost simplicity, but the days of the past usually were not all that attractive. A simple life of drafty houses, cold privies, dusty or muddy streets, and isolated, dull, and lonesome settlements is a life to which not many would choose to return. A Victrola in the corner, a stereoscope, and a deck of cards in the cupboard were undoubtedly simpler than a modern stereo hi-fi and the assortment of games presently found in the typical family-room of the middle-class home, but they did not provide much in the way of cultural and intellectual stimulation.

Once it is decided that material goods are valuable in achieving some liberal-left values, then the middle-class ethic of hard work and frugality is more understandable. To work hard develops skills (the formation of human capital), and turns out the capital goods employed in factories, on farms, and in households. Save and accumulate, the results of human effort, rather than consume in immediate gratification. The consequences of hard work and frugality often produce a better life, and security for the future.

Needless to say, it can be argued that striving sometimes

becomes an end-in-itself and that too much is sacrificed in the present for the sake of the future. It should be pointed out, however, that there is a trade-off here, that a better life in the future requires sacrifices in the present, and that a great many of the possibilities of today (which tend to be taken for granted) represent the hard work and frugality of a middle-class past. The economist interested in institutions can also point out that it is under capitalism that people (those above the level of subsistence) are left largely free to decide for themselves how much they will live for the present and how much they will work and save for the future. In the Soviet-type economies, however, the Party oligarchy determines an individual's present and future. Are cramped apartments, recalcitrant plumbing, and a dearth of household appliances an appropriate price for people to pay for the benefit of future generations?

Competition

The *competitive* striving for *status* particularly appears to gall the critic of the middle class in suburbia. In substantial measure we see here the clash of two different value systems. Some people glory in the competitive environment; others prefer the quiet life. Often, it is the ones who are confident that they can win or place who prefer competition, and perhaps it is the ones who are not so sure of themselves, the ones who feel the strain, who call it the "rat race." The objective observer will recognize that in a genuinely competitive environment, in which informed participants and spectators follow a good set of competitive rules, the striving is for excellence—excellence of product and service, excellence, for example, in the design, interior decoration, and landscaping of the suburban home. With numerous suppliers committed (or constrained) to full disclosure, and a critical audience of consumers and neighbors who know the difference between the excellent, the good, and the shoddy, the winner often is one who excels.

One other point about the competitive striving of the middle class: Market economies offer a wide variety of events in which to compete, and these activities call on a broad range of interests and skills. For example, an individual can try to design or construct a better building, invent a better mouse trap, improve the quality or lower the cost of a high-fidelity phonograph, run a better automobile repair shop, or teach a better class in swimming or home decoration. And market economies provide quite a variation in degree of competition. One may choose the hectic life of work in high-fashion clothing, or the placidity of a quiet backwater in a declining rural area. The qualification required here is that in a free enterprise system no sector is completely free from the threat of a competitive incursion, but perfect economic security probably would be attained only if technological progress somehow were nearly forbidden. It is probably true that market economies provide less economic security than do most alternative sets of institutions.

A word might be said about cleanliness. When youth rebels, it is not too surprising that this includes a rebellion against all those past admonitions to take a bath and get a hair cut. And it is not surprising that the need for peer approval should cause these fashions to spread rapidly. A little attention might be given here to middle-class preferences for the clean and orderly. One obvious point is that cleanliness is hygienic. A second point is that when people dress nicely and bathe, they may be doing it out of considerateness for others as much as for themselves. To test whether the middle-class individual is seeking conformity or considerateness in his cleanliness, one might ask if he is as averse to the clean eccentric as he is to the unwashed hippie. The widespread adoption of cleaned-up versions of hippie clothing styles suggests that the middle class may not be as staid ("square") and conservative as its critics have made it out to be.

Then there is tidiness, not exclusively middle class, but much of the time preferred by the middle class—tidy yards, tidy homes, sometimes even tidy closets. Tidiness is orderliness, and order is valued by many people. It is the aesthetics of form and it provides the security and comfort of the known and predictable. Probably it always will be appreciated more by the old than the young, and probably there will be in most systems a tendency for the spontaneity of youth and the disorder of the new and the raw to give way to the tidiness and the orderliness of "establishment" life.

Finally, the critic of the middle class frowns on the conventional morality of the suburbs. It would be difficult to establish statistically that the middle class is more hypocritical in matters of morality than other classes. Most people find it difficult to live up to their ideals.

That the suburbanite impinges on the privacy of his fellow residents and induces them to participate in community activities when they would rather not is frequently argued by those who criticize life in the suburbs. To begin with, we should recognize that some people prefer more privacy than others and that in any case the degree of privacy in a particular culture would be hard to measure. Perhaps most people would agree that life in the middle-class suburbs is less private than the anonymity of the downtown apartment, but more private than the familiarity of the small town. The loneliness of the big city has been discussed frequently, as has the gregariousness of the small community. Because the desire for privacy varies from one person to another, we might conclude that a range of alternatives in privacy—from the central city to the suburb and through the small town and countryside—may be a desired feature of modern life.

As for the pressure on people to share in community activities and social affairs (even to the point of making people feel guilty if they do not participate), the force of such pressure would be hard to measure. The pressure may be smaller in the suburbs than in small towns, and almost certainly it is greater than in the central city. It is interesting to observe that social pressure of this kind is what is proposed as the principal device for control of behavior in socialism and in communal anarchism.

And indeed when one reflects upon the matter, it is surprising to discover how much of what one observes in the suburbs is what the old-time socialists dreamed of for the workers. Take suburban leisure-time activities. The socialists, particularly the communalists (the anarchists), intensely disliked a "de-humanizing" specialization and division of labor. But the suburbanite often is a generalist. He may be a craftsman with all sorts of hand and power tools; he may be a gardener; he may also be quite a sportsman. To a considerable extent, suburban life is the return to nature which was the dream of the utopian socialists and the suburb is the garden city in which anarchists like Kropotkin were interested.

Then, there is in the suburbs a good deal of neighborhood mutual aid. Families help one another during and after the arrival of new babies, phone calls are made and assistance is rendered when there is illness in the family, mutual baby-sitting arrangements are not uncommon, and the men get together when the heavy-labor part of a remodeling job is underway (with a little of the spirit of the old frontier barn-raising).

The Deficiencies of Suburban Life

Suburbia is a long way from utopia, and we will turn now to what appear to be its most serious shortcomings.

The strongest criticism of suburbia is its exclusiveness, the exclusiveness of the old and fashionable suburbs that would prefer to exclude the nouveau riche; the middle-class suburb that would exclude the lower middle class and skilled workers; and, all the suburbs that would exclude the poor and the black. Whether it be with a frigid social exclusiveness, the zoning out of small lots and houses, or the exclusion of large public housing projects, some suburbanites do what they can to keep out what they consider to be undesirable elements. This tells us a lot about suburbia—about the people living in it as well as the people wanting in who see it as the good life or at least the better life. Liberals might hesitate before they condemn out of hand these aspirations of the masses. They might even conclude that the problems of the middle class and the suburb are as much problems of the distribution of wealth, particularly the distribution of attractive and scarce spatial locations, as they are problems of a deplorable quality of life.

To be sure, there may be a rationale for the suburbanite's desire for exclusiveness. The middle class may be trying to exclude others in order to avoid associated spillovers: for example, the untidiness and uncleanliness of people with different cultural traditions, rough kids as playmates for their children, perhaps a higher incidence of crime.[27] The scholar cannot as scientist condemn these motives for exclusiveness, although he may be able to point out objectives that can be achieved only through cultural diversity.

Closely allied with the exclusiveness of suburbia is the suburbanite's concern for people outside of suburban life. Some *do* have a smug satisfaction with their own good fortune and an insensitivity to the plight of the ghetto dweller, the aged poor, the down-and-out drifter. While society is probably better organized than it ever has been to alleviate the sufferings of these people, the suburbanite appears not to be concerned enough to move over and make room for the outsider, and is most reluctant to consider changes of substance in his own way of life.

Having said all this, we must remind ourselves that parochialism is not confined to the middle class in the suburbs. Most of us are willing to make only marginal changes in our lives for the benefit of others. The liberal-left itself, for the most part comfortably ensconced in suburban life, has been insensitive to the feelings of the skilled and semi-skilled workers as they find their way into the suburbs. Frequently living in closer proximity to the central city, and less firmly protected by zoning ordinances and high property values from the spillovers associated with new, low-income migrations, these people have worries which the liberal-left has been slow to comprehend.

[27] H. E. Frech III, in a private communication.

Along with exclusiveness and unconcern for those on the outside, suburbia lacks many of the attributes associated with the communalists' view of a community. While neighbors do help each other, they seldom come to one another's assistance in a substantial way when major problems occur. Mutual aid is lacking for major illnesses and serious financial reverses. Apart from relatively minor and temporary help, the household is pretty much on its own when catastrophe strikes. The suburb does not fulfill the age-old dream of the communal anarchist for a system of mutual aid and support that would be stronger than the household and family, and yet lack the coercive apparatus of government.

Critics of the middle class, moreover, tend to think of the suburb as a phenomenon of capitalism. Yet a middle-income group, middle-management, and professional staff, exist in all industrialized urbanized economies. Some critics of the Soviet-type economy, particularly Yugoslavs, believe that they have identified in this kind of economy a "new class" made up of government officials, Party cadre, and industrial managers. (Since classes have been officially abolished in the Soviet Union and Eastern Europe, sociologists who follow the Party line speak only of "strata.") Moreover, suburbs and suburban life may be a phenomenon of urbanization, coming into existence under socialism as well as capitalism.

It is difficult to imagine that the middle class and suburban life will disappear in socialist systems with central planning and government directives. As in the Soviet-type economies of today, a class of government officials and plant managers will exist, and they probably will dwell with their families in suburban locations and live much like the suburbanites of today—with appliances, competitive striving for status, smugness, and so on.

An intriguing thought is that suburban life may be a middle way between country and city—a middle landscape somewhere between the loneliness of the city and the lack of privacy of the village and countryside.[28] The individual, both constrained and supported by neighbors, can at times escape into the anonymity of the city and enjoy some of the many options open to the city dweller. And perhaps suburbanites themselves may learn to become more sensitive to people's differing and varying needs for privacy and propinquity.

Marx was interested in the achievement of material gains for the working class. In fact, the material comforts found in the suburbs

---

[28]See William H. Whyte, *The Organization Man* (New York: Simon and Schuster, 1956), pp. 286, 355, 361, 364–65; Robert C. Wood, *Suburbia: Its People and Their Politics* (Boston: Houghton Mifflin, 1958), pp. 15–16, 105–8, 295–96.

constitute a great deal of what the traditional socialists wanted for workers. In the view of Edward Shils, much of the criticism of suburban life is a criticism of industrialization, rationality, and progress, and consequently is close to the classic conservative criticism of the culture of industrialism.[29] For the liberal-left, as we have seen, a cultural critique has largely taken the place of the old critique of the distribution of income. It is materialism rather than the distribution of wealth which is decried.

A Moderate View of the Suburban Middle Class
Life in the suburb is far from perfect, and the scholar who observes an emotionalism among those who scorn the middle class in the suburb should be careful not to react to the point of becoming an apologist for suburban life. The suburb is not utopia and is not likely to become so. On the other hand, it is probably visions of utopia that obscure the sight of many who examine the life of the middle class in the suburbs. Dreaming of a golden age in the past, if conservative, or a utopian future, if radical, the disenchanted observer is so contemptuous of reality that he dismisses it out of hand as being beneath consideration. And in so doing, he foregoes opportunities of pressing for smaller, unspectacular, but perhaps more enduring gains. The old-fashioned pragmatic liberal might properly ask the liberal-left to reexamine middle-class life in the suburbs, recognizing that it has achieved some of the goals of the working-class movement (and some goals of the upper class)—material comforts, handicrafts, outdoor life, a certain beauty, and some neighborly mutual aid. Then, having observed its positive values, the left might think about what might be done to make the middle-class suburb less exclusive, less parochial, and less smug. Simultaneously it might think about how to make suburbia more of a real community, and on how to inspire the suburbanite's concern for those on the outside.

And yet, probably still absent would be a lack of common purpose, a lack of community, a lack of national, all-embracing humanitarian objectives. It may be, however, that devotion to the household, to hard work and accumulation, to law and order, and to a pluralism of voluntary associations with bargaining and untidy compromises would do more to improve the lot of mankind than an all-embracing cause, a transcendental faith, or a charismatic leader. A middle ground, a humbler way that is secular (with faiths and dreams private and voluntarily embraced), that recognizes

---

[29] Cited in Berger, *Working-Class Suburb*, p. 102.

scarcity, constraints, and the impossibility of perfection might do more to reduce the pain of life and meet a larger set of diverse aims than would a "higher" culture embodied in a "monotheism" of a single national or humanitarian goal.

Political Economy

Part VI

Introduction to Part Six

The impact of economic systems on political institutions and vice versa has intrigued, and perplexed, many scholars. The subject is one on which it is difficult to write confidently. One can examine hypotheses, yet offer conclusions that usually are only tentative. But the questions dealt with are as important as any treated in this book. So we will enter, cautiously, a difficult terrain.

Chapter 18

The Relationship between Political and Economic Systems

Marxians hold that under capitalism the capitalist class rules politically even when elections are held and other apparently democratic practices are followed. According to them, the only true democracy is to be found in a socialist system. Conversely, there are those who argue that socialism is the road to serfdom, and that capitalism is a necessary condition for the existence of democracy. Similar to these disputes are the contentions that economic reforms in the Soviet Union and Eastern Europe require political reforms if they are to be successful, or, alternatively, that economic decentralization will lead to political liberalization. Moreover, there is also the thesis of convergence, that suggests that both communism and capitalism are changing and moving toward each other in economic and political institutions.

The Power of the Capitalist Class

According to the Marxians, democracy under capitalism is a facade behind which the capitalist class dominates. The Marxian, for example, points to the huge funds the wealthy can offer the compliant candidate for office, campaign funds and even funds for his or her personal use. He points to dishonesty in government and ballot-box stuffing. And the Marxian may argue that the electorate is ignorant and emotional and can be easily persuaded to vote against its interests.

Those who are skeptical of this view of capitalism and democracy point to the political activity of the unions and note how they educate their members on the issues. Particularly in the United States, a "bread and butter" unionism that shuns revolution and supports politicians from any party who act in the interests of the workers, may counterbalance pressures from businessmen. Then, public education increases the sophistication of consumers and makes it more difficult for politicians to act for the capitalist when it is contrary to consumer interests. An educated electorate also can insist, most of the time successfully, that procedures be followed to protect the ballot box and insure honest elections.

Most difficult for the Marxian to counter is the observation that governments, allegedly dominated by capitalists, frequently pass legislation that is contrary to the interests of capitalists. In the United States, there are laws to regulate the rates charged by the railroads and public utilities, antitrust acts, progressive income taxes, pure food and drug acts, laws to protect labor unions and collective bargaining, "truth-in-lending" acts, and many others. In argument the Marxist replies by pointing to the success capitalists often have in stopping legislation unfavorable to their interests. This argument, however, merely establishes that businessmen, like other interests, have some political power. It does not support the view that under capitalism all power rests with the capitalist class. The Marxian also argues that legislation favorable to workers and consumers is allowed to pass as a means of mollifying these groups, thereby enabling the capitalists to maintain capitalism and keep the levers of power in their own hands. But this argument is unscientific, because the Marxian is using both favorable and unfavorable evidence to support his (or her) thesis. If businessmen defeat legislation favorable to workers or consumers, this success may be cited as evidence of the power of the capitalist class. If businessmen fail to defeat such legislation, this failure may be cited as evidence of capitalist power, employed to pacify the working class. At the least the Marxian can be asked to indicate what evidence would refute his hypothesis that under capitalism democracy is a facade for the rule of the capitalist class. Unless the Marxian can clearly indicate the kind of evidence which would disprove the hypothesis, it is not a scientific one.

In the final analysis, the Marxian view of the power of the capitalist probably rests on the idea that workers and consumers do not know their own interests. Indeed the Marxian actually must argue along these lines as a consequence of his belief that through the expenditure of large sums the electorate can be persuaded to vote for candidates who govern on behalf of the capitalist class. Consumers and workers, however, are experts in their own lives. They know whether or not the streets are paved, whether they can buy automobiles, in what kind of housing they live, and so on. Administrators and legislators who serve capitalists at the expense of workers and consumers risk being voted out of office. On the whole, it appears then that workers are more likely to have power (shared of course with other groups) in a capitalist economy with a democratic political system than in a socialist economy where the leadership of a Marxian party rules in the name of the working class, forbids opposition parties, and controls the means of production.

Democracy and Socialism

Critics of socialism have argued that it may, or will, destroy democracy. We can consider the impact of socialism on four different facets of a democratic system: (1) on the rule of law, (2) on an independent judiciary, (3) on free elections with multiple political parties, and (4) on free speech and press.

The Rule of Law

Hayek in his book, *The Road to Serfdom,* is concerned with what he believes must be the arbitrariness of government officials in a socialist economy. He contends that laws often will be drawn up in general terms, leaving too much room for arbitrary administrative interpretation.[1] A statute, for example, may call for prices that are "fair" or "reasonable," with officials then free to decide what these words mean in particular instances. Why might the laws of socialism to be drawn up in general terms? First, governments under socialism try to do more than governments under capitalism: They appoint enterprise managers, plan output, investment, and distribution, set prices, ration foreign exchange, and so on. Legislators find it difficult to agree on so many things, and, therefore, paper over their differences with general rules. In addition, the cost of drawing up statutes is high, and the tendency is to hand to lower-level agencies generally stated laws which in turn are interpreted in individual cases. (To be sure an aggrieved party usually can appeal to the courts, but the appeal is costly and the court itself exercises discretion in deciding whether an agency has acted in accordance with a law stated in general terms.)

[1] Frederich A. Hayek, *The Road to Serfdom* (Chicago: University of Chicago Press, 1944), pp. 62–66, 78.

It seems undeniable that the rule of law becomes more difficult to preserve as the role of government expands. Socialism with extensive central planning, then, probably would increase the incidence of arbitrary government action. Market socialism—with output, input, and investment decisions in the hands of the managers of government enterprises would appear to be a less serious threat to the rule of law.

An independent judiciary should be about as easy to maintain under socialism as under capitalism. In both systems judges are paid by the government (and may be given tenure).

Electoral Opposition

As for free elections, one must start out by recognizing that in both systems elections are conducted by the government. But socialism and capitalism may differ significantly in the capacity of independent opposition political parties to survive and function effectively. Political parties require party workers and they, in turn, require salaries. In a highly centralized, planned economy with government as the only employer, people who work for an opposition party or contribute to it might find their jobs in jeopardy.[2] To be sure, any workers discharged for such work or financial contributions would probably find some pocket of autonomy, a niche in which they could make a living. Even so, opponents and the families of opponents of the government in a centralized socialism would be more likely to suffer cuts in their standard of living than they would in a capitalism having a multiplicity of employers. As a consequence effective conduct of opposition parties would be more difficult. Market socialism, a system of many autonomous enterprises, would be less inimical to democracy in this respect than would a tightly planned socialism.

Freedom of Speech

Speech may be inhibited and the press less free in a socialist economy than under capitalism. When the government is the only employer, people may feel less free to speak out in criticism of governmental actions. Newspapers and magazines may be cautious in what they publish when they have to buy paper from the

[2] Lord Robbins, *Politics and Economics* (London: Macmillan & Co., 1963), p. 39; Milton Friedman, *Capitalism and Freedom* (Chicago: University of Chicago Press, 1962), p. 16.

government[3] or sell advertisements to government bodies. Once again, however, market socialism, with competing autonomous enterprises, may be more conducive to democracy than a centrally planned economy. Under market socialism the outspoken individual might have more potential employers; the forthright newspaper might have more possible advertisers (and perhaps alternative sources of newsprint).

It appears that those who have argued that socialism will inevitably destroy parliamentary democracy have not made their case. The proposition, however, that democracy will be less secure in a socialist economy probably is correct. The rule of law will be more difficult to maintain in a system of many laws. With individuals having fewer employment opportunities and newspapers fewer alternative purchasers of advertising, parties not in the government probably will find it more difficult to get workers and funds, individuals probably will be slower to speak out, and newspapers may be cautious in their opposition.

Soviet Reform, Economic and Political

It is sometimes argued that economic reform in the Soviet-type economy must be preceded by political reform, and it is often suggested that economic reform will lead to political reform.

Those who argue that substantial political changes must precede reform of economic institutions assert that a change in political leadership is necessary in order to give people confidence in proposals for economic reform. But, of course, a change in leadership within the existing governmental structure, a palace revolution for example, might be enough to give people hope. Then, too, it is contended that political reform is necessary to get rid of a bureaucracy that would otherwise obstruct desired changes. It is not certain, however, that a more democratically chosen government would be in a stronger position to fire obstructive government officials. Though such a government might be better able to do so, it might fear a loss of electoral support from the dismissed officials and their families. It may be significant that in Yugoslavia political reform *followed* economic reform, and followed it slowly at that. (Yugoslavia is still a one-party state; only in the autumn of 1970 did Hungary ever so slightly dip its foot into the cold water of political change, and then later pulled back.)

Perhaps the more interesting question is whether economic

[3]Friedman, *Capitalism and Freedom*, p. 18.

decentralization always, or usually, leads to political liberalization. Many people think that the one will almost inevitably bring about the other. An important consideration is that if enterprise managers are given larger powers of decision, then critics and opponents of the government may have more job alternatives. Dissident journals might even sell advertisements to autonomous firms. The advocates of reform in the Soviet economies proposed that markets should play a larger role in the economy, and we suggested earlier that market socialism is more conducive to political democracy than is the traditional Soviet-type centrally planned economy. Still, the economic decentralization proposed a few years ago in the Soviet Union and Eastern Europe was a long way from the pluralistic institutions of west European and North American democracies. Economic reforms might lead to political changes, but the latter are far from certain, may come slowly, and conceivably might not come at all.

The Convergence Thesis

It is widely believed among Western intellectuals that the Soviet and Western systems are tending to become more alike, that the economies as well as the political structures are converging. Observers who see a convergence of economies pointed to the proposed decentralization of decisions in Eastern Europe and Russia, where some enterprise managers were freer to make assortment, input, and investment decisions. Observers also noted proposals to make a greater use of profits and markets. At the same time, they see in Western Europe and North America a greater centralization of decision making—monopolies, cartels, and trade associations, the regulation by government of prices, smoke emission, farm acreage planted, and so on. They point out that the progressive income tax makes incomes more equal. Advocates of the convergence thesis, moreover, forecast that these trends will continue. In the East "we may expect more freedom for managers and scientists and less central planning of production and central pricing.... In the West we may expect more central planning, further restrictions on unearned income, and further financial aid in education."[4]

[4] H. Linnemann, J. P. Pronk, and J. Linbergen, "Convergence of Economic Systems in East and West," *Disarmament and World Economic Interdependencies*, ed. Emile Benoit (Oslo: Universitetsforlaget, 1967), p. 258. Reprinted in Morris Bornstein and Daniel R. Fusfeld, *The Soviet Economy: A Book of Readings*, 3rd ed. (Homewood, Ill.: Richard D. Irwin, 1970), p. 457.

Rational People with Common Objectives

Some who believe Eastern and Western economies are converging contend that there is an optimum set of institutions—an optimum combination of government and private enterprises and an optimum role for government. They expect economies in the East and West to move toward the optimum, and assert that "since their deviations in most elements are on opposite sides from the optimum, a tendency for convergency can be expected."[5] Supporters of convergence say that people in different countries have about the same objectives,[6] and they appear to believe that people are rational. One writer argues that a "new-found devotion to social science ... will surely shake communism to its base."[7] In general, advocates of convergence seem to believe that changes, when they occur, are for the better.

It is, however, highly improbable that objectives in the East and West are the same, nor is it likely they are becoming so. (We must consider here the objectives of those having power to change institutions.) In Russia and Eastern Europe, the authorities aim at the development of heavy industry (with lately some increase in consumption goods) and the output of things like steel, cement, oil, and so on, while in Western Europe and North America electorates and other (pluralistic) centers of power prefer the output of goods purchased by consumers. In the East, there is an ideological attachment to equality (with substantial departures from equality in practice) and to decision making by a highly centralized government. Conversely, in the West, there is a pragmatic willingness to allow for a considerable inequality, and a devotion to the making of decisions at the periphery, by consumers, workers, businessmen, and local government officials. This ideological difference is between Marxism-Leninism, with a considerable remnant of Stalinism, on the one hand, and pragmatic pluralism, with a strong residue of Jeremy Bentham and John Stuart Mill, on the other.

But, argue the advocates of the convergence thesis, the present oligarchies in Russia and Eastern Europe will not stay in power and when they are gone there will be a movement toward political liberalization. Before we turn to the subject of political conver-

[5] Ibid., pp. 454–55.

[6] Ibid., pp. 443–44.

[7] Peter Wiles, "Convergence: Possibility and Probability," in Alexander Balinky, et al., *Planning and the Market in the U.S.S.R.: The 1960's* (New Brunswick, N.J.: Rutgers University Press, 1967), p. 98.

gence, we may note in passing that a belief in steady movement toward optimum economic institutions assumes that people are rational in their choices of institutional arrangements. Such an assumption closely resembles the nineteenth century belief in inevitable progress.

Obstacles to Change in the Soviet Union and Eastern Europe

People in the West who expect a political convergence between East and West maintain that most of the political change will occur in Russia and Eastern Europe. (Russian leaders have their own version of convergence; they expect the West in the long run to be submerged by the East. "We will bury you.") Soviet political liberalization is expected by some in the West to occur because of the requirements of modern science, technology, and industry, and because of the growth of education and habits of reason. Such observers expect a diminution of revolutionary fervor and an end of ideology.

It has been noted, however, that a politically repressive Soviet system did in fact develop a modern science and technology of space. Moreover, it has also been observed that education can be and is used for indoctrination.[8] Those who believe in political convergence do not seem to realize that the Soviet leaders have substituted a quasi-religious ideology for reason, and that they have at their disposal the entire mechanism of a totalitarian state to keep themselves in power. It is significant that the convergence theorists do not describe the Soviet mechanism of power—the single political party, the licensing of all other organizations, control over the press and assembly, the ubiquitous police and informers, the subservient courts, the dismissal of dissidents and their relatives from jobs, eviction from apartments, and deprivation of educational opportunities, to say nothing of exile, confinement in mental hospitals, and imprisonment. Nor do these convergence theorists describe the actions by which this elaborate mechanism of control is to be overcome. They do not appear to know how discouraged people become when repeated efforts fail to change the system. Men and women withdraw into their private lives, do the minimum amount of work necessary to keep their jobs, and go in for bridge, chess, skiing, boating, and the like. Holesovsky de-

---

[8]Tibor Szamuely, "Five Years After Krushchev," *Survey* 72 (Summer, 1969), pp. 65–68. Other valuable criticisms of the convergence thesis are the following: Zbigniew Brzezinski and Samuel P. Huntington, *Political Power: USA/USSR* (New York: Viking Press, 1963), pp. 9–14, 435.

scribed the aftermath of the "Czech spring" of 1968 as moving "from revolt to resignation."[9] A similar phenomenon was observed in Poland after the "Polish October" of 1956. After an unsuccessful attempt at reform some people simply withdraw from the political arena and leave political activities to the leaders of the Communist Party. "The greatest achievement of the Communists," a Polish graduate student said to me, very bitterly "has been to convince us that they are inevitable." Westerners who believe in convergence fail to observe that not one established totalitarian system has been overthrown by internal forces. Reading and listening to commentators who expect a fairly steady erosion of the power of the Party oligarchy, reminds one of people in the nineteenth century who believed that progress was inevitable. But, in the words of Andrei Amalrik, an outspoken opponent of the Soviet system, a man who has experienced imprisonment and exile asserts, "we know ... that history, and Russian history in particular, has by no means been a continuous victory for reason and that the whole history of mankind has not followed an unbroken line of progress."[10]

---

[9]Vaclav Holesovsky, "Planning and Market in the Czechoslovak Reform," in *Plan and Market*, ed. Morris Bornstein (New Haven: Yale University Press, 1973), p. 338.

[10]Andrei Amalrik, *Will the Soviet Union Survive Until 1984?* (New York: Harper & Row, 1970), p. 28.

Chapter 19
Conclusions—Brief and Prosaic

In the final analysis, what may we say about alternative economic systems? What advice can economists as scientists offer to people who choose between alternative institutional arrangements for their economies? It would seem that only a modest set of propositions can be supplied with any degree of certainty. Below we consider such propositions.

When free choice is an objective, prices must be market clearing.

When the objective is efficient production, with an assortment of goods to meet the preferences of consumers (or industrial users) and with an assortment of high quality goods, then current-output decisions might best be made by autonomous units. Such units might be privately or governmentally owned, respond to prices, and be motivated by profit. Current-output planning in the Soviet-type economies probably should be abandoned, as the Hungarians once hoped to do and as the Yugoslavs have already done.

As an alternative to investment planning, there is a strong case, when the objective is growth, for the use of an interest rate (a norm of growth) that would be the same for all sectors of the economy. Projects would be selected in response to expected prices so as to maximize present value or expected value, and all decisions would be unified through a capital market. Late returns would be discounted, and heavy industry would not be favored over light industry.

When it is suggested that output, input, and investment decisions be made in response to prices rather than as part of a set of plans, what is being proposed is that market socialism rather than a Soviet-type economy is a more promising kind of a socialism. The advocates of reform in Russia and Eastern Europe in the sixties were moving toward this position.

Insofar as it is desired that production and consumption decisions be decentralized, money (the bearer of options) will be employed.

Private instead of government ownership of the industrial means of production will be chosen (1) when private rather than governmental appointment of top management is preferred, (2) when private rather than governmental risk-taking is desired, and (3) when a time horizon longer than the tenure granted a socialist manager is sought. Whether or not private risk-taking is chosen over government risk-taking, may depend on either the existence or the possibility of the existence of an entrepreneural class.

The Soviet experience with collective farming and the private sector suggests that at least in intensive farming (in vegetables, fruits, nuts, poultry, and the like) private agriculture is likely to perform better than collective or governmental agriculture.

The principal obstacles to reform in the Soviet-type economy are fears and vested interests. The authorities fear that they may lose economic or even political power, and managers and workers have vested interests in obsolete methods of production. There is also a confidence gap: Workers do not trust the authorities to hold norms constant over an extended period of time so that harder work would lead to continued higher pay.

If a system of capitalism or market socialism is selected, then government action probably will be desired to deal with indiscriminate delivery (spillovers), natural monopoly, and the distribution of income. Regulatory bodies will impose ceilings on the prices charged by privately or governmentally operated natural monopolies, ideally employing a system of incentive rate-determination. The progressive income tax and death duties may be used along with government outlays to alter the distribution of income and wealth, with due regard being given to their possibly adverse consequences on incentives to work, save, and bear risk. Should equality of opportunity be recognized as an imprecise goal, reformers may accept minimum levels of achievement in basic skills as a more promising objective (along with minimum living standards for everyone). Beyond this, the objective might be development of individual potentialities as fully as possible (given constraints on available resources).

The shift from criticizing the distribution of income under capitalism to criticizing its culture may be reversed as critics recall that material well-being is much of what the old-time socialists wanted for the workers, while suburban life is a realization, albeit imperfect, of the dreams of a large part of the working population.

The Israeli kibbutzim along with the traditional and contemporary communes should be watched by the student of alternative systems in order to see whether or not the secular commune is a viable alternative system.

When political democracy is desired, it should be recognized that socialism does not make totalitarianism inevitable. However, the achievement and preservation of democracy probably is more difficult with the economy highly centralized. It is easier to work for and finance opposition parties when there are numerous alternative independent employers, as may be the case in market socialism and as is almost certainly the case under capitalism.

Is private enterprise, government ownership, markets, profits, fears and vested interests, regulatory bodies, observation of the Israeli kibbutz and other communal movements all that remains after the utopian socialists and anarchists' dreams? Where has the revolution proposed by Marx and Lenin gone, with its hopes of an entirely new order? The answer appears to be that no one has done the hard necessary thinking to convert the dreams into realities. The anarchists and the utopians mostly have rested their proposals on the emergence of a new person, who will be concerned with the community and with all of mankind rather than merely concerned with himself or his family. They have not, however, thought out and specified the precise steps that would produce such a person. The Marxians mostly have believed and still do that a powerful government that plans the economy will produce an abundance of goods, but they have not considered the cost of acquiring the knowledge necessary for planning or the cost of computation. The old socialist slogan of "production for use and not for profit" has filled Soviet warehouses with unusable goods.

We cannot rule out the possibility that someone might someday, with prolonged and difficult thought, find an entirely new way of getting the world's work done, but economic progress in general is likely to come through piecemeal reform, through small carefully selected changes which are indeed prosaic but that do achieve precisely stated objectives.

Appendices

The Pareto Criterion as a Defense of Market Economies

Appendix 1

Many, if not most, economists believe that the notion of a Pareto optimum can be used in defense of market economies, in defense of a competitive capitalism, and perhaps in defense of a Lange model of market socialism. But when the matter is examined closely, it turns out that the Pareto criterion is not very useful in the study of alternative economic systems.

We will start out with two definitions:

1. *Pareto superior:* A state of the economy x is superior to a state of the economy y if at least one individual prefers his position in x to his position in y, while all other individuals are indifferent between the two states.

2. *Pareto optimum:* A state of the economy is an optimum if there is no state which is (Pareto), superior to it.

What value judgment underlies the belief that a Pareto optimum is a desirable state of affairs? A person who wants to see the attainment of a Pareto optimum values a system where individual preferences count and where changes occur which are preferred by one or more persons, while others are indifferent. Such a person values a world of individuals, where beneficial, non-hurting changes occur, and he believes it a pity to forego changes preferred by some and objected to by none.

Beneficial, Non-Hurting Changes

Economists demonstrate that markets achieve desired, non-damaging changes, at least under special conditions. A competitive equilibrium is a Pareto optimum. When the marginal conditions are met, an optimum is attained. Hence the private, free, competitive markets of capitalism, as well as the socialist markets of the Lange model, are said to produce the changes preferred by one or more individuals.

Some economists seem to think that in unregulated market economies *only* beneficial, non-hurting changes take place. Take the following statement by Boulding:

> From any point not on the contract curve, agreement can be reached by trading, moving toward the contract curve.... Once the contract curve is reached, however, agreement by trading becomes impossible, and any move along the contract curve represents conflict—that is, a bettering of the position of one party at the expense of the other.[1]

Boulding here clearly suggests that trading does not involve conflict, does not move individuals to less preferred positions. That he believes trade to be mutually advantageous to all parties can be seen in another statement:

> The real significance of the Paretian welfare economics, then, is that it sets forth explicitly the distinction between those changes in variables which can take place through "trading"—i.e., through a mutual benefit of all parties—and those changes which involve "conflict," or the benefit of one party at the expense of another.[2]

According to Boulding, trade mutually benefits all parties, and does not hurt people. He goes a step further in his claims here for the market economy than would many economists. Along with the assertion that beneficial, non-hurting changes occur is proferred the suggestion that in unregulated markets *only* non-hurting changes take place. Many economists who work with the Pareto criterion have thought along similar lines, have believed that the allocation of resources produced by a market economy mutually

---

[1] Kenneth E. Boulding, "Welfare Economics," in *A Survey of Contemporary Economics*, vol. 2, ed. Bernard F. Haley (Homewood, Ill.: Irwin, 1952), p. 17.
[2] Ibid., p. 18.

benefits all parties, and that hurting changes need be considered only under the heading of distribution, when, for example, a redistribution through taxation is considered. But markets do move individuals to less preferred positions, and the hurting properties of markets need to be examined.

Markets Hurt People

While changes to Pareto superior positions occur en route to a competitive equilibrium, it is not true that *only* changes to Pareto superior positions take place in a market economy. One can easily find examples of individuals who are moved to less preferred positions during the course of market adjustments. Suppose that an economy is at an equilibrium and an optimum. Suppose that one worker-consumer then changes his preferences while the preferences of all other individuals remains unchanged. This worker decides to supply less labor (e.g., he will not go to work on Saturdays), and he decides to reduce his outlays correspondingly (e.g., he will cut back on expenses on Saturday night parties). As a consequence of his actions the buyers of his labor and the sellers of party supplies are moved to less preferred positions. Now the reader may state that an analysis using the Pareto criterion assumes that tastes and technology remain unchanged. But if this were so, it could be applied to the empirical world where tastes and technology do change. The analysis cannot be used to suggest that, in a world of changing tastes and technology, markets do not hurt people.

It turns out, however, that even if tastes and technology are constant, individuals may be moved to less preferred positions in a system of free markets. Suppose that a shirt manufacturer is at a position, chosen from his (or her) set of production possibilities, that is not at equilibrium. Suppose that to reach a point of maximum profit the manufacturer cuts back the production of shirts and lays off workers. Shirt purchasers and labor suppliers may be in less preferred positions. Alternatively, suppose that to reach a point of maximum profit the manufacturer expands the production of shirts and hires additional workers. Now other suppliers of shirts and purchasers of labor may be moved to less preferred positions.

In the markets of the Lange model of socialism, individuals also find themselves moved to less preferred circumstances. As a socialist manager adjusts his output to the point where marginal cost equals price, for example, he might lay off workers who then have to take less preferred jobs.

The notion that the decisions made in a system of markets are mutually beneficial to all parties will not stand up to close examination.

The market adjustments which shift individuals to less preferred positions are not exceptional. Indeed, they are probably more common than changes to Pareto superior positions. While it is actually difficult to find a plausible example of a change that moves an individual or group to preferred circumstances while all others remain indifferent, here is a possibility: Men with rising incomes prefer to buy more shirts. Existing suppliers prefer to invest in plant expansion, buy more raw materials and labor, and turn out more shirts. Suppliers of cloth, thread, and buttons prefer to expand their outputs, and workers just out of vocational school prefer to take jobs in the garment industry. The set of changes described are moves to a Pareto superior state of the economy. The scenario is plausible, barely plausible, but probably is not typical of a changing economy. Most adjustments probably have mixed consequences, and do, in fact, transfer individuals to positions which are less preferred.[3] In practice, somewhere along a chain of inputs, supplies are likely to be inelastic, so that an increased demand bids goods or services away from other people and as a consequence such persons end up in less preferred positions. In the foregoing example, the shirt manufacturers may attract skilled workers away from related industries, thus leaving them shorthanded.

As a dynamic economy constantly adjusts toward an equilibrium which is itself moving, changes in supply and demand regularly push individuals into less preferred circumstances. Increases in supply when demand is held constant take customers away from rivals. Decreases in supply deprive purchasers of goods to which they are accustomed. Increases in demand with supply constant bid goods away from others, while decreases in demand deprive suppliers of customary sales. *All* price changes move someone to a less preferred position: price increases adversely affect buyers, price decreases hurt sellers.

The hurting characteristics of markets are suggested by the popular denigrations of market activity, which often is called a

---

[3]Economists cannot assert as scientists that the gains of those moved to more preferred positions exceed in value the losses of those moved to less preferred positions.

"rat race," a system of "dog-eat-dog." Much legislation is put on the books to prevent markets from shifting people to less preferred positions: tariffs and import quotas, measures of resale price maintenance, regulations preventing railway branch lines from closing down without government permission, and so on. Upon reflection, it seems clear that changes to Pareto superior states of a market economy are relatively scarce, while changes to situations with mixed consequences are common.

Why have economists been inclined to think that trade is mutually beneficial to all people? First, they frequently look at a single transaction alone, compare it with a state of affairs in which no transaction occurs, note that free individuals would not enter the deal unless it were advantageous to each of them, and leap to the conclusion that trade benefits everyone. They do not seem to realize that the transaction in question may have succeeded a transaction which was more favorable to one of the parties, or that withdrawal of one party from trade that has been taking place regularly in the past (withdrawal of "custom") moves the other party to a less preferred position, or that entry into trade or expansion of trade may hurt third parties who are competitors. Moreover, economists who use the Pareto criterion to defend market economies uncritically apply to the empirical world their studies of equilibrium positions (comparative statics) and fail to examine movements to and from equilibrium.

Some readers may argue at this point that too much has been made of Boulding's assertions that trading mutually benefits all parties, and does not involve conflict. Yet, most economists simply set aside the obvious fact that markets hurt people, while they determine the conditions under which beneficial, non-hurting changes take place. The position being taken here, however, is that in market economies changes with mixed consequences are far more common than changes to Pareto superior positions. At the least, users of the Pareto criterion should, after they have looked at non-hurting changes, make clear that many changes in market economies shift individuals to less preferred positions. Better still, those who employ the Pareto criterion in defense of markets might reassess their thinking in light of answers to the following question: Which feature below is more characteristic of a market economy? In other words, which feature is most useful in deciding on the value of markets: (1) that beneficial, non-hurting changes occur, or (2) that most changes have mixed consequences, putting some individuals in more and some in less preferred positions?

Marginal-Cost Pricing

Appendix 2

Lange, Lerner, and others contend that enterprise managers in a system of market socialism should produce to the point where marginal cost is equal to price. Hotelling and others argue that agencies regulating the rates of natural monopolies in a capitalist economy should set prices which are equal to marginal cost. In this book, however, the operational model of market socialism and discussions of regulated capitalism do not employ marginal-cost pricing. Rather, a sort of "average cost" pricing is proposed. Under conditions of natural monopoly, ceiling prices are to equal unit costs plus the profit which it is judged will induce a desired amount of risk-taking. Since all costs are to be covered, such an approach is sometimes called "full cost" pricing. In this appendix, the rejection of marginal-cost pricing is explained.

Marginal Cost as a Measure of Opportunity Cost

When the objective is to maximize the rate of growth in wealth, opportunity cost should be minimized whatever the system. Advocates of marginal-cost pricing want to minimize opportunity cost and believe that marginal cost best measures the value of foregone alternatives. Lerner asserts that "if we so order the economic activity of the society that no commodity is produced unless its importance is greater than that of the alternative that is sacrificed,

359

we shall have completely achieved the ideal that the economic calculus of a socialist state sets before itself," and he concludes that "the guiding principle that we seek is none other than the equation of price to marginal cost."[1]

When one looks at the troublesome case of a decreasing-cost industry, however, one clearly sees that the price equal to marginal cost will not cover opportunity cost. When marginal cost is equal to price in an industry like steel or aluminum or electricity, that industry will be operated at a loss. Its losses will then be covered by a subsidy, by the profits of governmentally owned increasing-cost industries or by tax revenues. (The opportunity costs of production in a decreasing-cost industry include the goods that might have been turned out with the resources paid for by the subsidy funds provided by the government.) Had the subsidy not been necessary, the government might have spent the profits of increasing-cost enterprises on highways, for example. Or taxpayers might have had more money to spend on clothing because they were being less heavily taxed. The highways or the clothes that might have been produced, had not the decision been made to operate the industry at (a loss-producing) marginal cost equal to price, are part of the alternatives sacrificed. It seems incontestable that the opportunity cost of producing where marginal cost is equal to price includes the value of the goods which might have been produced with the resources purchased out of subsidy funds. It may be that the reason most governments have so stubbornly resisted the advice of economists and clung to prices that cover "full" costs is that they are more aware of the costs involved, of the alternatives sacrificed, than are economists who have thought that an output rule can be chosen without looking at the resources represented by the subsidy funds required when the rule is applied.

Distributional Consequences

Marginal-cost pricing will not realize the distributional objectives which an electorate or a legislature or an executive is likely to hold. Moreover, the very idea of taxes being collected to subsidize consumers of the products of decreasing-cost industries is not an appealing idea to some people. Should an electorate or legislature be inclined to redistribute income through taxation and govern-

---

[1] Abba P. Lerner, "Statics and Dynamics in Socialist Economics," *Economic Journal* 47 (June, 1937), pp. 253, 257.

ment expenditure, it would seem more likely for it to be interested in a movement toward equality or in a distribution based on need. In the 1970s a legislature with government funds available for subsidies probably would choose a special education program for disadvantaged children over a program which increased the real incomes of consumers of the products of decreasing-cost industries. And an economist could not, as a scientist, argue against this choice.

Marginal-cost pricing, therefore, can be defended neither on grounds that it minimizes opportunity cost and hence maximizes the rate of growth, nor on grounds that it provides a distribution of income likely to be preferred by an electorate, legislature, or executive.

Indiscriminate Delivery of Output as a Substitute for the Concept of Externality and Social Cost

Appendix **3**

Economists commonly say that the market fails to perform well when there are externalities. This conclusion, however, has become a matter of definition, since the concept of externality has been extended to cover all non-market interdependencies. It appears that a return to the older Marshall-Viner definition of external economies, along with a different characterization of the phenomena of smoke, noise, odor, and the like, would give a more accurate description of the properties of the empirical world.

For Marshall and Viner, external economies and diseconomies were external to the *firm*. "External economies are those which accrue to particular concerns as a result of the expansion of output by their industry as a whole, and which are independent of their own individual outputs."[1] This idea is clear and has been useful. But present-day economists write of economies (or effects) which are external to the *market*.[2] The image of something "outside"

---

[1] Jacob Viner, "Cost Curves and Supply Curves," *Zeitschrift für Nationalökonomie* 3 (1931). Reprinted in Committee of the American Economic Association, *Readings in Price Theory* (Homewood, Ill.: Irwin, 1952), p. 217.

[2] J. E. Meade, "External Economies in a Competitive Situation," *Economic Journal* 62 (March, 1952), p. 56; Tibor Scitovsky, "Two Concepts of External Economies," *Journal of Political Economy* 62 (April, 1954), p. 144; Francis Bator, "The Anatomy of Market Failure," *Quarterly Journal of Economics* 72 (August, 1958) p. 358; E. J. Mishan, "Reflections on Recent Developments in the Concept of External Effects," *Canadian Journal of Economics and Political Science* 31 (February, 1965), p. 6.

the market is not a clear one and does not point to an essential property of the empirical world.

Let us consider a different approach. Suppose a factory has three outputs: pig iron, slag, and smoke. The management wants the first product and would prefer not to have the other two. Usually, the smoke is said by economists to produce external effects, while the slag does not lead to externalities. But what is the real difference? The smoke represents an *indiscriminate delivery of output to recipients,* while the delivery of the slag is controlled. The factory "dumps" the smoke indiscriminately on the surrounding countryside, while it dumps the slag only on selected land.

Where delivery is controlled, the market performs well (apart from problems of monopoly, income distribution, and so on). With delivery controlled, the government can assign property rights and then let the parties trade out their conflicting interests. An individual has the right to prevent the dumping of trash on his land. The steelmaker must buy that land if he wants to dump trash on it, or he must pay the owner for the right to do it. If the delivery of smoke to recipients could be controlled in the same way as delivery of rubbish, then economists would not have singled it out for special treatment under the heading of "externality." This is true also of noise, odors, impurities in water, pollen, and so on. It is clear that the cause of market failure in all of these cases is indiscriminate delivery of output to recipients.

Economists who want to identify the exact properties of the empirical world which cause the market to fail should define external economies (and diseconomies), as did Marshall and Viner, as changes in costs which are a function of industry output rather than firm output. They should then use the concept of indiscriminate delivery to deal with phenomena like smoke and noise. If the two phenomena—"changes in costs which are a function of industry output" and "indiscriminate delivery"—are to be put in the same class, the class should be the precise category of "causes of market failure," rather than the amorphous one of "factors external to the market."

The phrase "indiscriminate delivery" is rather like the often used terms "spillover," "side effect," and "neighborhood effect."

A characterization of a phenomenon like smoke as a "social cost" is no better, in my view, than its characterization as an externality. There are two sets of individuals concerned with smoke: (1) those who prefer to emit smoke, and (2) those who prefer that smoke not be emitted. To refer to the desires of those who prefer that smoke not be emitted as the costs of society is to suggest that the preferences of those who dislike smoke have greater validity than the preferences of those who want to discharge smoke. The economist, however, cannot arrive at such a conclusion. Moreover, the words "social" and "society" should be used cautiously. They frequently connote the idea of a source of value over and above the preferences of the individuals in the economy. Rather than speak of smoke as a social cost, the economist need observe only that some people prefer not to have smoke emitted and that, because the delivery of smoke is indiscriminate, the market does not perform well in satisfying these preferences.

Indiscriminate delivery, then, is a better explanation of government action in matters of smoke, noise, impurities in water, and the like than either the modern concept of externality or the older notion of social costs.

Index

Ability of consumers and workers, 338-39
Abouchar, Alan, 64
Accountability
　versus autonomy, 152-53
　and efficiency, 152
Accumulation, capital
　during early NEP, 6-9
　primitive socialist, 13
　in Soviet development model, 89
Advertising
　and the capacity of the consumer, 283-84
　governmental control over advertising copy, 298
Aggregation
　increased under some proposed reforms, 95
　problems of, 18, 21, 25
Agriculture
　in China, 262-65
　climate and soil in Soviet Union, 86
　future of socialist, 86
　"parity," 293
　policy in the US and USSR, 292-93
　private, 348
　recent developments in Soviet, 83
Altruistic motivation, 182-84, 186
Amalrik, Andrei, 79, 345
Amanas, the
　disbanded, 214-15
　economy, 213
　erosion of community life, 214
　organization and control, 213

Ames, Edward, 55
Anarchism. *See* Communal anarchism
Ashbrook, Arthur G., Jr., 259, 262, 266
Assortment
　in an operational market socialism, 143
　problem in Soviet-type economy, 44-45
　under capitalism, 281
Autonomy
　and efficiency, 152
　versus accountability, 152-53

Bakunin, Mikhail, 180
Barone, Enrico, 127
Bator, Francis, 363
Behavioral engineering
　alleged basis for a communal science, 238
　development of Skinner's thought, 237-41
　incentives, 240, 241-42
　irony in behavioral engineering in Walden Two and Twin Oaks, 243-44
　objectives imprecisely stated, 239
　role of experiment, 237, 238-40, 242-43
　at Twin Oaks, 241-43
　in Walden Two, 207
Behavior of people under capitalism, 274, 275
Bellamy, Edward, 189-96

Bellamy's *Looking Backward*
  absence of corruption, 194
  centralized planning, 189
  conflicts of interest disappear, 193, 195
  draft of workers, 191-92, 193
  failure to recognize interdependencies, costs of data collection, costs of computation, 191
  functions and costs of government reduced, 195, 196
  human nature, views of, 193-94
  industrial army, 192
  organization of, 190-91, 193, 194
  prices, 192
  reduced scarcity, 194
  wages, 191-92
Berger, Bennett M., 324, 325, 332
Bergson, Abram, 56, 57, 58, 62
Berliner, Joseph S., 35, 67
Bill of goods
  in current-output plan, 19-20
  dated, 50
Blueprint of socialism, 4, 127
Bobrowski, Czeslaw, 20, 22
Bonus. *See* Reward
Bornstein, Morris, 68, 69, 70, 107, 114, 116
Bottlenecks, 4
Boulding, Kenneth E., 30, 302, 354
Brzeski, Andrzej, 72, 75
Brzezinski, Zbigniew, 344
Bureaucracy
  as obstacle to reform, 124
Burks, R. V., 116
Businessman, role of, 274-75

Campbell, Robert, 116, 120
Capital market
  under capitalism, 274
  under operational market socialism, 140, 142-43
  unify investment decisions, 347
Carden, Maren Lockwood, 209-12
Clarke, Roger A., 85
Clemens, Eli Winston, 318

Chinese Communism
  agricultural teams, 263
  attempt at a Soviet-type economy, 254
  believed malleability of man, 256, 265, 266
  a Chinese model? 259
  decentralization, 255, 257, 260, 260n, 266-67
  goal of equality, 253
  from heavy to light industry and rural enterprise, 259, 261-62
  historical sketch, 253
  intensive farming, 262, 264
  investment in agriculture, 262
  the likely future, 266
  people's communes, 256
  planning and control, 259
  regional self-sufficiency, 260, ideology, 261
  rural household, 262
  uneasy balance, 265
  unique, 253
Coefficient of "deficitness," 69
Collective farm ("kolkhoz")
  delivery targets, 78
  farm market, 81
  income of members, 78
  organization, 77-78
  private agriculture. *See* Private plot
  property in, 77, 79
  workers' residual claimants, 79
Collectivization, 10
Commercial banking theory (real bills doctrine), 74
Communal anarchism
  absence of cities, 186
  absence of conflicting interests, 181-82
  absence of scarcity, 184-85
  altruistic motivation, 182-84, 186
  decisions, unanimous, 181
  description of, 179-180
  family and friends in, 182-84
  a proposed leap in the dark, 187
  small-scale production, 185-86
  social solidarity, meaning of, 182

specialization, absence of, 185
what communalists do not like, 179
Communes, conditions for viability of, 249
Communication
   horizontal, 22, 32, 53
   vertical, 32, 53
Communist party. *See* Party
Complexity of an economy, 17
"Computopia," 55
Conflict of interest
   absence of, in anarchism, 181-82
   absence of, in Bellamy's *Looking Backward,* 193
   between levels in the Soviet hierarchy, 26
Consistency
   of central plan with lower-level plans, 31-32
   in current-output plan, 23-24
   defined, 23
   of lower-level plans with one another, 31
   in multiperiod plan, 52-53
Consumer, rationality of, 282-83
Control by the ruble, 73
Control figures (preliminary indicators), 22, 25
Convergence thesis
   economic, 342-43
   political, 343-45
Cost
   opportunity, in a centrally-planned economy, 29
   planned reduction, 42
Criticisms of capitalism, traditional:
   income distribution, 321
   a cultural critique, 321-23
   lack of a common purpose, 332
   the middle class, 325, 326
   middle-income group in non-capitalist economies, 321
   suburban life, 324-32
   suburbia, a middle way, 331
Crook, Frederick W., 262-63, 266
Cultural revolution, 258

Decentralization
   the basis for effective, 266-67
   by decree, 110
   violations of decree, 110
Deficit commodities, 69
Democracy
   under capitalism, 337-38
   under socialism, 339-41
Dernberger, Robert F., 258-59
Destler, Chester M., 289
Development in the Soviet-type economy
   government as risk-taker, 92
   heavy industry, 90
   housewives enter labor market, 90
   increased accumulation, 89
   low procurement prices, 89
   output of consumption goods restricted, 89
   planned investment, 90-91
   reduction in services, 90
   role of coercion in, 92
   turnover tax, 89, 90
Development under capitalism, 93
Dialogue, top authority and Planning Commission, 20
Dickinson, H. D., 128, 150
Directives, governmental
   cost of enforcement, 298
   inequalities, 298
   objectives, 297
Dobb, Maurice, 3
Domar, Evsey D., 108
Donaldson, Scott, 324
Donnithorne, Audrey, 254-55, 257, 260, 262, 264
Due, John F., 316

Eckstein, Alexander, 255, 257, 259
Economic reform: Does it require political reform? 341
Efficiency
   autonomous units promote, 347
   bargaining for, 27-28
   defined, 26
   in multiperiod plan, 52-53
   through input substitution, 28

of trade, 30
under capitalism, 272, 277
Entrepreneurs
in development, 93
Environmental concerns
costs of reducing spillovers, 295
impact of regulation on income distribution, 295
markets and indiscriminate delivery, 295
Equality
complete and total, 312
in credentials, 313
in income, 313
in knowledge of basic skills, 313
"Equality of opportunity"
and economic progress, 311
footrace metaphor, 309
and individual differences, 308, 311
investment in human capital, 310-11
lack of precision in idea, 309-10
Erlich, Alexander, 111

Fairfield, Richard, 235, 244-49
Fondy, 22
Foreign trade
in Soviet-type economies, 107
Frech, H. E., 330
Free choice
require market-clearing prices, 347
under capitalism, 271, 277
under market socialism, 156
Freedom of contract, 273
Freedom of speech under socialism, 340
Free elections under socialism, 340
Friedlaender, Ann F., 316
Friedman, Milton, 315, 340, 341

Garfield, Paul J., 318
Garvey, George, 72, 75
Gerschenkron, Alexander, 67-68
Gies, Thomas C., 318, 319, 320
Glass walls, socialist enterprises in, 150

Goals. *See* Objectives
Gray, Ralph, 294
Great Leap Forward, 256-57, 263
Gregory, Paul R., 78
Grossman, Gregory, 55, 116, 120, 124
Group-marriage communes, 248-49

Hardy, Earl O., 291-92
Harrington, M., 294
Hayak, Friedrich A., 127-28, 339
Hippie communes
anti-intellectualism, 246
austerity and disorder, 245
average duration, 246
crash-pad mentality, 246
emphasis on leisure, 244
lack of knowledge, 244
lack of organization and structure, 244, 246
lack of responsibility, 244, 246
need for structure, 247
open-door policy, 246
rejection of consumption, work, and capital formation, 244
seasonal fluctuation in population, 245
short time-horizons, 246
source of livelihood, 245
Hirschleifer, Jack, 131, 151
Hirschman, Albert O., 91
Hodgman, Donald R., 72
Holding companies, under socialism, 139
Holesovsky, Vaclov, 116, 120, 345
Holzman, Franklyn D., 72
Horvat, Branco, 159, 165, 167-70, 171, 175
Hubbard, Leonard E., 77, 78
Huntington, Samuel P., 344
Hutterions
child rearing, 217-18
duration and numbers, 215
economy, 216-17
organization and control, 215-16
viability, explanation of, 218-19

Ideology
    in China, 261, 264
    in industrialization and
        collectivization, 13-15
    as obstacle to reform, 124
    party, 2, 5, 9
    tentativeness as an alternative,
        267
    versus pragmatism in kibbutz,
        226-27
Indiscriminate delivery (spillovers)
    alternatives open to recipient
        of, 280
    concept superior to concepts
        of "externality" and "social
        costs," 363-65
    in Lange's model, 135-36
    manners, a substitute for
        regulation, 202
    regulation in an operational
        market socialism, 153
    under capitalism, 280-81, 297
Individual differences, 314
Industrialization, 9, 11
Inevitable progress, 344, 345
Information, inaccurate
    because overfulfillment
        rewarded, 41
    broken promises, 122
    concerning technological
        coefficients, 26
    as a consequence of input
        norms, 42-43
    secrecy, functional, 150, 276
    secrecy under capitalism, 276
Innovation and short-run
    monopoly profits
        capitalism, 276-78
        operational market socialism,
            149
Institute for Industrial
    Reconstruction (IRI), 141
Interdependencies, 17-18, 23, 28-30,
    33-34, 82
Interest
    as an alternative to planning,
        347
    in calculation of present
        value, 65-66, 69
    in Soviet-type economy, 59-60,
        62-63, 65
Inventories, excess, 68
Iteration
    administrative, 24, 32, 53
    in drawing up the central
        plan, 24
    in multiperiod planning, 53, 54

Jarrett, James L., 310
Joffe, Ellis, 259
Johnson, Harry G., 91-93
Johnson, Ross, 117

Kanovsky, Eliyahu, 219, 221
Kaplan, Norman, 57
Karcy, Jerzy F., 84
Kelf-Cohen, R., 146
Keren, Michael, 147
Kershaw, David N., 316
Khachaturov, T. S., 58, 143
Kibbutz, Israeli
    assistance, inter-kibbutzim,
        223
    attraction of the household,
        228, 229
    child rearing, 221
    consumption, 220-21
    future of, 225
    hired labor, 222-23
    ideology versus pragmatism,
        226
    incentives, 221-22, 229
    individuality, 223-24
    kind of people in kibbutz,
        224-25
    objectives, 219
    organization and work, 219-20
    possible loss of members to
        city, 226
    role of women in, 226, 228
    role of Zionism in, 228-29
    the separate kibbutz and the
        movement, 227
    unpleasant jobs, 222

Kindleberger, Charles P., 91
Kinkade, Kathleen, 229-37, 238, 241-44
Kolkhoz. *See* Collective farm
Kolkhoz (farm) market
   inefficient, 81
   volume of sales in, 81
Kontorovich, L. V., 54, 63, 64
Kristal, Irving, 323
Kronstadt Island revolt, 5
Kropotkin, Peter, 180, 185-86, 261, 312
Kulak, 8, 10

Lange, Oskar, 30, 128, 130-38, 150, 154-56
Lardy, Nicholas R., 260
Leeman, Wayne A., 164
Leon, Dan, 219-28
Lerner, Abba P., 30, 128, 131-33, 360
Levine, Herbert S., 34, 46
Lewin, M., 3, 8, 9, 10, 11, 12, 14, 15
Liberman, E. G., 65, 96, 97, 101, 106, 111, 258
Linbergen, V., 342
Link (work gang), 115
Linnemann, H., 342
Lovejoy, Wallace J., 318
Lutz, Vera, 141

McKean, Roland N., 66
Marginal-cost pricing, 359-61
Market socialism, operational model
   appointment of managers, 142, 147-48
   autonomy versus accountability, 152
      indiscriminate delivery in, 153-54
      value of actual competition, 154
   capital markets in, 140, 142-43
   competitive sector, features of, 139-40
   creation and destruction of production units, 139-41, 146, 155-56
   efficiency, 156
      more promising than Soviet-type economy, 348
   enterprises, government, 139, 145
      government departments, 139, 140-41
      holding companies, government, 139, 140-41
   free choice, 156
   government corporations, 145-46
   natural monopoly, 145-47
      price ceilings, 146-47, 154-55
   profit as incentive and success indicator, 143-44, 145, 148, 154, 155
   profit, risk, and innovation, 148-52, 156
   rationale for, 139
   reward of supervisors, 144-45
   secrecy, 150
   standards of quality, 146
   trademarks, 140
Market socialism, static model
   accounting prices, 130
   idea of, history, 127-28
   indiscriminate delivery (spillovers), 135
   industry managers, role of, 136
   investment rule, 132-33
   large model, description of, 129-37
   managers, supervision and reward, 133-35
   $MC = P$ rule, 131-32
   price determination, 130
   rules imposed on managers, 131
   scarcity prices in, 138
   statics and dynamics in, 137-38
Markets hurt people, 354-57
Marx, Karl
   income distribution under communism, 186
   little to say about socialism, 127
   on withering away of the state, 179
   worker has property rights in his person, 285-86

Material balance
  defined, 22
  an example, 23
  first efforts, 4
  perspective, 49, 51
  strained, 27
Meade, J. E., 363
Merret, Stephen, 101, 105
Method of balances
  flexibility of, 25
Mieszkowski, Peter M., 315, 317
Migration from the countryside, 86-87
Millar, James R., 13
Minimum skills, 314
Mises, Ludwig von, 30, 127
Mishan, E. J., 363
Monetạ policy
  budget surpluses in lieu of, 75-76
  none in Soviet-type economy, 74, 76
Money
  degree of moneyness, 73
  need for in Soviet-type economy, 71
  minimization of idle balances, 72
  promotes decentralized decisions, 348
  Soviet bank deposits, 71-72
  Soviet currency flows, 71
  tension in Soviet monetary system, 71, 73-74
  tied, 73
  two monetary circuits in Soviet economy, 71
Móntias, John Michael, 33, 45, 49, 50, 55, 63, 116, 120, 124
Multiperiod planning
  consistency and efficiency in, 52-53
  knowledge required, 50
Mumford, Lewis, 196, 325
Mundell, Robert A., 202

Negative income tax (guaranteed minimum income), 315-17
Nemchinov, V. S., 97, 99, 106
NEP. See New Economic Policy

"New class" of government officials, 171
New Economic Policy (NEP)
  beginnings, 5-6
  capital accumulation, 6
  demise of, 6, 8
  Nepmen, 6
  position of peasants in, 7
  role of market in, 6
Norm. See Technological coefficient
Nove, Alec, 3, 4, 5, 6, 9, 12, 14, 15, 57, 60, 70, 84-87, 115
Noyes, John Humphrey, 209-12.

Objectives
  Israeli kibbutz, 219
  laissez faire capitalism, 271-72, 277
  party, 2, 18, 49
Obstacles to reform
  confidence gap (reserved trust), 122-24
  fears of inflation, 116
  fears of loss of power, 116
  fears of lower pay and unemployment, 116
  low-wage philosophy, 123
  opposition from underdeveloped regions, 120
  piecemeal, 122
  pressures for recentralization, 121
  taut plans, 120
  weight of bureaucracy, 124
  weight of ideology, 124
  who might be hurt, 117-20
Oneida community
  demise, 211-12
  economy, 210
  establishment of, 209
  marriage, unconventional, 211
  political structure, 210
  prospective members screened, 210
Open land communes, 245
Optimum economic institutions, 343-44

Pajestka, Jozef, 33
Parrish, William L., Jr., 263
Party
  capture of power, 3
  in conflict with peasantry, 3, 5-11
  urban-based, 3
Patent rights, 273
Peasant
  middle, 6
  poor, 6
  rich, "kulak," 6
Pechman, Joseph A., 315, 317
Pejovich, Svetozar, 164, 165
Perkins, Dwight H., 254, 256-58, 262-63
Peters, Victor, 215-19
Peterson, John M., 294
Phillips, Charles F., 318
Plan
  taut, 120
  convergence toward best, 34
  drawing up, 18-34
  execution, 34-47
  Five-Year, 51
  knowledge required, 19-21, 28
  lower level, 21, 31-32
  revision of, 46-47
Planned obsolescence, 282
Planning
  bargaining in, 27
  in Communist China, 259
  concrete, 97
  current output, 16-34, 347
  during the NEP, 6
  first Five-Year, 11
  flexibility in, 32-33
  from above, 27
  informality of, 22
  mobilization, 12-13, 27
  organization and procedures, 19-23
  rolling, 54
  simultaneity, 34
  spacial factors, 18
  upward, 27
  versionism, 34
Planning Commission, State, 19-21
Political reform: Does it follow from economic decentralization, 341-42
Powell, Raymond P., 74

Preferences of the top authority, 19
Preliminary indicators. See Control figures
Price controls
  followed by rationing, 299
  objectives, 297
Prices
  farm prices in Soviet economies, 113
  list and actual, 275
  market-clearing under reforms, 98-99
Prices, inflexible
  in Soviet-type economy, 68
  at times under capitalism, 279
Prices, scarcity (market-clearing)
  explicitly used to obtain cost reductions, 43
  and free choice, 69, 347
  implicit in input norms, 42
  impossible to obtain efficiency when these are not known, 30
  in market socialism, 130, 140
  retail, in Soviet-type economy, 68
Prices, wholesale, in Soviet-type economy, 69
Private ownership of means of production, objectives served, 348
Private plot
  and collective production, 82
  in Communist China, 254, 255, 257, 262, 265
  output of, 80
  party attitude toward, 80
  size of, 80
Procurement, grain, 4-5, 6, 8-10
Procurement prices, 89
Productivity, ethic, 286
Profit
  implicit in material rewards associated with physical planning, 44
  not important as Soviet success indicator, 70
  in operational market socialism, 140
  and plan, under proposed reforms, 100, 100-06
  profit bonus formula, 100-03
  reduced through pooling, 93
  Soviet, normal, 69

turnover tax, as, 70
Project selection (investment choices)
    alternative processes, 55
    coefficient of relative effectiveness, 57
    impatience not the consideration, 63
    minimization of total costs, 56
    norm of relative effectiveness (interest rate), 59
    present value of costs, 62
    present value of net income, 65, 347
Pronk, J. P., 342
Property
    and courts in Soviet-type economy, 112
    defined, 108-09
    and due process, 272
    and human rights, 273
    and independent courts, 273
    not absolute, 272
    not unchanging, 272
    rights of decision, 108, 166-67
    a set of rights, 272
    "social" ownership, 109
    in Soviet-type economy, 109
    tenure, 112-13
    under capitalism, 272
    under socialism, 108
    in Yugoslavia, 165-70
Proposed reforms
    in agriculture, 113-15, 121-22
    elimination of seller's market, 100
    farm prices, 113
    a large role for profit, 100
    link (work gang), 115
    market-clearing prices, 98-99
    obstacles to, 115-124
    output directives with free choice of inputs, 97
    in price formation, 98, 121-22
    profit and plan, 100
    reduction of inputs subject to rationing, 97
    reduction of output directives, 93-97
    reduction in subsidies, 106-07, 108
    reward for the sale of goods, 99-100
    role of competition in, 99, 122
    sheltered enterprises and foreign trade, 107
    voluntary purchases, 99
Prybyla, Jan S., 255

Queue (waiting line), 68

Rationing
    enforcement, 303-04
    point, 299, 302-03
    separate-commodity, 299, 300-02
    in Soviet-type economy, 69
Rawski, Thomas G., 261-62
Regulation
    cost-plus pricing, 291
    farm price support programs, 292
    limitations of government, 298, 321
    populism, an ideology, 289-90
    pragmatic, 289, 296
    railroad, 290-91
    versus government ownership, 296
Religious-occult communes, 247-48
Rent
    in Bellamy's *Looking Backward*, 192
    in Soviet agriculture, 114
    in Soviet-type economy, 69
    in Wells's *Modern Utopia*, 198
Requisitioning. *See* Procurement, grain
Reserves
    concealed, 27
    distribution of materials held to meet shortages, 45
Revolutionary force, 9, 15
Reward, managerial
    for cost reduction, 42-44
    for fulfillment of plan, 35
    for overfulfillment, 40
    for plan fulfillment and volume, 36-37
    for volume, 36
Risk
    of private ownership of capital goods, 271, 278

profit and innovation, 148-52
reduced through pooling, 93, 151-52
Risk-averters
    managers, 27, 36, 39-40, 40n, 45
Risk-takers
    authorities, 27, 39
Robbins, Lionel, 127, 340
Roberts, Ron E., 232
Robertson, Ross M., 290-92
Roll, Charles Robert, Jr., 263
Rule of law under socialism, 339-40

Sacks, Stephen R., 162, 165
Safety factor. *See* Risk averters
Samuelson, Paul Anthony, 300, 302
Samurai (voluntary nobility) in Well's utopia, 199
Schran, Peter, 256
Schroeder, Gertrude E., 120, 124
Schumpeter, Joseph A., 134-35, 138, 149, 276-77
Scitovsky, Tibor, 363
Second-order linkages, 33
Seeley, John R., 324
Service communes, 247, 248
Sheltered enterprises, 107
Shepherd, William C., 318, 319, 320
Shortages
    distribution of reserve materials, 45
    revision of the plan, 46
"Shuttle technique," 22
Sigurdson, Jon, 260
Ota Šik, 98, 106, 107, 116
Simhoni, Yehudit, 226
Skinner, B. F., 203-07, 230, 234, 237-41, 244
Skinner's *Walden Two*
    behavioral engineering, 207
    capital accumulation not considered, 205
    complexity of economy not considered, 206
    economy, 204-05
    organization and government, 203-04, 240-41
    uncertainty and risk not considered, 206
Slansky, Rudolf, 167n

"Slavish adherence to plan," 45
Smolinski, Leon, 17
"Social capital" in Yugoslavia, 165, 165n
Social influence in Yugoslavia, 167-70
Spillovers. *See* Indiscriminate delivery
Spulber, Nicholas, 49
State farms, 83, 85
Strong, Anna Louise, 10
Structure of industry
    under capitalism, 276-77
    in Yugoslavia, 164-65
Stuart, Robert C., 78
Subsidies and grants
    impact on leisure, 307
    in money or kind, 307
    unit, 304-05
Substitution of inputs, 28
Surplus, agricultural, 13-14
Szamuely, Tibor, 344

Taut plans, 120
Taxes
    death, 306-07
    income, 306
    sales, 304-05
Taylor, Fred M., 30, 128, 130n
Technological coefficients (norms)
    average-progressive norm, 26
    a forecast, 25, 27
    over time, 51
    unrealistic, 27
    vary with output, 21, 25
    a weighted average, 25
Tenure
    in operational market socialism, 140, 142, 147-48
    and property, 112-13
Terminal capacity, 50-51
Time horizon under capitalism, 277, 278
Tobin, James, 315, 317
Tocqueville, Alexis de, 308
Todorović, Mijalko, 117
Trademarks, 140-42
Turnover tax
    defined, 70
    first introduction, 12
    price determined, 70

Twin Oaks
  consumption and leisure valued, 233-34
  disputes, 234-35
  the dream of not being lonely, 236
  economy, 231
  lack of capacity to rear children and care for elderly parents, 235
  membership turnover, 233, 235-36
  organization and control, 229
  outside work, 232
  poverty of, 233, 243
  responsibility, need for, 237

Urbanek, Leda, 116
Utility rate determination
  incentive rate determination, 319-21
  regulatory lag, 320
  traditional method, 317-19
Utopia, defined, 196
Utopian dream, 178, 207

Viner, Jacob, 363
Voline, Lazar, 84

Wädekin, Karl-Eugene, 79-83
Wagner, Richard E., 316
War communism, 4
Ward, Benjamin, 159, 161, 165
Welfare programs, 294-95
  from private charity to governmental actions, 294-95
  problem families, 295
  war on poverty, 294
Wellisz, Stanislaw, 34, 47
Wells, H. G., 196-203
Wells's *Modern Utopia*
  to be achieved gradually, 197
  costs of capital accumulation not considered, 200
  government and laws, excellent, 199
  government by elite, 202
  a happy land has no history, 201
  life still imperfect, 196-97
  limited knowledge not considered, 201
  a mixed economy, 199
  people saturated with consideration, 201
  role of government, 198-99, 202
  role of money and prices, 198-99
  samurai (voluntary nobility), 199-200
West, Geoffrey, 203
Whyte, William H., 331
Wilber, Charles K., 90
Wiles, Peter, 17, 343
Wood, Robert C., 331
Workers' control, 4
Workers' control in Yugoslavia, 159-61
"Working collective" in Yugoslavia
  bonds as inducements to invest, 161-62
  conflicts in interest, 171-73
  disinvestment possible, 161
  investment decisions, 161
  a new class? 171-72
  not communal anarchism, 170
  organization, 159-60
  profit sharing, 163
  solidarity or conflict, 170-75
  solidarity versus efficiency, 175
  time horizon of workers, 163
  versus the capitalist enterprise, 174-75
  workers' control, 159-61

Yambura, Barbara, 213-15
Yeh, Kung-Chia, 263
Yugoslavia. *See* Working collective

Zauberman, Alfred, 57